The life o... ...cious. Why do people work there? Their reasons for doing what they do are startling, touching, shocking. But the Street has a code, a system, a vitality, a hierarchy just like any other social group. Here the misfits can come and be part of a group—a whole world to itself—a grey society living off the needs and greeds of people they fundamentally despise.

Robert Benni, restaurateur: "If I don't go to church on Sunday, I feel rotten . . . even though I might walk out of church and bust a guy in the head with a hammer . . . I have to go to church first."

Jessica King, cocktail waitress: "Streetwalkers give us the most. They say 'Why don't you get on your ass like us?' and I go, 'Huh?' And they go 'Here, honey,' and give me money."

Jim Flaherty, police detective: "I sent him to the state penitentiary twice, and he's one of the dearest guys I ever met. He paints like an angel, but he'd rather steal."

Merle Farquhar, retired prostitute: "I got tired of being busted and ripped off at the same time. I got a couple of fancy cops demoted to flatfeet. It took two years of gossiping but I did it. I'm the worm that turned."

In their own words they tell you what living in the grey society really means—ferociously competitive, tender, rough, poignant—a life for survivors only.

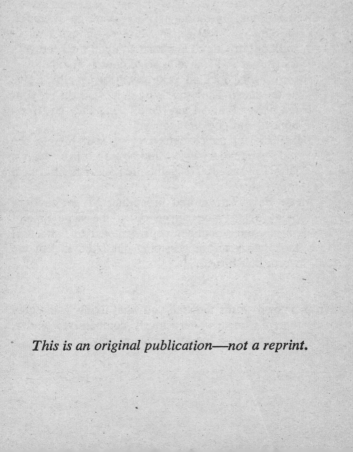

This is an original publication—not a reprint.

Copyright © 1974 by Ballantine Books, Inc.

All rights reserved.

SBN 345-23825-7-150

First Printing: January, 1974
Second Printing: March, 1974

Cover photo by Hank Dunning

Printed in the United States of America

BALLANTINE BOOKS
A Division of Random House, Inc.
201 East 50th Street, New York, N.Y. 10022

SWEET STREET

The Autobiography of an American Honkytonk Scene

Jack Olsen

BALLANTINE BOOKS • NEW YORK

For Su

"Sweet Street" is a name assigned arbitrarily by the author to a single block of a major American city. To protect its residents from public embarrassment and harassment, official or otherwise, all names have been changed except those of historical places and personages.

CONTENTS

PROLOGUE

LATE IN THE AFTERNOON, a few wan creatures, pale and bleached, scuttle about in the lee of the drooping sun, slipping from bar to bar, blinking their eyes like lemurs. These hard-core spectators have arrived too early for the evening performances, and now must busy themselves under the cold and unlit signs of Sweet Street:

> THE WORLD-FAMOUS FRENCH LOVE ACT
> BATTLE OF NAKED LADY WRESTLERS
> TOTALLY EROTIC YOUNG DANCERS
> SEDUCTIVE STEWARDESS STRIP
> HE AND SHE NUDE LOVE

Most of the street's gaudier business establishments will not open until dark, but already the faithful employees are arriving. The males are dressed for their evening's work, their hair parted and sprayed, their faces and necks splashed with heavy colognes, their breaths improved with mint and chlorophyll, the better to conduct business mouth-to-ear over the din of the music. The women retain the sheen of the scented oils and avocado creams that protect their skins off duty. Their eyes, ungarnished by the customary flecks and streaks of foreign matter by Maybelline, look curiously birdlike and opaque. Bright scarves enshroud short hair-dos that soon will be concealed in fancy wigs, and knee-length raincoats scarcely cover long, muscular showgirl legs.

Sweet Street is momentarily still. Indoors, bartenders check their banks and slice lemon peels. Dancers limber up their muscles and apply blusher and rouge and body cosmetics. Waitresses squeeze into their sequined uniforms, briefer than jockey shorts, and stuff Kleenexes into their decolletage, each

1

according to her need. Barkers clear their throats, sip final whiskeys, and pop stimulating pills, like professional athletes. In the evening's action, they will bear the brunt.

As night arrives, neon tubes flicker and glare, and banks of unfrosted bulbs go off and on like heat lightning. Marquees are seared in giant splashes of hot color, eye-straining combinations of scarlet and cobalt, flamingo and herring-scale blue, electric green and Bessemer yellow and strobotron white, a massive assault on the optic nerve, the whole recalling a flakship at night, or H. L. Mencken's words: "On certain levels of the human race ... there seems to be a positive libido for the ugly, as on other and less Christian levels there is a libido for the beautiful. . . . Here is something that the psychologists have so far neglected: the love of ugliness for its own sake, the lust to make the world intolerable. Its habitat is the United States."

Certainly the lust for ugliness is apparent in honkytonk environments: Bourbon Street in New Orleans, Broadway in San Francisco, Rush Street in Chicago, Newport in Kentucky, the Sunset Strip in Los Angeles, the smaller nightclub sections of Bangor and Sheboygan and Tampa, Springfield and Buffalo and Boise, all those public temples consecrated to Pan and Bacchus and the accumulation of money. There is hardly an American city or town without an enticing, noisy casbah where lonely old men and roistering young studs and fresh-paid soldiers and sailors on weekend passes can see the geeks and the strippers, the strange and menacing creatures of both sexes that wander back-alleys at night, the painted women who make promises with their hips. The various versions of Sweet Street are patterned on one another, and their journeyman laborers and artisans frequently trans-ship to a new scene, seeking more salubrious weather, or higher income, or a change of venue in behalf of the spirit. Wherever they travel, there is always an availability of customers, of "marks" and "johns" and "tricks," the naïve and immature and impetuous.

Here they come up the hill from the financial district, carrying their pigskin attaché cases. More spill out of hotel bars downtown, martini bravado under their belts. Some arrive in cabs from convention meetings, where they have been bored all day by stultifying addresses and seminars, and some chug into town in pickups and four-wheel-drive vehicles, fresh from the land, the smell of corn and lettuce and cattle and hogs still upon them, fingers stained with the juice of tractors and grapes. Here come the early marks, the clerks and hard-hats and students and an occasional cleric with his collar left behind in the friary, striding briskly along Sweet Street as though they were en route to a place of greater moment, waving away the more aggressive barkers disdainfully. They ogle the pictures from the corners of their eyes, and pretend not to hear the blandishments: "Come on *in*! We'll put a furry one right in your eyeball!" "No cover, no door charge, just acres and acres of quivering flesh!" In a few minutes, red velvet drapes will be yanked open with a flourish by the doormen—"Take a free look, *on me*!" as though they were offering a priceless value and Green Stamps to boot—and just as quickly snapped shut, unloosing a faint scent of bourboned air, and providing subliminal peeks at nearly naked dancers gyrating with early-evening energy to the ear-twisting music of two-hundred-watt jukeboxes.

"We're opening in just a few seconds!" a barker says, and four young men in college jackets step shyly into line. A tiny Oriental man passes a club entrance, slows almost imperceptibly, and resumes shuffling along in his threadbare black suit, the pants and jacket of which appear to have reached maturity at different times, his head a random collection of oiled cowlicks. Five minutes later he shuffles back from the opposite direction, quickly looks both ways, and steps to the entrance. "I have met them all," the protagonist says in Edna O'Brien's *Night*, "the cretins, the pilgrims, the scholars, and the scaly-eyed bards prating and intoning for their bit of cunt." On Sweet Street, a mere look will cost the scaly-eyed bards five dollars and fifty cents, the going rate for a mandatory pair of weak drinks. Or the street might offer something more, but at correspondingly higher prices, up to and possibly including life.

"If there was anything the customer wanted that was not in stock, the Montmartrois would gladly improvise it," Robert Wallace writes in *The World of Van Gogh*. "The steep, crooked streets teemed with cutthroats and pickpockets, pimps, prostitutes, drug peddlers and homosexuals of both persuasions." Sweet Street is identical. Panders stroll about in clouds of musk and patchouli oil, trying to smell like the runaway teen-agers they hope to "catch" before the night is over. Some of the pimps look like Mardi Gras celebrants in blackface: they wear pirate hats, safari helmets with sapphire stickpins, silken turbans, solid gold cocaine spoons on solid gold chains, diamonds as big as the Ritz, suede boots with four-inch heels, bellbottom pants that trail a foot behind them and sop up puddles, black leather maxi-coats with panels of mink, and little touches of purple here, carmine there, and high-visibility aeronautical orange on the side. They strut and preen, "styling," attracting the attention that history cruelly denied their ancestors.

"Shuckers and jivers," wails a young barker, Billy Wilson. "It's getting so that's *all* you see around here. And the old folks that live in the upstairs hotels: sick, sad. One lady, her hair's green with mistreatment, she dresses in rags, she drags herself up and down the street mumbling, doing obscene things. A very deranged person, but there's so many deranged people here it's hard to tell who's straight any more. Psychotics walking up and down, smiling at you. Walking time-bombs."

Mickey Martin, a salesman and habitué of the area, is newly nervous. "All these weirdos walking around in packs," he says. "It's a different world. When trouble starts, guys are always going to their pockets, which means they're holding some weight, youknowwhatImean? When I see three guys on one side of Sweet Street, I naturally cross over. I seen guys rolled five feet from a doorman. I know some cops that if they see trouble on Sweet Street, they go the other way."

"The place already has a bad name," says waitress Lydia Rubini, a street veteran at twenty. "I've talked to cabdrivers that won't take a fare here. The clubs are all hurting. The Lion's Tail does the best, and it's running in the hole."

"We're in the death throes," says Josey Costello, a dancer and heroin addict. "Nudity is everyplace these days. The new generations have all the sex they can handle, free. Sweet Street's down to the lowest forms of life: freaks, perverts, and fools."

Freaks, perverts, and fools. One is reminded of the gentle advice of T. S. Eliot, offered in a similar context: "To regard this group of people as a horrid sideshow of freaks is not only to miss the point, but to confirm our wills and harden our hearts in an inveterate sin of pride." Or Stephen Dedalus in James Joyce's *Ulysses*: "Every day is many days, day after day. We walk through ourselves, meeting robbers, ghosts, giants, old men, young men, wives, widows, brothers-in-love. But always meeting ourselves."

A swirling gray cloud swoops down Sweet Street, and whipping winds drive gusts of rain that drench the tourists and lash the barkers' eyes. The glow from millions of candle-power is picked up and reflected in spray, hanging in the air like puffs of colored chalk from a blackboard eraser. Then just as quickly the cloud moves on, silver wisps of steam curl up from the asphalt, and one can almost feel the stars pop out above the neon canopy. A barker shakes himself like a wet spaniel and booms out his announcement: "Right inside, folks, the hottest show in town! Topless and bottomless, AND ALL AT EYE LEVEL! *Come on now, take a free look!*"

Sweet Street is open for business.

The Glad Cafe

Beggar

Je maintiendrai
—motto of William of Orange

THE EVENING RUSH HAS not yet begun in Raffaele's indoor and outdoor café. A barman polishes glasses, holding them high to ensnare the lavender light from the night club across the street. A narrow-waisted waiter primps in front of a mirror, wiping away a hint of too much make-up, and an Oriental busboy applies a clean new rag to an already gleaming steamtable, pausing every now and then to brush his shirt sleeve across his forehead. Toward the rear, a widening pool of water seeps under the men's-room door. Lately the night manager has become angered by the popularity of Raffaele's toilet facilities and has decided to let the bathrooms go untended for a while, out of pique.

A man walks in from the street, looks at the puddle, and changes course to head for a table occupied by a lone tourist. He grabs the tourist's hand and pumps it heartily.

Hey, man, where you been? I ain't seen you in a long time. Where you *been*? Yeh, *sure* you remember me! Toby Gomez, the former ex-fighter? Sure, I'm a little drunk, but I remember *you*. Cleveland, wasn't it? No? Solly your name was? No? Frank? Wait, I'll guess it.

This book here? It's the stubject, the study, it's the subject of law. It's by Elliot Brown, the lawyer. I like him, I'm trying to learn his technology. I want to read law, even though I know it ain't gonna do me no good, but I want to experience everything, oh, God, yes! *Everything!* Why should the white people know everything there is in the world? Why can't the Spanish people have the audacity to understand things? It tears me apart! But I met a lot of people. Once I met Marilyn Maxwell, this beautiful doll, before she died. I met a lot of people in life: Marilyn Monroe, the mayor. One time in 1964, October 20, I left the city and I went to Washington and New York City. I was in Washington city during the inauguration of President Lyndon B. Johnson. I've done so many things, pathetically. Why? There's no end to me! I want to know everything. I been that way all my life.

Sure, thanks; I thank you very much! *Salute!* I don't know what makes people like me so much. I got a personality that won't quit. But sometimes I feel kinda down and out. I got a good family, indubibably. I'm Mexican-Italiano. My daddy was Mexican, my mother died. No, my daddy died. Now you got me all confused! I fought under the name Brock Wilson, I was a rated fighter, oh, my God, yes! I was a welterweight, and I fought in New York City, Boston, Chicago, all over the country. I fought Joey Giardello; he knocked me on my rear end. I won thirty-two, lost seven. My last fight was in Portland, Oregon, oh, my God, yes! Years ago I was knocking everybody out in the third round, the fourth round, but I'm a has-been now. I tried to find something, but I never found it. My manager, Nappy Berg, he was a Jewish person. He stole all my money, pathetically.

When I was fighting, I didn't care about nothing. I give a lot of money to a lot of people. I built my mother a nice house. I didn't think about later on when I'd need money. Now, *ma donna mia*, I have nothing.

I always wanted to be in pictures, but I could never make it. I was around the set of *Fat City*, but the policeman made me leave. I tried to get a job as an extra, but I didn't belong to the Screen Extras Guild, and the cop said, "You better get out of here!" I was in one picture with John Wayne. Duke, I called him. All of us used to call him Duke. *Yeh, Duke!* He liked all us Mexican people. I don't think Duke's ever liked anybody but Mexican people. Oh, my God, you got me going now!

I have pride, indubibably. I have pride that won't quit.

Very much so. Oh, my God, yes! I have the audacity to understand people, and I'm not a dummy. Tell me something, and I'll respond to you. Just try it once! But it's better when I'm sober.

As Toby Gomez speaks, his arms flail the air, scoring points, but when he tries to keep still, his hands vibrate hopelessly, sending miniature tidal surges back and forth across the ruby surface of his drink. He says he fought at 137 pounds and now weighs 152, but he looks wan and wasted. His hair is coal-pit black and full of vitality, but his complexion is contrastingly sallow, the dark gray color of moist sand. He has a small, undernourished mustache and a three-day growth of cactus-apple stubble. It is evident that he was once handsome, and he is proud of the fact that his often-broken nose is perfectly straight; "I made the doctors fix it up, I didn't want no ruined nose like the rest." He makes an effort to dress correctly, but he lacks too many resources. His sports jacket is devastated along the shoulder seam. An expensive angora waistcoat has lost its nap and taken on the texture of a shaved rat, and a thin, knitted tie is stained with flying food. His warm black eyes watch the watcher. "Well," he says, "do I pass? They tell me I look a lot like Ricardo Montalban."

After a few sips, the power of the grape begins to gush from his mouth, and he makes great leaps into Spanish with an Italian accent or vice versa, creating a new Italo-Iberian hybrid with expressions like "*muchas grazie!*" and "*buena sera!*" Accustomed to being rudely interrupted both by his coevals on Skid Row and the "marks" from whom he makes his living, he tends to blurt out his thoughts as though he may not have time to finish. In the process, he levels the peaks and valleys of pronunciation; Los Angeles becomes "Lanlez," Cincinnati "Snatty," and San Francisco "Sancisco." His favorite word seems to be "indubitably," which he customarily pronounces "indubibably" and which he relentlessly foreshortens as he sips his zinfandel, until finally he is pronouncing it "boobaly" and "doobaly" or sometimes just "blee."

Human relations are his forte, and he is proud of his ability to get along with people—i.e., cause them to relinquish money. But underneath the benignity that he has cultivated professionally, there are a ferret's tenacity and singlemindedness. He reads faces anxiously and comes up with instant conclusions, which he passes along with unremitting pressure. "Why are you smiling? You're not paying attention! Why are you looking over at that table? You're *always* looking over there. You're doing it again!" Toby Gomez, alias the hardpunching welterweight Brock Wilson, demands the fullest attention.

I been panhandling ten years off and on. My people think I go out of town to work, but I panhandle and drink instead. Everybody's so nice to me, real nice, so sincere, oh, my God, yes! I panhandle about four hours a day, that's enough to keep me in wine. Once I made forty dollars in four hours. Other times I can't make nothing. God, yes! The most anybody ever gave me was twenty dollars.

I've made my living by being nice to people, very much so, yes, and if they say, "Beat it, bum," I just walk away. And I says, "Thank you ever so kindly for being so . . ." Very much so. I was brought up that way.

Even though I'm a wino, a drunkard, I have a philosophy. I came back from Korea with one philosophy: to live and lev . . . to lev and live . . . I'm all mixed up. To *live and let live*, that's it. And I came back with a lousy disposition, a *lousy* dis'sition. I was mad at *everybody*! But I finally got away from that. Oh, my God, my God, I learned how to be . . . nice.

When I ask, I receive. People don't seem to care that I have the audacity to be even able to ask them for a dollar. One guy said to me, "You know, Toby Gomez, you talk so nice, I'm gonna give you three dollars." And a lot of the tourists that come here, they have the audacity to be so nice to help me out with whatever I need. If you got a good face, you can do anything. Oh, my God! Everything is just wonderfully!

Once I asked some people across from the Holiday Inn, "Would you be nice enough to help me out, because I just got into town, and I don't have no money whatsoever. I'm broke and busted."

"Sure," he says, and real quick he gave me money. Indubibably. I've been fortunate, thank the Lord.

All you have to do is be a little original, to attract attention, because there's a lot of bums to compete with. Like when I was in Las Vegas, I would say, "Forgive me, sir, but could you give me maybe a quarter, a nickel, fifteen thousand dollars?" Nine times out of ten they would help you out with a five-dollar bill, a ten-dollar bill, fine, wonderfully! And they would laugh at my humor. I put 'em in a good mood!

Or I'd be sitting nonchalantly in a bar, and the guy next to me would say, "Here, here's twelve dollars," and sincerely he'd give it to me. Why? 'Cause I asked him for it! I don't steal. He gave me the money with all his heart.

Or you walk up to people and act like you know them, the way I did tonight, and they give you money every time, if you're nice. Once I bummed a police sergeant in uniform. In uniform! Oh, God, yes! Nobody else bums a police sergeant, just Toby Gomez.

Oh, God, I've done so many things. I've been bumming the last fifteen years. I like to travel, I'm a gypsy, but I always come back here to the city. My dad told me one time before he died, God rest his soul, he says, "You know, Toby, you're gonna be just like me, die with nothing." And I said, "Yes, Daddy, I know." And it turned out to be the truth.

I'm a tramp. I lost everything I wanted in my life. God, yes, I did! I don't have nothing whatsoever now. I'm a tramp because I loved a woman very much, but she didn't really love me. We had two beautiful daughters, a handsome son. My daughters are twenty-two and seventeen now, and my son's fifteen, and he's getting good grades. Here, here's pictures of my daughters, if you want to see them. Thanks! Thank you very kindly for being so nice. I have the audacity . . . I met the mayor one time, no, three times.

It still bothers me about my wife. She's a barmaid now, and I know I still love the lady. She looks so nice, so pretty, and she's the mother of my kids. I love her because of my daughters and my son, Toby, Jr., and he's doing real good in high school, nothing but As and Bs, no Fs. Oh, God, yes, and he loves me, too! He loves me.

While I was overseas in Korea, my wife began doing bad

things. I was the one taught her how to drink, and then she became a ... I don't want to say the word. She became a woman who sells herself. Should I say it? A *whore*! And she likes to go to bed with women. A lesbian. *The worst kind of a whore*! So I had to leave her. Oh, God! I still loved her. I tried to kill myself two times, cut my wrists, but it didn't work. All I wanted was sympathy, sympathy. I wanted it from her. She says, "What'd you do it for?"

I says, "I just felt like doing it."

But I still love her. Very much so. God, yes! You never forget your first wife. But I can't go back with her again, very much so. That's why I'm drinking. So many things on my mind, pathetically. I haven't been right since I lost her. It's always on my mind, even though I had the audacity to have the consideration of loving her, and I still love her.

She remarried, oh, yes, very much so. And her new husband killed a guy—three bullets right in the back. *Wham wham wham*! Now he's serving life for first-degree. So I said to myself, "Oh, my God, how lucky I am. At least I don't have to serve a sentence."

This panhandling can be a terrible life sometimes, a lousy life. You're walking the streets, somebody approaches you, you ask them for a measly nickel or a dime, and all this after you've been an ex-fighter! It's a downfall for me. But then somebody'll say, "You have such a wonderful personality. Here's two dollars." Beautiful! So I say, "Thank you, thank you, thank you."

One good thing, I have a room for tonight. I go down to St. Timothy's church and they always seem to be real nice enough to give me a lodging ticket. Father O'Rourke, I think. You take the ticket to this hotel and they give you a room for a night, and St. Timothy's pays the whole three-fifty. Indubitally. Indubibibly.

I used to live on Skid Row. I got stabbed down there, right in the back, by a Peruvian person. Sitting down drinking a beer, and you know what I did? I stole his dollar. I shouldn't have done that. When I got up he stabbed me in the back. I walked into the restroom and I felt the blood, and the barmaid said, "Toby, you're bleeding all over." But I was drunk. I spent fifteen days in the hospital.

I always keep one sandwich in my pocket, there's one there right now. 'Cause I know I'm gonna get up in the morning with hungriness. Who was this writer who one time said . . . I forget, I forget. I forget that right now offhand. I don't know.

The wine I get cheap. Old Castle brand, forty-seven cents a quart. If I got money I'll drink two or three quarts a day, but I don't get smashed. I maintain. I maintain, and I'm gonna keep on maintaining, dutably. Dubably. As long as I can keep on drinking and maintaining, being nice to people, I got it made. I just have to try to have a little audacity of understanding.

I think I'm going back to Hollywood to work. I know I'll change. No, let me refrain that. What I mean is, I *hope* I'll change. Something in my heart'll click. Oh, my God, I don't know how. But it'll click, and I'll get a job, and oh, God, yes! I'm not really a bum. I'm not really a bum. God, no. I hope to God I'm not. Did I show you my daughters' picture?

Café Manager

For better than the minting
  Of a gold crowned king
Is the safe memory
  Of a lovely thing.
                    —Sara Teasdale, "The Coin"

ROCCO CARDI, THE NIGHT manager at Raffaele's, is tall and broad and muscular, with hands the size of hockey mitts and a disposition that changes abruptly from early Mohandas Gandhi to late Joseph Goebbels. Sometimes Rocco glides about the café like a demure dragon, his easy stride belying his bulk, and strangers are hardly aware of his presence. But then some dissonance intrudes: a mendicant drops in from the street and fails to pay him proper homage; an employe holds back fifteen cents from the cash register, or a freeloader freeloads to excess on that soft touch, Raffaele. At such times, Rocco says softly, "I gotta tangle-ass. I feel it coming." He tangles-ass with mighty blows, kicks and butts (his "rap sheet" at police headquarters lists seven assault charges), and then returns to his original role: Raffaele's domesticated crocodile, docile and tractable and sometimes even friendly.

Rocco is a charter member of the *macho* club that meets nightly in the café to exchange tales of masculinity. With his close friend Mickey Martin and a rotating squad of others, some of them high business executives and some of them low criminal types with records far longer than Rocco's, he sits in the corner table reserved for the staff and favorite customers and tells stories whose dramatic high point always seems to be ". . . And then, *pow!*" followed by a graphic description of how far the victim flew across the room and how long he was unconscious. One almost never sees these supertough *hombres* with women, although their stories redound with seduction and submission. They go to the movies with one another, to steambaths and workouts and golf matches together, and they would not dream of missing a boxing match or a professional football game. When they are not discussing their exploits as avengers of the weak and upholders of the tradition of Edward Teach, they are discussing whores, "black motherfuckers," the availability of stolen goods, con games recently perpetrated, sports results, and the ease with which homosexuals are taking over the city, so that a man is no longer safe in the streets. Rocco is not entirely pellucid on the problem, as exemplified in his remark, "Once in a while you're gonna run into anything around here—the whores, the fags that dress up as women, heterosexuals, *anything!*"

Rocco's head is arresting, every feature competing with every other feature for dominance, with abrupt angles and planes that look like an almost-finished bust, as though the sculptor had been called to the telephone. His face is the despair of a local caricaturist. "I just can't do as good a job of caricature on his face as nature has already done," she says. "Every expression is an exaggeration." One night Rocco donned a pair of Charley Chaplin black-rimmed glasses, whereupon the frustrated caricaturist announced, "Contrary to public opinion, the nose and the mustache do *not* come off with the glasses!"

The nose is long and pulpy and tipped up at the end, as though to catch rainwater. The mustache is dense and black and stiff. The full jaw juts straight out in defiance of every other human being. The black hair is oiled and slightly pompadoured, the greased strands so thick that they look like wrapping cord. The over-all impression is of an outsized Etruscan warrior, the kind of physical specimen the Bolognese reverently call *un gigant*. But inside this intimidating presence beats the heart of Steinbeck's Lenny. Says Fatso Cohen, one of the world's five greatest press agents, self-ordained, "Don't let Rocco bullshit you how tough he is. He cries when a snake gets runned over." There does seem to be a certain close kinship between Rocco and the lesser orders of the animal kingdom. "Quieten down!" Rocco orders, and mighty beasts are silent. He has been known to approach vicious dogs and calm them by his simple presence, reaching out to stroke Alsatians and Dobermans and Danes that are known as biters. "I don't know how I do it," Rocco modestly explains. "I just got a way. I get down on my hands and knees and jolly 'em a little bit, and they always seem to like me. And I'm very *very* fond of them. More so than your average asshole people."

Like the old sea dog that he is, Rocco walks slightly on the bias, having worked below pitching decks for years as a cook and steward, bearing what he calls "the stimulated rank of lieutenant commander" perhaps a retroactive promotion. In his spare moments, he has also been a pickpocket, a con artist, a card cheat, a pander, and a receiver of stolen goods, and he doggedly and loudly maintains his proficiency in several of those pursuits. To be in the same room with Rocco is to invite the loss of wallet, watch, or fountain pen. Some consider it a mark of esteem to be victimized by the quicksilver fingers of the night manager, and besides, he usually returns the stolen items within a few hours. Rocco also shows his affection by frequent "goosings," friendly jabs at one's genitals, and other hypermasculine showings of strength and style. It is not unusual for him to unzip his trousers and display his large penis in furtherance of some rhetorical point or another ("You want to see my credentials? *Here's* my credentials!"), and it is a rare night when Rocco's personal plumbing is not placed on public exhibition at least once. The management (i.e., the tolerant Raffaele Pirini) feels that any woman who faints or any man who protests did not belong in the café *a priori*.

Unsurprisingly, such a contradictory human being as Rocco Cardi excites confused responses in his acquaintances. Robert Benni, a transplanted New Yorker who runs a restaurant down the street, says, "Rocco's a nice man, a good guy, a real man's man, but he lives like a degenerate, a dirty animal. What's he do with his money? He lives in a dump, he never spends a cent. If I'm lying to yeh I'm dyin to yeh, I've known him six years and I've never seen him spend a fuckin' nickel on anything. Not even on cig'rettes. He gets cig'rettes from the busboys and the waiters that work for him. Tell you the truth, I think he might be a little goofy. Why don't he clean up his act? Goosing everybody and pulling out his dong and dry-humping the lady customers—he acts like a fuckin' fool. But don't get me wrong—I like him. He's a good person, Rocco."

One summons the angelic vision with difficulty, but it is true that Rocco drives to his widowed mother's home every Sunday and trims the lawn and cleans rooms and runs errands. He neither drinks nor uses heavy narcotics, settling for an occasional marijuana cigarette and two or three packs a day of bummed cigarettes, aggravating the chronic emphysema that stalks him. He chases fires at all hours of night and day, and keeps an ancient pickup truck parked near Raffaele's so that he can dash out the door and follow the engines. Raffaele smiles patiently when his night manager disappears in the wake of the clanging and the sirens. "Rocco's a little boy still playing on the corner," he says, "and that's beautiful. I hope he stays that way till he's eighty."

With so strong a mandate from the owner, Rocco rules the tiny empire of Raffaele's sidewalk café with an iron hand, and sometimes foot, and anyone who disputes his harsh dictates is invited unceremoniously to "get outa here, ya fruit ya!" at the top of Rocco's lungs. Sometimes he takes an instant visceral dislike, and one is greeted by a smiling behemoth shaking one's hand and saying, "Good evening, nice to see you, sir," followed by a stage-whispered "ya crummy lousy rotten motherfucker prick ya!" Unlike Toots Shor, the New York restaurateur who fawns on his favored customers by pretending to insult them, Rocco means every word. The patron so insulted remains in Raffaele's at his own risk.

Dining with Rocco can also be traumatic, since his gustatorial habits most closely resemble those of the giant warthog. When he is called away from the table, he spits into his food, an old Florentine reflex aimed at keeping others from sampling. But he is not correspondingly scrupulous about the portions of his tablemates, reaching across with his chisel-shaped fingers to pluck some treat like a maraschino cherry or a button mushroom. Raffaele finds this habit endearing. "Oh, that Rocco," he says, laughing. "All day long he fools around with his joint, and then he'll reach out and touch your food. But he doesn't mean anything by it."

Such emetic idiosyncrasies notwithstanding, Rocco is awesomely proficient at his job, which consists largely of keeping order in a place where disorder is a way of life. With his long, uptipped nose and his cavernous nostrils, he sniffs out discord before it happens, and rumbles across the room like an angry elephant, juxtaposing his large frame between troubler and troublee, and sometimes ousting them both, depending on his spirits and the phase of the moon.

Of all the offenses that test his patience six nights a week, the crime that irritates Rocco most is larceny, his own favorite pastime. Mickey Martin, a close friend and the only living human permitted to call him "Horseface," is as puzzled as anyone about this contradiction. "Rocco figures that he can steal from anybody," he says, "but God help anybody that tries to steal from him. Nobody can be as righteous as Rocco when somebody tries to hold a penny back from the register, or takes a pastry." The sweet-natured Raffaele is exactly the opposite, extending so much credit to deadbeats and compassion to petty thieves that he often succeeds in totally unbalancing his books, leading to constant squabbling between him and the unforgiving Rocco. "Goddammit, that fuckin' Raffaele is the world's biggest patsy," Rocco says. Only rarely does he succeed in convincing his patron of someone's essential ill-worth, and he speaks of such occasions with pride.

Altogether I've caught five bartenders and nine waiters stealing in here. I can spot a crooked bartender a half a mile away. When I'm sitting over here at the corner table and the bartender keeps looked at me, then I know he's up to something. Raffaele don't give a fuck, but I do. When I suspect a bartender's stealing I put the eephus on him right away. I slip over and wash the coffee machine, rinse out a coupla cups, anything to get closer to the bar, and I dig his action.

I caught a black bartender the other night, working a girl outa the joint here. I threw him out, and Raffaele said I was prejudiced. So the first night after we rehired the guy, he started pouring free drinks for his buddies, and I caught him cold. I said, "Raffaele, you say I'm prejudiced against the nigger here, but I caught him point-blank."

Raffaele says, "Don't use that word nigger. I don't like it."

I says, "He's still a fuckin' nigger, and I don't give a fuck. Now here's the proof," and I showed him the cash-register tapes. "Now am I still prejudiced against the nigger?"

Raffaele said, "Do what you have to do." So I fired the nigger's ass for good. Raffaele's funny about that word nigger, unless he has to throw one of 'em out himself, and then he calls 'em nigger motherfucker, jive-ass black motherfucker, nigger bastard, and he keeps right on saying it. Then he tells me not to use it.

Sure, some blacks are good. I'm not prejudiced to the extent that I hate 'em all. But I am prejudiced when a black is hatred and he acts like a nigger. Then to me he's a nigger, and I'll call him nigger to his face, 'cause I want to get him angry enough to put up his hands and I want to beat the shit outa him. When they come in the place and they wanta beat me for a piece of pastry or a meal, then I just wanta take 'em out in the back and beat the shit outa them. I got a lot of whites that do the same thing, too. In the old days you dare not see a nigger on Sweet Street. There was this one old-timer that used to shine shoes in a shoeshine box, Rufus his name was. No, Rastus. He was the only one. Any other nigger come down here, they'd tear him limb from limb.

When I see somebody acting up in here, somebody that's undesirable, I always talk nice to 'em, try to ease 'em out without trouble, if necessary take 'em arm in arm and stroll out with 'em. And if none of that works I spin 'em just a little half spin and throw a punch in their kidneys. A short hook, takes all their breath away. But I don't like to hit people. Well, sometimes I do. Sometimes I go two, three weeks without a good fight and I'd really like to tangle-ass with some black or white or Chinese or whatever.

Last night some fuckin' creep was panhandling the customers, and he gave me some lip. I bent his arm behind him and rammed him into the wall head first and knocked him cold. Then some asshole customer said, "You didn't have to do that."

I says, "Don't give me none of your shit, too, mister. Pay your check and get the fuck outa here!"

The other night a guy walks in, a pack on his back, and he's over at a table talking with a sailor. When the sailor turns his back, this stiff reaches down and grabs a piece of bacon off the sailor's plate and starts eating it. I jumped the bar and grabbed a hold of him, and I says, "You fuckin' asshole," and *ba-doom*, I rush him out. I says, "You motherfucker, stay outa here! Where in the fuck you think you're at?"

He says, "Well, I—I—I'm hungry."

I says, "Well, come over and ask *me* if you're hungry." I says, "If you're hungry, sit down, you fuckin' asshole, and I'll bring you out a sandwich and you can take it on the road witcha." So I went in the kitchen and made him a sandwich and he took it and left.

You gotta use discretion is all. Every case is different. Like the old Hebe that used to sell second-hand dishes, cups, and saucers around here, stolen from other places on the street. He'd walk into a place in his big overcoat and clean 'em out—ashtrays, cups, mugs, silverware, anything that wasn't tied down. Then he'd go to the next place and try to sell it. A little hunchback Jew.

One day he comes in and he's trying to sell something to Raffaele, and I says, "Don't listen to him, Raffaele, he's been stealing from us all along."

Raffaele says, "Bring the stuff in, I'll look at it."

I says to the old man, "You dirty cocksucker, I'll bet you got some of our ashtrays in your pocket right now," and I'm standing right alongside him, next to his overcoat pocket, and while he's talking to Raffaele I pull my zipper down and put my balls and prick right in his overcoat pocket. I says, "Come on, show us what's in your pockets."

"Okay, *goniff*," he says to me. "I show you. I no steal nothing," and he starts reaching around in his pockets, and he grabs my prick and balls, and he's stroking 'em, trying to figure out what they are, and all of a sudden he lifts my balls out of his pocket and sees what they are, and he says, "You goddamn schmuck, you fuckin' asshole cunt motherfucker!"

He's shaking his hands, wringing them out like he's just

dipped shit, and Raffaele and I are laughing our fuckin' heads off. Raffaele gets down on his hands and knees, he's laughing so fuckin' hard. He's saying, "I'm gonna die, I'm gonna die!" So the thief never came in the joint again, and that's how I solved that problem.

Right now I'm trying to figure out what to do about the toilet. We got the most ardent users of the toilet on this block I ever seen. They don't go to Vino's, they don't go to the Crystal Palace, they don't go to the fish and chips, they always come to Raffaele's. You'll see a line sometimes, there's so many toilet customers, and they'll keep flushing over and over, on *our* water bill, and they'll get in there and just sit, and we got a couple jackoffs that'll go in there and fall asleep. Look, there goes two more. Raffaele's public baths. Watch. See that black guy parking out in front, right by the hydrant. Watch. See that? Into the toilet and out, and not a penny changes hands. *Hey, you black motherfucker! Don't come back*! He'll be back tomorrow afternoon, same time, same parking place, same toilet. If it was up to me, we'd have a lock and an electric button. A regular customer, you push the button and the toilet unlocks. Otherwise nothing doing.

The other night I saw a guy take something from the pastry cart and I followed him into the toilet. I grabbed him and said, "Hand it over, motherfucker, or I'll beat the shit outa you." He says, "You ain't beating the shit out of anybody." *Pow*! I knocked him across the seat. The cop runs in and I'm hitting the guy and the cop says, "Don't break his head, Rocco! Don't break his head!" I found two pastries on the punk, turned out he was an addict on weekend leave from the hospital. Took him ten minutes to come to after I got through with him.

Well, I keep control. I move my ass, I'm up and down, and I got eyes all over the place. I know when somebody's not paying a check, I know everything that's happening. I only ever got hurt once, doing my job. A panhandler was going from table to table, and I went out to move him along. I told him he had the whole Sweet Street to work on, but he didn't leave, so I gave him a good shove. He fell off the curb and he pulled a penknife and said, "You motherfucker, you come close to me again, I'm gonna cut you up!"

I says, "That's good enough for me, baby. Come on!"

With that, he come right at me. I picked up a chair and jammed him in the face, like you do a bull, and he went backwards, and I jammed him with the chair again and spun him around and hit him across the mouth. Then I hit him with a left hook and he went down. But I made the stupid move of wait for him to get up instead of kicking him when he was down, and he came up and slashed the back of my hand open. That enraged me double, and I knocked him down and kicked him in the head three times. That was it. I broke both blades off the knife and threw it on top of him. We still see that bum on Sweet Street once in a while, but he stays on the other side.

Rocco is sitting at the corner table when suddenly he is up and out of his seat, through the door, and to the farthest corner of the sidewalk portion of the restaurant, all in a matter of seconds. "Pay your bill, you motherfucker!" he says as he grabs a thin wisp of a man and yanks him back onto the premises he had been vacating. Rocco bends the man's arm behind him and marches him up to the cash register. "Now pay up!" he says, and the faded specimen of manhood reaches into his pocket and pulls out a crumpled dollar.

Back at the table, Rocco explains, "A hype." *Hype* is short for hypodermic and signifies a user of heavy narcotics. "He don't know what he's doing," Rocco says. "He just got up and forgot he had a check."

A little girl comes in with her mother, apparently an old friend. "I wanna sucker, Uncle Rocco," the child says.

"I got something for yeh," Rocco says.

"What is it, Uncle Rocco?"

"A right hand." But when the child appears not to understand, the W. C. Fields of Sweet Street reaches in his pocket and pulls out a quarter. "Here," he says. "Go buy yourself a fix."

A young man with a beard and long hair walks up to the table and passes around a card: I AM A DEAF MUTE. PLEASE HELP ME. Rocco says, "Get outa here! Take a hike!" The young man says, "Fuck you!" and sprints away, and Rocco, veteran con man and bunco artist, snickers at the inept performance. "One night I threw a firecracker under one of them guys," he says, "and he jumped three feet."

Another long-haired straggler enters, looks around with glazed eyes, and walks to the corner table. "Rocco," he says in a faint voice, "do you remember me?"

"Yeh."

"I was wondering perhaps if you have any scraps."

"Jeez, we don't have any scraps here tonight. We just don't have em. Go to Vino's next door. They'll give you all they have. Just walk in. They got buns and everything over there."

"*Ommmm.* Thank you."

"Or the Crystal Palace, down the street."

"Thanks, Rocco. See you later. I'll get you something, man."

"Okay, brother. Right. Right on."

For a while, Rocco watches quietly as three young blacks panhandle in front of the café. The blacks are mildly persistent, trailing their marks up and down the street, entreating. Rocco beckons to a policeman eating quietly in another corner. "See them guys?" he says. "They're blocking the sidewalk, grabbing people, and then holding 'em by the fuckin' collar and won't let 'em by. I saw 'em grab a girl and practically had her crying, the motherfuckers. I don't want 'em doing that kind of shit again."

The policeman strides toward the door. "Don't worry," he says. "They won't."

A few minutes later an elderly man with bluish skin and a stubble and a filthy old jacket and battered yellow hardhat walks silently through the door and deposits a bag of evergreen cuttings in front of Rocco. Without speaking, he turns around and walks back into the night. Rocco explains, "That's the flower man. He used to own the highest class flower shop in the city, just for the socialites and the wealthy. Long-stemmed roses used to cost you twenty-five or thirty dollars the fancy way they boxed 'em. Then he lost his mind and his business. He's always bringing me flowers, trees, anything he can find. I have a feeling for him. I know it's a sickness. He's just a wandering fool."

The night bartender wants to take a break, and Rocco heaves his lengthy frame up from his favorite seat and goes behind the bar. Soon the scene becomes *opéra bouffe*. "See that guy?" Rocco says. "He's been nursing his beer a half an hour." The customer turns his back to talk to a young woman, and Rocco quickly grabs the bottle and his penis and rubs them together. "Maybe that'll make him drink up," he tells his laughing cronies, while Mickey Martin all but falls off his stool in high amusement.

"Tell 'em about the night you made the gin fizz," Martin says between spasms of laughter.

"Yeh," Rocco says. "Well, I made a real nice gin fizz and the guy at the table said it didn't have enough booze in it, so I put some more gin in and he still complained, said I didn't know how to make a gin fizz. So the waiter brings it back and I dip my prick in it, swished it around, and said to the waiter, 'See how he likes that.' The guy said, "That's perfect. Tell the bartender to make 'em like that all night.' So I did. Got a nice tip, too."

"Tell em about the night at the Steake Shoppe," Mickey Martin orders.

"Yeah," says Rocco, warming to his role of minstrel. "I was cooking at the Steake Shoppe, and a guy wants his steak charred on the outside and rare in the center. So I did it just beautiful, and the waiter brings it back and says it's not charred enough. I put it back on the grill, put the weight on it, turned it over and put the weight on it again, sent it out, and the waiter brings it back again.

" 'Hey, c'mon,' I says. That motherfucker! What the fuck, I'm busy. 'C'mon, don't break my fuckin' balls!' So I took the fuckin' steak and I threw it on the floor, I stepped on it, stomped on it, and then I took my dick out, I rubbed my dick all over it, so help me God, and I spit on it, and I sent it out with a little butter on top and a little parsley. The guy said it was the best steak he ever ate in his life. So help me God, that dirty motherfucker!"

Rocco tells his stories with great animation, adding doubtful dialects and dubious sound effects and vocal intonations. His imitation of women is done in a peculiar alto, and makes them all sound like children. Bright women become stupid, dull women sound downright cretinous, and all tend to approximate Stan Laurel talking to Oliver Hardy. Raffaele, who has studied Rocco for two decades off and on, swears that this has nothing to do with any inner hostility toward the opposite sex, that Rocco in fact is very much enamored of women and is a sweet and gentle lover. "I got that information from some of the girls who've slept with him," Raffaele says. "They tell me he's even kind of withdrawn in bed, and yet he's always playing the man's role, so there's nothing queer about him." Rocco can talk all night about his rewarding relationships with women, and often does.

The greatest day of my life was when I was sixteen, seventeen years old, working in a small-town hotel, and four girls checked in, twenty-three, twenty-four years old, taking a census for the state. They sent down for room service and I brought 'em up breakfast. When I got there, one was sitting in bed with nothing on. I'm shaking so fuckin' hard, the coffee's going all over the tray, the orange juice's spilling.

She says, "What's the matter, haven't you ever seen a naked girl before?"

I said, "Y-y-y-y-yes." I couldn't talk right. I was fucked up, man.

She asked for another coffee, and I ran down to get it, and I ran back up the stairs, *da-dum da-dum da-dum*, and she says, "Have you ever been with a girl?"

I said, "Oh, yes, I've been with a girl, yes." It was true. I nailed a woman that used to wash my mother's clothes when I was fourteen, and then she turned out to be my cousin Maria. So I was telling the truth.

The next morning it's Sunday, and there I go bringing up their breakfast again, on my day off. *Da-dum da-dum*. She says, "Come here. Have you really been with a girl?"

I says, "Oh, yes, but nothing as pretty as you."

She says, "Well, thank you very much. Would you like to touch my titties?"

I said, "Well, yes." So I sat on the bed and started caressing her titties and she says, "Would you like to kiss my titties."

I said, "Yes, I would."

So I lain down and started kissing her titties, *ba-boom ba-boom*, and I got a fuckin' hard-on that's bursting through my pants, and she's kissing me, and then she touched my dick. She touched it three times and I come all over myself! Man, I just couldn't stop. There was a big splotch soaked right through. She says, "Oh, honey, I didn't know you were this ready! I'm sorry."

All this time the other girls are sitting in bed reading the Sunday paper! Not paying the slightest attention! This is the fuckin' truth. She picks up my pants and takes 'em to the washbasin and starts washing 'em, and I said, "Hey, that's the only pants I got!"

She says, "You're not going anyplace. Isn't this your day off?"

I says, "Yeh, but I gotta go to mass."

She says, "We'll go to mass later." And we did. That was my happiest. That was the greatest thing that ever happened to me.

Okay, forty years go by, and the other night I have another greatest night of my life. I'm sitting there at the fuckin' table, and the fuckin' joint is dead, absolutely dead. So in walks this beautiful blonde, about eighteen years old. She says, "Hello, don't you remember me? You taught me how to play dominoes."

I says, "Yeh, yeh, yeh."

She sits down and after a while she says, "You got a pad around here?"

"Yeh."

"You know something, I been running up hills and down hills and I feel like a goat. I'd sure like to freshen up."

"Yeh? Want a shower?"

"Yeh. I have my overnight bag with me, and I'd like to change my clothes, too."

So I took her home, *ba-doom*, and I showed her the towels and the soap, and she goes in there and starts whistling, *ba-bom ba-boom, ba-bom ba-boom*, and then she open the door and she's got a towel wrapped around her, and *ba-BOOM*! my dick stands straight up. Automatic! She says, "You're in for a surprise."

I says, "I am?"

She says, "Yeh, I'm gonna rape you."

I says, "Just a minute." I tiptoed away, I kicked my shoes off, kicked off my T-shirt, I jumped in the shower and washed my back, everything, and I come back and she's sitting up in bed watching TV. And *ba-bom ba-boom* all night. She comes from a wealthy family, too.

Those were the best times, now I'll tell you the worst. Twenty years ago I got paid off in Baltimore, and I had to lay around waiting for a ship. I got paid off $5,850 cash and I already had two-thousand dollars from cheating at cards, so I went into town with about eight-thousand dollars in my suede money belt. I checked into a little hotel, got a room for eighty-five dollars a month, went out and bought all new clothes, and finally around ten o'clock at night, I'm sauntering down the avenue near the Gaiety Burlesque Theater looking for some pussy. But there wasn't any free pussy around, so I decided I might as well find me a whore and get my prick unloaded and forget about it. A guy told me where most of the Baltimore whores hang out, so I saunter in and sit at the bar and right away I spot this beautiful fuckin' blonde down at the other end. Oh, God awmighty, just absolutely beautiful! I'm looking at her, and she's looking at me, and I says to the bartender, "Would you ask the young lady if she'd like to have a drink with me?"

So we drink champagne cocktails, and after a while I can tell I'm in like a burglar. She says, "Would you excuse me? I'm part of the show, and I go on next."

She sings three numbers, and I'm clapping and applauding, the loudest motherfucker in the joint, clapping my fuckin' hands off, the fuckin' people are all staring at me. Now she comes back and she's changed into a blue thing, beautiful fuckin' cleavage, a navy blue shimmering dress. Oh, Jesus Christ, she looked so fuckin' good! She sits down and she says, "Now may *I* buy *you* a drink?"

I says, "Hey, honey, it's all right, I got money," and she says she'll have the same. We talked for forty minutes or so and then she went off to sing her last set. "You won't run away, will you?" she says.

I says, "Honey, wild horses couldn't drag me away."

She winks, and she says, "I'll be back," and man, when she touched me my dick came up *boing*. Automatic! *Boom*!

So they do their finale, they sing "Good Night, Sweetheart," and then the MC introduces them, this is Yvonne, this is Mary, this is Frances, this is Joanne, good night, good night, and the curtain comes down. Joanne comes back dressed in another beautiful outfit, and she says, "I'm ready to leave."

I says, "Can I take you home?"

She says, "Is that what you wanted?"

I says, "Yes, absolutely!"

I holler "Cab!" and she says, "No, we'll take my car." Oh, man, I'm in! She hands me the keys and *ba-room, d-r-r-r-rp, drrrrrrr* we're driving down the street, and I'm humming and singing to myself.

We walk into this lush apartment, first class all the way, and she says, "Do you know how to make coffee?"

I says, "Honey, I told you, I'm a ship's cook. I can make anything."

So I make the coffee while she changes. In she walks and oh! she's got a negligee with white ostrich feathers criss-crossed all the way down to the floor, and that blond hair streaming down, and I'm saying to myself, how fuckin' lucky can I get? If I told those guys aboard ship they'd never fuckin' believe me!

After a while she leans back and I take her hand and squeeze it, and she sticks her little tongue out and wets her lips. Beautiful lips! *Ummmmmm. UMMMMMMM*! Pretty soon we're French-kissing and sucking tongues, and I can't hold back much more, so I loosen my pants and my belt.

She says, "Are you excited?"

"What do you think?"

I kiss her some more, and I reach down and put my hand under her chemise and stroke her legs, and I get closer and closer to the V, but she keeps crossing her legs real tight or pushing my hand away, real prissy. Pretty soon I just forced my hand closer and closer, and she's saying, "Oh, please, don't do that! Oh, please, please! *Don't*!"

So I says to myself, "Ah, fuck, man," and I worked my

hand around her legs, pulled up the chemise, and I forced my hand up between her legs and—oh, my god, no! NO! I pulled away, man. She had two—great—big—hairy—*balls*. I was just sick.

I stood up and I said, "You dirty motherfucker, you!"

She says, "Well, didn't you like it, honey?" Now she's giving me the voice change, real deep, instead of the high voice she's been giving me all night.

I straightened her up with my left hand and *boom*!, I got her with a fuckin' right hand. I picked her up and *ba-room*, I hit him about five times and he's out. The first punch he was semi-out, the second punch I put him clean out, and then I just pounded the living shit outa him.

Then I go in the toilet and I take a gargle, and I get the dry heaves. Every time I think of that guy's tongue down my throat I get sicker, and I'm trying to throw up and nothing comes out, and oh, man, I'm sick, I'm so fuckin' sick.

I came back in the living room and I kicked him right in the fuckin' head. I wanted to get it all outa me, so I kicked him again. Then I put my coat on, and then I say to myself, Well, fuck me, this motherfucker cost me twelve dollars at the bar, so I go into the purse and take eighty-five dollars out of the motherfuck. I come back and I pulled her wristwatch off, and I looked inside her jewelry case and found two men's watches and took both of those.

I blow down the street, jump in a cab about four blocks away, so the cops can't trace me, and I go back to the fuckin' hotel. I says to the night clerk, "I just got bad news from home. Can you refund me my money?" So they gave me seventy-nine dollars back, and I packed my bag and I'm outa that town in forty-five minutes. I took a cab to the bus station and took the first bus out—to Chicago. Then I transferred to another bus and went to New Orleans and picked up a ship. I never heard a word about it. Not a word.

The other bad time was right here in the city. As much of a rounder as I've been, here I've been robbing people all my life, cheating every which way I can to make a buck, one night *I* get taken. *Me*!

A gorgeous absolutely gorgeous little girl comes in, and she's hungry and she tells me she's from Wisconsin and she's looking for her relatives, which she can't find, and she tells me how she went into the bus depot to wash her face and some lady rifled her coin purse and her wallet and left her penniless.

It's eleven o'clock at night, an absolutely beautiful young thing, oh, my God, so I says, "Well, I can help you." I give her a bowl of clam chowder and a tuna sandwich on white bread and a cup of coffee, and I sat down and joined her. We get down to the bare essential facts. She tells me she stayed with only one man in her life and she's very naïve. I says, "Well, look, honey, I won't touch you, but I got a flop up here above the café. You can stay with me till you get yourself straightened out." Which I was very much in earnest.

She says, "Oh, I think that'd be wonderful."

So about four in the morning I take her upstairs and show her her bed, and I'm sitting in bed reading the morning paper, and all of a sudden she comes in and she says, "I'm a-scared to sleep by myself. Can I sleep with you?"

So I says, "Sure, honey, if that's what you want." Jesus Christ, now I can't read any more, because my mind is concentrating on this half-dressed little thing in bed with me, and pretty soon she starts rubbing my stomach and then things start to happen and *ba-room*!

Afterwards, she goes to the bathroom, and I had a cigar box underneath a bunch of magazines with six hundred and fifty dollars in it, so just for safekeeping I take the money and slip it way under the mattress, and I put my head down and I'm out like a light, asleep.

I'm out. Snoring away. I hear a creaking noise. I wake up, and I realize it's the door downstairs. I jump and I say, "Karen." I yell, "Karen? *Karen!*" but she's gone, and so is my money. I jump out of bed, I run to the bathroom, I'm bare-ass naked. I reached out and grabbed my shorts and put 'em on. Her coat was on the hook, her dress was there, her purse was there, everything was there but her.

Ba-room! I run down the fuckin' stairs and I see her just making it around the corner, and I start chasing her. I'm bare-ass except for my shorts and she's bare-ass except for my pajama top, and she's running right down the middle of the street and me after her. Up comes the patrol car and it's

Ted Rollins, a friend of mine, and I says, "Ted, that fuckin' cunt down there just grabbed me." I get in the patrol car, and *ba-room*. We chase her into the Triangle Hotel, which is a haven for narcotics, dope addicts, pimps, and whores, that's all it is, and we go inside and there's one little Chinaman downstairs. Ted says, "Where'd that girl go?"

The Chinaman says, "No see no girl."

Ted grabs him up by the shirt and he ripped all the buttons off his shirt, and the Chinaman says, "Twenty-one! Twenty-one!"

Ba-room, up the stairs and into the room. There's four mattresses on the floor, no beds, and five hypes laying all over the fuckin' floor, all knocked outa their fuckin' minds. The window's open, the broad's standing there shaking like a leaf. I grab ahold of the cunt and I says to her, "Come here, you motherfucker. Where's my fuckin' money?"

She said, "I ain't got your money. Leave me alone, you bastard!"

I grabbed her and threw her up against the wall and I got her by the throat and I'm killing her, *killing* her. "Where's my fuckin' money?"

She says, "*Ugggggh.*"

One of the hypes says, "Hey, man, her old man just went out the window with the money. A nigger pimp."

So Ted sticks his gun out the window and says, "Halt or I'll fire," but the pimp was gone. So we call the wagon, and they find about forty balloons of heroin and cocaine and four or five lids of marijuana, and they throw 'em all in the city prison.

The next afternoon I'm too fuckin' embarrassed to go into the café, you know? The word is out already: I've been grabbed by a teen-age hustler, and I fell for it. Then she calls me up. "Rocco, I set you up, but my old man made me do it."

I says, "Who's your old man?"

She says, "You know him. It's Harry." I knew Harry well. A cheap motherfuckin' pimp on the street.

I says, "Where you at?"

She says, "In jail. My old man won't bail me out. I called him five times and he won't bail me out, and he's gonna skip on me. Come and bail me out and I'll be your old lady and I'll earn all the money back."

I says, "Go fuck yourself, motherfucker!" and I hung up.

I got a subpenee to go to court and tell the story, and the girl got six months. And when she got out, the cops made her recopense—re—reconvince—recompensate my thing there, so she came in one time and gave me a hundred dollars, she gave me sixty, then a hundred and fifty, and another two-hundred, and that was the last I seen of her. But for something like that to happen to me! The rounder of Sweet Street! I was the laughing stop of the whole fuckin' street, I'll tell you.

MIDNIGHT AT RAFFAELE'S. THE early crowd has come and gone, and the late crowd, the leftover customers and Sweet Street establishment members that spill out of the strip joints at the 2:00 A.M. closing, have not yet arrived. Rocco, comfortably cast in the role of his own amanuensis, sits at the corner table, spinning his tales, stopping every so often to dash across the room and attend to some problem, and always keeping his "eephus" on the outdoor section of the cafe, where trouble often strikes first. His eye is caught by a chunkily built man of about thirty or thirty-five who appears to be kneeling behind one of the tables, so that only his head and his broad shoulders and muscular arms are visible above the surface. The man makes a short speech to the scattered customers sitting outside, and when he struggles through the door on foreshortened, widely bowed legs, it is seen that he is crippled. He begins to speak in a clear, loud voice: "We're trying to find a thirteen-year-old girl. She's got long black hair. She's real small, very very petite. She disappeared from her home tonight, less than an hour ago. Will you tell her if she does show up—" The man's voice begins to falter. "Will you tell her that everybody at home—" He pauses. "Everybody at home wants her to come home." He blurts out a name— "Laura!"—and rushes into the night on his crooked legs.

Rocco turns from his tablemates and mutters something. When he turns back, his brown eyes are moist and half-shut. Thirty years before, his first wife bore him a daughter, the only issue of his five fractured marriages. Is he remembering now? "What a big motherfucker that guy woulda been," he says softly, "if he wasn't crippled."

The girls come to this street because they think it's showbusiness, and ninety-five percent of 'em are small-town girls and they think they're gonna strike it big, instead of working for the phone company and becoming an operator. When they hit this street, they never have a happy ending. Suicides, everything. Maybe one outa fifty'll have a happy life. Three outa fifteen will become whores, with nigger pimps and so forth, and be hustling their body the rest of their life, till they're completely worn out and the pimp kicks 'em out.

The black pimps go down to the bus depot and get them right off the buses, young girls that come in, and they catch them and put them to work on the streets, hustling their ass. And those black pimps are all mean motherfuckers. Dog eat dog. I seen some of the pimps where his old lady'll come in out of the pouring fuckin' rain, and she didn't break luck yet, and he'd just whack her across the side of the fuckin' head with his hand right here in Raffaele's. Or he's sitting outside in his Cadillac and she didn't break luck and she says, "Honey, it's cold outside. Can I come in and warm up a little bit?"

He says, "How much money did you make?" And *boom*! Whacks her right on the side of the head. "Get out and make me some money, bitch!" When a girl gets picked up by a pimp, that's the end. I know. I did a little pimping myself, so I know. That was a long time ago.

When I came out of the Marines I didn't want to work. All the four-Fs were driving around in big cars, they had money to burn, good clothes, and it just tore me up inside. I said, fuck it, I'm not working. I had twelve hundred dollars mustering-out pay plus three thousand I'd won cheating in card games. I used to cheat all the GIs that come in fresh from the farm.

So I bought me a panel truck and put a mattress in the back and went out to see the country. When I was broke I'd go to work for a week, mostly picking fruit and picking cotton, but picking cotton was tough.

One night I met a hustler and we got real chummy. He says, "You got an ideal set-up with that panel truck and all. How'd you like to go into business with me?"

I says, "Well, it depends on the business. I've done a few county jail raps and I hate being in jail. I can't stand being locked up. I like my freedom."

He says, "Man, this is legit." He says, "You know how many whorehouses there is in this state? There's got to be two-hundred."

I says, "Wha-wha-wha-what?"

He says, "We'll go down to the wholesale outlets and buy clothes, seconds and irregulars and whatnot, nightgowns, negligees, underwear, stuff like that there, and truck it around to the whorehouses and sell it to the whores. We'll make a mint, a mint. There's a guy in town that he's got counterfeit Chanel Number 5 and Coty's all put up in special boxes, we pick 'em up at six bits a bottle and sell 'em for five dollars. He makes the stuff with two or three drops of the original plus a lot of junk and water. The perfume don't last, but it lasts long enough to sell."

That sounds pretty good, so I tried it. We bought six hundred dollars' worth of stuff and started hitting the whorehouses, and we made a pile of money, believe me! Later on the guy said he wanted out, he wanted to make it for bigger things, and I was doing it all by myself, working out of the mattress in my truck, instead of paying for a hotel every night. Once a week I'd take a cheap room in a small town and shower and wash up and change my clothing. Sometimes twice a week.

One night I'm in this place in the country, and it had seventeen whorehouses for the lumbermen and fruit-pickers. It had a three-dollar house, a five-dollar, and a ten-dollar house. The ten-dollar house was for the businessmen of the town. You took your time in the ten-dollar. You sat down with the madam, she'd give you a drink or two, and you showed a little bit of class. So I hit this ten-dollar house run by an old madam named Fanny Kubelsky. She says, "Vot vot vot you selling now?"

I says, "I got some clothes and perfume and stuff like this here."

She says, "You ain't got a little something for me?"

I says, "Well, confidentially I got a nice present for you. I bought you two beautiful bottles of Christmas Night."

She says, "Dank you, dank you." She says, "Do you play canasta?"

"Yeh, I play cards occasionally. I love to play canasta."

"Do you like to gembel?"

"What do you mean by gamble? I don't gamble heavy." I'm giving her the con now.

Well, in the long run I stayed there for five days and five nights, living in the whorehouse, shacking up with a different broad every night, playing canasta with the old lady, eating the wonderful food, and all she wanted me to do was play canasta, believe me, at a penny a point and five dollars a game. I was holding out jokers and deuces like mad, she was so stupid, and I'm stacking the deck every time, and once in a while I'd let her win one game for twenty, twenty-five dollars, and I'd end up with fifty, sixty dollars a day and all expenses, and different pussy every night, which I didn't pay a dime.

One of the girls got pregnant, and she wants to have an abortion and she doesn't know where to go, and I talked to her, which I knew of a doctor in the city. So I drove her back to the city and on the way she says, "You're the most decent man I ever talked to in my life."

I says, "Yeh, okay." How little she knew.

She says, "Rocco, I don't have anybody with me now. I'm what you call an outlaw broad. I've had a few old men, but all they wanted was my money, and you're the first hustler I've seen that really worked for a living, and I'd like to stay with you. If you don't have anyone."

"I'm listening."

She says, "How are you at saving money?"

I says, "I'm very frujal."

She says, "Well, while I'm having my abortion and all, I want you to handle this for me." She hands me an envelope, and I open it and I almost choked. There's twenty-eight hundred dollars. She says, "This is your money. I want you take care of it for me." She says, "We'll take a small apartment and I'll pay the rent and the food and whatever money's left over I'll split with you."

"Hey, baby, you got a deal. Lovely!" And that's how I became a pimp.

After the abortion, she began bringing in a whole lot of money, and I decided to quit the road and take a job in the city on a little higher ekelon, so I went to work in a straight ten-dollar whorehouse hotel. And I also worked as a bartender in a strip joint, a bust-out joint. I was good. Out of a fifth of whisky, I'd pour sixty or seventy drinks, where the normal guy would only pour twenty, twenty-five.

Between my old lady and me, we're piling in the money. I'm making $125 a week plus sixty or seventy dollars in tips and all I can steal. Like I'd wipe some guy's ashtray and pick up a five-dollar bill sitting in front of him and throw it on top of the ice, or run a rag over his change and pick up half of it. By the end of the night I'd have fifteen, eighteen dollars on ice, and I'd take a lot more than that from the drunks.

Then we found out about a fancy new house opening in another town, and Jeanne says it's a train stop, and all those horny engineers and railroad men have big money, a bonanza, and so she goes to work there, and I called her up once a week at the house, but the madam preferred that you not call too often. One night I called her and she says, "I have a surprise for you when I come home. I'll be home on the twenty-eighth with my flowers." That meant she'd have the rag on, "the flowers," going through her ministrating period. She takes off four, five days at that time. Of course, a lot of pimps make their old ladies work when they got their flowers, make 'em work with a sponge. "I need that money, bitch. Just keep your ass on the street," so they'd work thirty days a month continuously till they're completely psycho cases, and then the old man'd kick 'em out without a penny and get a new broad. I seen many a case like that. But I wouldn't treat a woman that way.

So I cleaned our apartment and went shopping and made the place all nice and I'm cooking dinner when the doorbell rings and there's my old lady Jeanne and another broad standing there holding a little nightie bag, and Jeanne says, "Well, here's your surprise. I got you an extra old lady."

So we got a big double bed and we're sleeping three in a bed, and I don't know who to lay where, or when. And all this without moving a finger and I didn't even want to be a pimp, believe me! I'd been a hustler all my life and I wanted to get out and make my own money, and now I'm a pimp with two broads!

Well, I give 'em what I could in return, and Jeanne brought me more old ladies, and pretty soon I've got four, five broads, bringing extra money into the house. And I gave them all protection. Once the head pimp at one of the whorehouses smacked one of my girls and I went to the place and I tore right into the motherfucker. I just about killed him. I never stopped, I never let up on him, and for the coop de grayce, he was laying down and I picked him up by the hair and I brought my knee up and smashed his whole facial structure.

Jeanne stayed with me four years, very nice years, and then one day she come up to me and she says, "Daddy, I met a trick and I just fell heads over heel in love with him, and he says he'll take me outa the racket."

I says, "Hey, baby, more power to you! Good!" So she went to the bank and withdrew $4,850 and gave it to me. She said, "Rocco, I want you to have this, because I spent four of the happiest years of my life with you."

I still think about her. Not that I loved her, no, but I had a strong feeling for her. You argue and you fight, just like being married, but it's not the same as—well, if I really loved her, she wouldn't have been hustling, I wouldn't have let her. But she was good to me. Every time she'd go shopping she'd buy me a shirt or a pair of slacks, a pair of Bally shoes, a suede jacket, something nice.

It tore me up inside the day she left. I brought her to the bus depot and I had to break away. I was in tears. I just—I just torched for her for three weeks. She wound up getting married, had three kids, lives in the Rockies someplace. Her husband was a mining engineer, made lots of money, and I'm very happy for her.

That was around 1950; I been pimping off and on ever since. I'm running a broad right now—or I was till last night.

A cute little blonde. I knocked her in, I copped her, I caught her from some pimp. She wanted me and she dug me. She said, "I like older men. I'll work for you." What the fuck, *she* was asking *me*. It'd be rude to turn her down.

I took her home and she says to me, "Don't you like me? Why don't you fuck me?"

I says, "I don't fuck for nothing. I'm not a chippy fuck. Bring me the money and I'll give you a fuck."

She says, "Oh, you're mean!" She says, "Can I play with you?"

I says, "It won't do any good anyway." So she starts, and so forth, and pretty soon we were winging it. Beautiful! I told her, "You know the house rules. Bring your money home, and no fucking around with narcotics, nothing like that, and no pills." Which I have Demerol and whatnot for my bursitis, and some more powerful stuff I got from the football trainer.

So I seen after a few days she was hitting my pills, and I hid 'em. Then I walked home unexpectedly last night and she's sitting on the toilet with one of my neckties wrapped around her arm and she's shooting heroin. I like to flipped my lid. A good little broad, too, twenty-one years old, good looking. I had a little feeling for her, too, but I threw her clothes right out the front window, and I threw her out the door. I didn't hit her, no. I couldn't bring myself to hit her.

That's the trouble with whores; you can't be nice to 'em. That's the first mistake, treating 'em like ladies. One time I was in Nice and I run into this famous American athlete, and we got to buddying around, but he didn't want to go to the whorehouse with me. So I told him we were going to a little after-hours joint, which it was a whorehouse only he didn't know it. The madam poured us enough drinks so he couldn't tell whether he was in a whorehouse or the Ladies Auxiliary, and then the broads came in and paraded.

I says, "Which one you want, Lefty?"

He says, "You fuckin' asshole, this is a whorehouse."

I says, "C'mon, c'mon, let's get laid. What are you, saving your love for your wife? Do you think she's back home saving it for you?"

Now he's doubly pissed off, but we finally go upstairs, me and him and a whore, all in the same room, and the girl starts working on Lefty *ba-room ba-room ba-room*, and he's red as a beet from being in the same room with another man naked. So I says, "Jesus Christ, Lefty, you're hung pretty good!" Then I turns to this little French broad. "Hey, honey, you see that little dick hanging there?" And I points to mine. "This is its father."

Oh, Lefty got embarrassed, bright red, and he goes limp. I says, "Aw, you fuckin' asshole," and I grabbed two pillows and threw them on the floor and I started to bend the whore over to fuck her, but I started to shove it in her bunghole by mistake. She screams, "AHHHHHHH!" like she's been stabbed. She jumps up and she says, "You clazy fuckin Amelican! Get the fuck away from me!" Then she screamed about seven more times, and she jumps around the room.

So we went downstairs and paid the madam forty francs, twenty francs for each of us, and the madam said, "Did you have a good time? What'd you do to that girl upstairs? She's mad."

I said, "What the fuck do you want me to do about it?"

She pours us another cognac, the buzzer rings, and she walks out. I says, "Lookit this fuckin' bar, isn't this beautiful?" It was all silver. And behind the bar there was a big silver box. I lifted up the lid and it was full of money, fuckin' francs.

Lefty says, "Oh, no!"

I says, "Oh, *yes!*" All those five-franc pieces, I'm filling both pockets with 'em, and finally the madam comes back, and I says, "Honey, we got to run, see you tomorrow night."

So we're walking down the street. Lefty says, "You fuckin' asshole!"

I says, "You don't think I was gonna let them get the best of me, do you?" I split the money down the middle, and I said, "Here's your half."

He says, "I don't want that."

I says, "Well, on second thought then I better keep it." Totaled 280 francs, about $70. He was talking about it all night. "You crazy cocksucker," he's saying, "I can't afford to get arrested over here. Can't you see the headlines: Famous

American Athlete Arrested in Nice Whorehouse?" But we never were arrested, so I guess he just blew thirty-five dollars and a nice piece of ass. You can't trust whores, so you might as well rob 'em.

Used to be, there was twenty-five or thirty whores came into Raffaele's, and I would tell em, "If you want to have something to eat, something to drink, fine, but don't use the place as a pickup joint, because as soon as you do I'll lay the fuzz on you and that's it, baby." They said, "Fine, okay, thank you, Rocco, we appreciate that, we like to come here and see the people. We won't bother anybody."

So one night I was off and two whores walked in with a trick and took him to a back booth and got him drunk, and one girl's playing with his dick, and he's kissing her, and the other girl's going through his pockets, takes his wallet, strips the money out, and puts it back in his pocket. In the meantime they had three steak dinners and all the trimmings and drinks, and then the broads disappear.

The waiter hits the trick with the bill and he's got no money, and they call the cops and it's a dirty mark against Raffaele's, and the guy's screaming he got rolled and *blah blah blah, ba-ba-boom,* and how they took $630 from him. He yells, "How'm I gonna explain this to my wife?"

I told him to dummy up and take it like a man, and I grabbed him and pulled the wristwatch off his arm, and he started to scream again, and I said, "Well, either I keep the watch or you're going to jail for not paying your bill, baby. You're defrauding an innkeeper." So I kept the watch and he never came back to redeem it, and I sold it for forty dollars, pocketed nine dollars and rang up thirty-one dollars in the register for the bill.

After that, we kept all whores out for a while, but you just can't do it. Who's a whore and who isn't? That's the first problem you gotta work out. Now they're in here all the time, and the cops got on me about it. But what'm I suppose to do with Raffaele? The other night I told him, "Raffaele, the sergeant was in last night, which he called me over and says, 'Rocco, too many fuckin' whores floating around here every night. I hate to make an arrest outa here, but I gotta do it.' " Raffaele says, "Don't tell *me* about it. Get 'em outa here."

Now lookit over there at the bar. See? Four of 'em, right there at once. One-two-three-four. No, *five*! What Raffaele means is chase away the whores, but don't chase away his favorite whores, don't send out none of his pets. That's different. Now I'm just sitting around on tender hooks waiting for the fuzz to bust somebody. There's a cop sitting right over there, eating. See him? A harness bull. Every harness bull that comes in here, we always pick up the check. *Always*. Every other restaurant in town makes 'em pay half price. And we give two sandwiches for the lieutenant and two for the sergeant on duty every night, 364 days a year, which we're closed Christmas. Every night two patrolmen come in to pick up the sandwiches for the loot and the sergeant, and maybe they stop and have a bite themselves, while they're waiting.

But that don't mean they don't come in here and bust people. They hauled out three whores from here Saturday night, and I'm gonna have to go see the captain about it one of these days to put a stop to it, and at the same time I'll promise to put a stop to the whores, all except Raffaele's favorites that've been long-time customers and they don't turn tricks in here anyway. I don't dig this business of coming in here and arresting our customers, I don't dig it a bit. I mean there's fair, and there's fair. This isn't fair.

ROCCO IS DOGGEDLY WRITING his life's story, working-titled *I Con Man*, on cardboard laundry panels in heavy black pencil. The opus begins with a description of a rigged lottery game when Rocco was eight. The winning number was always held by a close friend, who would split fifty-fifty with the game's *éminence grise*, Rocco Cardi himself. One day the young schoolboy is ordered to stand in the cloakroom in expiation of some minor infraction, and thus discovers the treasures that abound in the lunchboxes of his classmates. Thereafter he manages to spend half his grammar school life in the cloakroom, stuffing himself with bananas and pastries and other goodies, and selling the students their own desserts.

A close friend and hanger-on at Raffaele's, Stanley Hamilton Briggs, has been listening to Rocco read from these memoirs nightly, the same ten pages over and over, and he is growing less fascinated. Says Briggs, a burglar by profession and self-taught philosopher by avocation, "He reads those fuckin' ten pages like they were Tolstoi. Night after night. To anybody that'll listen. *Anybody.* It's really not that bad, considering his education and all. It says something about the melting pot, the American culture. But does he have to keep saying it over and over?"

Pending completion and publication of *I Con Man*, one must settle for a fuzzy picture of Rocco's life in crime from certain sources at Raffaele's. Says Stanley Briggs, "There's a lot of myth and legend about him, a lot of bullshit. He says he never steals from his friends, for example, but he's taken a pretty good income out of Raffaele for years, and I doubt if even Raffaele knows how much. He also runs an occasional broad, and of course there's his fencing operation."

Rocco's public image is of the friendly fence, the warm-hearted pal who will turn up an IBM Selectric typewriter or a Curta Calculator at a special low price, but only as a personal favor. His pickup truck is always parked nearby, a convenience in chasing fires and hauling away illicit purchases, which often are made on the spur of the moment, following some heroin addict's desperate timetable of need. Briggs says Rocco's apartment looks like "a men's store, with jackets and pants and fur coats all row after row, stuff he's fencing. That's why he never invites anybody there." At night in Raffaele's, pro athletes sit around and discuss hot goods. A policeman comes in and says, "Hey, Rocco, when you getting me that color TV?" The chairman of the board of a major conglomerate is handed a computer, and a journalist is told, "You shoulda been here yesterday. I had a terrific pocket tape recorder." Everybody loves a bargain, and Rocco abounds in clients, some of them with sterling financial ratings.

A slightly jaundiced view of Rocco's smooth fencing operation is held by Diego Darby, a well-known criminal-about-town. Diego, a placid and friendly little man on the surface, turns turkey-wattle red when Rocco is mentioned. "That lousy fuckin' son-of-a-bitch motherfucker," Diego comments.

"I *hate* that son of a bitch. He's in good with the cops. He does things for them, so they let him have his little fencing operation. He's a rat, a stool pigeon. About four o'clock one morning I'm burglarizing a car, and he comes roaring by in his pickup truck. I'm trying to get a camera outa the car, me and another guy, and Rocco honks his horn and I holler, 'Fuck you, man! Take a walk!'

"Pretty soon here comes two police cars, and me and the other guy run up to an apartment building and hid in some ferns and watched. Rocco drives up, and that's how I know he gave us up to the cops. Why else would he show up like that, two minutes behind the patrol car? Trouble with him, he's got this thing about him belonging to Sweet Street and Sweet Street belong to him, and anybody else is riffraff, an intruder. Yeh, he'll buy a hot item now and then, but he won't give you no money for it. He's the cheapest fence in town. I come by there once with a super tape deck, a Sony four-track zero zero zip zap, a big beautiful thing in a leather case. He wanted to buy it, but the price was ridiculous. I had to take it to the jeweler. Another thing I can't stand about Rocco: he's a trick. He goes to whores. Nobody likes a trick. Tricks are shit."

No one knows the exact extent of Rocco's fencing operation, nor does anyone know his total yearly take from held-out jokers, six-ace-flat dice, and the technique of double-pegging in dominoes. Rocco claims he never cheats his friends, but the claim is open to debate, especially by his patron, Raffaele.

RAFFAELE: You never played a legitimate game of cards in your life.

ROCCO: I play legitimate with my friends.

RAFFAELE: You shit play legitimate.

ROCCO: You're a bad loser is all.

RAFFAELE: Why, you cheated me when we were playing here, not even for money! You have to win.

ROCCO: No, I have to aggravate you, that's all.

RAFFAELE: You remember the day we were playing double solitaire? I thought to myself, how unlucky Rocco is, his jack's under his ten, if he only had that jack he could get rid of the ten, and then there was a nine you could get rid of, and you could do a lot of other things. So I said to myself, "I'm gonna give him the opportunity to cheat," so I turned around and talked to somebody, and sure enough I turn back around and the jack comes up. I said, "Gotcha!" You cheating motherfucker! I berated you, don't you remember?

ROCCO: You shoulda called it before that, you shoulda called it.

RAFFAELE: *Called it?* I called it just as you put it up there, you cheating bastard. You say you don't cheat at gambling, you don't cheat your friends? You cheat, but you just don't admit it!

Well, I never was no saint, but one thing, I would never never *never* steal from a friend. From anybody else, yes. When I was a kid we used to steal everything. We even used to go to the old Thrifty drugstore and trade batteries for our flashlights. Just open the back end and trade the dead ones for new ones. The next customers would get dead batteries, and up their ass. That's their tough fuckin' luck.

I worked New Orleans at Mardi Gras one time. I was down there waiting for a ship and I run into this pickpocket and I watched him in action for a while. I said, "Hey, man, you're pretty good. You got pretty tough fingers. Pretty george, baby."

We got to talking. Mardi Gras was in three weeks. I says, "Did you ever work with a partner? I'm already fairly good, but what I don't know you can teach me."

He taught me plenty, how to give people a bump and a shove, a bump and a shove. You play the drunk in a hotel lobby or a dinnerhouse, or you spill a drink on your pigeon, and while you're rubbing him off with your handkerchief, you're grabbing his wallet. The rubbing ties him down, see?

My partner was very good with a razor, and he taught me that. It was a little straight razor, without the handle, and he held it between his fingers. He'd zip out a whole wallet pocket before the guy even knew it happened. He'd be in a crowd and he'd lift the coat up and make two slashes, one up and one down, and take the fuckin' wallet out. Or do it on a bus, with the jostling back and forth, and it's "Excuse me," and a shove here and a shove there and you got the whole fuckin' pocket.

He and I worked Mardi Gras together, and we scored good, very very good, and he was pretty honest with me, too, about splitting up. I know he gave me a good count, fifty-fifty all the way. I held out on him, though. I grabbed one pigeon for seven crisp new hundred-dollar bills, and I sunk that money away in my backpocket and my partner even knew about it. But other than that, I never stole from a friend. Of course, that was strictly business.

You'd have to look far to find a better spot than Sweet Street for hustling. It goes on night and day here, right out on the street in front of the naked eye. Paddyhustling goes on every night, *every night*! I stand outside and watch 'em. I say, "Mickey, watch this motherfucker, he's gonna roll this guy right here on the street," and *ba-room*, there he goes, right in front of us.

Everybody that comes on this street is a pigeon in one way or another. These poor fuckin' servicemen, they're the worst. They get their mustering-out pay, and they got twelve hundred, fifteen hundred dollars in their pocket and a plane ticket home, and they're fuckin' young punks and they don't know shit from Shinola about the big city. *Boom*! Some broad'll latch onto him, she puts her hand in his pocket and starts jacking him off, and at the same time she's going through his pockets. She says, "Oh, let me get my hands in your pants, honey," and he says, "Oh, yeh, go ahead," and that's it. There goes the money, bye-bye. One hand on his joint and the other in his wallet, and he's too enthralled to notice.

I don't handle nothing seedy like that. An occasional odd job, yeh, but never anything like paddyhustling or rolling a drunk. Here's the kind of job I do: I have this friend who shall be nameless 'cause his name is Bob Carbon, and he comes to me and says, "Rock, this fuckin' foreign car I bought is a lemon. I had it five weeks, and four weeks it's been in the garage, in and out, in and out, in and out, in and out. What am I gonna do?"

I says, "Dump the motherfucker for the insurance."

He says, "I don't wanta dump it close by here."

So we work it out. He's gonna give me the keys that night, go to bed, and get up the next morning at ten o'clock and report the car stolen from in front of his house. Meanwhile I'll be dumping the car at Hell Slide.

Fine. I got my pal Tom Andrews, which he's now a cop, and we drive all the way down to Hell Slide, hairpin curves and drops of three hundred, four hundred feet, straight down. I drive Carbon's car, and Tom takes his own Buick.

Five o'clock in the morning we get there. I says to Tom, "Go up the road and wait for me. Put your lights out. I'll be right there."

So I put the sportscar in gear, I step on the gas, I head it straight for the drop-off, and I jump out and make a beeline for Tom's car. I turn around and the car is half on, half off, hanging over the edge. The crankcase is stuck on a big rock.

I run back down, I get behind the car and push it. *Uggh!* It won't budge. A guy comes driving up and he says, "Hey, you're in a bit of trouble there, huh?"

"Yes," I says. "I been trying to hold it. I'm scared it's gonna go over any second. Can you do me a favor?" I asked him to go to the nearest gas station, which I know is about forty miles away, and get me some help, a tow truck or something. *Ah-room!* he takes off. So I get behind the wheel of Tom's car, and I rammed that little sportscar twice from the back, pushed it off, and that son of a bitch went over, and we took off. A nice clean morning's work, and Bob Carbon collected the whole price.

Now look what I got in the office here. Cost me thirty dollars, must be two hundred dollars' worth of marijuana in that bag. Somebody asked me what it was, I told 'em it was peat moss for Raffaele's flowers. They get a half a buck a joint for this here peat moss.

You know, sometimes I think I'm getting a little stale around this place. I'm not going anyplace, doing anything, and I'm not keeping up on my collections. I got an ivory collection that's worth twelve thousand, fourteen thousand dollars. I picked up all the pieces when I was at sea—Macao, Siam, Hong Kong, Singapore, Bombay, Calcutta. I got the only one in the U.S. now, a circle with twenty-five balls all carved one inside the other in ivory. I paid dear for that, $140, in Macao. The largest ball is nine inches in diameter, and it scales down to three-quarters of an inch. All inside one another.

People don't understand why I collect things like that. I collect 'em for the beauty and the aging and the coloring, to see the fine lines, the features. I've got the seven gods of wisdom in ivory, *truth* and all the rest of the gods. I've got the fisherman and the god of love. The fisherman's the most beautiful one, he's got a delicate nose, his nose and his chin and his beard, *so* beautiful, and he's got a goatee that's so realistic and beautiful, and almond-shaped eyes. Just lovely. Ah, lovely!

On some of the voyages, I doubled my income cheating at cards and doubled it again with jades and ivory and things like that I'd bring back and sell. We'd dock in Hong Kong, and I'd make up three days' menus for the crew and take off, go to Macao, take a junk, and go out there with six or seven of my shipmates, about a seven-hour sail. That's the best place for buying hot stuff. Last trip out, I picked up about four pounds of jade for four thousand dollars, and I resold three pieces of it to a department store for fifteen hundred dollars apiece, and two more pieces to a Chinese restaurant for $850 each, and I wound up making five times what I paid, and I still have two pieces the size of baseballs in my collection. It's clear profit. I don't have to pay any customs. I know one of the inspectors, and I bring him back a half-dozen boxes of Philippine cigars, Supreme Corona Coronas from Manila, big huge cigars, and I treat the other customs agents to a big meal on board, and I'm home free. *Dum—dum—dum*—they put the stamps on my packages, and one hand wash the other.

I miss it, the bargaining and the sailing and the card games and the good times. I been ashore twelve years now. Too long. Of course, I've always got a place to go. My daughter's thirty now, and she come up to me three years ago and she says, "Dad, I have something to talk to you about, and I'm embarrassed."

I said, "What are you embarrassed about? Hey, honey, I'm your dad! Just talk to me."

She says, "Well, we want to move into a larger house, what with the three kids and all, and we have our money tied up, and we need four thousand dollars to swing the down payment."

I says, "No trouble." I had the cash inside my safe. I said excuse me, took out forty one-hundred-dollar bills and gave 'em to her.

She started crying and whatnot. I said, "Hey, will you dummy up! Forget about it!"

She says, "Dad, were getting a five-bedroom house. There's a bedroom for each of the kids and one for us, and one reserved for you." So there'll always be a place for me to stay.

But I'm restless, tired and restless, and I enjoy the sea. Especially on those hot summer days. There's great peace of mind. You finish your duty and grab your cot and go out on the afterdeck and strip down to the raw and lay there and take your sun. Your little portable radio's with you, bringing in stations from all over the world, and you get black as a bear. It's ideal. I tell you, I'm going! Fuck Raffaele! And fuck Raffaele's! Which I'd miss 'em, yeh, but not that much.

RAFFAELE PIRINI, 51

Restaurateur

A STRANGER SITS POP-EYED watching a display of ill temper by a stockily built man in a black beret and tennis shoes, seated at the corner table in Raffaele's. The man in the beret slams his fist down on the table, rattling cups and spilling drinks, and emits a long string of Tuscan curses. "What's his trouble?" the stranger asks a waiter.

"Oh, that's Raffaele," the waiter says.

"What's he so excited about?"

"They were talking about the distances between stars, and Raffaele's mad 'cause he can't comprehend something."

Just then the violent man jumps up and says, "Yes, god-dammit, I *know* it's 720 fuckin' trillion miles! But how far is *that*? Who the fuck knows? *Nobody*! And that bugs me."

Raffaele Pirini wants a total grasp of every concept, to pick it up in his hand, turn it around in the light, and see through its secrets and mysteries. Since this is unfeasible with anything except fishbowls and marbles, he is chronically frustrated. He plumbs a subject till he can no longer stand not knowing all that he does not know, and then passes on to the next. At one time or another he has been addicted (as others become addicted to dope or alcohol) to astronomy, music, anthropology, pathology, agriculture, painting, sculpture, philately, animal training, microscopy, paleontology, and dozens of other subjects. Someone interested him in cancer research, and before he had lost his impetus he was spending half his time in laboratories, peering through high-powered instruments, and attending post-mortem operations in the city morgue. Then the passion ended as quickly as it began. "I love the guy," says Rocco Cardi, "but he never follows through on anything. If he put all his good intentions to work, the man would have been a genius."

At fifty-one, Raffaele is beginning to expand around the middle, and he has long since gone bald, a subject on which he is touchy. He owns drawers full of berets, and he never goes anyplace bareheaded. He abhors suits and ties, and customarily is seen about his restaurant in sweater and slacks. He will wear a tie, but only on threat of exclusion from some beloved event, such as a violin concert. For thirty years Raffaele has practiced four hours a day on his violin, and for a single purpose: so that he will sound better when he performs for himself. Rocco says his boss plays as well as most professionals, but Raffaele is far from satisfied. "My life's ambition is to play a little bit better than Heifetz," he says. "For that, I would sell my soul to the devil. Honest, I'd make a deal!"

His ancestry is mixed Mediterranean, with traces of Spanish and a predominance of Northern Italian. Like Tennyson's Ulysses, he is vexed by an aging wife, and she by him, and he takes solace in a lovely young woman with chestnut hair who sits quietly with him at the restaurant and holds his hand. He withholds none of his feelings from friend or enemy, often shifting in a single speech from polemic to panegyric, and expressing both with fanatical energy. He has a blind adulation of his friends. "If Raffaele really likes you," says his good customer Mickey Martin, "I don't care how much you do wrong to him, he'll still like you. He's just one of those guys that's forever forgiving."

Stanley Hamilton Briggs, the ex-con philosopher and sometime helper at Raffaele's, refers to his employer as "the de' Medici of Sweet Street," and talks about him emotionally. "He's a constant teacher of humility. He has an ability to extend attention to people almost unendingly, even if he knows they're insane or stupid. Somebody'll come in and act obnoxious and I'm about to throw him out and Raffaele sits him down and gives him a cup of coffee and starts talking to him. Hours later you look around and they're still talking, and Raffaele's completely into the guy's trip. What this teaches me is not to be so hard on people, to try to understand them no matter how they look on the surface. Raffaele's my daily lesson in the humanities."

The indoor and outdoor café and restaurant, known simply as "Raffaele's," is a mélange of styles and smells and little boys' dreams. It serves hard whiskey and hot fudge sundaes, thick capuccino and espresso and *café au lait*, light herb teas and tamarind coolers from India, exotic fruit punches and whipped-cream agonies. Pots of rich black coffee send aromatic steam twirling out of sight into the cavernous ceiling, and a dessert cart creaks under the weight of thick cheesecakes, Napoleons, vanilla and chocolate éclairs, cupcakes, apple crisps, and eleven-layer chocolate cakes. The bar is small and off to one side; narrow racks set into the brick wall hold bottles of Metaxa, calvados, Courvoisier, ouzo, Amer Picon, and Grand Marnier, while the working-stiff Scotches and bourbons and gins are down below.

Near the entrance a baroque red coffee-making machine, retired long ago, serves as a decorative companion to a large, round table that is shielded from any possibility of indoor thunderstorm by a brightly striped beach umbrella. Dotted around the rest of the room are old-fashioned marble-top tables, with leather booths lining the walls to the rear. Above, beyond, and beside everything are plants—big potted plants that look like young redwoods and small potted plants that hang in wire baskets from the ceiling and shed occasional leaves into the refreshments. A single red rose in a narrow vase is centered at every table.

Through an array of plate-glass panels one can see the sidewalk portion of the restaurant, almost always busier than the inside. Yellow heat lamps are banked along the ceiling, casting a soft glow on the customers' hairstyles, and cars whip around the corner just outside and splay their headlights across the tables, creating strange surrealistic effects. Seen from the inside, the backlighted sippers and diners turn into cardboard cut-outs, as starkly outlined as the black-gowned woman in Toulouse-Lautrec's poster for the Divan Japonais. From directly across the street, to the dismay of Raffaele and Rocco and the restaurant's establishment, a bright sign flashes the word NAKED, and calls attention to a smaller sign billing "The Battle of the Naked Lady Wrestlers."

The occupants of Raffaele's, inside and out, are usually a mixed bag of pimps and whores and burglars, bank presidents and politicians and industrialists, social workers and clergymen and newscasters. Raffaele himself welcomes the raffish assortment and encourages it, and is particularly fond of four or five of the "working girls." "I don't judge them as whores," he says. "I've found that what people do for a living has very little to do with what they are. Besides, there's lots of respectable women that'd like to get a hundred dollars for going to bed with somebody. My wife said, 'Gee, I'd like to try it.' I said, 'Honey, you like it so much you'd give 'em ninety-nine dollars and ninety-nine-cents change!' "

The financial future of the place is never assured, despite its popularity. Raffaele's is the central meeting point for all Sweet Street types, many of whom are capable of whiling away two or three hours over a cup of coffee, tying up a table all the time. Another reason for the lack of financial security is Raffaele's softness. As Mickey Martin put it, "On a street that's full of hustlers, Raffaele couldn't hustle his mother. He's too poor an actor. He doesn't have the heart for hustling. So he gets hustled unmercifully himself."

"Look at the poor patsy!" Rocco says disgustedly. "Sitting over there eating with the rich again. Yeh, they're rich Hebes from New York. He just met 'em tonight. He'll pick up the check and then they'll go outside and laugh at him. Jerk-off freeloaders!"

In Raffaele Pirini's philosophy, the underdog deserves pity and assistance, and an underdog is defined as anyone who does not own a restaurant. He sets up drinks and dinners for financiers and bums, and his wallet is always being turned inside out for someone he hardly knows. "He has false friends that'll come in here and sit for hours in front of a glass of water," says Mickey Martin. "Then Raffaele'll come in and say, 'Hey, you want something to eat?' and the guy'll say, 'Yeh, gimme a steak sandwich, the works, and a little touch of cognac.' And Raffaele buys! There's one writer ran up an eighteen-hundred-dollar tab. Then one day he sold a book, and he came in and showed Raffaele a check for ten thousand dollars. But he didn't pay his bill, and he still hasn't. Ask Rocco! Then some broad'll come in that she'll be so dirty and smelly that nobody wants to come near her, and Raffaele'll pick her up like a poor dog and feed her and console her, youknowwhatImean? This is his way. He's an animal-lover. But he helps people to the stage where he's hurting them. It's not good for people to get too much help. And it's certainly not good for his financial rating. I told him once, 'Raffaele, I only hope that if God forbid anything ever happened to you and you got down, that all your friends'll help you. Don't hold your breath.' "

The worst bum, that's still a human being. I often think about what a man looked like when he was a little baby, a cute little baby with pearl-like skin and his mother and father so proud for him to be born, and he turns the wrong ways and he gets caught in the traps of life. I'm not gonna turn my back on him just because he's a little drunk or he's in trouble.

People say I'm tolerant, but I hate that word. I don't want to tolerate, and I don't want to be tolerated. The word should be "understanding," to understand everyone's plight. It's like Mort Sahl said about the girl at the party that kept staring at him, and she finally said, "I noticed you were Jewish, and I've been tolerating you." That word is *terrible*!

When I started my restaurant fourteen years ago the idea was sables and sandals. I didn't want any one set of people. It's the mixture that's beautiful. I want human beings in my place, not just certain people that have neckties on and look good. It took a while to get the idea into some heads. Like my wife's. When we first opened, my wife comes running into the kitchen in shock. "There are four guys here with beards. They look terrible! They're gonna ruin the whole party!"

I said, "Beards are gonna ruin a whole party?" Can you imagine?

I was at a business meeting the other day and as usual wearing my beret and no tie, and all the businessmen were dressed in ties. One of them took a dislike to me, and I could tell it was because of my beret. He asked me why do I always wear it. I told him, "Well, some people wear false teeth or a wooden leg. I have no hair and it bugs me, so I put a hat on it. I like it better that way, okay?" I said, "What do you care if I wear a hat? Does it bother you?"

He lost faith in me then. He questioned everything I said throughout the evening, just because I wore a beret. Some people are stupid. That kind of a guy I couldn't get along with for two minutes.

There aren't many things that make me mad. I guess mostly they come under the heading of deliberate cruelty. I can't stand deliberate cruelty to anything. The maddest I've ever been in my life was the night some kid, twenty-six or twenty-seven, came walking by the restaurant and broke a limb off a tree in front. I hollered so loud they thought I was shot, and I chased that kid all the way down the bottom of the hill and brought him back, and I beat him within an inch of his life.

Why, we wouldn't even be alive if it wasn't for trees! They're the most beautiful thing that God's created. Why, there are trees two-thousand, three-thousand years old. It makes man pretty puny. I have an arrangement with a mortuary here, and we've already picked the tree out, where I'm gonna be buried by the roots. Just my ashes. It's against the law, but he's gonna sneak me in. A tree's the most glorious thing that lives on this earth. Sometimes when we close the place up at night, I go out on the sidewalk and play my violin to our outside trees. They like jigs and tarantellas, happy music, because they have to stand so still. They don't want to hear a love song. So at four in the morning, I play and I tell 'em that I love 'em.

I don't like scenes like beating up that kid. Things like that upset me for a long time. I'm a little upset with myself most of the time anyway. The way I react to people—do I want them all to love me, or am I just afraid of being hated? In some ways I think I'm better than I really am, but then I put myself down more than I should. I'm not thorough, I learn things, but I don't get to the bottom of them. And my English isn't good. I love expressing myself, but I'm frustrated because the ideas come into my head and I can't express them properly, and I get embarrassed at some of the things I say. And then I get depressed, dwelling on past hurts.

I don't see anything strange about wanting to be better, to know more, to know everything there is to know. I don't care if it's impossible or not. I'm gonna keep on trying just for the fun of it. The thing I hate more than anything else in the world is the group that talks on one subject and studies one subject to the total exclusion of everything else. I used to belong to a music study group, and I used to say, "Don't you fellows ever talk about girls or something?"

Once they had a seminar and they told me, "Bring your favorite record." So I brought the Heifetz recording of the Brahms violin concerto, and when I got there they said, "Brahms? Are you kidding? We don't play Brahms. That's Gypsy music!" I picked up my record and left. What a lot of shit!

Maybe I'm stupid, maybe that's the problem. Maybe I'm just a simple soul. I like *all* music. Why, there's even some rock and roll that knocks me out. I started out in life on western music, on a ranch where I was brought up, and I still like some of it. I guess I'm just not sophisticated. I was thrown out of the sixth grade, and I never went back. We were hungry a lot of the time and worried the rest; maybe that's why I went into the restaurant business, to make sure my stomach's always full. One time during the depression my father came home and the food was on the table and he was angry at my mother, and he kept talking about the food we were eating and how there was no money, and how hard he had to work to keep our mouths full, and I couldn't eat. The food stuck in my throat, and I was hungrier than hell, too, but I couldn't swallow. I felt like he was mad at me for eating *his* food. He was probably just tired, but who sees that as a kid?

There were hoboes that used to come around, and I'd sneak them food. My mother was a meticulous housekeeper, so clean she was almost dirty, going around picking up invisible lint, so we could never have hoboes inside the house. But I used to like to talk to them. They were great philosophers. One winter one of my favorites came by with four others and I was about nine years old and nobody was home, so I invited them in for a home-cooked meal. I knew it would bug my mother if I served them on the kitchen table, because that's where we always ate, so I set the dining room table that we never used, and I fixed them a beautiful spread of spaghetti and meat balls. I knew I was doing wrong, but I still did it. The hoboes were kind of uncomfortable, and right in the middle of the meal my mother walked in. Holy Christ, did I get it! *Ai yi yi!* Those poor guys felt so sorry for me!

Maybe that has something to do with the kind of place I run now, where everybody's welcome and anybody can sit anywhere and get the same kind of food service. The trouble is, the atmosphere around the street is getting so schlocky that people are beginning to stay away. The main thing that's lacking is taste. I don't mind nudity, the human form has been shown for ten thousand years, but can't it be done with some degree of taste, some degree of style?

This street, the signs and the garishness of them, the colors, the everything—it's abominable. Somebody told me about a barker the other night trying to lure him inside and saying something about "dripping cunts." Oh, I wish I'd heard him! I'd have had that barker arrested in about two seconds. How dare him!

The club owners come in and they just block the rest of us businessmen out. They take care of themselves and nobody else, and they don't realize that we all have to live together. They're hanging themselves. If they did their business in good taste, it'd be better. Why can't you show beautiful bodies gracefully? Why must it be bawdy and gaudy and smell like perspiration and defecation? These strip joints are toilets. *Toilets*!

There's no telling what kind of advertisements they'll put in their windows, where everybody that comes driving by can see them—little kids, nuns, old ladies, everybody. It's like the guy saw a store full of clocks, and he goes inside and he asks for a new clock and the merchant says, "I don't sell clocks, I perform circumcisions." And the guy says, "Well, what the hell's the clocks doing?" The merchant says, "What *should* I hang in the window?" That's the way Sweet Street's going. Any day now they'll have girls screwing in the windows and performing sodomy and all kinds of things to get the people in. If you didn't put any controls on these owners, *they would do it*! That's how bad off they are mentally. They're really sick! They're ruining this street. I hate to see it. It was a good street for a while.

Salesman

If you have to keep reminding yourself of a thing, perhaps it isn't so.

—Christopher Morley, *Thunder on the Left*

MICKEY MARTIN IS ALMOST the same size as a hundred-gallon drum, and just as robust. Each evening he drives home from work and catches up on sleep squandered the night before. Around nine or ten P.M. he wakes up and begins his toilette. He slicks his short brown hair tightly to his skull, buffs his face to a candy-apple sheen, and applies the faintest hint of a masculine cologne. His head barely visible over the steering wheel, he drives his super-powered Detroit smog-belcher four blocks from his apartment to Sweet Street and patiently circles the block—sometimes for fifteen or twenty minutes—until he gets the parking space of his choice. Then, bathed and freshly scented like Blanche DuBois, he enters Raffaele's.

For the rest of the night, his raucous debates and his even more raucous laughter rattle the dishes and dominoes at the corner table where Raffaele and the other insiders sit. Mickey's closest crony is Rocco the night manager, and it is one of his proudest boasts that he alone can call Rocco "Horseface" and survive. "Hey, Horseface!" he calls across the room, then says to a companion, "See? Not a beef outa him. I can call him that name any time I want. Now *you* try it!" The companion demurs.

At thirty-four, Mickey has been a fixture at Raffaele's for ten or eleven years. He grew up in Chicago, where he learned self-defense from the cradle, and he is renowned along

Sweet Street for the number of men he has anesthetized with a single punch. Now, in the late afternoon of his career as an avenger of the wronged and oppressed, he sits for hours trading *machismo* stories with the burly Rocco and others. When Mickey tells such tales about himself, the pitiable opponent is usually cast as a boorish bully who kept insulting Mickey or one of Mickey's friends or any lady of Mickey's acquaintance until "Pow! He asked for it. What else could I do, youknowwhatImean?" Mickey does not mind being characterized as tough, so long as he is characterized as fair.

He also likes to think of himself as cool under fire, but even the most judicious have their limits. One night a female customer with the tongue of a mamba was sitting with Mickey and Rocco and a few others. As she recalls the incident, "Mickey was rapping some very racist remarks, and none of the so-called men at the table were answering him back. So I finally said, 'Mickey, I think you should shut up. The jock strap is too tight on your mind.' He reached across and slapped me as hard as he could with a rolled-up newspaper. We haven't spoken since." Mickey has not added the event to his collection of anecdotes.

As befits an aging warrior with a good won-lost record, Mickey says he no longer feels that he has to prove himself to everyone who comes along. "It was because of my short height," he says. "I always felt inferior for a long time, and I had to show people I could handle myself." He was a star football player in high school and a bruising rugby player on the sandlots, but he butted so hard and so often that he ground away part of his neck vertebrae and had to have a fusion operation. As a nonparticipating, almost neckless sportsman, he makes a specialty of striking up friendships with professional athletes, and travels far to watch them perform, as though to prove his loyalty. Occasionally one of the athletes will reciprocate by stopping into Raffaele's, and Mickey is careful to introduce him around and make him feel at home and guffaw at his jokes.

Sometimes there is an aura of Willy Loman about Mickey; being liked is not enough, he has to be "well-liked." But in situations where Willy Loman would fold up and brood, Mickey lashes out with his formidable fists, and still somehow manages to retain an image of himself as the little choir boy, now grown up. He tells proudly about the Chicago woman who told her son a few decades ago, "Wally, how come you're not like little Mickey? Look at him. He's an angel right out of heaven!"

Violence is never far from this particular angel, as it is never far from anyone on Sweet Street, even the most venerated of the elder statesmen, even street gods like Raffaele himself. One night Raffaele concluded a sullen game of dominoes, and Mickey shouted across the room, "Who won?"

Raffaele grunted, "Rocco."

Mickey applied the needle. "Excuse me, did you say Rocco won?"

Raffaele stood up and shouted, *"Rocco won! What the fuck do you want me to do, make up a placard? Rocco won, Rocco won!"*

"Fuck you, Raffaele!" Mickey said.

"Fuck you, too!" Raffaele answered.

"You don't have to get hot about it."

"Fuck you, Mickey! You're horseshit anyway."

The two old friends moved nose to nose, trading masculine pleasantries, till the towering Rocco pushed between them. Mickey stormed off to Vino's for dinner. When he returned a few hours later, Raffaele met him at the door. "Here, Mickey," he said, handing over an umbrella. "You forgot this. I been saving it for you."

"Oh, thanks, Raffaele," Mickey said, smiling beatifically. "Nice of you."

The two men retired to the corner table, and within a few minutes Mickey's laugh could be heard around the room. He does not have to prove himself any more.

I'm a loner. I mean, I know a lot of people, but I'm a loner. Most people like me, and the ones that don't like me, most of 'em I *forced* 'em not to like me. I developed this philosophy of life a long time ago, that if I don't like somebody, I just insult 'em and pretty soon they stop coming around, youknowwhatImean?

When I was a kid, I used to dream all the time. We were

poor and hungry, and I used to ditch school because the seat of my pants was so worn you could see through 'em. One Christmas my mother gave me a thirty-five-cent pair of socks. She said, "I really feel bad, but this is all I can give you. Merry Christmas, and I love you."

I took the socks and threw 'em down and I said, "How come everybody else gets clothes and presents and I never get nothing?"

She said, "I'm sorry. All I can give you is my love." But that wasn't enough for me then.

I went out and shined shoes and sang for pennies when I was seven years old. At nine I was selling ice cream on the beach, at twelve I was moving furniture, and at thirteen I was working for the city. I musta had something special, because it would never fail that people would look at me and they would see something in me. One guy always used to look at me and say, "You're gonna be somebody someday, kid. You got that magic." I was seven or eight! I had a God-given gift. People liked me.

It's still that way. When I went back to see my sister after a long time, she sat me down in front of her kids and she said, "There he is! Look at him! That's your Uncle Mickey. He's the one we always talk about!" That little niece of mine, she used to sit on my lap and tell me how much she loved me, out of all her uncles.

Well, I never entertain the thought that people don't like me. The ones that don't like me, it's because I forced it that way. I have *reepport* with everybody. At work, I'm the only one that can go in and whack the boss's secretary on the rear end. She's an older woman, and she looks on me like a son, youknowwhatImean? Just like I'm the only one can call Rocco "Horseface."

I know a few people say I'm racist, but I'm not. It's the individual I'm interested in, not the race. Why, when I was younger I'd go in joints people should never go in. But, see, I'm smart enough when I go in a joint, I know how to handle it. Like I used to go into colored joints. The first thing I'd do is wheel up to the bar, order a drink, and I'd say to the bartender how's everything going youknowwhatImean? Fine, youknowwhatImean? and he'd pour me a drink and I'd give him a dollar tip, and I'd give the cocktail waitresses a dollar, and from then on they'd take care of me, not let anybody bother me.

Around Raffaele's, I sit and watch a lot, and most people that don't know me think I'm just some real square guy that isn't hep. But I observe many things in Raffaele's that no one else does. I see the way colored guys hit on white girls. Maybe no one else will notice it, but I notice it. It's hard for me to stomach. But black and white's the trend now. There are nights in Raffaele's when that's all you'll see. It's hard for me to accept.

Me, I don't go for the women around here. They either turn into two things: they marry some barker and go through life fighting with each other, or else they get involved with a colored guy and become his old lady, and of course that cuts 'em off from the white environment, because the white guys all go dead on 'em after that. The white guys all say, "Well, I understand, I can dig race-mixing," but inside they don't accept it at all.

I don't think I'll ever get married. My standards are way too high. I'm satisfied to be a salesman, a good salesman. I've got it made, I've got it made. If I want to sleep in till noon tomorrow, I can do it. The way my boss feels about me, I can do anything I want. He likes the way I do things, and he likes my results.

When I wake up in the morning, I'm really happy to be alive, youknowwhatImean? I'm so happy because I've come so far in life, further than I ever dreamed when I was a kid. If I was to pass away tomorrow, God forbid, I would say, well, I really lived my life. Just about everything I dreamed as a kid, I went out and did as an adult.

I have just one ambition left. I'd like to be invited to the White House for dinner, and then be invited to dinner with the biggest bum on Skid Row. That way I'd know I was accepted by everybody, I could get along with everybody from the president to a bum.

Restaurateur

Where do they get the money? Coming up redheaded curates from the county Leitrim, rinsing empties and old man in the cellar. Then, lo and behold, they blossom out as Adam Findlaters or Dan Tallons . . . Off the drunks perhaps. Put down three and carry five. What is that? A bob here and there, dribs and drabs. On the wholesale orders perhaps. Doing a double shuffle with the town travellers. Square it with the boss and we'll split the job, see?
—James Joyce, *Ulysses*

A MAN WHO LOOKS like a movie star enters Raffaele's, causing a stir among the nonregulars. He is of medium height, with wavy black hair, gray-blue eyes, and the profile of a young Rock Hudson. His face bears the sweet look of success, the satisfied smile, the smooth, unlined cheeks. "Hey, look who it ain't!" Rocco says, and greets the newcomer with a tweak of the testicles, Sweet Street's ultimate sign of friendship and approval. The two engage in mock combat, and Rocco keeps clutching the man about the waist and repeating, "Where is it? Where *is* it? I know it's somewhere!" Finally the newcomer swirls back his jacket and reveals the stubby handle of a small revolver, tucked neatly into the waistband.

"Hey, I've seen that guy in the movies," someone says to Rocco a few minutes later. "What's his name?"

"His name is Robert Benni," Rocco answers, "and you never seen him in no movie, 'cause he's never been in one."

Robert "Bobby" Benni, twenty-eight years old and already a respected elder statesman, takes his seat at the corner table, and there is a short, respectful silence. "Well, Bobby," Raffaele says, "how they hanging?"

"Foin," says Robert Benni, "everything's foin on this field of wheat."

Bobby and some of his intimates have perfected a rhyming code, to enable them to exchange secrets in front of outsiders. "This field of wheat" means this street. "Foin" is the way a survivor of East Harlem says fine. Bobby has been on Sweet Street for six years, not long enough to rid himself of his foin New York overtones, but long enough to become an accredited Sweet Street businessman, owning and operating a flourishing restaurant and bar. He is articulate and quick, with a rodent's high metabolism. His grammar is undisciplined, but he is never at a loss for a street idiom or an emphatic retort. He spots a handsome woman entering Raffaele's, and he tells Rocco, "Piper Heidseck at the Borden Company," meaning look at the breasts.

"Yeh," says Rocco, who is not quite at home in the strange tongue. "I already Piper Heidsecked 'em."

After a while, Bobby answers a visitor's question. "Sure, I always carry a lady from Bristol," he says. "It's right in my naps and aunts, whenever I need it. The guys on this field of wheat know I'm saying I always carry a pistol right in my pants. A lump of lead's your head, your I-suppose is your nose, your minced pie is your eye, north and south your mouth, whip and lash your mustache, and ones and twos your shoes. One and another's your mother, and twist and twirl's a girl. We talk that way 'cause a lotta times there'll be a rootin tooter sitting at the counter, that's a fruit, or a scooter and bike, that's a dyke, and we don't want them to know what we're talking about, or there'll be some boats and oars, that's whores, and fish and shrimps, that's pimps, or some tea leafs, thiefs, and we can carry on a whole conversation in front of 'em."

Bobby's personal hallmark is an intense neatness and orderliness, in all areas. Now that he no longer has to labor for a living, he wears immaculate suits with matching shirts, ties, and socks, all cut in the same patterns and weaves and differing only in color tones and the direction of the grain. His black boots are polished to a drill sergeant's shine, and his monogram RMB is likely to show up on his person in three or four different places, including his shorts. "All I ever had was hand-me-downs," he explains, "so I'm making up for it."

His other mark of distinction is his pistol, a stainless-steel Smith & Wesson .38 with jacketed hollow points for maximum penetration. When the pistol is not secured in his belt or a shoulder holster, Bobby is sleeping, the weapon alongside him on the table. He is incomplete without it.

"Yeh, and that ain't all," says Rocco. "Don't let him shit you, because he carries two pistols, he just won't admit it. He'll show you the .38, but he's packing another one elsewhere on his premises. I just happened to bump into it one night when I was picking his pockets for a laugh, and I said, 'Hey, man, whattaya need two pistols for?' He acted annoyed. He said, ' 'Cause I got a cold.' Never fuck with him, man. He's a crack shot."

"I respect the guy," says Raffaele, "but there's one thing that enters my mind. What about a man that is never without a pistol in his belt, and sometimes two? Does this really mean he's a tough guy? I was just wondering."

There's ugliness and beauty on this field of wheat. I have a great love for it, 'cause I make my living here. There's people here that I dig, and there's a lot of pukes, too. The cops are pretty good guys, from the captain down, nice people. I don't think they're very hip, no. I don't think the toughest cop in this town could walk a beat in Harlem for ten minutes, but I'd rather have these cops than the New York ones. Nine out of ten cops here will tell you, if a guy wants to go out and get himself jacked off, there's nothing wrong in it. They'd rather see a guy fuck some broad than go out and rape my sister. That's exactly my attitude, too. But no, the laws fix it good for the pimps and bad for the whores, which is exactly the opposite of the way it oughta be. So we got a bunch of nigger pimps turning broads out. Lunchbucket pimps, I call 'em. They're not even good pimps. Your local pimp, he grabs himself a runaway from Bumfuck, Kansas, parties her, puts a little cocaine under her horn, and gets her geezing something. Once he traps her, he tells her she's got to bring in a hundred a day. Her expenses are thirty bucks for shit, twenty to live, so he's making fifty off her. He's a fifty-per-cent pimp. He's a piece of shit.

I don't see anything wrong with a legitimate pimp or a legitimate whore, but not these nigger lunchbucket pimps. They've got their broads turning seven dollar tricks, so a legitimate pimp can't make any money. And everybody's afraid of these black motherfuckers, and that *kills* me. Nobody touches 'em. That fuckin' *kills* me!

You should hear me talk to a nigger pimp, a nigger whore. When I find out a broad's got a nigger pimp, a fuckin' raboon pimp, I really get rank with 'em. I really degrade 'em. I talk to 'em like I'm talking to a teamster. I really get dirty-mouth with 'em, and I'm proud of it.

About six months ago a whore came in and tried to work my joint, and this ain't that type of joint, right? I told her, "No unescorted women allowed," which isn't my rule, but I make up my rules as I go along, to allow for cases like her.

She says, "Fuck you, motherfucker!" She's a ranky fuckin' whore, and she started badmouthing me, "Fuck you, you motherfucker, you cocksucker!"

I said, "Hey, don't talk like that! If you're gonna talk like a fuckin' man, I'm gonna treat you like a fuckin' man."

She said, "Fuck you!" and went to hit me, so I just cold-cocked her and threw her into the street. She got up and she said, "My old man'll take care of you!" She's a white broad, see, but she's living with a nigger, and that makes her a nigger, too.

Later that night I'm walking to my apartment, and I reach the big steel gate in front of the garage and this big Mark IV Lincoln whips around and comes straight across the street for me. I can't do nothing, right? I push against the fence and the man upstairs is taking care of me. Somebody had forgot to lock the gate, and it swung open. Otherwise I'd have been crushed against it. So I ducked into the garage area, and the Lincoln had to stop unless they wanted to bust up their grille.

Okay, by this time I got my piece and I see where two niggers in the front seat are getting ready to come out, because the courtesy light goes on. So I raised up the difference and screwed two shots right into the windshield. One hit the back of the rear-view mirror and shattered glass all over the inside. With that, the fuckin' guy put the car into reverse and backed across the street and rammed his rear end into a light pole, and then he goes screeching down the hill and away.

A few weeks later I'm walking on Sweet Street and I see this spade cat walking by and I bunk into him by accident. I'm just about to say excuse me, and he says, "Hey, man, I don't want no fuckin' trouble wit' chew!" so I know he's one of the cocksuckers that tried to kill me. I grab him by the scuff of the neck, I take my fuckin' gun and I shove it under his chin, and I walk him up the street to my apartment. I say, "Man, I'm gonna blow you away!" I'm really talking bad, but I ain't gonna do nothing to him. Maybe pistol-whip him a little bit, but I ain't gonna kill him. I ain't a fuckin' idiot.

I says, "I'm gonna give you a fuckin' break. Just tell me who was with you."

So he gave me two more names—the pimp and another guy the pimp had hired to kill me, three of 'em altogether. I says, "Well, where *is* this motherfuckin' pimp? I'm gonna take care of him."

He says, "You don't have to, man. When we got back to the black district, we took care of him ourself. We worked him over good! He told us he wanted us to do a simple job on some little cocksucker that ain't worth a shit. We didn't know it was you, man, or we wouldn't've done it." So I talked to him awhile and I let him go and now all the niggers know me and respect me, which they better.

I'm not huge, but I can take care of myself. I'm in perfect shape at all times, ready to mix with anybody. If a guy comes at me, automatically my hands go up. I cock, I move around, I got my moves, I know where my hands are going, what I'm doing. When I walk into a place, I look around at the people, and I say, Well, if this cocksucker hits me from the side, there's an ashtray over there, a chair at the bar, and I'll use those on him. Unconsciously I'm figuring out exactly what to do if anybody jumps me. The same thing when I work the front door of my own joint.

I'm into karate six years now, and I have a gym in my house, weights, a bench, boards to punch, a speedbag. I've perfected a ten-count karate chop I can do in like a few seconds. Here, stand up! When you throw a punch at me, I step forward like this with my right foot and I throw both sides of my hands against your forearm, to catch the nerves up there. Foin! I *snap* my hands in there, and it's that snap that causes the tearing and the busting and the broken bones. Then I start throwing chops so fast you can't even see 'em, one on the side of your neck, then I bust your nose with my left hand, hit you in the groin, then another nose shot, an elbow into your jaw to bust it, and one more into the nose, to make sure it's broken and make sure you're blinded so you can't fight back, and then I drive the broken bones into the face with my fist, and then snap a half-fist into the throat, and usually that's enough. Any *one* of those moves is usually enough, but what the hell, if you kill him, he ain't feeling it, so you might as well finish the sequence. And if he's just knocked out, you can keep on till you do kill him. Costs the same, right? The whole sequence takes a second or two, if you do it right.

The other way I protect myself is with weapons. I love gun shows. It's just you and the guy you're dealing with—no registration, no nothing. "Here, you want the gun? You got the gun!" No waiting. A lot of shit goes under the table that way. Like a friend of mine bought a sawed-off exterior hammer ten-gauge shotgun. With that gun he can remove a wall. But he didn't get it for hunting, just for people. I have thirty-six guns in my collection, and every one is functional. They're the best pieces made, polished and oiled and fully loaded with the foinest ammunition at all times. I have my own private armory, stuff like whips and swords, clubs that convert into swords, billies, saps, blackjacks, bludgeons, ax handles and maces and guns, and almost everything in my collection turns into a sharp sword in a second, and I keep them all honed. My burglar alarm system is so delicate I can hear an ant pissing on my windowsill. Nobody comes fucking around my apartment without me knowing about it, plus there's an outside lock and an outside burglar alarm they gotta get through to get near me.

I fear nothing on earth, but I do fear God if nothing else. I get a great personal satisfaction out of going to church. I drag my ass out of bed after three or four hours sleep and I go to mass, regardless. Look, here's my beads. I carry them always. I'm not by any stretch a good Catholic, but I enjoy church. I sit right in front. I know all the ritual. I can serve at mass. I donate. There's something called intentions, and like I'll pay for intentions, I'll make a promise to God, and mostly I promise money, and if one of my intentions comes out—if something happens that I asked for—I'll donate to the church. A hundred, one fifty, two fifty, depending on the intention.

If I don't go to church on Sunday, I feel rotten, really rotten, even though I might walk out of church and bust a guy in the head with a hammer, it wouldn't bother me. But I have to go to church first. Maybe I'll be shacked up with some little chickie, and we'll be getting it on all night long, and then she'll say, "Where you going?" and when I tell her I'm going to church, she thinks I'm kidding. I don't elaborate on it, because I don't want her to feel guilty about what we did all night.

I have my own arrangements with God. I go in and talk to God like anybody else. I don't do formal prayers and things like that, but I sit there and talk, and when an answer pops in my head, I figure it's from Him. I enjoy my church, it still has the organ music and the traditions that I like, and the priest does good sermons. He's against the nudie scene, and every once in a while he'll preach that he hopes Sweet Street will be restored to moral sanity, and all that kind of crap, and he'll say, "There's a young man that comes to this church who's a good man, and he takes care of his mom, and he owns a nice restaurant that has fine atmosphere." That's me he's talking about. When I first opened the joint, he came down and blessed it, which has got to be a first on the street.

I've brought him a lot of kids to be baptized, and I keep the pictures of all my godchildren on my dresser, in nice frames. They were all children of unwed mothers, and I figured it wasn't their fault they were illegitimate. Every illegitimate kid in town is my godchild. The mothers were fucked up and didn't even know who the fathers were, most of the time. So I take 'em into church, and the priest says, "Who's the father?" and I say, "Man, what's the difference?" At least

I give the kid a little foundation, 'cause he's got a hard way to go running around without a last name for openers.

I try to be a decent person, I try to do the right thing. I'm no fuckin' saint, but I have a moral code of my own, and I live by it. I bought my mother and father a home in the country; that was a life ambition for me. Another life ambition was to say to my father—he was a truckdriver—"Here, Dad, here's a brand-new car," 'cause he never had a brand-new car paid for. He paid on a car three years and then he traded it in. And I always wanted to say to my mother, "Here, Mom, here's a house. This is *your* house." So I bought 'em both the house when I started making a little money, but my dad died two weeks after they moved in, so I never got him the car.

My mother wants for nothing! Her house cost me thirty-eight thousand dollars, and I don't even live there. Three bedrooms, two baths. Do you know what that means to a fuckin' kid that used to have a potbelly stove in his kitchen and a bathtub that we use to have to fill with a fuckin' pot? You know what a home means to my mom? Do you know what happiness is to my mother? *Vacuuming the rug*! Who the fuck ever had carpeting to vacuum? That's happiness! When we first got the house, we'd sit there and look at the fireplace, 'cause who the fuck ever had a fireplace in East Harlem? A wall oven, who ever heard of that? And a two-car garage.

Well, I love my mother, and I'm not ashamed to say so. There's nobody can call me a cherry, no one can say I'm anybody's sissy, right? But like I'll see my mother and I'll kiss her. Like every time I see her I'll kiss her hello, I'll kiss her good-bye, I don't give a shit who's there.

One day when I was nineteen my mother and I were shopping for a Christmas present for my father, and the clerk showed us something, and I said, "Gee, do you think Daddy'd like that?"

The clerk said, "*Daddy*? I haven't heard anybody call his father Daddy in I don't know how long." I didn't like the way he said it, so I walked my mother outside to the car and I said, "Jeez, Mom, I think I dropped my comb in there," and I went back in and laid the guy out. I gave him two shots: a sternum shot and when he went down a whack on the side of the head. I left him unconscious.

I called my father Daddy till the day he died. I still call my mother Mommy. To my aunts or my sister, I'll say, "Where's Mommy?" Never "Where's Mom?" or "Where's Mother?"

I call my mother up every day, I'll show you my phone bill. Every single day, even if it's just to say, "Hey, Mom, everything okay? Well, I'm busy. Talk to you later!" One day a week, sometimes two, I'm at my mom's for dinner, and I take her out like she's my girl friend once a month. I'm very close to her.

I guess it's because when I grew up my mother and father gave me nothing but love. They gave me maybe a dime a week, but they could only afford a nickel. So these cocksuckers that can afford to give their kids three hundred and only give 'em two hundred, well, fuck 'em! My parents gave me till it hurt. Who's a better mom? You tell me! I grew up in a house where there was nothing but love. I had the happiest childhood there ever was.

No pansies ever come out of my neighborhood, I'll guarantee you. At least not alive. All we did was fight on the streets. Not only did I have to fight the niggers, I had to fight the spics, the Irish, the squareheads, the Polacks, the Germans, and even some of the Italians. Fighting is all we had. We played games like knucks, mumphreys, Johnny ride a pony, nick, all brutal games. In nick, you take knives and one guy nicks the other—zzz! You take turns till somebody gives up. We played chicken. Two guys would stand on top of an elevator in the projix and another guy would press the top-floor button inside and whoever ducked first when it reached the top of the shaft was the loser, and we'd all beat him up. We played the cig'rette game, where you put bare arms alongside each other and drop a lighted cig'rette into the crack, and whoever pulls away first loses and gets the shit kicked outa him.

Fighting is all we had. We never had any money, so the only thing we could play for was pain. It sounds sick, but it made sense. We had to play for pain or the game would mean nothing to us. And these were your friends, your closest buddies, guys that eat at your house, sleep at your house. Imagine what we did to our enemies!

East Harlem was great training for life. These guys out here in this town never had our experience, and they're soft. Why, we'd get broken noses, broken jaws, broken hands, arms, and legs. It was common, everyday stuff. If our mamas walked by and we were pounding each other to bloody pulps, and three of my friends are on toppa me beating me to death—*boooooooom*!—and the fuckin' blood is running down, and my mother'd call out, "Bobby, your father'll be home by five-thirty. You better be home!"

That was training, we needed it to survive. My dad, may he rest in peace, he was two hundred fifteen pounds, and I'd be sitting at the table and he'd spin me around, pick me up, and *whack*! He'd lay me out! He'd point down at me on the floor and he'd say, "That's for nothing! *Don't fuck up*!" He knew that I was twelve years old, going to school, I weighed a hundred thirty pounds, and I needed to be tough. He knew that if some punk came up to me and said, Gimme your lunch money, gimme your algebra book, I could say, Well, I just took a grown man's best shot, so why be afraid of this asshole? *Fuck you*! It was training for how you was gonna live. Survival. If I hadn't learned these lessons, I'd be dead today, twenty times over. I was never big, but to beat me up they had to keep coming at me and coming at me and coming at me, 'cause I'd never give up. One day a guy told me, "I'd rather fight your brother all day long before I'll fight you." My brother weighed two-forty!

Later on we had gang wars, and I was always either president of my gang or war councilor. If you walked into the wrong gang area, *bop*! We used pipes and belts and guns. We had gangs that lost one member out of every five, *every* year, either killed in a car accident or a gang war. Twenty-five or thirty of us would be in our candy store discussing a gang war and we knew that if it was a good fight, we knew that the average was that one of us would get killed and five of us would make the hospital. But we alway figured it would never be me.

Death is nothing. I been stabbed four times, I've had nine concussions, my left shoulder's been dislocated seven times, my right shoulder twice, my wrist busted, my kneecap shattered. I've been hacked with a machete by the spics, I've had fifteen stitches in a cut, my nose broken four times, and I'm one of the luckier ones. I really didn't get hurt.

My brothers were terrific guys, really killers. My brother Danny and Dale the Whale and Bootsie Butler used to go into a neighborhood Puerto Rican bar and they'd order a drink and say, "Hey, Bootsie, do you smell anything?"

Bootsie'd say, "Yeh, what is dat?"

Dale the Whale would say, "Jeez, it smells like a buncha spics in here."

Or they'd go to a black neighborhood, and they'd say, "Jeez, it smells like a dead nigger." They were out looking for trouble. Imagine a guy like that, my brother Danny, and he's a fuckin' cabdriver now! What a letdown!

Me, I always wanted to amount to something, and I knew that education was the answer. Look at the guys I grew up with: Fat Dickie Quercia, Richie Nabors, Tommy the Chink, Sally the Jew, all the guys I grew up with, Billy Garbage Pail, all those different fuckin' guys that were heavyweights when I was a kid, and you know what they're doing now? One of 'em's a Con Ed repairman, another's a TV repairman, and they're all making between seventy-five hundred and ten thousand a year, and they married the girl upstairs in the apartment who's ten pounds overweight, and they've got two to four kids, and they live in an apartment, and they'll never live in a home. They'll move into the apartment that the mother and father dies out of, and that'll be it.

That was never my scene. I never wanted to be ordinary. When I was a kid I was always a war councilor or something I could be proud of. It was never my number to be a truckdriver, like my father. I'm proud of my father, and I loved my father, but no truckdriving for me. I'd seen generations of truckdrivers.

Out of all the kids in my neighborhood, I was the only one graduated high school. Out of my neighborhood, ninety-three per cent of the kids quit school, and most of the ones that graduated were girls.

I got a job driving a catering truck, going around to the factories and the offices with sandwiches and doughnuts and coffee and stuff like that. I'd go to Con Edison and give a guy his coffee and cake free, and he'd give me a ratchet wrench, and I'd take the wrench and trade it for something else. Like my first morning stop was in a raincoat factory. Some Puerto Rican would give me a box of ten raincoats that retailed for ten or twenty dollars apiece, and I'd take that to Con Ed and give a guy a ten-dollar raincoat and he'd give me thirty bucks worth of tools, and I'd take the tools to a construction job and he'd give me material that I could sell at a body and fender place. By the end of the day I'd turned a few orders of coffee and cake into merchandise worth three hundred bucks, and I did that *every* day.

Plus I worked scams on the accounts and fucked the boss a little bit. I had a way of turning the numbers around. Like I could turn an eleven into a four, and nobody'd know the difference. I'd turn in two sandwiches for credit, and I'd make the two into an eight and get credit for returning six sandwiches extra. I rejuggled all my books to make up for it, and I earned a very handsome living. I had one big guy on the payroll at each stop, and if somebody got behind on his accounts this big ape would go collect it for me, and all for free coffee and cake.

I did this for four years, till I was twenty-one, but then it began to get to me. I couldn't take a day off, 'cause I couldn't let anybody else go on my route 'cause they'd see what was going on. So finally I had to quit.

I went on a trip around the country and when I got here I really liked it, and I had a second cousin named Amadeo that ran Amadeo's on Sweet Street, and he said he needed a guy. Right from the jump, I knew my cousin Amadeo was an asshole, and I went to work for him, checking ID, and here's the difference between me with my training and the locals with their training: the kids that showed me how to check ID are *still* checking ID on Sweet Street. I worked like a fuckin' dog, I came out of a competitive background, I fought eight million people all my life. These people in this town fight *nothing*, and they're soft.

When I first went to work, Amadeo said to take it easy, I was too small, I might get hurt. He paid me seventy-eight a week. One night there's a beef in the joint, and somebody gets dropped, a guy Pearl Harbored him in the side of the jaw and laid him out, and then he turned to get Amadeo. I stepped in, I spun, I gave the guy a sternum kick, turned him around and gave him two chops in the fuckin' neck, and I drove his nose into his fuckin' eyes, and Amadeo was impressed. He made me a barboy, washing dishes, and the joint was making two thousand bucks a night at one-fifty a drink, so figure out how many glasses I was washing.

Well, I worked my way up, from dishwasher to floorman to barboy to assistant bartender to service bartender to head bartender, *rip rip rip*, all in a year and a half, and then I was running the joint for my cousin, doing everything.

We put in an act called Bonnie and Clyde, the first male-female act on Sweet Street, and the cops busted us. Amadeo fell apart, and for a year and a half he didn't come around the club because he was afraid of going to jail. Such a chickenshit!

He just didn't know how to handle himself in fast company. Like I installed a little bullet trap that I could shoot anything up to a .357 magnum into, and I used to practice every day, and I'd be shooting and Amadeo'd come down and he couldn't even handle a pistol! Pathetic!

One day he says, "Look, we're not doing enough business. We gotta make some money. I don't care how you do it."

I says, "Look, 'Deo, if you want me to run a bust-out operation, I'm gonna hire a guy and pay him twenty-five a night and he's gonna be the manager when the cops come, and the only thing he's gonna do is *he's* gonna go to jail, not *me*. 'Cause I got a big future on this street and I don't need a police record."

So we put in more strippers and we began pumping champagne, and then it got so lucrative, and he got so chickenshit, that he just said, Fuck it, and practically turned the whole joint over to me, and of course I made a few nickels from time to time.

We always had a few boats and oars around, and lots of B-drinking. We did the thing with the champagne where the waitress'd say, "Oh, *thank* you! How'd you know it was my birthday?" and pretty soon the sucker's buying her a case of champagne at twenty-five bucks a pop. When he's tapped out, the girl goes into the back and disappears, and we close his account. We used to open the champagne bottles by shaking 'em up, turn 'em around and pop 'em, and three-quarters of the fuckin' bottle would spill on the counter. And the broads would spit their drinks back into special glasses, and I'm constantly refilling, refilling the glasses, and the trick's getting drunk, sick, the room's spinning, while he tries to keep up with the broad.

If the broad's really alive, she throws a fuckin' party out of the guy's wallet. She says, "Send champagne to the waitresses, to the bartender!" And like the guy's nearly out by now, and he gives me two twenties for the twenty-five-dollar bottle, and I put the change in front of the broad that's working the champagne, and she grabs it and throws me back five bucks tip and says, "Here, honey, that's for you." The guy's got a hard-on, and he doesn't give a shit. She takes the other ten and she tries to slough it. If the mark doesn't go for it, she gives it back, 'cause we had rules: no stealing.

If the guy gets outa line when the broad disappears, we'd beat him up and dump him in the hotel stairway next door, pour wine all over him and then call the cops: "Say, some wino fell down the stairs of the hotel." We had big ax handles and clubs in strategic spots. Like say I'm fighting a big guy, am I gonna do the Marquis of Queensbury rules? I'm there to win, not to fight. So I'd back up from the guy, reach my hand up, and there'd be an ax handle, and two or three shots with that and it's all over. I'd put the ax handle back up and the guy'd look like he was hit with a train, and we'd dump the wine on him and throw him out and call the cops.

I used to have a spring-loaded sap, a flat steel encased in leather, that I kept up my cuff, and when a guy got out of line I'd slap him with it and practically break his jaw, and then the asshole'd look at me and he'd say to himself, If that's the way he slapped me, what'll happen if he ever *hits* me? He'll *kill* me! And he'd cool it. This would happen after we'd robbed 'em when they'd wind up with a hard-on and nothing else, and the broad's gone and his wallet's just about empty. And if they wouldn't quit, if they just kept fighting and fighting and getting out of line, why, they'd end up in jail for drunk and disorderly. It never missed!

We had rules. We never took a guy for everything he had. We always made sure he had cab fare, and we'd call a cab and throw him in it just to get him off the street. The biggest problem with a bust-out operation is if you take every dollar the guy has and then he can't get away from your club, which is exactly what you don't want—you want him out of there, off the premises completely, because the next thing he's gonna do if you keep him there is go to a cop and say, Hey, I haven't even got fuckin' bus fare, and then the trouble comes down.

One time I had to take a guy's wallet out of his pocket to put a fin back in. We took all his money by accident, and we thought he had more, but the cocksucker was empty. So I go to dip him, and he turns around and tries to nail me, and I nailed him, but I made a wrong fist and tore up some cartilage. Trying to give a guy some money back!

What the fuck, we tried to do things on the up and up. If people want to give you their money, fuck it, take it! They'll just give it to somebody else anyway. So I really didn't feel like I was doing anything wrong. I worked hard, and it was my living, it was the only living I knew at the time, and it's better to work for a living than to be a fuckin' criminal.

We had a crazy bunch of guys at Amadeo's, a real rogues fuckin' gallery. Our barker was a guy called Crazy Kennie that was in the Marine Corps. A sad case. Kennie was a violinist who was in the Korean War, and he got shellshocked, really insane. He was six-foot-three, with beautiful hands, but after he got outa the Marines he got into so many fights he couldn't play no more. A tragedy of war. They took a kid that won the National Violin Championship and reduced him to a blithering fuckin' idiot.

Then we had a big fag bouncer that was six-five, named Shorty, naturally, and he couldn't fight his way out of a paper bag, but he was so big he'd go over to the guy and the guy'd say, Fuck it, I ain't fighting *this* mountain.

Then we had a garbage man named Lucca, a scavenger, that looked like Tough Tony Galento, a fireplug, and a guy named Pete Harrigan, a Section Eight from the army, a fuckin' berserker. He'd start twitching and blinking his eyes, and I knew there was gonna be a beef. I was the only one that could handle him.

For females, we had two cross-eyed sisters that were cross-eyed in the same eye, Luba and Vera, and we had a sex-change named Lucille that used to turn tricks on the side, and one day she came in with a mink coat, and I says, "Baby, where'd you get that?"

She says, "I get mink the way mink get mink." Once she showed me her cunt, and it looked just like a regular cunt, as far as I could tell.

Then we had a broad named Sherry Wine, built like a sumo wrestler with two big tremendous tits, and she was the best bust-out broad I've ever seen. She used to go through two or three cases of champagne a night. She'd do an act where she'd bounce her tits off this massive chest, and then she'd suck her own tit, if you can believe anything that gross. She'd ask a square from the audience to come up, some guy with glasses, and she'd tell him to undo her bra, and then she'd snatch his glasses and stick 'em in her G-string, and she'd say, "If you want 'em back, take 'em!" He'd reach in, and she'd say, "No hands!" and he'd have to pull his glasses out of her G-string with his teeth, right out of her pussy, see? Just *gross*!

Then we had the supergirl, Lana, that used to do a supergirl number with cape and all. She was a little goofy. And we had a couple of scooters and bikes eating each other, putting on shows for us, in between when they weren't waitressing and selling champagne. But none of 'em was as good as Sherry Wine. Once Sherry was in the backroom with a sailor and he got out of line. Now she was just like a man, she carried a .45 automatic and she shot a twelve-gauge shotgun, and you didn't fuck with Sherry Wine! Somebody called out on the PA, "Bobby, the back room, the back room!" So I know there's a beef, and I go running back there and here's Sherry Wine sitting on top of a guy with her blond wig cocked to the side like a fuckin' George Raft would wear his tit for tat over his eyes, right? She'd knocked this sailor out with her fuckin' fist, and we drug him into the fuckin' street, poured wine on him, and called the Shore Patrol.

We always had ways of protecting ourselves from smart

tricks like that. We had a temporary bouncer named Mean Gross Gene that I seen pick up a guy by his throat and the pants and slam him down across the fire hydrant, just break him right in half. Mean Gross Gene had something he called the Hollywood Smile Treatment. He'd knock you out and then he'd put your mouth against the curb and kick you in the back of the head and break out all your teeth. Mean Gross is still around. He just got outa jail. He's tough. He was a Green Beret *before* the war. He's the closest thing to a modern mercenary. He takes the toughest jobs, hires out to bars, and he works all the big cities, special protection jobs, and moving on from place to place when the heat gets on.

We were always hiring new bouncers. The joint was bust-out all the way, it ain't like these fuckin' cherries around here now. We had a powerful one-legged bouncer named Burt Peterson that had his leg blown off with a shotgun and once fought Jake LaMotta. One night a guy walked in and Burt was in a bad mood and the guy was giving Burt one of those rubbernecks, staring at him, and Burt said, "Could I help you?"

The guy just kept on looking, so Burt says, "*Can I help you?*" The guy still didn't say anything, so Burt grabbed him and put his head against the fuckin' bar, and started punching him with this gigantic fist, breaking the guy's head open. I was on the other side pushing against Burt's huge enormous shoulders, he wore about a size fifty jacket, and I'm yelling, "Burt! *Burt!* What'd he do? *What'd he do?*"

Burt finally let the guy drop, and we threw him in the hotel stairway. I said, "Burt, not that it matters"—'cause you had to be very tactful with him—"but what did he do?"

Burt said, "He didn't acknowledge me."

Another night one of the bartenders went into the shitter to take a hit and miss, and two muggers go in there and they try to get his money. Who walks in but old Burt Peterson. He drops one guy and the other guy runs. Burt started pulling him back into the toilet and the guy dug his nails in the wall, screaming, "Please don't let him take me in there!" and then Burt stuffed his head in the toilet bowl and flushed it, and then really fucked him around, nearly killed him, a big fuckin' tough guy, too. Oh, that Burt! He was something. He liked to walk by the door and spit a big lunger into the street, regardless of who was walking by. An incredible man! He died of a heart attack.

Then we had a little Southern kid, my barboy, Roy, a diabetic, a real Southern bigot. He weighed about eighty pounds and when anybody started fucking around, Roy'd grab a stick and he'd go after anybody. One time I'm hassling with these two mountainous sailors at the front door and they're giving me some shit, and then I hear, "Excuse me," and I move to one side and it's Roy with an ax handle, and he lays the fuckin' sailors right out. He's shouting in this high-pitched Southern accent, "Now that's enough of that bullshee-it! Ah got work to dew! Ah got glasses to wash!" And he turns around and goes back to work.

There were guys we nearly killed. There was a big Samoan, about five-foot-six in all directions, that we clubbed with ax handles the whole length of Amadeo's and threw him into the street and he sat there and shook his head like he'd just come up from a deep dive and starts getting up to come back in. I grabbed my gun and told a girl to call the police, 'cause I knew I had to kill this cocksucker. Luckily he took a hike before I had to shoot him.

It wasn't till I'd been running Amadeo's for a few years that we started turning tricks in the back, because we were having too fuckin' many fights the other way, with just plain bust-out and no satisfaction for the customers. We were having two fights a night, and we were getting scarred up by all those guys with hard-ons. They didn't mind spending their money, but they wanted to come, you know? So we started having broads jacking guys off at the bar, and then we decided to turn a few blow-job tricks in the back, and that worked so good that we started fucking a little bit. But the fucking got to be trouble, because the guy couldn't always come right away, and the broad had to go onstage and dance her turn and we'd have to go back and pry the guy off her, and there were *more* fights. Then we had a broad that was always giving people clap, and the Board of Health was giving us shit over her, and finally one night we took a raid, sixteen vice squad guys and the FBI. The reason for the raid was one of the broads that had worked for us went to work at a whorehouse in Nevada, and the fuzz thought we were sending broads back and forth, which makes it interstate, the Mann Act, but it was really a big misunderstanding, because we weren't doing any such thing. It was a big waste of time, but we still took a bust behind it. It got dismissed. They arrested everybody but me, and they all had to go to court.

Well, after a few years I'd put a few dollars in my sock, and then I bunked into this deal where I could buy a used restaurant for a certain amount down, and I figured I'd had enough bust-out, and I bought this joint I got now. I may come from a bust-out operation, but this joint is run as classy as any place in town. You notice how clean my bar is. Everything is like that. You can eat off the men's-room floor. I'm a straight operator now. My next move is gonna be a bigger joint, and my final move will be a supper club like the good old days. They're coming back now. It'll be like this, but bigger and better, the finest joint in the city.

I do a lot of talking, but I get by on work, on guts and balls and nerve and plain hard work. Most of the Sweet Street guys see me around at night, in and out of Raffaele's, playing kissyface with the broads, but they forget that I'm also here all day, doing the janitor work, changing signs, fixing ice machines, washing ashtrays, cleaning syrup guns, and things like that. Nobody around here sees that end of me. I'm not complaining, 'cause I make a good living. But I work! I'm a worker! I've always been a worker.

Amadeo's, I'm not ashamed what I did there, but I feel better here, 'cause this is a quote legitimate unquote operation. Amadeo's is history, that's the past, that's where my head was at one time, and I'm not ashamed. I did the best job I could. I only know one way to work: the best.

Now that I've got my own joint, I hardly ever fight any more. I'm the hardest guy in the world to get into a fight. I've fought enough. I'm not insecure no more. I mean, fuck, if a guy says to me, You're an asshole, I say, Yeh, man, you're right! If a guy comes to the door and he says, Fuck you, I'm coming in whether you like it or not, I just say, Look, man, I couldn't stop you anyway, but I just got a job to do and a wife and a coupla kids, so whattaya want to fuck over me? I try to appeal that way, and if it doesn't work, foin!

'Course, if it's a guy that'll take kindness for weakness, I go the other way. You look him straight in the eye, and you speak softly but directly. You never yell at him: yelling at him, you've already lost the fight. If you're a yeller, you're not a fighter. So you just look him right in the eye and tell him if he comes in it's got to be over you, or I just say, Look, man, I ain't bad, but the bad don't fuck with me. If he keeps coming, I got to knock him out. But that's rare.

Inside the place, I have to improvise, 'cause I don't like rough stuff in there, it ain't classy, and it distracts from the joint's image, which, believe me, is triple-A all the way. I try to get the job done as quietly and peacefully as possible, but if I got to take care of some asshole, I take care of him. Like one night a big asshole, about six-three, comes in with a hooker, and I knew her, so I said hello. The big guy says, "Fuck you, you asshole, don't talk to my girl," like he's with a virgin or something. One thing leads to another, and he throws a drink on me, and it hits Mickey Martin, who is a fuckin' killer himself.

Mickey wants to tear the guy up, so I says, "Hey, man, I don't want no trouble in my joint." So I pick up a drink and throw it on the guy, and I say, "Now, look, asshole, you threw one on me and I threw one on you. Now fuck you and your girl friend, just leave and there's no problem."

The guy grabs me by the scuff of the neck and starts rubbing a rag in my face, like he's trying to degrade me, and I don't degrade too easy, so I slide around the end of the bar till I see the two boiling-hot coffeepots, and evil shit came into my mind, and I just grabbed his waistband and pulled it out and dumped a whole pot of steaming coffee right down his balls. He screamed like a Comanche! Everybody started laughing, Mickey Martin and all. The guy ran into the streets, screaming and screaming and screaming, asking for fuckin' mercy. But he started it. All I did was say hello.

So I've done a few things like that, and I've also done a few things that are against the law, little misdemeanor shit, but I don't consider myself a bad person. I'm not throwing bouquets at myself, but I take care of my family, and I'm honorable with people that're honorable with me. Anybody on Sweet Street that says I fucked 'em is a liar. I worked hard for everything I get. I quit the bust-out business when I brought my mother and father out here, 'cause I knew I was on borrowed time, especially after that big raid. As good an operator as I was, I knew eventually it had to catch up with me. Then my dad died, and I was responsible for my mother and my sister, and I got into a legitimate business as quick as I could.

But I still worry. When will it stop, the worrying? I know what it is to be poor, and I don't ever want to be that way again. My dream is to shower my mother with real good things. I have no ambitions for myself. When and if my mother dies, maybe I'll look for a family of my own, but right now I'm satisfied. Most of the broads you meet on this street are very unexciting, blankos, plastic. Look at Annette De Ross, that just went into retirement. She'd had her teeth capped, her lips split and widened, her nose done, her skin bleached, her hair bleached, her tits blown up with silicone, she's had a fuckin' rib removed to give her that smaller ribcage, she's had her back teeth pulled to give her that hollow cheek look. The chick is really a plastic doll! And they're all trying to imitate her. The big deal on the street now is Connie Lea, and she's plastic from top to bottom, her tits are courtesy of the Dow Chemical Company.

One night I slept with a beautiful blond dancer, big tits and all, and the next morning I woke up and I look over at the next bed and here's this toothless broad with short brown hair, looked like the syphillated drippings of a Mongolian gangfuck. I said, "Where'd *she* go?"

The broad said, "I'm her." Turned out she'd had special tapes holding up her floppy tits, she had false teeth, a whole plate, she had a blond wig, false eyelashes, and a special pair of nylons that made her bad legs look good, and she was a drunk and a lesbian besides. That's a Sweet Street broad for you.

Well, I try to find my social life with a better class of women. I'm a solid citizen of the fuckin' town now, and I want to go out with solid citizens, not these cheap strip artists made of rubber and test tubes. I want to be straight arrow.

I've never been in trouble anyway, I've always been lucky or smart, and I don't want to start fucking up now, plus it'd break my mother's heart. That's why I don't drink; it's been ten years since I took a drink. I don't smoke, and I don't use dope, and I never took an upper, a downer, or a sideways in my life, 'cause where I came from it was the creeps and the niggers that did things like that. I don't even take an aspirin without a note from the doc. I try to live my life like a man, one hundred per cent a man. I'm by no stretch of the imagination a bully or a tough guy, and I'm not big and overpowering. But when I walk into a place, I want people to know a man walked in. I don't want anybody to think a boy walked in. That's something I could never stand.

SERVING LADIES

Next to us owners, it's the waitresses that make the big money on Sweet Street. They make triple and quadruple what the dancers make. The dancers get twenty-five bucks a night, and the waitresses make more like seventy-five, a hundred, a hundred and ten. If the dancers ever find out, they're gonna be nagging me for waitress jobs, so I try to keep it quiet, and so do the waitresses.

—Bill Gold

Waitress

IN THE SULPHUROUS, ACRID, ear-jarring evening at the Lion's Tail, a buxom young woman with a chignoned puff of bright hair dips and darts from table to table balancing trays of drinks. She seems on a warm personal basis with her clientele, risking the instant unleashing of her bustline by leaning over to nibble the ear of a dark old man with sprigs of hair growing from the lobe, lightly slapping the face of a wounded pink-cheeked soldier who dares to cup her posterior with his one remaining hand, and laughing and lollygagging with the band and the dancers and the bartender.

But as each evening goes on, the young woman slows and nearly halts, and as the two A.M. closing time approaches she often is seen standing along the wall by herself, her eyes narrowed as though focusing far away, her body quivering to inner beats, her fingers popping lightly to the final gasp from the bandstand. "Jess," another waitress says. "*Jessica!* Snap out of it!" But the waitress remains against the wall, a strap going awry at her shoulder, transient coils of red hair shaking loose from her chignon, hints of frowns and smiles flicking off and on her reddened face. She is still a waitress on duty at the Lion's Tail, but only physically.

In those increasingly rare moments when Jessica King is fully attuned to reality, she has a queenly air. She is nearly five feet eight inches tall, large-boned, with green eyes that pick up and repeat the glint of red from massive winding sculptures that she forms on her head with several pounds of hair the color of brushed copper. Her head is leonine, her cheeks and jowls firm, her face full and well fleshed-out. She speaks finishing-school English, rounding her o's in the British manner, and sometimes talking through her nose. Her conversation is peppered with charming little assumptions and interrogatories, as though the listener possesses a Ph.D. in her personal mythology. "I wasn't right for Bill, don't you think?" she says. She talks about Bill Gold often. Her three-year romance with the boss of bosses dominates her memories of Sweet Street now that she has become a middle-aged woman by local standards.

Gold himself is busy demolishing any vestiges of reports that he was deeply in love with Jessica, love being one of the few words considered truly obscene by Sweet Street males, as though to love or be loved is to be shamefully traduced and exploited by another. "Yeh, I lived with her for almost three years," Gold tells anyone who will listen, "and she was gorgeous, young, built like gorgeous, a fantastic lover, alive, and all that, but it was only an accommodation. I did it for convenience to myself. I wanted somebody to take care of my laundry. The broad was dumb. I mean *dumb*!"

Jessica King donned the proceeds of the dead affair—one floor-length ranch mink coat—and wobbled around from lover to lover, plumbing lower depths until she married a barker, the local equivalent of a peon. Now the other waitresses point her out as a sad example, and gossip about her over tamarind coolers at Raffaele's: "Talk about temper tantrums! She pulls the most outrageous scenes. And she's always crying! Breaking down and crying, like a nervous breakdown every night. I'd feel sorry for her, but it's ninety-nine percent bullshit."

"Yeh. She's always coming in with these stories that her husband is gonna kill her. She's weird, poor girl. She's so hyper and unrelaxed. She needs help. She's very pathetic."

"She tells Pete, 'Oh, Pete, I can't work tonight, he's threatening to kill me again!' Till it reached the point where Pete would be really cruel and cold to her. He'd say, '*Who* threatened to kill you, Jessica? Did somebody get killed? Who? *Who*! Where's the body?' And she'd cry all the more."

Once Jessica King's closest friend was Carrie Hess, the star waitress at the Lion's Tail, but their fellowship was sundered by Jessica's quixotic behavior. Now Carrie says, "She's nothing but a Sweet Street waitress at heart. I just can't see her in any other setting. She's impossible to work with. She's freaked out half the time, pills, marijuana. She's run the gamut on pills. For a long time it was speed, I don't know what it is now. They used to call us the Twins, we were so close, but lately I hate her. She talks to me and I walk away. She's been on the street too long. I don't see where she can go from here. It's like that song, 'Have I Stayed Too Long at the Fair?' The rest of us, we can go back to being housewives or secretaries, but this street is Jessie's whole life. She won't get off the street till she's thrown off, and when that happens, she might as well head for the bridge."

I've been on Sweet Street since I was seventeen years old. That's a long time. I'm the best waitress you'll ever see. I know how to read the customers and play on their feelings, do you follow me? Some nights they're just hostile. It depends on where the moon is. I always look outside to find out. When the moon's in Aquarius it's always very groovy at the club, and also in Taurus and Aries and Leo. But in the others it's bad. When the moon's in Libra, people are very grouchy. The tips are best when the moon's in Taurus, my sign. Taurus people are very generous.

Soldiers are the ones that just flip over me. They give me money all the time. I even tell 'em I'm married or I have a boy friend and they still give it. I have good money karma, don't you think so? I'm the only waitress at the Lion's Tail that gets customers to give her cash money. A hundred dollars one night, two fifty another night. A soldier gave me three hundred one night in traveler's checks. I've gotten hundred-dollar bills plenty of nights. So the other waitresses are super jealous of me. Guys like me. And they don't want anything from me. A soldier came in one night and he said, "I like you, you're a groovy lady, I want to do something nice for somebody," and he gave me a hundred dollars. He said, "Would you like to go to the car show with me, no strings attached?" That was *after* he gave me the money.

I said, "No, my boy friend owns this place," and he still let me keep the money!

Not too long ago a drunk came in and gave me three hundred dollars, and he said, "Are you gonna meet me later?"

I said, "We're not allowed. But maybe if you come back in again I'll talk to you some more." He kept giving me money, and the other girls were watching. Oh, they hate me! None of the other girls have this happen to them. People have given me money outrageously! A group of young kids were tipping me two, three dollars a drink, ended up giving me fifty dollars, because they liked me so much, and every single week! And the guy that gave me three hundred, he was an older guy, he just thought I was cute as hell. None of the other girls get tips like that. All they get is sleepers. It's just my personality, don't you agree? They like me. I'm such a sensitive person, and when I'm hot, I just charm anybody to death, don't you think so?

I'm top lady when I'm hot. Bill wanted me to train all his waitresses because none of 'em are pros. They're like a bunch of teeny-boppers. I know how to handle the feelings of people, how to talk to them, make them feel at home. I tell people they have bad breath, or BO. I give them gum to improve their breath! They love it! They're the ones that give me the biggest tips. I tease around with 'em, joke with 'em. If they're cute, I tell 'em, and I pinch their nose. The other waitresses don't do these things.

Of course, we're bound to have conflicts, the four of us. We're all Taurus, for one thing, all earth signs. We're all very aggressive and we hate each other's guts. The other night an old customer of mine came in, and Carrie took him to a table. I said, "Carrie, he's *my* regular customer."

She said, "Who the hell are you?"

I said, "You bitch!" and I waited on him. But there's no friendship any more, no respect for each other. Too bad! Nobody'll do anything for you, or help you out. They slice each other's throat; there's no sense of family. The other girls are experienced but not professional. They're rude to customers that don't tip 'em, and I think that's horrible, don't you? Carrie calls 'em cheap bastards to their face, and Olive'll say, "We live on our tips, you motherfucker!" I've heard her!

The most I'll ever say is, "My services are not included in the price of the drink," and if they don't respond to that, I just say thank you and go away. You're not gonna get a tip by insulting anybody. Don't you agree?

I don't know how I got here in the first place. I was a surfer girl, raised on the beach, all healthy and tan and outdoorsy. I was raised a Catholic, and I'm still a Catholic, although I don't believe in going to church to prove that I believe in God. I had a lot of fathers—four, I think—and all I ever knew was rejection. My mother used to beat me up and then hug me and say she was sorry. She'd say, "Oh, what have I done?" Once she almost choked me to death. My fathers were always younger men, almost my age, that's why I go after the male older figures now. My mother is beautiful, more beautiful than I am. I love her very much.

I think of myself as intuitive. Don't I seem intuitive to you? Maybe I'm not intelligent. I have a lot of passions. I love flowers, I love foreign movies, Fellini, Ingmar Bergman, I just adore them. *The Virgin Spring, Wild Strawberries, The Passion of Anna,* movies like that. I love classical music: Bach, Mahler, when I'm in a certain mood, Handel's *Messiah*: church music, harpsichord music. I love the theater, the arts, modern dance.

I love to eat. I love to cook. I'm a gourmet cook—that's one of my greatest pleasures, next to sex. I—love—to—*eat*! Sour-cream baked potatoes, bagels, cream cheese, lox, steak. If I could have only one meal on earth it would be cheese, fruit, a big piece of steak with potatoes and sour cream and chives. I'm a health food fanatic, but I don't practice it. I like to dissipate too much.

I'm very expressive. I believe in anything that comes naturally. But I'm not into bisexuality. I would like to experience everything before I die, but I still enjoy having one man at a time. I don't like orgies, and I've never been to one. I'm a one-man woman.

I was seventeen when I came to the city. I hitchhiked here because my boy friend was stationed here in the service. I hit the road with cut-off Levis and a Jacobs surf board and T-shirt and pigtails, in my junior year of high school, and I never went back. When I first got here, I was a little hippie girl. I panhandled, sold newspapers, slept outside, took my baths in the park with the beatniks. It was groovy, the beginning of the flower-children era.

I got to be a good panhandler. People love to be hustled if

you're artistic about it, and if the vibrations and the warmth are right. I used to have great days panhandling, and then I'd take all my Bohemian friends out to dinner. My girl friend and I would work opposite sides of the street, see who could make the most money. I used to do pretty good at the Playboy Club. Streetwalkers used to give us the most. They'd say, "Why don't you get out on your ass like us?" and I'd go, "Huh?" And they'd go, "Here, honey," and give me money.

I was very innocent and naïve in those days. I moved into the Triangle, and I didn't even know it was a junkie hotel. I just thought everybody looked kinda tired and run down. Fifteen dollars a week for one room, and junkies all over the place. Later on I moved out, and I crashed around from place to place. I met a pimp, and he protected me and he told me, "You have two ways to go in this street, young lady. You can go down and fool around with everybody in town, down the line with the rest of the girls, straight to hell, or you can make it. Stay away from bad people!"

At that point, I was puritanical, even when I was living with the pimp. I wouldn't let him touch me! I didn't put out those vibes. He ran his women and just let me live there for a while, and he protected me like his baby. I traveled around with a lot of strip dancers in those days, and they were almost as puritanical as I was. Most dancers have high morals. I'd say your secretaries and your airline stewardesses sleep around far more.

One day one of the dancers said, "Hey, do you want to make money dancing?"

I said, "Oh, no, I could never dance topless!"

She said, "It's fifteen bucks a night to just stand up for a few minutes. Easy!"

I said, "No, I couldn't do it." But fifteen dollars was a lot of money, I was only making about five a day panhandling. So I got dressed up and my friends took me to the Paris Lido. The topless rage was still hot and strong. There were lines outside, waiting to get in. It was amateur topless night. I went out onstage with my eyes closed, scared to death. I turned purple, green, and I made the fifteen dollars. I took a steady job at Amadeo's, began to eat right, and I moved out of the Triangle and into a decent place. I began dating a musician, and I threw over my Coast Guard boy friend that I came here to marry. I told him, "Honey, I've been around now. I know the whole scene." I was still the most insecure woman on earth, but I wasn't letting on.

Somebody gave me speed one night when I was dancing, and it was wonderful. They couldn't get me off the stage! I wanted to dance till six in the morning. I got freaked out, I got really weird, and I couldn't sleep. I began taking speed all the time, and I lost weight, and I became a very strange lady and went home to mother and ended up in the hospital, cleaning out. I slept for two weeks straight when I was coming down.

Then I came back to Sweet Street and began hanging around with this crazy dancer named Dodie. She was real popular in those days. She and her sister did a dynamic duo bit. They called themselves the hundred-inch sisters, because their bust measurements totaled a hundred inches. Dodie took a lot of speed; she was a very sad lady. She had this beautiful house and we'd go there and talk all night and pop meth-tabs. Night after night we stayed on the pills, and I thought, Wow, this is groovy, dancing and dancing and talking and talking. I ended up in the hospital for a month. But Dodie wouldn't clean out. She was a super speed freak, and she shaved her head and tattooed a flower on her forehead, and flipped completely. I understand she's crazy now, living with her mother. The old lady takes care of her.

So many of the girls I knew six or seven years ago have either flipped out or they're still on drugs or alcohol. I used to dance with a very nice girl, very pretty, and she got mixed up with a pill freak. A few years ago I saw her on Sweet Street. A vegetable! She used to be a beautiful blonde, but now she was twenty-two, twenty-three years old, and finished. She couldn't talk right, she couldn't see, one eye was closed, it was just horrible! Her hair was straggly, she was skinny, she was covered with pimples. I tried to talk to her, but she couldn't communicate. I said, "Do you remember me?" She just made guttural sounds. I ran to get away. I blocked it all from my mind, because it was so upsetting. Wouldn't you?

Even the successful women on this street are losers, as far as I'm concerned. You can see it coming, even if they can't see it themselves. I've got an old friend, the Vampire, and everybody on Sweet Street points to her big success as a call girl. Here's her success: she lives in a mansion downtown now, and she has minks and everything she wants. The last time I saw her she was deep into downers and God knows what else, and she can't get the man she loves to marry her, and she has these tricks that fly in for blow jobs for big money, deals like that. She's had the silicone treatment, and she's still very young, maybe twenty-six. But she's headed down, down. It won't be much longer.

My first disastrous love affair on the street was with Tommy Lynch, Bill Gold's predecessor. I told you I was into older men, because I never had a real father. Tommy made me go to the beauty parlor and stop being a hippie chick, and I loved the man so much I let him take control of me, and I lost my identity, and I was molded into what he wanted, an imitation of his dead wife who'd shot herself in the head. Then he left me flat on Christmas day. He said I wasn't good enough for him, I was too young and I was embarrassing to his friends, too freaky.

I went back to my mother in pieces. Slowly I got my old identity back. I stopped dressing in his ex-wife's clothes and with bubble hair-dos and things like that. I stopped wearing all the straight clothes he'd bought me. *Terrible*! Skirts down to here, just when miniskirts were in fashion, and I have good legs, too. He had me dressed up like an old matron.

Then I met Bill Gold, and I didn't like him. He was the one who brainwashed Tommy into dropping me, I just know it, and I hated him for it. They used to call him the Shadow, because of the way he followed Tommy all around, and we all used to laugh at him. I hated him! What a creep!

One night he got me drunk and we went to his place and he wouldn't take me home. I slept on his couch and he came out and started making love to me, and that was it. *A guy I really didn't like*! I'm nuts, I'm nuts!

The first thing he did was to run down and tell everybody on Sweet Street. "Oh, I got this girl!" Later on I moved in with him. I said, "I'll live with you for a while till I get my own place." I said, "I'll pay for half the groceries and take care of my share." I wasn't working at the time, so he put me at the Lion's Tail as a waitress.

Well, after three years with that man, I grew up a lot. I began to resent paying for the groceries. I mean, here this man was making love to me, and he was making a *lot* of money, and I was paying my own way and being treated like a dog. I said to myself, "You're really a sucker!" But it was an ego trip for him, having a young girl living with him and paying her own way. So I left him for a month, and he phoned me every day. He said, "Come back! I'll do anything! We'll go to Miami Beach, and *you won't have to pay for groceries any more!*" I moved back in, and I learned to love him in my own way. I saw the good side of him. He's a very cuddly, soft person. He cries when he sees a movie, that's what I love about him. I used to say, "That's the only time you show me you're human, when you cry at the movies."

He talked to the other guys about me all the time. "Young broad, a nice piece of ass." It hurt me, but that's just the way they talk on Sweet Street. Haven't you found it to be true? Anyway, that wasn't the worst thing about living with him. He was *always* right. He wouldn't listen to anybody. He was very egotistical, and very stingy. It was always a bartering relationship. "If you take me to Las Vegas, I'll do this and that." And he thought he was Sigmund Freud, super psychiatrist. He thinks he has no problems of his own, and he has many more problems than any of us, but he hides them. *Nobody* can get through to him.

I think he loved me, even though he hated the expression. He never cheated on me. Never never never never! And I never cheated on him. Never never. He was always home for dinner. There he'd be, sitting in front of the TV, drinking wine, smoking a joint. To this day he's never been with another woman on Sweet Street. I think he still has deep feelings for me.

I always told him when I left him I'd do it quietly, just get up and leave. I visited my mother, and while I was there I went out dancing and things that I never did with Bill, because he wouldn't take me out. So I decided, "Well, I'm going."

Everybody on the street thinks *he* left *me*, and he told

some people that he did, but actually I left him. He called me every day after that, and then he began going with these cheap women. I thought, "Ugh, cheap! Awful women!" I thought, "God, Bill, you can do better than that!" Now I realize, I was probably the most interesting part of his life, and he'll never forget me. I was probably the only special thing that ever happened to him.

Well, after I left Bill I went out with *everybody*. I was going with fifteen different people at a time. I just went berserk. I dug being free. Then this barker began hanging around my door, you know, Gig? I didn't like him, but he kept coming and calling. So we became friends, and I'd let him come over and cook for me and clean my place. He was always there, so I thought, the hell with it, why don't I marry him? After all, he loves me so much. I married him in a moment of weakness. That killed Bill. He said, "You were my friend till the day you got married." He meant it, too. That was six months ago, and ever since then I've felt my days are numbered. I can feel it in my bones.

Well, Gig turned out to be a very nutty man. I thought he was a lovable guy, but as soon as he got me under his wing he turned on me violently, and totally put me through hell. He made me a basket case, he put me in the hospital with a nervous breakdown, and I never was a nervous person before. Two weeks after we were married he drove me out on the big bridge and put a gun to my head. He was high on something, and he told me he was gonna kill me if I left him. He played a game of Russian roulette with the gun against my head, and it didn't go off. You know what that's like when somebody pulls a trigger when a gun's against your head? You're dead but you're not dead.

Then he drove me across the bridge and parked and made me shoot heroin. I begged for my life, and he made me shoot up, because he knew I was afraid of it, scared to death. I thought you'd be hooked if you used it once, and I was petrified of needles. He'd been chipping a little, so he had some in the car, and he shot it in my arm. It was fantastic! I got *so* high! Very groovy!

It was like that for months, him acting crazy and threatening to kill me, and me having to go to work every night acting like a basket case. Finally I just broke down completely, and I went in the hospital for two weeks, and Gig went to Mexico and cleaned out completely. Now we're trying to make a go of it again. He doesn't want to lose me, so he's gotten a straight job, and he's stopped beating me up, and he hasn't taken any dope for two weeks. I do love Gig, and I *am* married to him, and I'm gonna try it again. But I don't think it's gonna work. No way.

Sometimes I don't think I've got too much longer to go. The way things are, I could be rolling around in the gutter in a couple of weeks, or I might be floating down the river by Gig killing me. He comes close sometimes. It scares me. I've also thought of suicide. I've been close to it; we all talk about it on the street. But a few times when I was just about at the end, I pulled myself together. I won't kill myself because I like myself too much for that. I go through fantasy periods where I pretend I'm a movie star. I see a Greta Garbo movie, and for two months I'm Greta Garbo. I've been Marilyn Monroe, and I identify with her. I also do a lot of dreaming: I'm falling, people are chasing me, I'm running. I get swallowed up in the ocean, and I can't breathe. I'm running from myself, running from my life, escaping reality.

Do you think I'm different than the other people on Sweet Street? I *am*? Oh, thank you! That makes me feel *good*! You don't know how *good* that makes me feel. God, you just made my whole year! I'd rather be me than anybody I know.

ON A FOGGY NIGHT of Spring, Jessica King is fired by Pete Stang, the manager of the Lion's Tail. "She lost her protection here," Stang says, "and without any protection, she had to go. It was a conglomeration of things, stealing from customers, causing internal problems, and she was just plain stagnant. The exciting trip was over. I'd already given her four chances to straighten up. She was always on dope, and showing it by midnight. I told her she was fired for smoking marijuana in the club, and she said she didn't, and I said I found a pack of her cigarettes and there was three joints in it, and earlier in the evening we'd smelled marijuana in the bathroom, and that was the same evening when the police were all over the place looking for Bill Gold. I told her cops can smell, too.

"She said, 'Well, those cops are friends of mine.'

"I said, 'It doesn't matter whether they're friends or not. Maybe they have a hard-on for Bill or a hard-on for me or someone else in the club, so you have to see the whole picture.'

"I showed her the pack of cigarettes with the joints, and then she said, 'Okay,' and she went upstairs and left."

When Bill and I broke up, he asked me to not be seen with anybody else on Sweet Street, and then he asked me to quit my job. He has a very big ego, and it was rubbing into his face for me to be around a club he owned. He said, "I beg you to quit!" and when I got married I knew I had to go for sure.

Pete fired me for smoking grass, but everybody smokes grass in there, including Pete. He said, "You're fired," and I said, "Fine thank you good-bye."

I saw him later on the street, and I said, "Pete, I know what happened and so do you. It's been building up since I got married, right?" And he goes, "Yeh."

This is a very lost moment in my life, and at the same time it's a very rich moment. I have to start all over again. Sure, I can! I'm not gonna go running home to mother. I'm gonna get some money and go some place, Hawaii, Mexico, New York City, *some* place. I've had it in this town. I've done some growing up here, and I've had a lot of sadness, too. It's time for me to go. Sweet Street and I have had our love affair, and it's over. I'm twenty-four years old. I can't believe I'm all finished. Can you?

Waitress

CARRIE HESS, BORN CARRIE Kashfi, is the epitome of the loyal Sweet Street employee, so taken by the honkytonk culture and its people that she lives diagonally across the street from Raffaele's, in a third-floor apartment whence she can survey the scene of her nightly trials and triumphs. "I couldn't live anyplace else," she says. "I've grown accustomed."

Carrie dashes through life at breakneck speed, always worried about "freaking out," but willingly flying back to the flame six evenings a week. In the two years since her divorce and her arrival on Sweet Street, her entire metabolic process has altered. She dashes about the Lion's Tail on long, racehorse legs, sometimes literally running from table to bar, her head filled with orders and demands, exuding efficiency and professionalism. Underneath she is nervous and afraid, seeking therapy at Raffaele's after work, imploring other Sweet Street types to help her sort priorities.

Befitting her Middle Eastern ancestry, Carrie has moments when she looks like a half-dressed Nefertiti waiting tables. Her eyes are light brown and heavily shadowed, her lips wide, her nose long and prominent. She smiles sweetly as she speaks, no matter the mood or occasion, and tight little dimples appear and disappear on her lower face like champagne bubbles. Her figure is lithe and slender, almost bustless, her hair long and black and rich, although usually concealed by wigs that are far less attractive.

Her three-room apartment, a block from the Lion's Tail, is kept bright and tidy. Carrie likes light colors, airy scenes, smooth lines and flow. Pictures of savage animals peer down at the visitor, tigers, lions, cheetahs, a congress of jungle beasts in session on the walls. Plants are spotted about, a split-leaf philodendron, a miniature palm, an umbrella plant, a wandering Jew. The kitchen is impeccably ordered and clean, a library of cookbooks neatly arrayed against one wall. In the bedroom is more reading matter: *Harper's, Cosmopolitan, Playboy, Glamour, Mademoiselle, Psychology Today,* Sylvia Plath's *The Bell Jar* (Carrie's current night reading), and works by Jacqueline Susann and Erich Segal that she calls "my junk." A loving cup bears the inscription FUCK HOUSEWORK, and the hostess proclaims, "I don't do nearly enough around here." Nevertheless, there is not a speck of dust to be found. "Sometimes when I get really freaked out," Carrie explains, "I lock myself in my apartment and do nothing but clean. That's been happening a lot lately."

Like many before her, she came to Sweet Street looking for thrills and excitement. "I'd been a suburban housewife, and I thought it would be a fun thing to work on the street, like being out on a date every night and getting paid for it." She still enjoys the frenzied pace, the crash and color, but she is finding herself less able to handle the personal problems that arise from juggling too many love affairs. "Everybody on Sweet Street runs around with a sign that says 'I'll fuck you, but I don't want to get involved.' I've become the same way. But you *do* get involved, and if you're like me, it leads to all kinds of hassles. Because you take things seriously. You can't just fuck for fun. Now I'm being punished for it."

Carrie's image of superwaitress is beginning to fade as her private behavior becomes more erratic, and fellow waitresses are sniffing the kill. "She keeps her job by sucking around the bosses," says Olive Calzolari, another Lion's Tail waitress, in a voice dripping with venom. "But she's beginning to blow it, little Miss Supershit. She's taken too much advantage of our patience."

"I like Carrie, even though we're not best friends any more," purrs the fired Jessica King. "But she's a cutthroat, too. All us waitresses get to be cutthroats. Carrie's a very lost girl, but she doesn't know it yet. She's been on the job two years, and she's getting more and more weird and paranoid.

The bosses *like* it that way. Carrie's gonna crack. Any night now. You just watch."

Few would believe it, watching Carrie pirouette around the night club, but she has already lost her job once. A manager fired her, but she ran to Bill Gold and pleaded for another chance. Gold recalls the incident with gusto. "She was practically on her knees! She said, 'I'll work free! I'll go and clean your place once a week, *free*!' So I let her do it, just to punish her. Now she thinks I'm God."

Carrie Hess is in a state of siege.

I was all uptight the other night. One of my boy friends is gonna get married, and I had other personal problems and I just didn't feel I could work, so I came in early and left a note on the bar: *Carrie will not be in tonight.* I didn't think anybody would care. The next night Olive laid into me. She says, "You aren't the boss around here! I'm tired of you making up your own hours and only working when you want to work!"

I felt bad about it, so later on I had a live one, a guy that'll tip you five dollars for two drinks, and I turned him onto Olive so she could make the money, and I said to her, "I don't want you to be mad at me."

But she was *still* mad. She said, "Fuck it! Forget it." There was a terrible scene, and Pete, the manager, tried to break us up and I said, "Pete, I just have to leave right now or I'm gonna freak out," and I left. It was around eleven o'clock.

Now Pete says I'm on the same list that Jessica was on. So I said, "Well, if you want to fire me, fire me now, but don't play these games."

He said, "You know I only say things like that to make you more neurotic so you'll work harder." It's true! They go out of their way to make you unhappy, and they wind up with a bunch of paranoid employees. Like last night Agnes and I were on Valium, and we were running into the closet and nipping at a bottle. Why, we're turning into a couple of closet alcoholics and pill freaks! And neither one of us is a pill-taker. But we were so uptight last night we were taking anything we could shovel down. I just got so loaded, and I was *still* nervous.

It's a regular system with these bosses. Like some nights we'll all be there at seven, we haven't opened the outside doors yet, and Pete'll gather us together and he'll walk around us and look at us, like General Patton inspecting the troops, and he'll say, "Agnes, go do something with your hair! Jessica, your ass is three times too big. Carrie, you have no tits!" He'd have us all in tears for the rest of the night. So I told him, "Look, Pete, wait for the end of the night to tell us things like that, 'cause there's nothing we can do about it, and you're putting us all on a bummer." I didn't say it, but I should have: there's nobody dirtier or sloppier looking than Pete. What a nerve, him putting *us* down! He has that oily, greasy, stringy hair, and yet he's always telling me I look like hell in my natural hair, he says it's too straggly. So I wear wigs, and the waitresses tell me I look like hell in wigs. I guess I can't win for losing.

But I don't feel like a slave. I was just upset for a minute. The bosses know how to be nice, too. When you're feeling your worst, they'll do something. Like Pete goes out and buys carnations and gives one to each of us. Makes us feel good, makes us want to work for him. And I'm proud of my work. I'm proud of being the best waitress on the street, of knowing more about it than any of the other girls.

People kid me about my running around the place, but you *have* to run to keep up. You take a busy night and you've got about ten tables all screaming for the waitress and then you look at the door and here's a tour group of maybe forty people streaming in. How else can you keep up without running? We're trained that way. I'm the fastest. They call me the roadrunner.

I thrive on pressure. The highest pressure is for reorders. Whoever has the most reorders by midnight or one o'clock can go home early, and it's usually me. Management watches the reorders carefully, and if you're too low, you're fired, or you're threatened. "Your reorders are down, what's the matter with you?" I thrive on that. I can't work except under pressure.

It's just like any other business: you play by certain rules and regulations, you take part in certain little games. Like you never, *never* call in sick. Sick isn't enough, Pete would never accept something that unimaginative. You have to call in and say you took uppers when you meant to take downers, or you have a congestive liver. There's a whole list of acceptable excuses, but Pete would never accept just a stomachache or a headache. You have to say your eyes are swollen shut from crying, or you lost your bridge. It's the same way with being late. You can't say the car wouldn't start or the bus broke down or your great-aunt died. I was late the other night and I'd already used up a whole list of excuses, so I said, "Pete, I have worms in my philodendron." It took! He said, "Gee, I hope you're okay."

It's better to be working at the Lion's Tail than anyplace else on this street. It's *the* place, and everybody wants to work there. We only get thirty dollars a week salary, but tips can be up in the hundreds. We make a lot more than the dancers—they get a straight twenty-five a night, except for Connie Lea, the star—but we keep our income quiet. When the dancers are around, we say things like, "Oh, what a terrible night! I only made fourteen dollars!" We also keep quiet for the IRS.

The problem at the Lion's Tail is the customers. Usually we get a lot of businessmen, and they can be the worst. Like last night a party of four businessmen, they got a bill for twenty-two dollars, and they took great pains to count out exactly twenty-two dollars, and when I said that my services were not included, I was told that my services weren't worth a shit. So I put two people at their table, blocking their view, and I was just generally repulsive to them. But on the other hand we have people who practically throw money at us, so it all evens out. Most of the customers are very easily intimidated. Give them a slight dirty look, and they'll dig for a bigger tip.

Doctors are bad, that's for sure. The frozen-food convention last year was terrible. Orientals and most other foreigners are good. They don't go overboard on their tips, but they're consistent, and they're polite. Women are the absolute *worst*. We should have a no-women-allowed sign! They bitch about *everything*, they order impossible drinks, brandy alexanders and all that kind of stuff that ties up the bar.

And if the husband doesn't grab the change immediately,

the wife will. If the husband tips too much, she'll say, "You know we have to make the car payment this week," and grab the money off the tray. There are very few decent women that come into the Lion's Tail, especially the women in minks.

But you've got to treat 'em all the same. No matter what happens, you never argue. It's not worth it. Because any customer might be a spotter for Bill Gold. Bill says, Yes, we have 'em. Pete says, Yes, we have 'em. I was in a spotter's report once. A man at the door asked how much it cost, and I said five-fifty. I was supposed to say two-seventy-five a drink, and let him find out about the two-drink minimum when he got inside. So the spotter wrote me up.

Usually you can develop your tips down to an exact science. Like there are certain amounts of change where you just say thank you and keep it. On a sixteen-fifty round if a man gives me a twenty-dollar bill, I don't give him any change. Some will call you back, but you can almost tell in advance whether he will or he won't. A lot of people figure we're overcharging them anyway, so they won't leave any tip. We get customers who'll have eleven dollars worth of drinks and then they'll try to pay three dollars for it and act surprised at the price.

The main thing around here is God bless the sleeper! The sleeper is when someone thinks they gave you a ten and there's two tens stuck together. That's the original meaning. We stretch it to mean any money that a guy gives us by mistake. Like if the drinks are twenty-two dollars, and they give you a twenty, a one and a ten, we call the ten a sleeper even though it isn't. It's just a mistake. The other night a guy gave me a fifty, and he thought it was a twenty and so did I, at first, so I gave him change for a twenty and kept the rest. That's a sleeper. They come in all denominations. Last night I just missed making a hundred-dollar sleeper, and that's when your heart kind of falls. The guy pulled out two ones and a ten, handing me twelve dollars for his drinks, and as he was doing it a hundred-dollar bill popped out from under the others. It was already in my hand!

Sometimes it's not worth fooling around. Like sometimes I've been a wreck for the whole night thinking they're gonna call me back and demand their right change. One night I picked up a fifty-dollar sleeper from a guy and he kept staring at me, *staring* at me, and I was so paranoid about it, I almost went back to him and said, "Here, you gave me too much." Almost, but not quite.

I'm too honest, myself. I have a funny little code that I won't steal from anybody who can't catch me. Like the foreigners that come in on the tours. Most of 'em think it's five-fifty a drink instead of five-fifty minimum, and it would be so easy to overcharge them and keep the change. But I don't do it.

You also have to gauge your customer, watch his eyes, and watch the other people at the table, because lots of times friends will point out a sleeper and you'll end up embarrassed for taking it. It's terrible getting caught! The other night, Jessica ran up to the bar and she said, "Oh, I just got a twenty-dollar sleeper!" and the guy was right behind her, saying, "Did I give you two twenties and a one instead of a twenty and two ones?" and she said, "No, I don't think so." She had to give the money back. You don't argue. Just say, "Oh, I'm sorry," and hand it over. It doesn't happen too often.

The only other rules about stealing are you never steal from the bar. If the bartender undercharges you, tell him right out. And if you see anybody else stealing from the bar, you tell Pete or Bill right away. But if a waitress steals from a customer, that's her business. You don't tell *anybody*! There's no finking around here.

After you live your life according to Sweet Street's rules for a coupla years, it's hard to think about doing anything else. I even find it hard to communicate with daytime people, even relatives. They don't understand me, and I've already been where they're at, and I don't want to fall back into it. Sometimes I think I'd like to quit Sweet Street and become an airline stewardess, but I don't know if I'm patient enough. We know how to handle troublemakers at the Lion's Tail, but you can't throw people off an airplane. Well, I try not to think too far into the future. I play it by ear.

I just wish I'd stop going through these anxiety fits, wondering what I'm doing here. This crazy street! I really should be somewhere else. I think like that sometimes, but mostly I've adjusted myself to this life. The people I know are interesting. They're characters. Jessica, as much as she irritates me, as much as I hate her sometimes—I wouldn't trade her for a whole office full of New York secretaries. That's the trouble, I guess. I hope I'm not here for life. I'd get the biggest kick out of putting my note back on the bar: *Carrie won't be in tonight, or any other night.*

But I won't.

Waitress

The girls nowadays display a shocking freedom; but they were partly led into it by the relative laxity of their mothers, who, in their turn, gave great anxiety to a still earlier generation.
—Edmund Gosse, *The Whole Duty of Woman*

SHE STANDS INSIDE THE velvet curtains at the Seven Seas' wide entrance. Just visible below the arras, her high-heeled foot and curving ankle perform the same life function as the modified dorsal spine of the angler fish, waving in the current to attract the unwary. The instant the barker splits the curtain to admit a customer or provide him with a free peek— "G'wan! Take a look! No charge, no obligation!"—she links him firmly arm in arm and rushes him to the back of the club, all the while cooing familiarities. "Oh, I just *love* your jacket! Where'd you get it? New York? Paris? God, I'm so *glad* to see *you*! You'll *love* the show! I've got a special seat for you, right up front." Another waitress approaches and is quickly waved away. "No, no, he's *mine*! I've been waiting for this man all *night*!" The customer's misgivings theoretically have melted away in the warmth of the welcome, and in a trice he will be presented with the mandatory two drinks and a bill for $5.50. Lydia Rubini has scored again.

Like so many other waitresses, she started as a dancer. Her daytime strip act, performed at the Heat Wave, is still remembered fondly by the the chronic satyriasis sufferer, Buddy De Young: "One of the great clit-shot dancers we ever had around here. She'd just have her box gyrating around like a windmill, and she has a terrific-looking clit."

By her own reckoning, Lydia is beginning to feel old, used

and tainted, dragged down by such attitudes about her body and her past performances, and she is in the process of making the jump from Sweet Street to other environs. "Can you imagine being known as the broad with the most beautiful clitoris on the street?" she asks. "What *is* a beautiful clitoris? Large? Small? *Purple*? God, it makes you want to barf, the way these creeps degrade every woman they can find."

Lydia Rubini has shed thirty of the 150 pounds that blighted her adolescent years, and emerged from her chrysalis as a slim and handsome young woman. She has long, heavy-textured red hair, a small nose, nearly invisible reddish-brown eyebrows, full lips, and strong white teeth. Her cheeks and forehead are splashed with freckles, and her eyes are close-set and large, dark blue in shade, but almost always concealed by a pair of oversize sepia-tinted spectacles that help retain her privacy. She is minor in the waist and major in the bust, disdaining the padded undergarments and stuffings of other Sweet Street waitresses. At work, she wears a simple push-up bra under her scanty uniform, the better to carry out her angler-fish function. "I have a fairly decent figure, I suppose," she says, and understates the case.

Except for Olive Calzolari, Lydia is without enemies on the street, even after three years in the martial atmosphere. Cappy Van Fleet, Olive's black lover, says Lydia is "a nice enough girl, but dumb," but he stands alone in this judgment, and is perhaps soured by recent developments. Olive herself says Lydia is "a bitch, a real bitch," but Olive is violently jealous of anyone who even looks at Cappy. The other Sweet Street inhabitants think of Lydia as the dependable professional, always on the job, always on time, always available for a favor or a kindness, one of the grand veterans of the honkytonks. Such types being rare on the street, no one seems to notice that she is barely 20 years old.

I came here from a carnival background. My mother tried to raise me for a while, but she had too many problems of her own. She drank, she resented me because she got pregnant with me when she was only fifteen years old, and she never got tired of telling me I screwed up her whole life. When I was fifteen and my mother was thirty, I went to live with my father and stepmother in suburbia, but before long I was into dope and acid and everything else, and I was cutting school practically every day and giving my father a bad name in his neighborhood, so they threw me out and I went back to live with my mother and my aunt.

For a whole year I just partied and jumped up and down. My mother had boy friends and we used to ball each other's boy friends, really wild! It was so funny, I had this boy friend and one night we were having a party and he came over and he said, "I don't know how to tell you this, but I balled your mother."

I said, "Oh, far out! How was she? She's pretty good, I hear." He was just blown out about it.

But, you know, enough is enough, and after a year or so I ran away. My mother never put out an APB on me because she was in hot water herself, running around with an ex-con and stealing credit cards and passing bad checks and robbing places and all kinds of outrageous things. She got busted in Oklahoma and spent thirty days in jail there, and the old sheriff made her ball him every morning, and she couldn't do a thing about it. Then she had to do another three weeks in another county jail back there. They were into using guns, shooting people, her and this dizzy ex-con boy friend. Everything but bank robbery. The guy got sent back to the penitentiary, but my mother got off pretty easy.

She's living with another ex-con now. She's amazing! All she does is attract these bad-news men. I tell her, "Ma, can't you look out?" This guy she's with now, he's taken her for every cent she's got, moved her out of her house and into a trailer so he could get the whole four thousand bucks she had.

While I was on the road, I came across this carnival, Ding Dotson's Road-Running Free-Wheeling Carnival. *Everything* was crooked. I think even the hot dogs were fixed. There was a party every night, and everybody popping bennies and speed to keep up. I traveled with them, working the concessions, cleaning out the donnickers, and my boy friend was one of the hawkers. Later on I went with the fire-eater for a while. They all called me "The First of May," because I wasn't born into the carnival life.

When I was sixteen, I ran off with a famous rock singer, twenty-five years old, and we spent an outrageous month. We went to Miami, Tahoe, Acapulco, blowing all kinds of money, chartering planes, going to New York and back all the time. We stayed in really neat hotels, got loaded, went swimming, played tennis, and had a good time. But it was like I was babysitting him. He was so childish. Imagine me, sixteen years old, mothering this guy of twenty-five! Then he wanted me to marry him, and there was no way, *no way*, and I left and went back to my mother. I quit school during the twelfth grade, and I never graduated. I figured what kind of a job could a dummy like me get, and I applied for a position as a cocktail waitress on the other side of town.

The place was owned by Mike Poulous, a handsome guy, and I didn't know it at the time, but Mike was a bad actor, always full of pills and alcohol, a real insane dude, with terrible mental problems. He had a little office and bedroom combined upstairs, and I followed him up there, and he locked the door. He says, "Take off all your clothes."

I went, Oh, wow, here we go! So I just played his game, took off my clothes, and twirled around a couple times when he asked me. Then he came over and started to get nasty. I said, "Hey, look, I'm here for a job." He was pinching my tit and stuff, and I felt very uncomfortable. No caress, no line, no advances, just pinching my tit. These men don't have any respect for women. They've practically turned me off women's lib. Now I'm all for male chauvinism and chivalry and courtesy and all that old-fashioned stuff. I *love* it! The men I know are so rotten, they don't treat a woman for being a woman. They're nasty.

I told Mike, "I'm here to work, and that's all I'm gonna do." So he let me go. He didn't have me figured out yet, and he knew he couldn't play his tricks on me. He says, "Go on downstairs and dance."

I'd never danced naked, but I was open-minded about it, and I got downstairs on the stage and started, and all of a sudden these guys were looking at my body, and this kind of blew me out. I'm blind without my glasses, so I couldn't see them, but my knees shook for the first five minutes.

I got the job. There were four of us in all. We danced, and

we waited on tables, and we B-drank the customers. We were paid twenty-five dollars a night, cash, no deductions for taxes, and we made another fifteen or twenty a night on tips, so it all came to about two-fifty a week, not bad for a sixteen-year-old kid.

I don't drink—I never have—and I told the bartender not to pour me drinks, but whenever he thought I was acting too uptight and not rapping right with a customer, he'd pour me a little booze and I'd have to drink it. Once he slipped something in my drink just before closing time and it made me feel weird for two weeks, a heavy head trip, paranoia, scared me half to death. They were always fooling around with stuff like that in Mike's. They thought it was great fun and games to turn somebody on to dope.

Most of the time I'd just drink straight orange juice. I'd order a screwdriver, and the bartender'd give me juice. If the customer started to get wise, he'd put a float on top. And anytime we were just sitting around doing nothing, he'd say, "Hey, go over and drink with that guy in the corner. Move your ass!" It was so hard. A lot of the guys just came in for a drink, and they didn't want to sit and rap to a girl, especially not at two-fifty a drink, but we had to approach them all. I'd say, "Oh, hi, what's happening?" and a lot of the times they'd just turn me right off. The girl on the door didn't have to sit down and talk to anybody to earn her money, and I used to fight to get stationed at the door.

I saw so many miserable people. There was another waitress there that was turning tricks on the outside, and I could see that she was really messed up, really burned out. She was down almost as far as she could go, and not seeing any light at all. I could see her just lying down and dying some night.

After I was there a few months, a straight girl friend of mine came to town. She was twenty-two years old, married, and living a very dull life. Well, I wasn't aware of the dangers on the street yet, so I invited her to see me work. She told me she wouldn't mind getting a job for a couple of weeks, and I told her to stay away from this part of town, she wasn't ready for it yet. So what does she do? She puts on this net see-through outfit, no underwear at all, and she starts checking around from place to place to find work. Pretty soon she meets a girl who says, "Well, yeh, I can get you a job, but first come up to my apartment for a minute."

They went up, and there were a lot of spades there, and they shot her with dope and nobody heard from her for two days. Finally I get a phone call, and it's from this dude who says he's her pimp now and she wants to stay with him. I said, "Let me talk to her."

He puts her on the phone, and she couldn't say anything, she was just crying and upset. This went on for a few more days, and finally I got the address and the room number out of her. I sent two friends down to get her out, and they knocked on the door and a woman answered. She said, "No, there's nobody here by that name." So my friends went to the beat cops and told them what was happening, and the cops went to the place and claimed they couldn't get in either, which was understandable, because all the beat cops are paid off.

Well, we had a great big huge black security officer at Mike's, and I put him on the case, and he scared the shit out of the pimp and made him real paranoid, and one day the pimp sent my girl friend back to my place in a cab. She could barely make it through the door. She told me they kept balling her in relays the first two or three days, all these pimps, and making her give them blow jobs, and if she objected, they'd slap her across the face. She had to scrub the floors and wait on them hand and foot and kiss their ass whenever they ordered her. She said they took her out to a restaurant a couple of times, but mostly they locked her in the room. After a few days, they began bringing tricks to her, and this really flipped her out.

Before that, I didn't really understand how heavy the scene was at night. All's I knew was what went on inside Mike's, and that was just straight B-drinking. But just outside the doors there was plain old-fashioned white slavery.

From then on, I was very careful what I did on the streets, and I usually asked our security guard to see me to a cab when I went home at night. But I wasn't so careful inside the club. I was doing my job, but I was losing my own self, my own soul. Nothing was real, nothing was sincere. The whole aim was to make money, say *anything*, get the marks to keep buying drinks.

You get to the point where you're bullshitting people so much and you're making up so many stories that you can't keep track of who you are yourself. When they have a question, you can never answer it negatively. You have to keep everything bright and positive, so they won't get up and leave and stop buying, and you're just lying, lying, lying from one end of the night to the other, and you walk out of there at two o'clock a total mental mess, with no personal sense of identity at all.

It was even harder for me than the other girls, because I really had nothing in common with the customers, and I had to lie all the more to pretend that I did. It got harder and harder. I'd constantly be contradicting myself, but the guy didn't even really notice this because all he wanted to do was come in and rap to a chick and make a score. But then I found out I was beginning to bullshit my friends, on the outside, and they began to say to me, Hey, what's wrong with you? You're not yourself.

I started daydreaming a lot, and making up stories to tell myself *about* myself. I actually *believed* my daydreams! I told myself I was this fantastic girl that everybody really liked, a good conversationalist, a wonderful hip chick. I'd tell myself that I wasn't having any problems at all, but then I'd get a strange feeling, like my subconscious telling me, "Hey, that's not *you*!"

After my seventh week at Mike's I began to realize I couldn't handle B-drinking. I was sitting around moping, not rapping with any of the customers, not making any money, just sitting there talking to myself. One night Mike says to me, "Hey, go sit with that customer!"

It was a slow night. I said, "No, I'm *not* sitting with him. I don't feel like it."

He said, "Take your glasses off!" He grabbed me, and I screamed, "I can't see without my glasses!" He just ripped 'em off and threw 'em on the floor. I went over and picked 'em up and started going upstairs to where we changed. I was finished. My glasses were all broken and bent, and I had to feel my way.

He came up the stairs and threw me against the wall. He said, "You bitch, get down there and get back to work!"

I said, "I quit. Get your hands off me!"

He started shaking me and slapping me, and I said, "Boy, when I get outa here I'm gonna get the cops!"

He said, "I'll kill you!"

I ran into the bathroom and locked the door, and Mike's brother came in and grabbed him and calmed him down. I left. I had three days' pay coming, but I didn't even ask for it.

I called up the next day to ask about my money, and Mike said, "You so-and-so bitch, you rotten so-and-so, if I ever see you again I'm gonna kill you!"

But it was good training for Sweet Street, right? That was my next stop, three years ago today, when I was seventeen years old. I got a job dancing in the Heat Wave, and it really was a change, especially after working in the other neighborhood. The place had a bad reputation, but it really wasn't so bad.

Every two weeks the Heat Wave'd look like the USO, 'cause the place would fill up with servicemen. At that time, we were the only club on the street that'd let 'em in, 'cause they were all under age. We'd have a full house, and maybe four of 'em would be over twenty-one. They'd throw their hats up on the stage, they'd get *so* excited, and we'd dance around 'em and jump up and down on 'em and everybody had a good time. It was very relaxing work, at twenty-five dollars-a-day salary plus huge tips.

There was only one thing I didn't like about the Heat Wave. There'd been a murder in one of the upstairs dressing rooms in the 1920s, but the owners wouldn't talk about it. If you mentioned it, they'd shut up. It's a very tender subject. Anyway, there's a ghost left over from the murder. One night one of the dancers came screaming down the stairs and said some guy in a flannel suit was walking up and down the halls upstairs, and that he just disappeared in front of her eyes. So the manager went upstairs with a gun and patrolled for the rest of the night, but he didn't see anything. It happened a coupla times after that: always a guy in a gray flannel suit.

Different girls would see him and flip out. We were all sure of one thing: he was the murderer. It gave you the creeps to go up there.

By this time I was living with Billy Wilson, and we're still together after three years. Billy was my age, seventeen, when I met him, and he was dealing dope for a living. A very sweet person, but much different than me. He's a very mental person, whereas I'm a very physical person. He feels sex in his brain, and I feel it in my body. He's under control, but my sexual impulses run rampant with me. So it makes me the aggressor in bed, the domineering one. I don't like it that way, but that's the way it is. So I have a lot of fantasy trips about balling other people. I've tried to stop, but I can't. And I've had a few extramarital affairs with very strong, domineering men. On Sweet Street, I don't see how you can avoid this. Everything conspires to dilute sex for you, and create problems. When I was younger, and I slimmed down for the first time in my life, I'd balled everybody that came into my sight, and I kind of lost the feeling for it, and that made the Sweet Street attitude about sex even worse for me, because they've lost the feeling about sex on Sweet Street something awful. Going to bed with somebody becomes like drinking a Coke, with no more meaning than that. And you wind up a mess. You wind up numbed to sex. That's why I have to go out and ball some very strong person every once in a while, just to get through to my desires, to get back in touch with them.

It's all so blunt and vulgar on the street, how can you possibly have a normal sexual relationship, really *feel* it? I mean, I have orgasms, but sometimes I won't have one for a couple of weeks, and when my old man balls me I have to fake one so he can feel that he's doing his thing, and I can never come out in front and say I'm not having one, 'cause he wouldn't understand. I find myself turning colder and colder.

There's absolutely no courtship on this street. If a guy takes you out, if you accept a date with him, that means he's gonna ball you. There's a coupla guys on the street that'll take you out and not try to ball you the first night, but they'll drop you if they don't get it pretty quick. *All* these men are obsessed with the subject of sex. They can turn any conversation into sex. You'll talk about Buddhism, and they'll say, "Yeh, I heard that Buddha was a pretty big stud!" It's fucking this and fucking that. They've wrapped their whole lives into one big sexual fantasy. I feel kind of sorry for them. I don't see how they can hold theirself above water. And their old age must be terrible.

Every man on this street has a high sexual ego, and when you reject 'em it really shuts 'em down to a level so low you can't even believe they're really men. Their ego is just shattered! They get very insulted. "How *could* you? How could you refuse *me*?" They just freak, they don't know how to handle it. The owners are the worst. They all have the attitude that since you're a cocktail waitress, you're a degenerate, and you don't have any smarts upstairs, and they don't give a shit about you.

Well, the whole street needs a blood transfusion. I give it another six months or a year to make or break it, because I happen to know that all these rosy financial pictures that Bill Gold paints are a lot of bullshit, and they're losing money fast. There's too big a gap between what the bosses are giving and what the customers want, and the people just aren't coming the way they used to. The street needs new blood, new managers, a whole new treatment. And maybe it's gonna get one. I heard a rumor about Miami buying in, the Miami mob, the Mafia. That wouldn't be so bad. Maybe they'd bring in some real entertainment. Maybe they won't do things so half-assed. I do know that two months ago Bill Gold was having a special little conference with a guy from Miami who looked very mobbish, very Cosa Nostra, a little old *Godfather* kind of man, and a couple of big toughs with him. And Bill's been making frequent trips to Miami ever since.

Well, why not the mob? I'd like to see it happen just for the sake of the people who like entertainment, and the people who work hard on the street. Why, somebody could make a fortune!

Not that I'll still be here. I just broke something off that'd been going on for quite a while, and now Billy and I are getting it together again, and our plan is to get out for good. I almost spoiled everything, though. I was working for Cappy Van Fleet at the Paris Lido, and he saw that I was having personal problems, and that I was easy to sort of manipulate around. He started probing around me without me even realizing it. I felt comfortable with him, so I talked, and pretty soon he told me he could help me with sessions on yoga and breathing and different exercises of the mind.

I really seriously believed him, and I went to his apartment and did what he told me. He told me to take off my clothes and lay down, because certain parts of your body perspire when certain things are wrong with you, and he had to see where I was perspiring to diagnose what was the matter with me. He sat there fully clothed and asked me questions and taught me exercises and made notes. I did these breathing exercises to the point where I was almost paralyzed, I couldn't open my hands or my mouth, and in that condition I started bluring out things from my childhood, and he was sitting there writing it all down.

Cappy taught me that there was a physical counterreaction for every mental problem, and that if you feel pain, a tightness, in between your thumb and your index finger, that's a sign of sexual pain, from sexual dissatisfaction at home. I was the unsuspecting one. I lay there and he tried to relax me, and I found myself, for the first time, not relating to him as a black man. We discussed my problems with Billy, and he said I had strong finger tension showing extreme sexual dissatisfaction at home. Maybe that's not really true, what he said. Maybe he was just trying to get into sex with me, I don't know. But all the time he was stressing that there'd be *no* sex, he was just trying to help a friend.

After a while he told me that he couldn't help me unless we were together a lot, and he started calling me up in the daytime, when Billy was at work. He'd call up and he'd say, "Let's go someplace," and he'd keep me on the go all the time. I'd come into work, and he'd be strongly affectionate, and if I looked a little down in the mouth he'd say, "Why don't you take a break?" And he'd come up and kiss me once in a while, little things like that, showing me a lot of affection when I really needed it and I wasn't getting it from Billy. One night Cappy told me, "There's no other man who can give you what I can give you," and he told me I should find an apartment and move away from Billy, and he threatened me that if I didn't move out on Billy, I'd lose everything. So it was a power trip he was on, and he began to show it. He'd take me out to dinner, and he'd treat me nicely, but he'd also order me around, as though he owned me.

For a while, I fell into the trap. Everything was the street and Cappy. I'd work with him all night and play with him all day. I closed my mind to the rest of the world; I wouldn't let Billy touch me for days at a time. That was the most dangerous period of my life. Sweet Street was wrapping me up, wrecking my normal relationships, making me become a Sweet Street person, which I'm not at heart.

My stomach gave me signals that it was all wrong. I began to develop a very nervous stomach, and the doctor gave me some tranquilizers. I had a month of total upset, pain, and that's when I really faced up to things, and I found it harder and harder to talk to Cappy. I realized that he was trying to get me under his power, *deeply* under his power, not just a roll in the hay, and then I'd be one of his girls, and maybe he'd turn me out to make money for him, or maybe he just enjoyed finding out where you're at, and then just playing with your mind. He's always doing that with one girl or another. He's got one named Daphne on that trip right now.

About a month ago I talked it all over with Billy, and Billy said, "Look, either drop him cold, or move out!" I said to myself I'm losing my old man, I'm losing my home, I'm turning into a street person, and *this is not what I want, this is not me*! And I said the hell with it, and I quit my job to get away from him. That's when I came to work at the Seven Seas.

I'm better now, but I still find myself getting paranoid of things around me on the street. I start looking at life, and questions come up: What am I doing here? Why am I working on Sweet Street? Where am I gonna go? What are all these other people doing?

A lot of times things make me paranoid, anxious, and I stop everything and go to work on a painting, and after a while I say to myself, Well, I have my painting, I have my music, I can watch TV, and this brings me back down to earth, and I realize I don't have to go completely nutty on the street.

My ID says I'm twenty-four, but I'm really only twenty, and sometimes I get the feeling that I'm really old, but in other ways I feel like I'm just growing up. I look around me and I see things coming down so fast, I feel like I'm still a little kid. Lately I felt myself coming to the end of my ropes again. Standing there at the curtain of the Seven Seas, I was losing my identity, telling people lies, telling them we have a great show and they're gonna have a great time, when all's that's gonna happen is they're gonna go inside and get bored and get taken for five-fifty or eleven dollars or whatever. I mean, how can you tell 'em night after night that you have a great show, when you really have a *shitty* show, shittily produced by Buddy De Young and shittily executed by clumsy tubs and that old blond lady with the three tits?

So I have an appointment for a job at the Hyatt House. I won't be on this street when I'm twenty-one. It'll all be a dream. Even bad dreams have to end sometime.

OLIVE CALZOLARI, 23

Waitress

There is no excellent beauty that hath not some strangeness in the proportion.

—Francis Bacon

IN A SHADOWED CORNER of the Lion's Tail, two men in paper hats and two women in fur wraps climb slowly to their feet and studiedly look away from the show as though no longer entitled. On the dollhouse-sized table in front of them, eight fresh drinks remain untouched, along with a check for twenty-two dollars. To one side stands a glowering waitress with yard-long hair and the features of a high-fashion model, her arms folded sternly across her ribcage, her ballet-slippered foot tapping silent remonstrances. The band continues to create cacophony at its customary 125 decibels, equivalent to the sound made by three subway trains pulling into the Times Square Station simultaneously, and to some ears even less melodious. At a slight break in the programed disorder, the screech of the waitress can be heard from one end of the club to the other: "Sit down, do you hear me? SIT RIGHT DOWN THERE! *Every* club on this street is the *same* price and you get *two* drinks minimum at *every* club and if you *don't* pay for these drinks I'M GONNA GET THE MANAGER! DO YOU HEAR ME? You *ordered* these drinks and you're gonna *pay*! If you didn't know how much they were gonna be why didn't you *ask* me before I set you down? And I *told* you I was gonna bring you two drinks each. I *told* you! Don't you deny it! NOW SIT DOWN AND PAY UP!"

The embarrassed foursome sits down, and one of the men

throws a bill on the table. The waitress smiles sweetly, snaps up the money and says, "Cheap motherfuckers!"

Later, Olive Calzolari explains in a soft, feminine voice, "I know I'm not gonna get a tip when I act like that, but I'm not gonna get a walkout, either, and walkouts are the worst. They fuck up the register, and they make the place look bad. Besides, the manager always figures if a customer walks out it's got to be the waitress's fault. It can't be the price of the drinks or the fact that they don't like black dancers or they don't like Connie Lea—oh, no, it's *always* the waitress! Pete'll say, 'Why'd that party walk out?' and he'll act real grouchy, real uptight. I don't like that, so I scream for the money. I have a very small percentage of walkouts, and a very small percentage of getting yelled at by Pete."

In the dimly lighted nightclub, Olive Calzolari's finer features are mostly unappreciated, especially by the victims of her tirades, but outside in the flickering neons and hot white headlights she is seen as a stirring specimen of womanhood, even in her street disguise of pinned hair and granny glasses and jeans. Her face is thin, her flat cheeks heightened by high, thrusting cheekbones. Her nose is a straight line from bridge to tip, and her teeth are even and shining. Her blue-gray eyes look like seawater at dawn, and her honey-brown hair is finely spun and worn back from her high forehead, all gathered and gleaming, as though tended by maids with soft brushes and combs. When the spare young form of Olive Calzolari appears on Sweet Street, cars jolt to a halt, and passersby turn to stare frankly over their shoulders. Beauty has passed, and it is permissible to gawk.

But Olive is anathema, an untouchable, a voluntary outcast from the street's social register. She is what the men at Raffaele's call a "ballbreaker," quiet as a steel rod in her customary dealings with others, and equally inflexible. She lives with a black, Cappy Van Fleet, in a liaison which some of her friends interpret as "Olive's way of telling the men on Sweet Street to go fuck themselves." She is also an avowed homosexual, actively on the prowl for new young dates, and perfectly open about taking them into Raffaele's and Vino's and the Crystal Palace for long evenings of sweet talk and hand-holding.

Olive as predator does not even exclude her colleagues at the Lion's Tail from her list of potential seductees. Before she began a vendetta against the troubled Carrie Hess for failing to keep a tight working schedule, Olive campaigned actively for the young divorcee's body. "She never let up," Carrie recalls. "It was huggy kissy all the time. She'd say, 'Listen, why don't you come to bed with me? I won't hassle you, and you won't have to do *anything.* I'll do it all!' She put the make on Agnes, too. Agnes went to Olive's place and Olive tried to attack her in the waterbed, and Agnes freaked out and didn't come to work that night. Terrible! It's enough to make you sick!"

Jessica King is more open-minded. "Sure, Olive's a lez. So what? I'm *not,* so it doesn't affect me. She's a bitch, too, but did you ever know a waitress that wasn't? She's very aggressive about getting her money. She'll move right in front of you in the line and take a customer away, and she'll say, 'If you want customers, move your ass!' She's a good waitress, and before she was a good waitress, she was a super dancer, just *super.* I admire Olive. Deep down underneath, the whole street does."

I was a very homely child, fat and homely. I was brought up in Detroit, in a neighborhood that was part Polish and part Italian, and *all* white middle class. My stepfather was the dominant figure in our family. He was a sheet-metal worker, very strong, the classic worker type, and he couldn't understand my brother and me when we started branching out. My stepfather and I used to fight, because he was a Leo and I'm Taurus. My mother's Capricorn and my brother is Sagittarius, so you can see the problems.

I'd have been perfectly willing to stay right there in my old neighborhood for the rest of my life, but my parents blew it. I wanted to move to a little apartment down the block, but my stepfather wouldn't let me. It just wasn't done. You lived at home till you got married, and then you and your husband moved to the suburbs. It had to be done that way, *his* way. He had a real heart attack the night I said I wanted to move into a place of my own. I freaked! I went every day to visit him at the hospital. When he got out of the hospital and I knew he was all right, I took my savings and left. I spent six months in a convent in Los Angeles, but it wasn't right for me. I was looking for pomp and ritual, and all the pomp and ritual was gone. The sisters wore short habits and no hats, high heels and all. Another beautiful tradition shot.

So I began traveling, and I came here when I was nineteen, in between buses, and I put on my cut-offs and loafers and decided to look around. I was amazed! There were so many young kids. I just loved it, so I got a job as a cashier, and then I went to work for the phone company as a clerk.

That was *so* boring! One day I met a couple of hip young girls that worked part time as strippers. They'd run down to the theater and dance for a week or two weeks and then take a few months off. I went, "Wow!" I was chubby then, 135 pounds, five-six, but I thought maybe I could try it. They said, "Quick! They need amateurs. Come on, you can do it! Be a stripper!" They said I could work Saturday and Sunday and go back to work at the phone company on Monday, and nobody would ever know.

I was scared shaky. I went down to the burlesque theater, the Joy, and it was in the worst part of town, really seedy. I had nothing to wear for amateur night, so one of the professional dancers gave me bottoms, and somebody else gave me a dress to take off over my head. They put make-up on me, and I felt like a clown, 'cause they didn't put it on right, it was just too loud. And they pushed me out on stage with only two things to take off. Some striptease!

There was a three-piece band playing "A Hard Day's Night" in the pits, and the stage was huge, T-shaped, coming out into a runway. I did the pony, and somebody applauded, and I felt this incredible energy and I just started flying around that stage. I really *dug* the applause. I was scared, but then you're always scared onstage. It didn't bother me to take off my clothes particularly. I just said to myself, "Well, I'm getting paid for this, and I'll probably never do it again." I danced and danced around, and I thought, the music's taking *forever*. I found out later, if *I'd* taken my clothes off sooner, *they'd* have quit playing sooner. One of my friends said later, "I thought you were *never* gonna take that dress off!"

I don't even know how many people were in the audience, but there were three or four of us amateurs there, and the M.C. brought us out and did the trip of putting the hands over the head and asking for applause. I was the last one, and the audience applauded and applauded, and the announcer said I won, and I said, "What'd I win?" He said, "Well, nothing. You just won, that's all."

That Monday at work I felt great! I was still hyper from the whole experience. I knew a big secret that none of the other girls knew. It was such an ego boost to me, because just a year or two before I'd been a gawky teen-ager, plain Jane, Miss Studious, and everybody said, Oh, she's too intelligent, and now I was a sex symbol, and all those men in the audience dug on me. So in the office I felt sexier, acted sexier, even *walked* sexier. I was just Miss Femininity, and the guys in the office began to pick up on my energy, and some of the girls did, too.

But I was never gonna strip again. It just wasn't me. I felt too fat, and I just marked it down as an exhilarating experience, never to be repeated. But then they asked me if I wanted to work again, and I got a regular job stripping nights after work. I'd jump on the bus from the phone company and do the dinner show at the Joy, and then I'd dance a few more shows till midnight and I'd make fifteen bucks a night. I was working from 8:30 in the morning till midnight, but I didn't care. I was Miss Energy.

But every time I did it, I said, Okay, this is the last night. I still thought it was a little naughty, and it tied up too much of my time. Like you had two or three hours between shows. but not enough time to really accomplish anything. A lot of the chicks used to go to the bars in the neighborhood, hang out for a couple hours, drink, goof around, yakkety-yak with the guys. We used to fall into this place that had all the great burlesque stars' pictures on the walls, back from the days when burlesque was big, and I really began to get a feel for it, like I was involved in some great historical cultural thing, and I was important. And I realized I was getting something emotional out of the dancing. When you strip, you take the people in the audience on your own sensual trip. The old bumps and grinds were where the old strippers' heads were at, but by the time I came along it was the girl-next-door act, little Miss Innocence, naughty but nice. You know what's going on, but you're shy, and still you do it. I enjoyed it.

When my vacation came up, I went on a trip around the country, and when I was in Washington, D.C., my money ran out, and I looked for a few nights' work. A little theater called the Gaiety hired me, and those dancers there really turned me professional. They put me in somebody's stretch gown, high heels, breakaway silver underwear, and tons of make-up, and sent me out. Well, my first show I took one step forward and the stretch gown unzipped from the bottom up. *Much* too quick! Instant strip! All I had on was bra and panties underneath. Another show, I was zipping down the back, and the zipper got caught in the lace of my panties, it wouldn't go up or down, and I had to back up to the curtain and stand there while the stagehand fixed it, and we did a little comedy routine all the time to cover it up. What can you do? You just wait for the act to end, and get off!

They told me I was great, and gave me a booking for the whole week. At first, I was still the studious kid from high school. Are you ready for this? I would leave the burlesque theater on breaks and rush over to the Smithsonian Institute! I *love* that place. But then I began hanging around with the other strippers, and that's when the trouble started. The feature's name was Tiger Fawn, a great big beautiful woman with flame-red hair, spike high heels, and a brand new silicone job. She got seven-hundred dollars a week, and she was worth it. Then there was Dixie, another stripper, and she was a butch, and she and Tiger Fawn were having a big affair. Till I came along. Then Dixie began bouncing back and forth between me and the feature, and there were big fights. Oh, God! It was torture! I lost fifteen pounds in one week worrying about it. Dixie knew what she wanted, and she knew how to get it. She carried herself like a man, she was *your* escort, she pampered you and spoiled you. She had day and night personalities, one for the theater, one for her private life. She had short butchy hair, but for stripping she'd tease it up a little, and she had a stocky waist, which a lot of butches have. She locked me up solid! That's when I *really* went gay. I was very young and impressionable, just ga-ga over her, and I thought that Tiger Fawn was gonna kill me at any moment.

When my booking was up, the manager wanted to book me into New York, with the other girls, but everything was so fucked up I said no. Dixie and I parted sadly. She gave me a two-hundred-dollar diamond ring, and she said she'd see me when she came here. Later on I met other butches, and I found out that Dixie didn't make love all that well. So when she showed up later, Dixie and Tiger Fawn together, maybe a year later, I wasn't interested in her at all. She broke up with Tiger Fawn and said she was gonna move in with me. I said, "Oh, no, you're not." She asked for her ring back, and I said no, and I made her leave.

By this time, the phone company was beginning to bore me, so I got a job dancing on Sweet Street, and I got another butch, and she took me to work and picked me up after work, and nobody else dared to lay a hand on me. I thought about being gay a lot, and I realized it was hard for dancers to be any other way, because of the aspect of how you work, traveling together, living together, a week here, a week there, two weeks there, and then you're sharing the driving and shopping together, and it becomes an emotional dependence and a physical thing, and you're locked up. I didn't find the physical end of it too overpowering at first. I mean, I had orgasms, but not tremendously. I was very high on sexual contact, but I couldn't really give to the other chicks, 'cause I didn't know what I was giving.

For a while, I felt confused, and I went to see a psychiatrist. He kept encouraging me to stop stripping, because of the way it was making me feel about men. I figured that men had nothing going for them at all! They were all beginning to fall into the same frame. We talked a lot about me and my stepfather, and I said I was gay, and he said, "You're *not* gay!"

I went, "Well, why am I going with all these chicks?"

He went, "You're doing that as an experience, maybe, but physically you are not a gay person." So I didn't know *what* I was at that point.

After a while I began to get tired of this pushy butch, Kenny, that had taken over my life. I was dancing at the Pink

Elephant and meeting lots of young, pretty girls, and I wanted to get to know them better, but Kenny wouldn't let me. She was too old for me, anyway, thirty-three, and she wasn't nearly as horny as I was. I was completely lesbian by now, solid. I wasn't even on the pill. I told Kenny I didn't want any more of her physical enslavement, and she said she was gonna lock me in the house. Well, it was *my* apartment, so I said, "Hey, I like my place, but I don't like you. I'll help you pack!" She like spun me around and threw me on the bed. I got up and put on a sweatshirt, and she threw me down again. I got up and put on jeans, and when she grabbed me again, I said, "Okay, you want to fight?" and I threw her across the room and into a table. She just sort of gasped. Then she said, "Oh, Ollie!" as if she couldn't believe what was happening.

I said, "I'm packing you right now. Call the taxi."

I just needed some freedom, that's all. We had two afghans, a Pomeranian, five cats, goldfish. It was a zoo, and I was going crazy, plus dancing every night, and Kenny not working at all. She used to be a feature stripper, but she's a female bartender now, and a hustler on the side. I haven't seen her in a long time. She came into the club one night after I threw her out and she said, "I'm gonna pull you off that stage and beat you up, and you're never gonna dance again," screaming all this right in front of the customers!

I said, "Get out, or I'll call the police!" She phoned me a few times after that, and then she stopped.

I got a job at the Paris Lido after a year or so, and that's when I first saw Cappy Van Fleet, the scourge of the street! He was working as light man, and I was scared to death of him, with that crazy shaved head of his and those big devil sideburns and those funny moves he makes, like a snake standing up. I'd been told that if the dancers didn't like their lights he'd throw them down the stairs if they complained, and it was *true*! He used to throw the feature down the stairs all the time. He'd say, "Shut up, bitch!" The first time I ever saw him, I walked into the club and he was sitting at the bar in his blue jeans and blue-jean jacket and shaved head, and my eyes got as big as saucers. I thought, "Oh, God!" I was *so* afraid of him, I couldn't even talk.

A few nights later I was dancing on the sheepskin rug on-stage, and Cappy came up and pinched me on the butt right in front of the audience. I freaked out! I had half a house, so I couldn't say much, but when I was finished I went straight to the owner and I said, "Listen, I'm not *that* friendly with him offstage, and I'm not gonna be that friendly with him onstage. You keep him away from me!"

Well, Cappy has this awful stutter. When he gets excited, he can hardly get a thought out. The owner ordered him to apologize to me, and he came up and said, "I-I-I-I-I-I-I-I'm sorry," and it almost *choked* him to say it. I knew they'd put too much pressure on him to apologize, and that I'd carried it too far, and I felt a lot of compassion for the poor man, that he had to do this unnatural thing of apologizing when he already had so much trouble just talking.

So after that I made friends with him, and I began to build a rapport with him, and I even started taking dance lessons from him. But I was still slipping out with chicks, too, and having a gay old time. His blackness didn't bother me at all. I had an open mind about that. I don't like black pimps, no, and I don't like the shuckers and jivers, you know, the young bucks that come out in their fancy clothes and say, "Hey, mama, yew sho' look good tonaht! Kin Ah woke yew a ways?" But Cappy isn't like that at all. He's revitalizing, full of energy and ideas, eastern philosophy, yoga, Oriental martial arts, things like that. He can talk to you for weeks at a time and never repeat himself.

It took quite a few months for us to get it together. One day he brought me to his place and he said, "Have you tried a waterbed?" I sat on a pillow, but I refused to try the bed. He'd brought me there on a pretense—said he had to pick up something—but he was really trying to feel me out, and I couldn't handle it.

But then I was really digging on him one night at work, and he could tell, so he said, "Would you like to come home with me tonight?"

I didn't know what to say. I realized this was it. Whatever I said right now would decide our whole relationship. It hung on a word. So I went, "Yes," and he went, "*What*?" I went, "Yes," and he said, "Okay."

I hadn't been with a man in two years, and I tried too hard, and I almost spoiled everything. I was just too phony in bed, I mean I was enjoying it, but I was adding to it, making sounds and all. I was very uneducated sexually, really. Cappy saw right through it. After a while, he rapped my leg with his hand, and he threw me to one side, and he said, "Hey, save all that noise for your girl friends!"

But little by little I worked my way out of it, and after a while Cappy and I found we were very compatible, in bed as well as out, and I realized I was spending more time in his apartment than I was in my own. One night he said, "Hey, how long do we have to support two apartments?"

I was shocked, because he'd told me he never wanted any chicks living with him.

I said, "Well, gee, if it's all that serious, maybe I better go back on the pill."

He freaked! I thought he was gonna have a heart attack! I mean, he'd already had six children, and lost three. He just sat there fuming.

I said, "Well, Cappy, I've been gay all this time."

He said, "But all the gay chicks take the pill!"

I said, "None that I know of."

He said, "Well, I'm not touching you till you get on it!" I've been on the pill ever since, almost two years now.

I still dig on chicks, but I can't find chicks that are to-gether enough to play with. When I was a dancer, before I discovered I could make much more money as a waitress, we were all so close, undressing in front of each other. Pretty soon you began to feel a closeness, and then you made it once or twice, as a relief, as a curiosity, just to get it over with. You *enjoyed* it, and it wasn't overdemanding. But with these girls at the Lion's Tail, we all tease and play grab-ass, sometimes to the extreme, but mostly they're so shut off from one another, it's "don't touch me!" all the time. They all seem too much within themselves to even try a lésbian ex-perience, and yet some part of them seems to crave it, too. That's why all the grab-ass.

Myself, I think I've grown beyond lesbianism mostly, but I don't let on. If the other chicks don't know where my head's at, then I'm not gonna be the one to tell 'em. I find it useful not to reveal exactly what I am sexually. I think I'll always like chicks, but right now I'm in love with Cappy, because Cappy is exceptional, and he's the only man that turns me on. I do like pretty boys, young hippy type boys that look so innocent and sweet and young, but they're not together enough to go out with, and I just end up all disappointed. Only one man has turned me on in the last year, other than Cappy. He's Pete Stang, the manager. He kisses me once in a while, and I like it. So I guess there's still hope. Cappy likes me to date, so I'll keep on trying. But I still like chicks, no doubt about it. I guess I always will.

The Establishment

Press Agent

IN BETWEEN THE SPANGLED entrances of two of Sweet Street's business establishments, a scarred wooden door leads up a long flight of worn stairs to the second-floor office that serves as headquarters for a small syndicate of strip-joint operators. The office is wallpapered in a pattern of silhouettes showing men and women coupling with hound-dog enthusiasm. A calendar from Harold's Club, Reno, decorates one wall, an assortment of nude pin-ups another. A stained curtain of red velvet hangs across three windows that open on an outside sign: NAKED DANCE OF LOVE, formed in red and circled by white bulbs, and a tall black profile of a nude man and woman: advertisements for the nightclubs downstairs.

One desk is covered with newspaper clippings and yellowed old files; the other bears a copy of a pornographic magazine called "Ball" and a box marked "Yahtzee." An antique Royal typewriter sits to one side, and there are telephones and adding machines and filing cabinets, atop one of which a long greenish-brown panatela cigar, soggy and cold and abandoned, is balanced on the edge of a grimy ashtray. An empty can of Pepsi-Cola and two stubby glasses smelling of whiskey rest alongside a postal scale.

It is early evening, and the three windows pick up and distort the magentas and royal blues and heliotropes of the signs outside, tinting the faces of the office's occupants. A young woman looks out a window at a large globule of mankind slowly waddling up the street. "Here he comes," she says. "That's him. That's our Fatso."

Natie Cohen carries almost four-hundred pounds on his short, overstressed frame, giving him the shape of a teed-up football. Atop this ponderous ellipsoid is the sweet face of an innocent child, framed by a full head of wavy, brown hair. The effect is to charm one totally, unless one has been forewarned that Natie Cohen's looks can be especially deceiving. This very day he has received a curt message: a bullet wrapped in tissue paper and captioned with commendable brevity: "4 U." Natie smiles his sweet smile, like a Bar Mitzvah candidate looking over his shoulder at the family, and drops the slug in the wastebasket.

"He makes people mad," says Mary Hawkins, Natie's part-time secretary and occasional movie date. "He just picks at you till you've had enough. You want to punch him right in his fat stomach. Once I called him a fat fucker. That was one of my good days. He stopped talking to me. Ha ha!"

"He's always antagonizing somebody," says the head of the nightclub operation, Bill Gold. "Natie's a very antagonistic and sarcastic person. You want to know his problem? It's his overattachment to his Jewish mother. That's what causes the overweight and all his problems. When he gets sick, he runs home to mother. Every Friday, sick or not, he eats with the family. At thirty-seven, he should be getting away from them, get married. A very strange person, Natie. You love him and you hate him at the same time. He can be a little boy, and he can be a terrible schmuck."

One learns quickly that Natie Cohen seldom converses. As befits a public relations man, he makes pronouncements. "Don't interrupt!" he says frequently. "Let me finish my thought," as though it deserved to be carved into marble. Sweet Street is the locus of his universe, the remainder of the world serving merely as an adjunct, existing to provide Sweet Street with fruits and vegetables and industrial goods and basic services. Natie is self-described as "The Archie Bunker of Sweet Street," but he is not that easily pigeonholed, and many consider him a total enigma. In one breath he will lambaste the blacks *en masse*, and in the next provide a sparkling defense of the most notorious black pimp in town. Some say that the motivation is pure contrariness, and that you can always get Natie Cohen to disagree simply by taking a strong stand in any direction.

Sometimes he holds court on the sidewalk, moving slowly

and imperiously along the crowded street bestowing the benediction of his hellos and his nods on the showpeople he has made famous around the neighborhood. He is fond of executing *mots* like "toplessness has certainly captured the public lack of imagination," but he is also capable of mangling his metaphors, as in "this business is right up my cup of tea." Despite the nature of his profession, he is still under the impression that the dark tips on human breasts are called "nibbles."

Friends say his life expectancy is short, which might explain a tendency to rambling, nonstop disquisitions on any subject, as though there were little enough time to complete the record. "The weight's killing him," says Mary Hawkins. "It's affecting his circulation. He's already having bad trouble with his legs, and they might have to cut one off. Sometimes he has to stay in bed, to get blood down to the ankle. He never sticks to his diets. You'd think he'd want to lose weight, but no. He likes the image of being a big fat publicity agent. Well, I certainly don't want to see him die. Not especially."

I'm no angel, I know that. I am no fuckin' angel by a stretch of the imagination, and I am not the easiest person to be with. I'm a maverick, in my business, but I love my business. I don't know many people who even know my name, but there are maybe fifty top press agents in this country, and I'm in the top five, and I'm only thirty-seven years old. Notice what I said: I'm not a public-relations man, I'm a *press agent*. That's my job. I'm a bullshitter by trade. I'm selling fantasy to the people. I get persecuted because of the business I'm in. I'm a fuckin' genius in my fuckin' business. I've pulled some stunts that you won't even fuckin' believe, and I get tremendous satisfaction even today, after ten years of it, when I get one of our stars' names mentioned in the papers, on television, radio. And I got all this publicity with no superstars to work with. I never had the Marilyn Monroes or the Mansfields or the Elizabeth Taylors or the Bette Davises, those kind of people. I did it with a cocktail waitress that took silicone shots.

I started the whole topless craze. I went to Nick Testi,

who owned the Lion's Tail at the time, with a newspaper clip
of a four-and-a-half-year-old girl in a Rudy Gernreich topless
bathing suit, and then Nick and I told Connie Lea if she
wanted to dance on our stage she should wear a suit like
that, and she said okay. She was dancing already as a go-go
girl, in between rounds of waitressing, and all she had was a
34-B cup, but big nibbles. It wasn't till a few years later that
she took the shots and went up to those balloons she has
now. That started everybody getting silicone. It got so bad
that one night I looked up and there was a girl dancing with
one breast pointing ninety degrees to the left and the other
ninety degrees to the right. This broad had just had fifteen
hundred dollars' worth of silicone inserts, and she looked like
she was wearing spaceships going to two different destina-
tions. I had to pay her off and let her go. I said, "Sorry,
honey, but it's just too obnoxious to look at." I said, "Really, I
think you should go back to your doctor and have them re-
done."

I don't know how she slipped by the manager. Normally
we try to audition all the girls. We take them downstairs in
the office, and we ask them what they look like underneath
their beautiful wardrobes, and all that kind of stuff. We go
through the whole shtick with them. But this isn't a vulgar
business, and these aren't vulgar girls. These are girls that
want to be in show business. Our greatest commodity is tits
and ass. That's what we're selling. I personally think we
should be picking up a better cream of girls than what we're
getting, weed out the hippies and get showbiz types again.

As human beings, the girls that dance on this street want
to be loved, like everybody else, and they do have a heart.
The first time somebody wants girls to dance for the Vet-nam
amputees in the hospital, these are the girls that're willing to
go. We took fourteen girls from the Silver Peacock, and
they'd never seen a man with no arms and no legs, the only
thing he has left is his penis and his balls, and that's it, everything else blown off by a mine, and you talk about guts! Guys
that'll never walk again, never see again, no arms, no legs.
Hey, these are people! The politicians that are always
bitching about the nudity on Sweet Street, they should spend
a little time with these guys, see what the Vet-nam war has

done to them. What guts! And our girls went over and put on a Christmas show, with all their clothes on, and then they went into the wards. Everyone of the girls broke down and cried. And the guys were telling the girls, "Look, please don't cry! We love you for coming! *Please don't cry!*"

I'll tell you, there's been many a superstar on Sweet Street, going back to 1964 when we went topless. This street was founded on superstars like Fran Dinkelman, topless mother of eight, at the Silver Peacock, and Fat Fritzi Myer at the Lions Tail. There was the Busty Hundred, two girls that measured a hundred inches between them. One was fifty-two, one forty-eight. And there was Mary Lou-Ann, the girl in the bedroom. She didn't fuck anybody, she just did a *beautiful* act in a bedroom. And I don't want to leave out the Katydids, our all-girl topless band.

But Connie Lea is still our super super super act. We spend twenty-five thousand dollars a year publicizing her. She's been in *Playboy* three times, in *Newsweek, Time.* She's the superstar of superstars. Every week in the world Connie Lea's name is being mentioned in print.

That's my job. I'm after that publicity day and night. Two years ago Rudy Gernreich came out with a frontless dress with pasties. I had one made up, a hundred dollars, and I took one of the girls with big tits on an airplane. We walked off the plane at the Hollywood International Airport and the whole press corps was there, including the police. I issued a press release, called it the Topless Skies of United. The girl paid a twenty-five-dollar fine, but the publicity you couldn't buy.

At one of our anniversaries, I had four topless girls draped all over a fountain in the middle of town at eight-thirty in the morning. I hid out, because at eight-forty-five they were arrested for indecent exposure and had to pay fines. Then I took two topless girls from the Peacock to a medical convention at the Hilton, and the general manager got very upset, and I was arrested for trespassing.

I'm the one who conceived the idea of footprints, handprints and bustprints all along Sweet Street. Mammary Lane, we called it. In front of the clubs I had fourteen topless girls laying their breasts in cement. Newspapermen all over the place! It made the wire services. I got arrested for disturbing the peace, but they dropped the case. We had to take the cement prints out later. They were too big. They looked like deep wells.

One Christmas I had Fat Fritzi Myer dressed as a topless Santa Claus, giving away kisses and candy canes in the financial district. We both got arrested for disturbing the peace. We had traffic blocked for miles.

Well, it's all fun and games and publicity. And honest business. There's no Mafia on Sweet Street, and nobody can say there is, because we're too well publicized. The Mafia wouldn't dare come in here. I wish they would. I would love to work for the syndicate. I could make a lot of money, and the Italian Mafia, those are beautiful religious people. That's their world, and they've got children and families, and they only fight among themselves. They don't go out and fight like a revolutionary that's tearing down a building or blowing up a bank or tearing up a school. Hey, they only fight amongst their own personal sectors.

I'd like to see a mob chick walk around with a black dude, the way they all do here. They'd cut his balls off. I know they say I'm bigoted, but I'm hot about that subject: black dudes with white chicks. You see them all over Sweet Street. It's so hypocritical. I know white chicks that've had abortions because they were knocked up by a black. I'd say, "Hey, you're a fuckin' hypocrite! Why don't you have the goddamn kid? Why don't you marry him? How come you like to fuck him but you won't take him home to mother? Isn't that being a hypocrite?" Drives them crazy!

On Sweet Street, a white broad is washed up when a black drops her. She's like living in a prison. She's branded. "Hey, that white broad," they'll say, "*she fucks niggers!*" No white man in his right mind would want to pick up with a chick like this, because the black-white affair is the white man's biggest nemis.

I don't like the women's lib movement, either. I go out of my way to antagonize them. They're more prejudiced than anybody in the country, those women's libbers. Their philosophy is one of the reasons today's woman is sexless. She doesn't want to stay home and be a housewife and dress pretty and put the perfume on. They'd rather be career women. They don't mind getting fucked once in a while by a man, but they don't want to get tied down in marriage.

I've always said I'll only marry once, and then it'll be for good. I don't know if I'll ever be able to do what I *really* want to do, and that's get involved in movies. Hollywood could revert back to its era of glamour and excitement, the Edward G. Robinsons, the Clark Gables, the Jean Harlows, Marilyn Monroes, these type of people. I can't believe we can't have a super-cowboy, a campy cowboy, a cowboy whose hat doesn't fall off in a fight, or another Johnny Weismuller playing Tarzan or the Abbott and Costello and Laurel and Hardy routines. We could bring it back easily.

All it would take is a good press agent. I'm available.

Secretary

"SHE'S THE TYPICAL DUMB blonde," strip-joint operator Bill Gold says without heat. "The world's worst secretary, bar none. She transposes numbers, she loses things, she's inefficient. When somebody leaves a number, I have her ask 'em to repeat it twice, and then I ask her to write it down and look at it and make sure she's got it right, and *still* she'll get it wrong. But what're you gonna do? After you know her a coupla days you're never gonna fire her. She's yours, she's on your side completely. And she hasn't got a bad bone in her. She's a sucker for every book company, every record company, anything you can buy through the mail, and she always owes me money. She works two jobs, seven days a week, and still never has enough money. So how the hell can I fire her? My partners complain, and I say to them, 'Okay, who wants to throw the rocks?' "

Mary Hawkins sits at the desk next to Natie Cohen's and idles her way through the day, conserving energy for her nighttime job as cashier at Vino's down the street. Sometimes she practices Yahtzee, a Chinese game played with dice. Practice consists of rolling the dice and keeping track of the results. "Oh, I'm getting good numbers today!" Mary Hawkins says after an especially lucky run. Every afternoon the old watchman from the Lion's Tail comes in to play a few games with her, and the dice fly back and forth while telephones ring and Mary tries to figure out which buttons to push and scrambles the incoming messages. Her main assignment seems to be to chat with the Sweet Street establishment and run down the block to get coffee and rolls for her various bosses, mainly Bill Gold and Natie Cohen.

Once she performed as a go-go dancer and later as the drummer in a topless band, but now she is twenty pounds overweight and firmly committed to the sedentary life. Her face is round, set off by gold granny glasses, and her nose is small and pug. Her hair is gold blond, her eyes light brown, and her complexion clear and glowing. Except in unguarded moments, she seems to "sparkle" like the Shirley Temple of forty years ago. She has the old catch-throat Temple style, and she giggles and laughs and falls just short of baby talk. Her voice and her vocal mannerisms are high-pitched, sometimes falsetto, like an actor in a grammar-school play, obeying stage instructions: MARY (*Laughs*)

Although she is frankly disappointed in her looks ("I'm average, I guess, kinda fat, kinda flat-chested, too old for everybody around here"), she does not worry about her personality. "One of my girl friends is always telling me what a nice personality I have," she says, and Sweet Street agrees. Mary Hawkins is a "nice" person, a put-upon, patient, kindly floradora girl, accepted by all, taken seriously by none, an early version of the faithful bunned-hair secretary who outlasts her bosses and never marries. "She's a beautiful person," says Natie "Fatso" Cohen. Natie says that about all the girls.

One good thing about my life, nothing sad has ever happened to me. Not even breaking up with my boy friend. Oh, I felt real bad the first day 'cause I had to go home to an empty house, but then I moved in with my girl friend and I didn't have time to be sad about anything. I guess you could say it was sad when they took me away from my mother, but I don't remember except crying all the way to the orphanage. I was four years old. I don't know where she is now. She's just gone. They took me from her because she wasn't a good mother, and she wasn't married, that's what it says on my birth certificate. I remember, they came to get me at the place where my mother and I were staying, and I didn't want to go, but I'm happy now.

I lived in the Catholic orphanage till my new parents came and got me when I was ten. It took a year for the adoption, 'cause they had to keep trying to find my real mother to sign papers, but they never could find her. And all the other kids would say, "Ha ha, they're not gonna adopt you! They didn't want you after all! Ha ha!" I fooled *them!*

I had a nice childhood in Idaho. My new mom and dad were nice, they taught me a lot of things. My dad taught me how to cry at the drop of a hat, and I can still do it. Like if I wanted to go to the show, he'd say, "Okay, if you can cry for me, we'll go." So I'd just think about something sad and cry. Ha ha! And off we'd go to the show. I'm still a good crier.

When I grew up, I couldn't stand it in Idaho any more, so I came here looking for work. I met a guy, and he brought me to Sweet Street and dared me to get into a topless dancing contest, so I did. Ha ha! I was twenty-two years old, and they offered me a job dancing barebreasted. That first night, my knees were knocking together. It took me three months to turn around and face the audience. I was scared! I was a nervous wreck! I'd have to play games with myself to keep on going, like I'd pretend I wasn't onstage, or I'd think about shopping. I'd be dancing topless and saying to myself, "I wonder what I'll buy tomorrow." Or I'd make eyes at my boy friend in the band. One night the boss told my boy friend, "Will you tell her to face the audience? We're not paying her to dance to you guys!" I worked seven days a week, from six at night till two in the morning, and I made $175 clear, after taxes.

I didn't mind it after a while, except for some of the customers. Once I came off stage topless and this guy pinched me right in the butt, and I just punched him all the way to the door. I said, "You jackass! Keep your hands to yourself!" He was six feet tall, and he kept right on walking.

The doctors are the biggest assholes you've ever seen. They act like they've never seen a broad—a girl. They do! I know! I worked when a medical convention was here, and they were so horny. They wanted to see the beaver shots and the whole works. They'd shout, "Hey, open your legs!"

I got pregnant, and that's when I put on weight. My boy friend and I couldn't get married 'cause he's already married and he's got two kids of his own, and the whole thing got me very depressed, so I ate three meals a day and whole cakes at a time. Ha ha! All I did was eat. I gained sixty-five pounds and weighed 190, and they fired me from my job, and I had to go on welfare. I gave up my baby, too, but that didn't bother me. April 14, 1968. She was cute. She had a tooth right here. Long eyelashes, and a little nose. She weighed seven pounds fourteen ounces. I was asleep when I had her, but I went down to the nursery to see her later. She was three days old, and she wasn't wrinkled like I expected. I gave her away to somebody that wanted her. Ha ha!

My personal life is pretty simple. I work seven days a week, five days here and five nights at Vino's. When I get off work at five o'clock and I don't have to go to Vino's I usually go right to bed, and I'm asleep by five-thirty. I'm tired a lot. I shouldn't be so tired, but I am. Maybe I need a vacation, but I don't have any money for one. I had a vacation three years ago, and it was fun.

If I don't marry, I guess my girl friend and I'll grow old together. We go out to dinner and we see a coupla little old ladies together, and we say we're not gonna be like that when *we* get old. Ha ha! Maybe we will! Maybe we'll *have* to. I don't have any money. I live from week to week, I only make $125 total from both jobs, so I can't save anything.

Sure, I'd like to get married. I'd love to get married. Just somebody, rich or poor. But I'm on the wrong street for that.

Show Producer

> In law, what plea so tainted and corrupt
> But being season'd with a gracious voice,
> Obscures the show of evil?
> —Shakespeare, *The Merchant of Venice*

Buddy's always telling me how he balled this girl and this girl and this girl. I said, "Buddy, you're very insecure about your manhood, aren't you?"

He says very nonchalantly, "Yes." I really loved him for that! He was being so honest about it.

—Jessica King, waitress

BUDDY DE YOUNG WALKS along Sweet Street with the slow and gouty gait of a dissolute old prince from the scores of Borodin. "He's like a sloth," a dancer says. "He just kind of mooches around." His head is adorned by a thinning patch of stiff hair that has been tortured and teased and redistributed in an effort to make it do a job too broad for its substance. The hair has been treated with various potions and philtres, and in rebellion has turned an odd metallic red in one light, orange in another, and the desired auburn only at a distance of twenty or more paces, or slightly less in the heavy fog that regularly enshrouds his creaking tugboat home. At fifty-seven, Buddy De Young is the unabashed masculine version of the little old lady with blue hair, and he is characteristically straightforward on the subject. "Fuckin' hair," he says in his tired voice. "No matter what I do, it still looks old."

Buddy is six feet tall and heavily built, with a swelling middle that increasingly limits his open campaign to bed every American female above the age of ten. His face is lumpy, his complexion mottled, his nose elongated and hooked, like a rutting salmon's. His teeth are stained from three daily packs of cigarettes, and his dark eyes are bleaching with age into a bilious tomcat-yellow. Except when he smiles his ingenuous little-boy smile, he looks wan and drawn, as though his vital juices had almost drained away. Ginny Thomas, who has lived on Buddy's tugboat for three years minus a few brief escapades ashore, says he is winding down fast. "He never used to look so tired," Ginny says. "I worry about him, the way he abuses himself."

Buddy De Young would be the first to admit that he has known brighter hours, and elements of his wardrobe attest to bygone splendor. On rainy nights, he walks Sweet Street in a Pierre Cardin maxi-raincoat made of a rust-colored material as soft to the touch as velours. "Just a little something I picked up in Paris," he tells the admirer. "Cost me two bills." No one on the street, least of all Buddy De Young, is shy about quoting price tags, or inflating them to fit the needs of the moment. "These set me back ninety dollars," Buddy says, pointing to a pair of patent-leather tassletop pumps, very much in vogue in the fifties. His jackets run to loud stripes and checks, materials like thick velvet and Billy Graham sharkskin, and satin linings and lapels. His ties and robes are of silk (prices available on request, and sometimes otherwise).

Almost every show on Sweet Street was produced or influenced by Buddy De Young, but opinions are sharply divided about his talents. Josey Costello, dancer and heroin user, argues that whatever Buddy's occasional lapses of taste, the street needs him "He creates the shows, he gets the girls, he holds it all together." Bill Gold, *capo di tutti capi* of a handful of Sweet Street clubs, calls his number-one aide and chief procurer "a positive genius." Pete Stang, manager of the Lion's Tail, says, "Buddy's shows are the shits, but they're so campy they're funny. He sees people laughing out front, and he thinks they're laughing with him. But what's the difference, as long as the street makes money?"

In a typical act, Buddy's hyped-up tape-recorded voice tells the audience: "Here we are at the Paris Lido, about to begin the show! So sit back, relax, fasten your seat belts, and fly

THE NAKED STEWARDESSES!" A brass choir blares, rear-projected jet planes roar across a screen, and three undressed young women mince onstage, entreating the audience to "Ride *me*! I'm Mitzi!," "Try me! I'm Gigi! I lay *all the way*!" and "Watch *us*! We fly United . . ."

Buddy's voice, complete with intermountain accent and rustic mispronunciations, proclaims, "And here they come, ladies and gentlemen, THE NAKED STEWARDESSES! We hope you left your troubles outside, because sex rules the world! And the Paris Lido is America's greatest, the city's *wildest* sex show! The Paris Lido is *girls*! The Paris Lido is girls, *girls*, GIRLS! We hope it's fun for you, ladies and gentlemen! *We love you*!"

A nude gum-chewing dancer climbs atop a swinging hammock and begins an unvarying routine that quickly becomes as repetitious as a Shostakovich coda. Back and forth, up and down, to and fro she swings, while Buddy De Young's recorded voice, blotted out occasionally by recorded cymbals and horns and drums, squawks an accompanying libretto. "Ladies and gentlemen, it seems that one of our flying stewardesses has flown out into orbit and bumped into the Star Trek gang in space! Ladies and gentlemen, may we interduce the heavenly body of our flying stewardesses and her or-ghee in orbit, as the Starship Intercourse attempts her rescue from space! The first two rows better move back! Here she comes!" The bored dancer continues to swing and exercise her mandibles as colored lights flash off and on, sirens wail, and voices cry out in panicked tones:

"Captain Smuck, the lights have gone out! We must get this girl out of orbit and into our or-ghee room."

"This is Smuck in the women's room on level four."

"Oh, no!"

"There's a janitor over there with a skeleton key. We should have her out any moment."

"But this is an emergency! Can't you do anything faster? Can't you blast her out?"

"How's the computer doing?"

"Fuck the computer! Smuck, look into this groove tube. We've got to get that naked earthling out of orbit before she gyrates herself into her ass-teroids!"

A typical Buddy De Young production runs slightly longer than an hour, and is performed six times a night. Five or six of the Sweet Street clubs use his material, and he boasts that he can rewrite and rerecord an entire routine in an evening, doing most of the voices and sound effects himself, like the old trouper that he is.

The bread-and-butter half of Buddy's job, and by far the more taxing, consists of troubleshooting the talent. As Bill Gold's major domo, Buddy gets the hysterical last-second messages that someone failed to show up, or a dancer fell off the stage and sprained her ankle, or a stripper was suddenly taken drunk or overdosed. At such times, Buddy leafs through the well-worn pages of his address book, sometimes calling as many as twenty or twenty-five women before filling the vacancy. He tries to relax in the late afternoons, before leaving his tugboat home for Sweet Street, but usually the jangling telephone will interrupt. Buddy answers in his weary off-stage voice, "Hello? What's up, Pete? Oh, God, don't tell me. Cappy needs two dancers, too. Okay, use Ya-vonne tonight. Did you call Ya-vonne? Well, what's wrong with all these dancers lately? Oh, shit. Well, I'll tell you, Monica might work, but don't make it too hard on her. She worked the Paris Lido last night, and some broad in the wrestling act kicked her right in the teeth and her poor little mouth hurts. Her lip was fucked up, and she's *such* a beautiful broad. I got her new number, yeh. And . . . Goddamn, Pete, I'd sure like to ball her, wouldn't you? Have you ever knocked her off? Yeh, Monica Corliss, 771-7711. Call her, will you, Pete? I'm busy lining 'em up for the Lido. Tell her the shows's real easy, and there's a whole bunch of time between the acts, and she can lay up there on the bed and rest. Tell her you'll give her some grass. She'lll be there. Okay? Right . . ."

Before I came to the city, I was king of the nightclubs. But out here I was nothing, and all these little guys were the bigshots. I needed a job, so I just went over to Bill Gold and I said, "Listen, you ain't doing no business on this street. You're paying a singer two hundred dollars a week, a band eight hundred dollars a week, and you got a bunch of strippers you're paying twenty-five dollars a night. I'll put in a show that all you'll have to pay is twenty-five dollars a night for the girls, one hundred dollars a night total. No band, no nothing, just tapes." I'd never made a tape in my life, but I knew it'd work, and it did. I charged 'em $150 a week while I was making the shows, and I stretched it out to three weeks. I coulda done it in four days. Now they have to pay me as long as my shows are in there. These tapes are my security. If the shit hits the fan someday, I can take these tapes and go to another town and open a bunch of clubs of my own.

Another thing I did that impressed Bill, when I first got here they were outa broads, and I wrote an ad that was great. It said something about, "Earn while you learn to dance. No personal involvement." That made the dancers feel they were somebody, and about fifty broads applied. My ads are still catching 'em. Here's one I wrote today:

> DANCERS, attractive, over 21, earn $150 a week while you learn. Costume shows, no personal contact involved. Apply after 12, Paris Lido.

Ain't that catchy? That'll bring 'em in, more than we need. When I'm pressed, I can find dancers right on Sweet Street. One night when I was first hired, I was desperate to hold onto the job, so I really put on a show for Bill Gold. I grabbed broads in Raffaele's, I grabbed 'em in the street, I created a pool of about thirty dancers for him to pick from. I even made a coupla hustlers into dancers.

These broads, they come into town looking for work, and they figure dancing naked is the bottom of the barrel. But then they get hungry, and they figure, Well, I gotta eat. They've waited till their last dollar ran out. But if you pay 'em right away they don't show up the next night, so you have to hold some money back. I'll say, "Here's fifteen dollars of your twenty-five. We'll pay you the rest on Tuesday." That keeps 'em dancing.

The main thing these broads have in common—they all need money now. *Now!* Not next Tuesday. They'll usually come in and say their rent's due, they gotta be paid. Fuck 'em. Pay 'em later. That way you keep 'em around a while, till they get used to dancing naked, and maybe they even begin to like it, they get turned on by it.

Some of them show up strung out on dope, and they're willing to dance naked to earn money for more. It don't bother me, even though I won't even take an aspirin, personally. Unless they act real goofy. I don't even *think* about their drug habits. That's *their* business, as long as they can get up there and show their beavers and move their asses.

You never know when you're gonna get a good dancer and when you're gonna get a real dog. I interviewed one the other night, a mulatto broad. I said "What nationality are you, honey?" and she said, "Half French and half nigger." I laughed so hard I hired her, and she's been going great. But that same night I hired this blond broad, over the hill, maybe thirty, thirty-five years old, and when I inspected her body I noticed that she kept her left arm just below her left tit, like she was hiding something. But what the fuck, we needed broads, so I hired her. When she got up on stage, it looked like she had three tits—she was suffering from a bad case of silicone slippage on the left side. I had to let her go. She turned all the customers off! But not me! I thought it was kinda cute. Something different, you know?

I probably wouldn't be doing this kind of work if it wasn't for the broads. If Sweet Street was a sawmill or a factory, I wouldn't be here. The broads keep me on the job. What a racket I got! I'm looking at a different beaver every night! Do you realize that? These new broads'll come in for a job, and I'll take 'em down in Bill Gold's office and tell 'em to strip, and they'll say, "Oh, do I *have* to take my clothes off?" I'll say, "Drop your laundry! We ain't running a sawmill. *Drop your laundry*! After that we'll talk."

HELEN LAWRENCESON'S DESCRIPTION OF Condé Nast matches Buddy De Young. "Certainly," she wrote, "I've never known a man who savored sex more raptly. It was his primary interest in life and he pursued it with wholehearted, shock-proof uninhibited enthusiasm." Sally Bob Tiner, the voluptuous dancer who follows the sun and the stars and the powerful pull of her own healthy libido, has had a long off-and-on affair with Buddy De Young, and she says, "He's an

Aries with a Scorpio moon, which means that physically he'll have a short, fast fire. He has a very sexual outlook toward life, which is true of a lot of Martian types. He likes to get it on with different people; he's *very* promiscuous. And he has to have new young blood all the time."

Buddy De Young does indeed prefer "new young blood," but mainly he craves female sexual action, whatever the type. Olive Calzolari, the beautiful bisexual waitress and former dancer, says, "Since he found out I like girls, he likes to come up to me and say, 'Oh, there's this chick you'd just love, Olive. You'd just want to eat her box out! Could I watch?' Those kind of things. He'd be content to watch, and then fuck the other girl, and not even get near me. He loves to talk like that, and I egg him on. I'll say, 'How's yours tonight, Buddy?' He says, 'High and dry.' I'll say, 'What? Not even excited? Come on, it's not even dripping yet! Oh, Buddy, come back when it's dripping!' He likes that kind of talk. He's our dirty-old-man-in-residence."

Buddy's gargantuan sexual talents are an inspiration to his diminutive boss. "That guy amazes me," Bill Gold says. "Ten years older than I am, and he has the ability to do more with women than any man I've ever seen. I thought *I* was good with women. I *am* good with women, I'm *fantastic* with women, obviously. But I'm not as good as Buddy. He's done things that were so fuckin' amazing that you just wouldn't believe it! Like he'll meet a girl on the street that he's never seen before, and he'll bring her to my office, and within five minutes he'll have her copping my joint and watching a dirty movie! Just like that! He *smells* it!"

Not everyone on Sweet Street is as impressed by Buddy De Young, and not everyone admires his ready concupiscence. Robert Benni, the gang-fighter turned restaurateur, says, "Buddy's out of touch with himself. He's sexually demented, the things he makes chicks go through. I've talked to some of his victims. He's lost concept of women as human beings, he's just trying to do a hurt number on them. Look at him—a guy that bleaches his hair at fifty-seven years old, and his big thing is to run around getting himself and everybody else fucked and sucked and turned inside out. That's gotta get you a little ill."

Says Mary Hawkins, faithful secretary to Bill Gold and Natie Cohen, "That Buddy! He sits around the table at Vino's and brags about the eleven-year-old girl he had. It's a dinner subject now! I mean, how could an old goat like that—he's *proud* of it! How would you like it if you had a daughter eleven years old and some old guy balled her? He says she came down to his boat and she looked older than she was, and *she* made all the advances. Knowing him, that's hard to believe."

Mickey Martin turns purple when Buddy De Young is mentioned. "If he was to go to the neighborhood in Chicago where I was raised in," Mickey says, his cheek muscles throbbing, "they'd have killed him a long time ago. He gets the young broads when they're down and out and hands 'em a little dope. He's the worst son-of-a-bitch around!"

Across the harbor from Sweet Street, Buddy De Young maintains a floating love nest, an eighty-three-year-old tugboat that has been on the bottom of the bay more than once, abandoned and left to the cypridinids and copepods and marine borers. Buddy spent four thousand dollars raising the derelict workboat, and now it serves as home for him and ex-stripper Ginny Thomas and two cats and a dog, plus assorted *objets d'amour* brought home by the master periodically.

The yacht harbor, like Buddy De Young, appears to be crumbling. His tug, *Venus*, rests in a greasy collar of oily wrack, its immediate neighbor an old two-master that sank into the mud years ago and is visible only as a set of bare ribs bleaching in the alternating sun and wind, like a leftover dinosaur on the Colorado desert. On the other side of Buddy's tug hundreds of faded anachronisms bob gently in the wakes of passing vessels. Ancient hulls are beyond scraping and painting, and styles are decades out of joint. There are long-snouted mahogany speedboats that Tom Swift would have called "runabouts," and listing old houseboats whose corroded bilge pumps have seized up and lost the battle against leakage. Every few weeks a boat expires in a froth of mud and bubbles. The *Venus* cannot be far behind.

Inside the worn wheelhouse and engine room, Buddy's tug is decorated with Elks Club antique. An ornate wooden sword covered with chipped golden lacquer hangs over the top of a monstrous bed. A yellow-bronze-painted cherub holds up a lamp, and a cuckoo clock by Schlockmeister of Zürich sticks out of the wall and chirps the wrong time at irregular intervals. A stained sheepskin throw rug adorns the bed. The furniture has been garnished in a leopardskin applique pattern. A bowl of waxen tulips rests atop a small table, and a pair of off-white cats with dichromatic eyes spit and snarl at a small mongrel dog that tries to curl up in front of a tiny standing fireplace.

Far forward, another double bed is tucked under the prow, and mirrors have been glued into strategic positions along the bulkhead. The bed smells of cat urine, and has been declared off-limits to humans. Buddy De Young and Ginny Thomas have standards about such matters, and all sleeping must be done in the big bed amidships. Female visitors are quickly encouraged to use the narrow head, and to press a button next to the toilet. Buddy De Young's recorded voice crackles out of a loudspeaker:

"To write is in fact to create. And to make love is potentially to create. To write provides a means of releasing one's intellectual and spiritual energy, whereas to copulate is a way of releasing one's physical energy. So the desire to write is at least as urgent and powerful intellectually and spiritually as a desire to make love on a physical plane. Composition is superior to lovemaking as a means of satisfying the need for self-expression. So will you kindly go up on the bed and remove your pants and get yourself ready, and I will come up and lay it to you, and I do hope you'll enjoy it, because it is a need for self-expression almost equal as to that loneliness which is in all of us, but especially the literary and artistic and musical creators, and a comfort and a solace."

That Bill Gold, he can't believe I'm for real! I used to give him bed delivery of broads. *Bed delivery*! One night I brought this super-innocent broad down to his yacht, and I was undressing her and trying to put her in the shower, so she'd be nice and clean for the bed delivery job. Well, it was a fuckin' comedy! I couldn't find the fuckin' light for the fuckin' shower. Finally I says, "Forget the shower! Just climb in bed, but don't wake him up." Bill's lying there wide awake, he can hardly wait to grab this innocent broad, he's got a hard-on that won't quit. So she gets into bed and he balls her. I had an idea earlier to take her home to my boat, but I didn't want to blow my image as getting broads for Bill. Later he told me she was absolutely terrific. I said, "Did she smell at all?"

He said, "No, not at all."

I said, "Well, I tried to get her into the shower, but I couldn't find the light."

But when I got home, I found out I had almost blew myself out of the water. By giving the broad to Bill instead of taking her home myself, I almost went without a broad for the night, and that is something I just don't do. I'd forgotten that I'd made a deal for Ginny, my old lady, to go fuck an old friend, and when I got home there was nobody aboard. Luckily I got in touch with Sally Bob Tiner. She said, "Oh, last resort again, huh?" but she came over and slept with me. That was a *very* close call.

I can't remember a night in my life when I didn't have a broad sleeping with me, since I left home. Wherever I go, whatever I do, there *has* to be a broad to sleep with. If there wasn't one, I'd lay there all night, awake. Maybe it's because my people were Mormons. My great-grandfather had eleven wives. I'll tell you, if I came home and there wasn't a soul on this boat, I'd leave and go over to one of my girl friends. I wouldn't stay! And I've got enough broads going, so I'll never run out.

I don't know what they see in me, but they flock around. Every time I see one of 'em on Sweet Street I say something like, Hey, let me see your wollybugger or your cunt or something like that, and I get away with it! I don't know how. Sure, I like 'em young. Doesn't everybody? It makes me feel younger to ball a young chick. Older women just don't turn me on, man. With an older woman, I couldn't get a hard-on no matter *what* they did. If they bought me a fuckin' yacht, I *still* couldn't get it up!

The youngest I ever had was this eleven-year-old hippie kid. I mean, I didn't fuck her, but we did everything else. Her brother and her mother and father, they were all kind of bums, lived in a box near the wharf. I took 'em all under my wing, gave 'em leftover food and stuff, and the two kids started coming over in the afternoon, and one thing led to another. One day I got word that the father wanted to see me! That was the first and only time in my life that I could see the prison doors opening. But it turned out he just needed money to get back to his home town. I was so happy that's all he wanted, I just peeled off bill after bill. "How much do you need? Can I give you more? Is this enough? Are you *sure*?" What a relief when he left.

I don't know what it is that makes the broads like me so much. I've had five, six old ladies at a time. Now I'm down to one, Ginny, but until a few weeks ago I had Sally Bob living here, too. Those broads were a great pair! Always fighting and arguing with each other, and then piling into the sack with me at night. I got sick, and I was in bed for twenty days, infectious hepatitis. I don't know how I got it, because I've never taken drugs, but anyway, those two broads, Ginny and Sally Bob, they got gamma globulin shots to protect themselves and slept right along with me, took care of me, waited on me hand and foot. Sally Bob is still faithful to me, even though we had to kick her off the boat. She'll come to work sick, night after night, rather than let me down. She says whenever she hears the word "supermasculine," she thinks of me.

I guess I just sort of inherited my old lady Ginny, because nobody else would take her two cats and a dog. I just moved all her animals in with me, and she followed along. That was three years ago, and she's been with me ever since. But I get tired of broads awful fast. I'm tired of Ginny right now. She won't let me bring broads home no more. I had this broad Felicia, and she's one of these broads, when you're fucking her she just keeps ooing and ahing all the time—*oooooo, ahhhhhhhh, ahhhhhhh*, you know? Well, it just drove Ginny nuts! She got so pissed about it, she said, "All right, no more of that shit!" That was four months ago, and we've had a new arrangement since then. If a broad's coming over to ball me, Ginny'll leave for the night. She's got a little action of her own, places she can go. I let her go ball some guy every Wednesday, anyway—it doesn't bother me in the least.

I don't know why it is I get turned off a broad after a while. I constantly need new—I'm like Dracula. Ginny has enough sense to give me rope. I can ball anybody I want, as long as I don't bring 'em home. But she's really a fine girl, she'd do anything for me. I don't like her housekeeping, no, and she's really super-stupid, but a wonderful girl. I could never do anything to hurt her, in no way. If I come into some dough or hit good on something, which I might on a movie or something, I'd lay some money on Ginny, fix her up in some kind of little business. Some kind of a Goodwill Industries type thriftshop bullshit that she's so freaky on, you know? She haunts all them places now, anyway.

I've always been fascinated by sex, as long as I can remember. They say it has something to do with your mother. Well, my mother died when I was a year old. I never had a mother. I had a bunch of chickenshit stepmothers. I left home when I was thirteen. My stepmother hated me. She used to say it right to my face: "I hate you." My father was a railroadman, but on the side he had some interests in show business. We lived in Salt Lake City, but I wasn't too thrilled by the place, so I went on the road. I started my business career at twenty-five dollars a week as a paint boy, and then I did lobby displays for Alexander Pantages in New Orleans. By the time I was eighteen, I had a half-interest in a burlesque theater, and I changed my name from Buddy Young to Buddy De Young, more classier. It was a shoe-string operation. Our theater was connected to the light plant of the hotel next door, so the lights were controlled by the hotel generators. If we didn't make enough money to pay the light bill by nine o'clock, they'd shut the lights off, which happened often. Then the union didn't like us 'cause we were nonunion, and they burned the place down, and I hit the road again.

When the old vaudeville days died, I found that I could take a bunch of people and put a nightclub act together. I'd steal my ideas. Like if somebody was hot nationally, I'd play on his name and fame. I'd get three whacky guys together and bill them as "The Three Scrooges." People would say, "Well, maybe it's those famous guys that go around whacking themselves over the head, and maybe it ain't, but we'll go see." That's the way I got by for years. I'd pay five hundred dollars an act, where a real act like The Three Stooges would cost about two thousand dollars in those days. I'd write the ads real tricky, so that the catchlines would infer it was somebody famous, and the people'd shell out the money, and they wouldn't get mad because they'd see a good show anyway. They'd go home and say, "I guess I was mistaken. It wasn't The Three Stooges, it was The Three Scrooges, but they were pretty funny anyway."

Sometimes there'd be a big scandal in the papers—some stripper'd shoot her boy friend and get a lot of publicity—and I'd make up a name similar to hers and work up an act that would simulate the crime, and people would assume it was the same broad. Even the newspapermen would come out and ask me, "Is this the same broad?" I made some pretty good money that way.

Right at the height of the depression I took a show on the road, and there wasn't much money around. I used girls sixteen, and seventeen years old, beautiful broads. We did the old burlesque routines. One time when I had the traveling troupe, we went into Ogden, Utah, and I didn't have a quarter to my name. Not a quarter. We had two Cord sedans, a LaSalle, and a Auburn, and we'd have parades. I'd put all the broads in one car, the band in another, and we'd parade through town. But this time we were broke, *nothing*! So I went out and promoted the gas for the cars, and I booked us into the Ben Lomond, the best hotel in town, and went on the cuff for all the rooms. Instead of eating in the coffee shop, I told everybody to eat in the dining room and sign for it. That was one of the few times I ever went in the hole— we had an Egyptian plot, and a lot of stripping, and we took in almost enough to break even, but not quite, not with all those expensive dinners on the arm in the dining room.

Then I got a chance to open a burlesque theater in Denver. I sent the whole troupe there in 1937, and I drove across the Rockies in a goddamn blizzard. I got there in eleven hours and it took everybody else three days. I tore up four pairs of chains, but I was a kid, and I just went *zoom*! I had three thousand dollars invested in the theater, and a partner put up all the rest. I contributed ten thousand dollars' worth of bullshit, how to get credit, things like that. I was always good at that.

At our theater we ran first-run sloughs, all the pictures that nobody else wanted, and every week I dreamed up a new stage show that would be strong enough to support the no-good movie. I wrote the wrong thing, choreographed it, rehearsed everybody, did the scenery and the advertising and the whole goddamn thing.

Well, I made a lot of money, and I got married, and I spent four nice easy years stationed here with the Coast Guard, and then I went back to Denver and I dreamed about opening a big nightclub, the biggest nightclub between New York and the Pacific coast. I was used to hitting the nightclubs, and now I was back home with my stodgy wife and she wouldn't let me out at night, so I figured if I opened a club of my own she wouldn't have no choice in the matter.

I bought an old hillbilly joint that used to be called the Dump. It was doing nothing. I called it the Sarong, after all them "Road" movies that Bing Crosby and Dorothy Lamour made, and I put it together with staples and palm leaves and junk, to give it a South Seas atmosphere.

I was determined to make that place into a real nightclub instead of the bucket of blood it'd been, but it wasn't easy. I'd sit there with six people in the joint and turn down fifty bums. That first year you'd thought I had a boxing license instead of a liquor license. My face used to look like hamburger, keeping them bums out. But I gradually changed the image of the place, and the bums stopped coming. I turned it into a club where you could get dinner, and where people came from the country club to see very fancy strip shows. The Sarong was one of the most unique places in the country—a strip place that attracted couples and decent people. After a while, I was running it couples only, and that's rare in the nightclub business. You couldn't even get in the door without a coat and tie.

Well, by the time I was thirty-seven I was a millionaire. I found that it ain't nothing to make a million dollars. And all you've got when you get there is everybody on your ass. Your money is in property and paper anyway, and you couldn't come up with more than fifty thousand dollars cash if your life depended on it. It's no big deal, being a millionaire, but it's preferable to what I got now.

I lie in bed at night and remember what I used to have. Every great American stripper except Gypsy Rose Lee and Ann Corio worked for me at one time. I had Kalantan, Candy Barr, Tempest Storm, I had all of 'em. I used to use —— —— all the time at the Sarong. She's a terrific person, as big as they get in the business, but she's a kleptomaniac. She'll wear a big fur coat into a store, and she'll buy some cheese and walk out with thirty dollars' worth of condiments. And she's never been in trouble for it! Not once! She was very active religious, and one night we were in the hardware store buying Christmas lights for her church, and I saw this little flashlight that costs five dollars. I said, "That's nice."

She said, "Well, cream it. *Cream it*!"

I said, "What does that mean?"

She said, "Put it in your pocket!" Sometimes she'd go downtown with my wife and steal great big things, candles, hats, boxes full of stuff, and scare my wife to death.

I tried out Tempest Storm in the old Sarong, $150 a week, one of the first jobs she ever had. I made that broad famous. She'd been working in North Las Vegas in a little dump, and a friend told me, "If you get her, she'll make you a lot of money." Well, in she came, and she had this beautiful perfect thin-boned body and these great big knockers. That's her secret: great big natural big tits on a small body, and she stayed sixteen weeks, packed the joint, a hell of an act. She worked for me for seventeen years after that, twice a year without fail.

A friend of mine run the college newspaper up at Boulder, thirty miles away, and he says, "Let's have Tempest come up and do an interview on the campus." The dean found out about it and wrote me, "We can't have Tempest Storm on the college grounds!" and I thought, Hot dog, this is *it*! Refusing an American girl that wants to look at a college campus, a poor hard-working girl that wanted to go to college but could never go. And whether she's a stripper or a nigger or *what* the hell she is, she's refused entrance! Oh, shit, that did it, man! I planned the visit for the same day some state senators were visiting the campus, and I brought her up there in a red Cadillac convertible, and she was wearing a low-cut deal, and there was a *riot*! The captain of the football team carried her around on his shoulders, and the students broke down a door getting at her. Oh, shit, it was a big day! Oh, shit, it was really terrific! It even got on the John Cameron Swayze news nationwide, and it made her famous. The next time I booked her I had to pay her twenty-seven hundred dollars a week.

Well, after that my personal life kind of went to hell. I got a divorce and remarried, then got another divorce and another marriage, and then that marriage broke up. All I had to show for my life was a little daughter that I loved dearly. And a million dollars. Then the nightclub business changed. The government took off the cabaret tax, and every bar in town put in a jukebox and a couple of topless dancers, and there were thirty joints where you could buy a drink for seventy-five cents and watch topless. There was no market for my kind of high-class operation, so I had to change my way of doing business. I had to operate bust-out like all the rest of 'em.

For a while, I went gung ho. I had one sucker that was spending a hundred dollars a night: ―― ――, he owned a big bank. He *loved* being taken. He wasn't even getting jacked off, he'd just drink with the girls and they'd bullshit him and pour the champagne back in the bucket, or pour it on the floor. I'd sell him a jeroboam of champagne for $160, and the girls could get rid of that in half an hour. The waitress would come by and the B-drinker would say, "Oh, can I have a glass? Oh, let's buy another!" She'd have ahold of his handle, and he'd buy anything she wanted.

Myself, I was very bad at bust-out, even though I ran that way for a year. I hired a tough kid to oversee the operation and I sort of shut one eye. But I'd never run no bust-out again. Some of the girls get used to it, they get good at it. I had one from Dallas, called herself Ginger Snap. I introduced her to an old friend of mine, and he cashed a check for a hundred dollars, and two drinks later he comes up to me and he wants to cash another check. I said sure, and a half-hour later he wants another hundred dollars. I said, "Who the hell you sitting with?" He says Ginger Snap. I found out she was stealing all the change from one of my old friends! I made her give it back. It just come natural to her to steal money.

Well, I don't know if you know Denver, but they run different out there. Here, the police and the laws are logical. They don't care if a girl gets up on stage and she's naked, but if you're hustling guys, stealing their money, jacking 'em off in the corner and all that bullshit, you're in jail. But in Denver, it's the other way around. The girl can't show her nipples, she can't show her box, but she can get a guy in a back booth and hustle him for five hundred dollars' worth of champagne while her and her girl friend are beating his meat, or almost balling in the booth. Of course you have to take care of the cops, and the vice squad is pretty tight with the club owners, believe me. Some of the owners even got girls for the vice squad. And they'd get nice pay-offs, too.

I always got along with the cops, and some of 'em I thought was decent people. I liked 'em personally. I'd go on trips with 'em. I'd help 'em out. There was one high-ranking cop, and if they got a groovy broad in jail, he'd bring her out to the Sarong and we'd both fuck her. Every Christmas I'd send the chief liquor, and he'd send a thank-you card. There was no sneaking around about it. You could send him liquor, or you could skip it, and you wouldn't hear nothing about it from him. He was a fine man, a beautiful person.

But with the vice, it was different. The vice was a little clique that had had its own way for years, just like those other Denver cops that got caught stealing all over town. The vice used to come out to the Sarong and I'd give 'em stuff. One cop, a big stupid oaf, he'd bring his neighbors, maybe twelve people, and they'd all have New York cuts with lobster, and they'd stay till midnight and take up two tables. That'd be at least once a week. And the rest of the vice would come in, two or four at a time, *every* night, and order New York cuts, and all the booze they could drink, plus I was paying them off at the same time. And this went on for twenty years. Figure it out! A lot of money! And a hundred dollars a cop bonus at Christmas, and none of it was ever refused, either.

Well, after a year or so of bust-out I got sick of running that kind of joint, and I converted to a straight operation, a little live rock and roll and reasonable prices and decent food at a fair price. No bust-out, no jerking people off in the corner, no nothing, and no payoffs to cops, either. I figured, "I ain't got nothing going, so why should I pay?" When Christmastime come, I paid off two of my old friends on the vice squad and ignored all the others. And I told one of the other vice cops—he was always trying to ball my wife—I told him, "Fuck you! Get out of my joint! You're not getting no booze, you're not getting no money, and I want you to lay off my wife!" I really got mad. It felt good, after putting up with his bullshit for a year.

Six nights later I was showing a ski movie at my house for some friends, and a couple of strangers that'd crashed the party kept saying, "Come on, put on the dirty stuff!" So I put on a skin flick, and as soon as the fucking started on the screen, one of the guys jumps up and holds a badge in front of the projector, and he says, "This is the police! You're pinched!"

I says, "Get your fuckin' arm down! I can't see the fuckin' screen!" I thought he was kidding! But then the other stranger opened the front door and the four cops came running inside like Eliot Ness busting Al Capone. I heard 'em say, "Wasn't that beautiful? The way we did that?"

They put me in jail for investigation of pornography. It was a weekend and I couldn't get out. There was no secretary there, nobody in charge of anything, and the D.A. was out of town. They had it all arranged so I couldn't get out. I called a former chief of police, a friend of mine, and he came down personally to get me out. They told him they'd let me out right away, and the second he left they put me back in the cell. I called a high city official that's even higher than the police chief, and he came down and looked the situation over, and he says to me, "Buddy, they've really got you fucked up. I can't do nothing."

The jail was filthy. A guy that had just held up a Safeway store at gunpoint got out in thirty minutes on bond. I sat there. I must have looked funny to the other guys in the lock-up. I had a three-hundred-dollar suit on, lizard shoes, and nobody seemed to trust me. One hardened gambler said, "If they ever get on you, they'll *never* let you alone." The cops were trying to get to me, and they got to me. I doubt if they knew how well they got to me. They kept me in that cell for three days, and I'd never been in jail in my life. They didn't even have a rap sheet on me before that.

When I got home, the one thing in the world that I loved was gone—my thirteen-year-old daughter. She'd had a hard life, but we were beginning to straighten things out together. She'd always been bad in school, but I was getting her interested. I'd talk to her about her homework, and I'd praise what she did, and I had a little deal with one of her teachers to tell her she was doing good when she really wasn't. She'd had a bucktooth problem, and she'd hold her hand over her mouth when she talked, and something like that hurts a kid. I spent two thousand dollars on an orthodontist, and we were solving that problem, too, and we were getting really close, for the first time in her life. Now she was gone. She'd run away from home. And I didn't have nobody but her in the world.

I started phoning her classmates, and they told me she'd left because she was embarrassed about her father being in jail and all that shit, because it was in the papers. Nobody knew where she was. Well, I was white as a sheet, I was green, I just looked horrible. I was so goddamned bitter. It changed me in some way. To be put in jail for three days by those rotten bastards I'd been paying off for twenty years, that changed me, changed my whole view of human nature.

My daughter was gone for two weeks. She told me she couldn't take all the questions at school. When she came back, we just hung around the house for a while. Then I got together all the cash I could, rathole money and money I'd stolen that the government couldn't check, like door money that nobody keeps count of. I just got all this money together, something like seventy-five thousand dollars, maybe ninety thousand dollars, I'm not sure, and I padlocked the Sarong and shut down the apartment and put my daughter in the car and called a moving van and drove off. I just got so fuckin' mad I turned my back on Denver completely. I still get fuckin' mad thinking about it. I just couldn't believe that anybody could be that fuckin' rotten.

I dropped my daughter off with relatives, and then I drove

straight here. I had it all figured out. I'd have the time of my life, I'd blow all my money, and when it was gone, I'd begin to worry. Then I met this girl on Sweet Street, she was in town for a Lutheran seminar, and we got to talking, and she said, "You know that people can never really hurt you, because you can always knock yourself off." She made it sound pretty good. So I thought, I'll spend all my money, and I'll drive up to the top of the bridge and jump.

Then I spotted this 117-foot yacht made in England, the *Thames*, and just for a lark I paid thirty thousand dollars down on it, against a full price of a hundred thousand dollars. What the fuck, it was only money. It was a last fling. I didn't know what I was gonna do, but I was gonna live it up, I was gonna have a goddamn ball. I started going with these Sweet Street broads, and they're all impressed by yachts. I had five broads living on the boat. Five old ladies! It was parties, parties, parties. I had a shore boat, everything. And new broads were always coming in and out. Altogether I had sixty-three broads in a year and a half! The *Thames* was like a floating whorehouse. It was a challenge to fuck that many broads and have five old ladies living with me besides. I'd fuck one every night, and one every day. Then my secretary joined me from Denver and she would detail the operation. She couldn't sleep with me, 'cause I snored too much for her, but she worked it out so that there was always somebody to sleep with me. If there was nobody aboard, my secretary'd sleep with me till I got to sleep, and then she'd go to her cabin, and then she'd get me my coffee and ball me in the morning.

Every day I'd walk around this little harbor town with all these Sweet Street broads, seventeen, eighteen-year-old cunt, all new to the town, and it bugged the shit outa the locals. And our parties bugged the people in the yacht harbor, too. The society assholes. They'd be entertaining for tea and crumpets on their yachts, and we'd be alongside having a party and hollering "fuck" and "suck" and running around naked. For a few months I had the excuse that I was making a movie, but then that didn't hold 'em any more, and they began putting on the pressure. My food bill every day would be eighty dollars for dinner, thirty or forty dollars for lunch, feeding all my broads. One final fling!

Then a few things fell my way. Some guy had a girlie film half made and he didn't know how to finish it, so I helped him and made a small fortune for three weeks' work. The film's still running in the skin-flick houses. I'd made my first film years before, with a burlesque star, and I knew something about making movies. Then I made a few more films on my boat, but of course I couldn't keep up those big payments, and they threw me out of the yacht harbor, and I cashed in and bought this tug I'm living on now, and I developed enough zest for life that I went up to Sweet Street and hit on Bill Gold for a job. That was four years ago, and I guess I'm set for life, now. At least I'm making a living, and I'm keeping my daughter in a good school, so who's to complain? If somebody came up to me and said, "Hey, man, you're an evil old man, you're in an evil business, strip shows and all," I'd just tell 'em I don't see it that way. I'd say, I'm really in the entertainment business, and I always have been. I like to write shows, I like to produce shows, and I really get my rocks off when I get a good show together. I get the same kind of thrill that somebody else might get on heroin. On the first night of a good show, there's something inside that kinda scares you and kinda thrills you at the same time. Burlesque or Sweet Street or whatever.

There's a 150-foot boat I been looking at, but I don't have enough cash right now to make the down payment. So that leaves me not knowing what I want outa life. I have no idea. I go day by day. Here, read this poem:

> I would rather be ashes than dust.
> I would rather my spark should burn out in a brilliant blaze
> Than it should be stifled in dry-rot.
> I would rather be a superb meteor,
> Every atom of me in magnificent glow,
> Than a sleepy and permanent planet.
> Man's chief purpose is to live, not to exist.
> I shall not waste my days trying to prolong them.
> I shall use my time.

Jack London wrote that. It's the code of my life.

THE TELEPHONE RINGS. "HELLO, Dominick, old pal. What's up? Yeh . . . Yeh . . . Oh, shit. Wow. So we got to have another girl for the Silver Peacock tonight, huh? And another for the Snake Pit? Oh, shit. Okay, I better get on the goddamned phone. I got a girl coming in for an interview tonight, she looks pretty good. She's got nice tits. Her thighs are a little heavy, though. Look, I've got a lot of calls to make, can you make one for me? Yeh, Mae Britten. Did you see her dance the other night? That was her first time ever. Nice body. You might say she's a cunning little stunt. Mae Britten. 741-6639. Right. I'm sure you'll like her. Okay, pal."

He pushes the disconnect button and dials another number. "Hello, Honey, this is Buddy . . ."

Homemaker

Where's the man could ease a heart
Like a satin gown?
—Dorothy Parker, *The Satin Dress*

SHE IS NEVER FAR from tears. Her eyes fill whenever she discusses crucial subjects: love, her three pets, her lost black paramour, her shaky future, the stolid mother who "didn't say much." She dabs at her eyes, composes herself quickly, and tries to smile. But soon another key word overwhelms her sentimentality, and she is distressed again.

In the blunt and simplistic language of Sweet Street, Boss Bill Gold describes Ginny Thomas: "She's a sad case, and she used to be a terrible dancer. It was the same step all the time. I heard she was a nymphomaniac and she loved to fuck. That's the reputation she had when she and Buddy got together. But we don't allow rumors about her now that she's living with him."

Physically, Ginny Thomas looks like a prototype hostess on a children's TV show: earth mother and playmate in the same image. Her brown hair is worn in a wind-whipped gamine style. Her eyebrows are unplucked and frank, her nose a button, her brown eyes wide and warm, her skin unmarked. She accentuates a natural, young look with unpretentious clothes bought in youth departments. "She's twenty-nine, and she looks like a fuckin' kid," Sally Bob Tiner says resentfully, and Ginny does not entirely disagree.

"I know I could never be beautiful," she says, "so I try to give the illusion of being childlike. I'd like to be beautiful, instead of cute, but I'm too out of proportion."

From the neck down she seems to have been constructed for the greater benefit of the child she never bore. Her bulging bustline is cantilevered straight into space, in flagrant violation of Newton's laws. Old-fashioned pedal-pusher pants follow her ample posterior contours like the skin on a sated boa. Although she is only two inches over five feet tall, her feet are size eight, and her hands are broad and thick, the hands of a young scrubwoman. Seen from a distance, she gives the appearance of a stack of larger and larger hemispheres, a body that borders on the obese, in full passage from voluptuous to overripe to fat.

Out of all this physical flamboyance and contradistinction comes a tiny mouse-sized voice that takes one by surprise—an indecisive, equivocating, tentative voice, soft and high-pitched, with the extra r's and localized vowels of the rural Midwest. She speaks of "*dee*-vorce" and her " 'partment," a "perfessor" she once knew, a visit to "Warshington." She tries to pick her words with care, especially on the ticklish subject of prostitution, but her vocabulary is too weak to allow great subtlety or nuance. She will never say flatly that she once was a prostitute, nor does she use the jargon of the oldest profession. "Davey tried to get me to go out," she says, meaning that he tried to establish her as a whore. "He lined me up a *thing*." She eschews words like "trick" and "john" as though she can avoid the stigma of prostitution by changing the nomenclature.

Ginny Thomas no longer solicits money from randy males, but occasionally a carnal opportunity is offered her, and if the sum is sufficient—in the neighborhood of one hundred dollars—she accepts. Money is her *raison d'être*. She lives to gain it, spend it, and gain it back. Buddy De Young says, "She's such a fuckin' pack rat, this boat'd sink in a month if I didn't have a rented room ashore for her stuff. All she does is shop for shit, see? I had to rent a room forty by forty to hold the overflow. It's amazing what she can get for a dollar. She's always got money, too, and I don't give her much."

Ginny earns pocket income by working two nights a week as a cocktail waitress and cashing in on her side chances. Her slight financial needs seem far out of proportion to her anxiety over money. Her major expenditure is thirty-five dollars a month for firewood; the *Venus* is damp and cold, and her aging dog treats its arthritis by nudging up to the fireplace. "Poor thing!" Ginny says, tears welling into her eyes, and picks the loved one up to stroke its thinning fur. A white part-Persian cat with six toes materializes out of the wet harbor air and meows for a share of attention. Ginny takes both pets in her arms, while a smaller white cat arches its sleek back and purrs against her ankles.

On a low table in the center of the tugboat's main cabin, several hundred soggy postage stamps have been laid out in neat rows. Ginny deposits her menagerie gently in front of the blazing fire, arranges herself demurely in the light of the amber rays, and begins to pick at the stamps with tweezers.

I just bought these at a thrift shop, and I'm beginning a collection. I soaked them out and pressed them, now I've got to sort them. I bought them because I like looking for bargains, and there might be a prize stamp in there. See my goldfish? I bought them as a bargain, and I've still got 'em. They were on sale, but then I had to buy an oxygen pump and everything else. Same thing with the stamps. You buy the stamps and then you have to buy albums and perforation gauges and tweezers and all that stuff, and that's where the money goes. Well, I have a lot of time on my hands, and maybe it'll give me something to do. Maybe I'll learn to dig it.

It's a little quieter around the boat now that Sally Bob's gone. She was Buddy's girl friend before he and I started living together, and she stayed right here with us, off and on, until the other day. She'd go away a lot, but she'd always come back to the boat. It's kind of like her home in a way, but in another way it isn't, because she didn't contribute anything. She took no responsibility. She lived out of her suitcase.

When Sally Bob lived here, all she did was cook our breakfast. That was her whole job. And Buddy and I did the rest, including buying groceries. I'd get groceries out of my own money and bring them home and Sally Bob'd eat 'em up. She'd say, "I don't eat much here, why should I buy groceries?" Meanwhile she'd be stuffing down everything in the place, even our vitamin pills, maybe five or ten cents apiece, and every morning she'd take ten of 'em.

So this kind of thing began to come between us after three years, began to gnaw on me. I feel sorry for her, sure, but she don't see that I'm the woman of the house. She thinks she's as equal as I am, you know? And she didn't mind whether I resented her or not, she kept right on coming back. I never could figure her out. She'd ball Buddy right there in the bed with me, but when he'd leave she'd reach over and grab me, and I'd just pretend like it was a joke, and it never came to nothing. But then one time I had a friend that I go out with, not for money, and he told me he'd pay another girl if she'd do it with me and he'd get a chance to watch two women together, which he'd never seen. I said, "Well, gee, I could get Sally Bob. She keeps making these little advances, and maybe she'd like to make a little money."

So I mentioned it, and Sally Bob acted very shocked, and she said, "Oh, no, no, *no!*" I was surprised. I would have thought she would have went for it. It would have given her the excuse and me the excuse to—you know.

The other morning she was back here again, and I called her "the perfessional visitor," and she said, "Well, what are *you?* You're a perfessional visitor. You've been visiting here three years now."

I said, "I don't see how anybody can be a perfessional visitor when they probably spend thirty dollars a week out of her own money for groceries." But I didn't say no more. I just went inside and waited for her to serve breakfast.

After about forty-five minutes I started asking her why it was taking so long. She said, "Stop acting like a queen bee around here! The only reason Buddy lets you stay is because you buy things."

That did it! I'd boughten two nice cups at the Goodwill, and she had eggs in one of 'em, and I just took this cup of eggs and I knew this'd burn her up, and I threw 'em down on the floor, right next to her feet. She really got pissed! She picked up a bowl and threw it at me, and I ducked and it went out the window.

That got me even madder. I walked over to her and started shoving her backwards down the stairs. I was gonna shove her right over the side. I said, "Okay, get off the boat!" Buddy told her she'd better pack her stuff and leave.

I saw her a few nights ago at the Seven Seas, and I told her I was sorry it all had to end that way, and she apologized, but she's not coming back. Well, love is important to me. I love Buddy, and I even feel a certain amount of love for Sally Bob, as though she were a sister, and I feel guilty about it. I'm sorry, let me compose myself . . .

I think, maybe Sally Bob's right, maybe she *shouldn't* have to buy groceries. Buddy came home and told me last night Sally Bob stopped him on Sweet Street and she said, "Well, gee whiz, it's just like you're *married* to Ginny. If I lived on the boat, you could bring home all the chicks you wanted." I guess she's trying to get in good with him again. Maybe she doesn't know it, but Buddy already brings home all the chicks that he wants, but I just leave when he does it. I go over to a bartender's house that I know, and I don't come back till I'm sure Buddy's finished. That's our arrangement, and it works.

Buddy and I may get a little jealous once in a while, but mostly I don't care what he does as long as I don't have to be there and watch. It used to be that his particular thrill was bringing another girl home, like a cat bringing in a mouse, like a trophy. At first I couldn't understand it, and then one of my friends that I go out with, he said, "I think he does it because he's proud of you, and he wants you to be proud of him, so when he goes out he brings back what he considers a big catch, and he wants to show you he can still get a young, good-looking girl." I think my friend is right. But I still had to tell Buddy that he wasn't doing *my* ego any good. I said, "I don't like to stand there and pass the towels, you know!"

Buddy's easy to live with. He's very undemanding. I like that. He doesn't say, I have to have my dinner at a certain time, things like that. He doesn't want me to stay at home ironing his shirts or nothing. He sends all his stuff out, except his warsh, and he used to send that out till he discovered they put in some kind of chemical that breaks out his skin. The only thing that he demands is that I'm around here in the daytime when he's here, because Buddy has to have a woman with him all the time, wherever he is.

I don't feel that he uses me. All things are equal. I have a place to stay, and I don't have to pay any rent or utilities. I buy the food, but only what I want to buy. I have a lot of time, so I go to the grocery store, the thrift shop, and I look for bargains. I buy the wood for the fireplace, do the warsh, buy things for myself. But Buddy and I keep our money separate. He pays the wharfage and the telephone himself.

I have a waitress job, cocktailing, twice a week. I guess I could go out and sell my body for more than I make as a waitress. There's been a few times when I called Buddy up and said I've got a chance to make a hundred dollars, should I do it? And he told me no, but I went ahead and did it anyway. And I'd come home and show him the money and he wouldn't make too much of a fuss. But he doesn't want me to do it because I might get caught, it might be a cop. And also if I did it all the time, it would deflate Buddy's ego.

I keep looking around for ways to make more money. Lately I've started learning how to mix drinks, how to tend bar. That way no matter how old I got, I could still tend bar for a living. I'm worried about getting old, you know. You can only dance for so long, and you can only cocktail waitress for so long.

My regular Wednesday night date gives me a certain amount of security. I don't charge the guy or nothing, but I know he has money, and I know if I needed two or three or even five thousand dollars, if I build up my friendship with him he'd loan it to me. He already takes me to really fancy places. If I want to go to a certain place, I can name it and he'll take me. Buddy used to take me to quite a few nice restaurants, but lately he's been busy.

A girl *has* to think about the future when she's involved with the Sweet Street crowd, let me tell you! I've got this girl friend up on the street, and she thinks she's gonna meet somebody nice up there. A rich man to take care of her, that's her goal. In my opinion, she's not gonna meet nobody up there that's gonna take care of her in her old age, because on that street it's hardly ever happened like that.

I was raised one way, that you grow up and get married and you have security. But I find in life that it doesn't work that way. The type of people I'm around, the people at the clubs, they don't get married. And the lack of security, it bothers me. If somebody said, "Okay, there's a lump of money in the bank in your name," I wouldn't worry so much. But nobody's saying that. I have a little money, but not enough to go for long, not with the price of pet food the way it is today.

Sometimes I think about going back to school, learn *something*. Or else go out and work really hard and salt some money away. You either have to have money in the bank or a perfession to stand on. You can't count on men. Buddy's getting close to sixty. He could drop dead tomorrow. Even if I could count on his character, I can't count on him to stay alive.

I'd be reluctant to marry Buddy, anyway, because he's so laxadaisical about his money, and if he died I might get stuck for all his lab bills, something like that. So it'd be a risk. I just don't know. If he came home tonight and said, "Let's get married"—well, I'd probably marry him, but I'm not sure there'd be any advantage to it.

And if it came to a choice between my pets and Buddy— Well, I like Buddy, but it's like my mother told her new husband. He didn't want her dog in the house, and she said, "You can take care of yourself, but this dog can't, and I've had the dog the longest." That's the way I feel about Alice and Puss and Spider. A human being is responsible to his pets, because the pet is at the mercy of its owner. I feel like once you get a pet, you're obligated to take care of him for the rest of his life. So if Buddy said, "You can either have me or the dog," well, I would take the dog.

I hope it never comes to that.

Club Operator

It seems to me that all of us, so far as we attach ourselves to created objects and surrender our wills to temporal ends, are eaten by the same worm.

—T. S. Eliot

"You are hereby ordered to immediately remove all signs that use the words 'nude,' or 'bottomless' or words of like or similar import, except that the words 'topless entertainment' are allowable. You are also hereby ordered immediately to remove all signs, photographs, paintings, and any pictoral representations that depict the human form or any portion or portions thereof in a nude or seminude state. . . . Police Department."

ALONG SWEET STREET, NO one is talked about with more *Sturm und Drang* than the elfin-sized operator, Bill Gold. He is either disliked or roundly hated; there is no middle ground, and the round haters far outnumber the mere dislikers. Even Buddy De Young, who had planned suicide before Bill Gold gave him a job, offers something less than total endorsement. "He's the biggest egomaniac you've ever seen," Buddy says in his usual tired voice. "To hear him tell it, he done everything, he wrote everything, he built everything, he put everything together. Whatever you ask him, he'll bring the subject back to his favorite subject: himself. But that's his happiness. What the fuck, I don't put it down."

Bill Gold lives on a 110-foot converted Coast Guard cutter that is exactly what Buddy De Young's battered old tugboat is not. The *Venus* is in exile far across the harbor, but Bill Gold's *Rapier* wharfs with society yachts in the city. It is the first boat in line, just inside the harbor mouth, and others point it out and cluck about its radical lines. The straightforward Coast Guard prow has been altered by the nautical equivalent of a putty nose: a false prow that sweeps up and out in a sharp curve, giving the vessel a rakish Norse line. Old salts point out that the first high wave would probably rip the *Potemkin* front off, but the matter is moot: the *Rapier* sticks close to its wharf and never goes to sea, like the Gilbert and Sullivan character in *H. M. S. Pinafore*.

The captain is always glad to conduct visitors on an inspection tour, the more so if the visitors are female, comely, and of tender years. "See this forward bedroom?" he says with pride. "I've got fifteen thousand dollars in it already, and I'm only half finished." The inner decks are covered with bulkhead-to-bulkhead rugs. Bill Gold is a jazz lover and twenty-five loudspeakers are dotted about, including one atop the mast and several in the heads. The galley is fur lined, and expensive dishes and glassware rest in soft, furry pockets to protect them against the harbor's buffetings. A wine rack shelters 120 bottles, mostly from California. A massive coffee urn decorates the main salon, along with a tiled *bracero* from Mexico, authentic Persian rugs, cherrywood furniture, a black leather sofa and black leather chairs, and a clipper-ship model provided by the employees of the clubs. A vivid painting on velvet decorates a passageway leading forward. "Not bad, huh?" the captain says. "I've got more than a hundred grand in it, but it's worth a hundred and a quarter. I put in two new three-hundred horsepower engines. In two days I could be ready to go to Acapulco, but I won't do it. I don't have time."

Bill Gold looks slightly like an updated Harpo Marx. His gray-blue eyes absorb the light, but seem to give none back. A beard and mustache and a circle of curly brown ringlets complete an impression of an ordinary face that has been framed for better viewing. Gold is short and quick, light on his feet, and studiedly informal in his attire. He often arrives on Sweet Street wearing jeans, and he is customarily shod in mod black boots. He walks in dense clouds of cologne, almost palpable.

In his speech, he retains traces of the Boston pushcart culture. "My first job was sigs dollars a week," he says. "Sigs dollars!" He dentalizes his middle T's, as in "I wan-ted this boat so bad I could taste it." He adds phantom New England r's: "The country that fascinates me is Asiar," and he some-times reverses the patterns of English: "Buddy I know for like fifteen years." His normal mode of speech is soft and pleasant and unhurried, as befits presidents and others who are accustomed to being listened to, and he can be a gracious and charming host, filling wine glasses and catering to his guests' whims. But he soon dispels the illusion of gentility with outbursts of braggadocio and tastelessness. It is almost as though he wanted to be reviled.

Bill Gold's roots are not deep in Sweet Street; he arrived four years ago, when a man named Tommy Lynch was the kingpin, and quickly set about adapting his own showbiz background to the new setting. "He used to follow Tommy like a little puppy dog," says his secretary, Mary Hawkins. "If Tommy'd ever turned around, he coulda bit Bill's nose off."

Robert Benni, the young sage and restauranteur, says, "We used to call him Droppy Drawers, the Shadow, the way he followed Tommy. Everything that Tommy knew, Gold cop-ied. Now he acts as if he invented the whole thing. He's got the other owners bullshitted. He conned them that he knows something, and he knows nothing. The only reason his clubs are making money is because this street made millions when the topless craze first started, and now the clubs are off the nut, so all's they're doing is keeping current with the current. If they had a mortgage, like me, they'd be broke."

Bill Gold's undisputed talent is the rapid manipulating of money. "Rake the bread in fast, and pass it out slow, that's his slogan," says a colleague, "and it works, it works." Gold is like the character in Djuna Barnes' novel, *Nightwood*: "He knew figures as a dog knows a covey, and as indefatigably he pointed and ran." Under Gold's direction, the nightly pay for a dancer has steadied at twenty-five dollars, no matter how vast her talents, or how big her following. Connie Lea, the street's "superstar," is the only exception. "He'll save five bucks a week on somebody's salary," Manager Pete Stang of the Lion's Tail says about his boss, "and when the broad quits, and maybe goes across the street to work for Sam Donahoo, Bill says, 'Who needed her anyway?' "

"He's a money-hungry asshole," says Josey Costello, a dancer. "He's on a big power trip. He's a businessman and not a showperson. Buddy is showbiz, but Gold's not. He'll pay you what you have coming, but not till you threaten to sink his yacht and beat him up."

A waitress who gravitates from club to club, Lydia Rubini, tells of an artisan who repaired the Lion's Tail's curtain and spent three days collecting his money. "But that's the way Gold operates," she says. "Put 'em off and put 'em off, send 'em all over looking for the pay-off, tell 'em to go see so-and-so and so-and-so, till they finally get sick and tired."

Among the females on Sweet Street, there is an unstated rule about Bill Gold: "Keep it impersonal." A waitress, Carrie Hess, explains: "I'm in good with him, and for one reason: I never balled him. I never let him play his little games on me. That's the only way to really get anything out of him, by keeping your distance. Several people thought they could ball him to get ahead, and they're all gone now."

"He balls girls just for the screwing," says Mary Hawkins, "and nothing deeper. They're balling him to get ahead in showbusiness; maybe they've read in the movie magazines that's how it's done. But if you do it you're through, because he loses interest."

Ginny Thomas has noticed something else in Bill Gold's relations with women. "We'll all be at the Heat Wave having a good time, Buddy and Bill and me, but if Buddy has to get up and leave, Bill can't just set there and talk to me, or even set there and watch the show with me. He'll stay a second longer, and then split, like he didn't know what to say. At first I thought he didn't like me, but now I just think he's not comfortable around girls."

Late one night Buddy De Young wanted to bring a young woman home to his tug, and he suggested to Ginny that she repair to Bill Gold's yacht. "They musta worked it out between them, Buddy and Bill," Ginny remembers, "but I didn't go for it. I said, 'Why do I want to go over to Bill's place? All I'd get is a quick fuck and get kicked out.' Because that's the impression Bill gives: like an invisible thing in the air. After he has his way, he just doesn't want you around."

If there is one subject that fascinates the citizens of Sweet Street, it is Bill Gold's sex life. Nightly at Raffaele's cafe, the opinions fly. His old girl friend, Jessica King, says, "He's insecure about his manliness. He'll make love with anybody, but young girls are a status thing to him."

Robert Benni is openly contemptuous. "I don't think Bill Gold could get laid in a women's prison on the prostitutes' ward with a handful of pardons, if he didn't own topless nightclubs. That's what a sex symbol he is. But he thinks he's Mr. Superstud of all times."

Nicki Brock, a predatory waitress whose attitude toward money is similar to Gold's, climbs her nightly soapbox to fulminate on her pet hate. "Bill Gold is the biggest asshole in the world! He *reeks* of bad karma! He stinks! He's poison to my system. He acts like he never saw a broad in his life till he came to Sweet Street. His big thing is to say to you, 'Let's go up to my place and smoke dope and fuck!' That etchings trip has been over for a long time. He said to me one night, 'You've balled everybody else on the street, how come you won't ball me?' I said, 'You're probably a lousy lay!' "

If Gold is aware of "bad karma," he shows no signs. He swashbuckles up and down Sweet Street as though he were the cynosure of every female eye, and his sex life long ago went public. "Wait!" he says to a group of business associates having lunch at Raffaele's. "I gotta go up to the office and get laid." Thirty minutes later he returns, sweating, a contented smile on his hirsute face. "That was great!" he says. "Now what were we talking about?"

A beautiful new dancer comes to town, and Gold interviews her for five minutes in his private office. He pokes his head out and whispers to a friend, "She wants to fuck me right away, but I won't let her. Man, they just keep coming and coming, don't they?"

One senses, after a time, certain contradictions in Gold's sexual timetable, certain exaggerations, and certain downright impossibilities. The same is true of the various recountings of his life. The narrative changes from one telling to the next, sometimes sentence by sentence. "I was in the Navy." "I joined the Army." "I was losing my shirt in that hotel." "I made good money when I ran my hotel." The contradictions flow on and on, and prices and values and details change at a whim. Bill Gold is manipulating his own life material, trying it out in Philadelphia, seeing what goes over biggest, exploiting a technique he uses in his strip-club operations. "My ability to making successes," he says, "is my staying power. That's the secret. *Try something often enough and quick enough,* and you'll get a successful formula. Then you bleed it. I'm in an enviable position: I have enough money. No, I *don't* have enough money. That's a lie. There is no such thing as enough money!" Just this once, Bill Gold has corrected his own misstatement.

My mother and father came from Poland. My father was a workingman for forty years. Originally I'm from Boston. I was a bum there. I ran away from home when I was fifteen. I hated Boston! I *still* hate Boston. Three days there seem like six months. I ran to Miami Beach, worked as a lifeguard, a dancing instructor, bellhop, dishwasher, and I starved, too. I used to do things like living three days on twenty-nine cents. I'd buy a loaf of bread and some bologna and eat it for three days. I'll never forget that. From that day on I said I'll never starve again, and I never have. That was 1939. Terrible! Sigs dollars a week income! Can you imagine living on that kind of money? Later on I went into the Navy . . .

I was a Pfc. in the Signal Corps during the war. But they busted me down to private. I saw how little I could do, and how many things I could get out of. I never did KP. I prided myself that I was sharp enough to get a backache or my arm was broken the day of KP. I did it once, like for an hour, and I said, "Hey, this is not for me! I'm no dishwasher."

When I got out of the service, I asked the VA what was the most needed thing, and they told me piano tuners. So I went to piano-tuning school, three years, and I was the highest graduate. Man, I love music! After I graduated I put an ad in the paper, but nobody called. So I started making money in other ways, and I always made lots of it. After that Miami experience, I wasn't *ever* gonna be without money. I had a couple of bad marriages, too; most women don't like to be married to people in the bar business. *Any* normal woman wouldn't.

I had this small nightclub in Denver for about eight years and then my old partner moved here and after a few months he called me and he says, "You gotta come see Sweet Street! Unblievable!" That was four years ago. No, less than four years I'm here. I took one look at the street and I said, "Yep, you're right. There should be a lot of business."

So I moved here and Tommy Lynch paid me a hundred or two hundred a week just to walk around with him and tell him the things I saw, and at the same time I learned the topless business. Then I got some money together and bought an interest in the Lion's Tail and some other joints. Some of us put up forty-thousand dollars for the Silver Peacock, and we almost went broke. There was a million people around but they weren't going into the Peacock. So we put in Latin music, cha-cha-cha, and the noise flowed out into the street and created excitement and the joint just exploded with customers. In fourteen months we sold the place for $107,000. That's how we started. I never used one penny of my own money. I got it all from the bank and my partners. We'd buy nightclubs that were doing badly and build 'em up. The Lion's Tail was losing money when we bought it, now it's worth half a million dollars. Altogether, the clubs that I run are worth a million and a half, a million six, counting their total assets. I'm what you might call one of the larger owners; there's one owner that has more than I have, but I make twice as much money as he does. There's maybe fifty owners in all, but I'm the working head. I call all the shots, and I get paid a huge salary for doing it. I mean a *huge* salary. I work Friday and Saturday and Monday and Tuesday, a four-day week, but I'm usually on the street seven days. My income is in the six-figure bracket. My partners are glad to pay it. The image that most people have is I'm a prick, but not on the higher echelons. My partners would vote for me for president. We got all our investment back in the first seven months. My partners loved me.

Mostly my job is to walk around and check the vibes. If there's something wrong, I can feel it. The bartender might be goofing, somebody's drunk on the job, something is amiss.

I can smell it when I walk in. When the places are running smoothly, it's like a well-oiled machine, and I can tell. Other times you'll see me sitting there for a long time to figure out what's wrong, and then I'll find it's a drape out of place, a light burned out, some wrong thing, but very *very* important to me.

They say I'm a mathematical genius, I have a computer in my head. It's true, I'm real good with numbers, but not that good. I have a memory about important things that's unbelievable, but I'm bad on little things. Last night I ran into a girl who worked for me in two nightclubs and also I balled her, and I couldn't remember her name. But when it comes to dollars and cents, I'm good. I can tell you the percentages, how to compute expenses, how a little savings in one thing can result in x amount at the end of the year.

I also have mind-blowing ideas about showbusiness and Sweet Street, but I can't expose them to my competitors. I know more about the nightclub business than anybody. I know what works, what the formulas are. I have sigs nightclubs to experiment with, and no other nightclub owner has anything like that. They can never learn what I know, unless they buy multiple places.

Like last night I tried something new in one of my clubs, and all of a sudden the club jumped two hundred dollars over the others, so obviously it's working. Those are the things that I know that nobody else can know. That's my edge. It allows me to make all the money I make. But don't make me out to be a braggart. I *am* a braggart. I *am* that type of person. I *am* an egomaniac, and I'm quite well aware of it, but when it gets printed that I'm a genius as an entrepreneur my partners get mad.

The formula? It's simple: *a good location plus a famous name is unbeatable*. In other words, you take a place that has a famous name either locally or nationally, and you move it to a busy location, and it explodes. Even if you have to buy a famous-name place and move it. Like if you took the Copacabana in New York and put it in a good traffic location, like Times Square, it would be almost automatically a big success.

That's how we capitalized on a dying industry. The nightclub business is dead. People are not gonna spend twenty dollars to go out when they can see all these stars on television. So the famous places have gone broke. We buy up their names and put on what's happening today, topless and bottomless entertainment, and we have an automatic success. All you have to do is follow the formula. Look at the Paris Lido—it wasn't always on Sweet Street. It got famous someplace else, and then we bought it and moved the name to Sweet Street. Same with the Snakepit, some of the others.

Of course, you'll always have that type of person that says we're making dirty money, we're in an evil business. Those people are sick in the first place. We live in a sick society, basically because of the church. The church says that normal things are bad. The church and the Jewish mothers, they'll cripple you. You don't have a chance. Before you leave home, you're told that everything's dirty. It's getting freer, it's getting more liberal, but I don't know if in my life it'll ever get the way it should be. My philosophy is anybody should let anybody do what they want as long as they don't hurt anybody else.

I mean, how can they knock Sweet Street? We don't have the Mafia here. Believe *me*, we don't have the Mafia here! One time there was a little misunderstanding about something I said in the press, and somebody got the idea we were gonna expand our nightclub operation into Denver, and a few days later three guys left a note for me in the Lion's Tail. It said, "Stay outa Denver!"

I found the three guys in a restaurant and I said, "Look, it's all a misunderstanding, there's nothing to it, I'm *not* going to Denver. I already lived there. I wouldn't go back there!" I bought 'em a few drinks, and we got drunk together.

The FBI found out about it, and it turned out these guys are murderers, and I don't get involved with murderers! I told the FBI, "I don't know nothing." They wanted me to testify that these guys threatened me. I said, "They *didn't* threaten me!" The cops showed me their rap sheets—they'd thrown bombs, *everything*! They were from a Texas outfit that bought topless night clubs in Denver and made bust-out joints out of 'em, where they have B-drinking and they sell the hundred-dollar bottles of champagne, rob the guys, that kind of stuff.

I'm in no danger from guys like that. They have their side of the street, I have mine. I'm in much more danger from the city, from the bluenoses. They're always attacking me for one phony thing or another. Right now it's my signs. They say the poor little kiddies will get contaminated driving along Sweet Street in their daddies' cars and seeing signs that say "nude," "naked," things like that. I refuse to take the signs down, and they arrest me about every third week. Don't worry, I'm gonna sue 'em for a million dollars. It's pure harassment.

Even if they had their way and closed me down, I'd still come out ahead. I asked my lawyers, "From the day I'm attacked and somebody's trying to close me down, how long before they can do it if I don't comply with their orders?" They said anywhere from a year and a half to maybe three years. Well, in my business the normal return is such that in two, two-and-a-half years I turn my money again. So the risk factor doesn't bother me.

It's a beautiful operation, it really is. In fact, I'd like to go bigger. I want to make more money! I want to put together bigger things. Like I started to buy the Desert Inn in Las Vegas, but I chickened out.

My only competitor on Sweet Street is Sam Donahoo over at the Purple Garter. He keeps me sharp, bless him! He paid for my yacht by putting his prices up when I didn't have the nerve. You know, when you're making all the money I'm making, why raise prices? But *he* raised 'em, and I said, If he's doing it, why can't I? What's the difference between $2.25 a drink and $2.75? Well, it meant six thousand dollars per month per club for a while, so figure it out.

Donahoo's the one guy on the street as bright as I am. He's from another planet. He bought a new Maserati and he started bragging about how it cost twenty-four thousand dollars and all. He didn't know about my boat, so I said, "Boy, that's something, a car like that. All I've got is a little Mercedes 450SL." I said, "But I do have one other little thing I wanna show you. C'mon!"

So I took him out to my boat. He couldn't believe it! He says, "Goddamn, this is class! Now you're talking!"

I love that little 450SL, too. I don't want anybody else driving it, so I keep a Lincoln for my guests to use. My boat's paid for, so is everything else. The rest of my money I put in apartment buildings, businesses, things like that. I just keep reinvesting it. I have a lot of clothes, maybe fifty different outfits, but space is limited on a boat. If I had space, I'd have five-hundred outfits. I own two hundred pairs of socks. I have fifty pairs of slacks, fifty sports jackets, all sort of mod. You'll very rarely see me in a shirt and tie.

For recreation, I do Kung Fu, the ancient Oriental philosophy, exercise, the art of self-defense, stuff like that. Kung Fu goes along with acupuncture. A master in Kung Fu knows how to do acupuncture, karate, the whole bit. I'm in physical fantastic shape. I enjoy grass immensely, wine, but mostly women. Women might be my number one pleasure, and there are hundreds of them available.

But it's still a lonely life, believe it or not. It's the room-at-the-top thing. You have nobody you can talk to. I can't find anybody on the street as bright as I am. I have a few friends out of the business, a businessman, a lawyer, that I can talk to. But that's the problem when you're somebody special. You have to live a lonesome life. And you can't stay married. What woman could take this life, with me always auditioning naked women and all? I have never seen a successful marriage in this business.

You use the street to keep from being lonely. That's why one of the fears I have of selling out is loneliness. Whenever I'm lonely now I can have my affair with the street, the most exciting place in the world for me. Even before I owned on Sweet Street, I spent every minute that I could down there. I loved it! And now I'm afraid if I get away from Sweet Street, if I sell out, I wouldn't have the power that I have now, and I'd end up as being lonely again.

The street gives me G-I-R-L-S! That's the name of the game. And my boat is helpful too. I've picked up *more* girls, right off the dock here. If it's a sunny day or Saturday or Sunday, there's ninety-two of 'em walk by here. And then you talk to 'em and you say, "Would you like to come in for a glass of wine?" and they come in and see how nice it is, and before you know it they're in the bedroom. One girl, it took seventeen minutes, I think, from the time I walked her on board till the time I got her in bed. And when I asked her what she did for a living, I was shocked. She was a psychiatrist. Isn't that a mind-blower? She was thirty-one years old, twenty-nine, something like that, worked in a hospital and had her own private practice. The other day I picked up an ophthalmologist, but I didn't score with her yet. On a sunny Saturday or Sunday, there's no way I *won't* pick up a girl and bring her on the boat. My sex record this year, I think, will be 114.

I do have trouble making steady relationships with women. I go with one girl, very nice, a gracious host, extremely charming, and after I spend twenty-five minutes with her I'm through. She's too strong, she comes on too strong. She dresses beautifully, she's a good lover, and to all outward appearances she's great.

The question is, After you fuck 'em, what next? I get this proved to me at least once a week. I'll say to myself, I'm never gonna see this girl again, and then I wind up seeing her again, and getting bored. There was one that I really liked, she had the humility I like, the niceness, and she was a fantastic lover. She'd come here at two o'clock in the morning. She'd massage my feet and make love, just fantastic! In the morning she'd make me a cup of coffee while I was still in bed, and then I'd drive her back to her apartment, and she'd never bother me otherwise. What a situation!

Then I made the mistake of spending three days with her. What a blunder that was! What a relationship! After "hello" we were through. I just hadn't realized—I'd never spent any time with her except sleeping time, and I thought I really liked her, but I spent three days at a ranch with her, and the intellectual level was like eight years old. She'd blurt out whatever she wanted to do whenever she wanted to do it, regardless of what you were saying, and then she wouldn't talk for hours at a time, just sit and say nothing, answer yes or no and shut up. There was no communication whatever.

Sure, I have all the girls I can possibly use; in fact I wish I had more than one body because mentally I would like more girls, and that's another syndrome of insecurity. But these girls don't know the president of the United States is Nixon. You talk about some item in the paper and they don't even know about it. They don't even know that I've been getting arrested on the street! I tell 'em about it, and they say, "Oh, wow! Right on! *Wow!*"

That's what I mean by lonely.

Straw Bosses and Geeks

CAPPY VAN FLEET, 40

Club Manager

SOMETIMES THE ARTISTIC AND sporting discussions in Raffaele's café are interrupted by a particular sequence of sounds from the street in front. The first indication is the squealing of several sets of tires, the second the sounding of horns and shouted imprecations. On the crest of the noise, a tall, lithe black man floats into the restaurant, performs an arabesque or an *entrechat*, and pulls up a chair. Cappy Van Fleet has arrived.

The former Broadway dancer is now the manager of the Paris Lido, "Home of the Naked Lady Wrestlers," directly across Sweet Street, and on a typical night he will make five or six excursions to Raffaele's, there to sip his favorite teas or conduct a bit of Byzantine negotiation or chat with his comperes from down the street. Cappy never fails to turn the simple process of going to Raffaele's into an ad lib choreographic spectacular. There are six lanes to cross, and a traffic light to control vehicles and pedestrians, but Cappy considers himself exempt from such earthly restraints. No matter how heavy the flow, he slips gracefully into the street and begins his personal waltz of the toreadors. A car skids toward him; Cappy slides smoothly away, slapping his open hand on the rear fender as it lurches by: a black Dominguin goading a young Detroit bull. From lane to lane, Cappy plays his dancing game with the ashen-faced drivers, stopping to point his finger at one, making a face at another. He prances across the right-of-way like an ostrich, legs akimbo, making long parabolic leaps among the headlights and the bumpers, his striped dashikis and saffron robes fluttering like wings in the mixed currents.

Raffaele himself is of the opinion that the public interests are better served by Cappy's mad flights than they would be if such a flashy figure were to walk slowly and majestically across the street. "He'd tie up traffic for miles if they got a good look at him," Raffaele says, only half-jokingly, "especially when he's wearing his purple skin-tight ass-huggers."

"It m-m-m-*must* be t-t-*true*," Cappy stammers. "I mean, I m-m-m-*must* have a sexy ass, 'cause everybody ta-ta-ta-ta-talk-talk-*talks* about it." Everybody also talks about his narrow clean-shaven head, his long protuberance of nose, his sideburns that curve down his -grayish-brown cheeks like scimitars, and his diabolical tuft of coal-black goatee. Cappy makes no bones about trying to look like Satan. He has also been known to act like the devil, shoving his dancers offstage, intimidating his waitresses, bullying and hectoring and threatening, entirely in the service of art. "S-s-s-*some* of them think I really *am* the devil," Cappy says with an air of pride and mystery, "and they may not be wrong!"

There are varying degrees of distortion in Cappy's troubled locution, and when he is at his worst, he pains the listener. The veins knot in his neck, and a slick nimbus of sweat forms on his razored scalp as he tries to wrench the stubborn words from his skull. "When he's like that," says Rocco Cardi, Raffaele's night manager, "you hate to talk to him. You suffer. You want to help out. You have to turn away." The stammer appears to be worst around policemen, rednecks, hard-hats, *macho* and pseudo-*macho* males, the ones Cappy must often deal with as a nightclub manager. His speaking problems are correspondingly reduced when the listener is soft-spoken and gentle, and nearly disappears around females, especially the patient, motherly variety. At home, he speaks smoothly and rapidly and almost without a trace of difficulty, except at times of high excitement.

Cappy lives with the waitress Olive Calzolari in a four-room ground-floor apartment midway between Sweet Street and the black section of the city. The entranceway is at the back of a damp one-car garage, and the door opens directly into a living room devoid of any sign of furniture. The floor is littered with twenty-nine overstuffed pillows of varying patterns and fabrics, out of which the visitor is told to create his own seating arrangement. The walls are lined in red and white synthetic fur, the doors vertically striped in panels of black and white, the ceiling covered with thick white fur that looks like the hides of a thousand pussycats. A helter-skelter arrangement of large mirror fragments is plastered into the lower part of one wall, and a collection of books on the flickering mysteries of the East lines another. A permanent infrared light has the effect of making everyone look the same color, while an expensive stereo rig plays cool jazz through every hour except the four or five that Cappy reserves to himself for sleep.

The man of the house is characteristically forthright about his decor. "You takes it or l-l-*leave* it," he says. "I've had some of the richest people come into my house. The most high society people! And one thing I don't do when they come: I don't change. They come to see *me*. If they eat, they're gonna eat what *I* eat, d-d-*drink* what *I* drink. If they want to eat caviar at the Ritz, then go to the Ritz and eat it. *Go back to your own house and eat!* Why should I change my habits so that you can come and t-t-*talk* to me? I give you Cappy! That's the god of this house. Cappy. *Me*. And Cappy doesn't change."

"Cappy is a pain in the ass," says the dancer Sally Bob Tiner, "but he's a good guy underneath. No, he's really a schmuck, and you have to know how to handle him. He's a Scorpio, and he's black, and that would make anybody insecure."

Lydia Rubini, the waitress who underwent several therapeutic sessions on Cappy's twenty-nine pillows, is equally ambivalent about her former escort, employer, and shaman. "I still don't know where his head's at," Lydia says in her most thoughtful, puzzled manner. "He's a fantastic talent as a dancer. When he does *Season of the Witch*, it gives you goose-bumps. He says he's from Africa and he's only been in the States ten years, but he has a typical southern United States black accent, no trace at all of African. Olive says he was brought up in Alaska. Then there's all that crap about his ex-wife being Persian and his mother being a Persian princess and his kids still living in Africa. Some of it doesn't add up. He can really put out awful vibes. When I quit partying around with him and taking my clothes off for his treatments, he began giving me these terrifying looks, made me feel really scared. After three days of it, I was afraid to go near him. When you work for Cappy, you become his personal property. He owns you outright, and you don't have a thing to say about anything. He loves to come up and pinch your butt or your boobs in front of other people. All the chicks say that about him."

"He's a power nut," says Buddy De Young, the producer. "He wants to show you that he has the power to make a white broad where you couldn't. It's silly. All the broads he hires have to be the kind that he can go up and grab their box, or kiss 'em in front of white people or customers. Maybe he never balls 'em, but they got to show that they don't care what he does to them in front of others. He has *nothing* to do with his own race. The other day I pointed out a little black dancer to him and he says, it was so cute, he says, 'Hey, I don't fuck spooks, man!'"

"Yeh, I've heard how they talk about Cappy," says Mary Hawkins, secretary to Bill Gold and Natie "Fatso" Cohen, "and it's all a bunch of bullshit. Sure, he likes to pat white women. So does every manager on the street. That's the way they keep the girls happy, ha ha, get sweet with 'em, all that personal bullshit. It's not fair to say that Cappy does it just because he's black. Besides, he's the best manager we've got."

During the early afternoon hours, when Sweet Street is empty and deserted except for its traffic and the luncheon crowd at Raffaele's, Cappy's station wagon is often to be found in front of the Paris Lido. He is inside the deserted club, painting a flat, rearranging the light gels, trying out a new movement. Of all the managers on the street, he is the only one who seems to take a daily pride in the smooth operation of his club. "Next week you come back and see how I've changed this p-p-p-*place*," he tells a visitor. "I'm gonna make it like a B-b-b-broad-broad-broad-*Broadway* production." Next week the customer returns, and things are much the same. At $165 a week, Cappy Van Fleet cannot be expected to work miracles.

I'm a double Scorpio, my moon and my sun. I have four houses in Scorpio and my nickname since I was nine years old has been the Black Devil. That's what they nicknamed me all over the world, wherever I'd go. A lot of people don't even know me by my name, only by the Black Devil. Businessmen, even. I *am* the devil. I *practice* being the devil.

I was born and raised in Monaco, Chad. I left there when I was seven, ran away, told my parents to go fuck yourself. I had seventy dollars. My mother's from Persia, she's a princess or whatever you want to call it. My father is an African dignitary, very high in the unions.

I jumped a freighter when I ran away, and I ended up in China, and I spent seven years in Tibet, that's where I got my training in philosophy, in a Tibetan monastery. I went through the whole rigamaroar of knowledge and foresight, change and mystique, Eastern philosophy, the devil, the white devil, God, the martial arts, the things you don't get over here. And all I ever wanted to be when I was a kid was a dancer and a philanthropist. *Still* do.

I left Tibet when I was sixteen, the year before the Chinese blew it off the map, and I went to P-P-P-Par-Par-*Paris* and worked two years with Marcel Marceau and his troupe, and then to Honigsburg, Germany, to the ballet academy, and then I came over to the United States and ran into a fifty-five year-old prostitute who took me in and taught me everything, taught me the *world*. Where? In Wausau, Wisconsin! Would you believe it? She had been a successful call girl, and she had money that wouldn't quit. She taught me *everything*.

When I was twenty I started dancing professionally, and then I played the gay role for a few years, in New York City, working as a dancer and a photographers' and painters' and sculptors' model. I always went to a lot of schools, and I got a degree in philosophy and another in dancing, and a degree in the black arts. I danced for a long time, in every major show you can think of. I was in *Hullaballoo, Shindig, Golden Boy* with Sammy Davis, Jr., *West Side Story*. But one night I hit a slippery spot in the stage and I slid off and wound up with two broken legs. That was the end of Broadway.

The only reason I played the gay role was for education.

I'm a funny person. I do things just to learn. I took seventeen shots of heroin just to learn, went through the whole scene, hospital and all, over a three-month period. I did it so I'd know what I was talking about when the subject came up. I was doing heroin and selling heroin, very heavy into the scene for a while. Then I went through the pimp scene. I had about five whores, but I didn't dig it. It's not a nice cup of tea. I tried to be good to my whores. I put something away for them. None of Cappy's whores died broke!

I came here December 9, 1961, and the first thing that happened to me, I walked into this little club on Sweet Street, paid my money, turned the corner and a guy decked me. Cold turkey! *B-b-b-bam*! I got to my feet and I said, "Are you a fool, man? What is *wrong* with you?"

He said, "You leave my wife alone!"

I said, "Man, you're thinking about somebody else. I just walked into this town. Here's my passport. I haven't been here three hours yet." That was my introduction to the street. It's a good thing I had my head together, 'cause otherwise that poor guy woulda been dead.

I was married all this time, married sixteen years to the same woman. We're divorced now. I made my living in various jobs: laboratory technician, cleaning pipettes in a hospital, landscape designing in the suburbs, laying carpet, and then I went to work in the Paris Lido, first as a dancer, doing the love act with some chick, and then as light man, choreographer, bartender, cleanup man, handyman, chauffeur, what have you. I lost three kids from sickle-cell anemia. My kids were five, ten, and eleven years old when they died. I have a son that's ten, and he has glaucoma, he's blind in one eye, and I have a daughter, eleven years old, and she's got a trace of sickle cell. I have sickle cell too: there's only eight of us in the world who've passed the age of thirty and survived. I keep it mostly in remission. When it breaks out, I get tired, move slow, sleep, there's blood in my urine, blood in my anus, and I cough it up. My body just totally goes wrong.

But I keep on going. I keep on going because my god is Cappy. I meditate for an hour every day. I'm my own religion. *Me*! Who else is there after you've lost three kids and the doctors tell you you're gonna die yourself? That's *it*, baby!

I've been on Sweet Street a long time now, and there aren't many of us blacks here, never were. This street has tried to beat me, but I won't let it. They've had me down, but I've never let 'em know it. Once I married a white girl and she began dancing on this street and they turned her head, started introducing her to white guys, telling her she'd have to d-d-d-*drop* me to get anyplace, and one morning in bed I rolled over and t-t-t-*touched* her and she screamed, "Nigger, don't touch me!"

I said, "Okay," and we separated. Then after a couple of years the street dropped *her*, and now she's off someplace, dying. So they tried to b-b-be-be-be-*beat* me, but I didn't let it show. For six months I was eating dirt, but I never let 'em know it. They *still* don't know it. We had a daughter, and she's six or seven now, lives up north someplace, I don't know where.

I laugh when they say we're all treated equally, black and white, on this street. There's heavy prejudice right now, right while we t-t-t-t-*talk*. Why, sixty-five to seventy-five percent of the people on this street are prejudiced very heavy! In some parts of the street it's almost ninety per cent.

A girl who dates a black guy on this street is considered a whore, or less. Even if she just dated the guy once. Nobody will touch her again. There's an old story that you're gonna have a black spot if a black guy ejaculates on you, and a lot of people around here still believe that! In the twentieth century!

A black person has less chance on Sweet Street than he would have in the Deep South. There are nine blacks working on the whole street, and most of them are dancers. 'Course, I'm not counting the musicians. That's a nice acceptable occupation for blacks, because musicians are not regarded as human beings, whether they're black or white. They're just musicians, something else.

Yeh, I talk to the white guys about prejudice! I jump into 'em! Like sometimes they call me a token spook, and that makes me mad. Wherever they want to fight at, I'll fight 'em. They really can't handle me, 'cause I don't give a shit. I'll put my balls right up on the table and I'll say, "Go ahead, man, smash 'em! Smash 'em if you can!" When they start telling me about their little es-es-es-esca-esca-*escapades* with black women, I laugh and I s-s-s-*say*, "Oh, but you know the time I fucked that white guy in the ass, boy, he screamed for *days*! B-b-b-b-*best* fuck I ever had!" They're fuming, and I just lay it on 'em.

The bosses, the owners, people like Bill Gold and Buddy De Young, all they're interested in is pussy. I don't know what they get out of it. You can only fuck one woman at a time. What can you get out of fucking fifteen women? I went through that. I tried. In one year I fucked three hundred sixty-five women, one a day, never the same one. I tried it out, to make sure I know what I'm talking about, and I got to the point, where after the fifteenth or sixteenth one, I preferred masturbating.

But these guys never quit. We had a meeting of the managers, and Bill Gold said, "We gotta have more cocksuckers around here. When I get horny, I can't find nothing." That's supposed to be one of the fringe benefits. He said he needed the kind that he could snap his fingers and they'd come running. He's strange, but they're *all* strange, the bosses. They can't handle me 'cause I won't fuck none of the broads around Sweet Street. I been on the street ten, eleven years and I've only been with four or five of 'em in all that time. So they say, "Cappy's different, Cappy's strange." I let 'em believe Cappy's gay, and they call me a punk or a sissy or a queer. Well, I don't fuck every broad I take out. Sure, I wine 'em and dine 'em, and next week I'll do the same thing, and then I *might* go to bed with 'em. Nobody can handle that kind of behavior on Sweet Street. They go around and tell the story, "He took me out for three days and *nothing*!" They can't understand me. They can't understand normal human beings.

SWEET STREET SEETHES ON a Saturday night, and the noise of the Paris Lido's tape-recorded show, Buddy De Young producer, is blaring out the front door like a jack-hammer chorus. Suddenly a florid man in an Al Capone fedora jumps up from a table. "Two seventy-five a drink?" he says. "Who do you think you're kiddin'?"

A lean black shadow intercepts the man and his party. "What seems to be the m-m-m-*matter*, sir? Can I be of assistance, sir?"

"What's this two seventy-five-a-drink bullshit?"

"Yes, sir, all the clubs have the same price, sir, and we have the best show."

"Two seventy-five for what?"

For the drink *and* the show, sir. You're p-p-p-p-pay-*paying* for the girls on stage."

"It's all included in the two seventy-five?"

"Absolutely, sir, there's no cover charge and no admittance charge."

"But two seventy-five's too steep."

"No, sir, when you b-b-b-*buy* the drink you're helping to pay for the overhead, sir, just like any other business. Tell me, sir, are you in business, sir?"

"I'm in the shirt business."

"Okay, when I c-c-c-*come* into your store and I see a shirt on the counter, do I scream out, 'Nine dollars for a shirt!'"

The man in the fedora reaches for his wallet, and the party sits down. "That bouncer," the man says, "he's a pretty reasonable guy, for a coon."

Our customers are the best human beings on earth, one hundred per cent better than the guys I work for. The whole world comes right through the front door. Why, ninety-five per cent of the United States comes to see our show. The extreme middle class, the nonchalant middle class, the upper middle class, and the high society. The high society are the cheapest, the worst. You have to slap 'em in the face to get any money out of them, the ones that wear the little mink coats and think they're Miss Bitch and walk out the door with a cigarette in her hand.

I respect customers. Some of them are trying to learn something, or they wouldn't be here. Searching, man, *searching*. They bring their wives in to see the show, man, and they're just so meek that you cry for 'em, you really *hurt* for 'em. Their lives are missing something and they're down here looking for it.

And then you get the grab-ass characters, the ones that sit at the edge of the stage and grab the girls and holler things like, "Boy, I bet she could suck a dick good!" The perverted ones. The dirty old men. We call 'em newspapermen, 'cause they bring in a newspaper to masturbate in. And real newspapermen and writers, they're the worst! Typical sex fanatics, man! Totally perverted cats, man! Somewhere along the line they've been denied something. I don't know if they've had too few beautiful women or too many, or whether they're just looking for power. These cats from the UPI, from the API, they're *something*. They think they can rule us around here.

We had one of those perverts, maybe sixty years old, coming in here when we had two little box seats right along the stage, sold for thirty dollars a seat. The dancers used to grind it right in those guys' faces in those seats, to give 'em their money's worth. So this old guy was there and our feature, Amber, was crawling naked closer and closer to him, and he timed it just right so that when she came down and sat right in front of him he just ejaculated right on top of her. Call me a liar, but they started up a friendship, and that's how we lost Amber. He married her and built her a sixty-two-room house in Wyoming, and she lived happily ever after. There you are, man, a Sweet Street love story! Ain't it sweet?

Well, there's more where she come from. We don't have any trouble hiring girls. Me, I try to hire only for paranoid girls, because they'll put out more for you. They learn to accept my idea that when you go up on that stage to dance I'm the lord and master and they have to watch me, take all their cues from me. So I whip, I use the whip-type action. I want performance, just like a finely tuned car, and I get it.

The trouble is, you're dealing with a freaky kind of girl on this street. When you hit Sweet Street, you stop existing in the United States, you stop existing in the whole rest of the world, you are a *nothing*, you totally stop existing. You drop your social security, you drop your name, you drop your family and your hometown. These are zero broads that can't make it nowhere else. They don't know what they're doing, they have no concept of day or night. They want money, *money*, and ninety-nine per cent of 'em are on dope or smoking a pound a day.

All of 'em have very serious personal problems. Right now ninety-five per cent of the girls on this street are either gay or bisexual, because of the way the guys use 'em. The guys make 'em do it with other girls so they can watch. I've been to parties where they take girls on the tops of bars, put whipped cream in 'em, and make the other girls lick it off. That's their kick. So naturally the girls turn lesbian. I'd say ninety-five per cent of these girls have hospital problems, mentally and physically, and since I have a lot of experience in psychiatry and therapy, they all flock to Cappy. I bring 'em to the apartment to do different therapies.

The dancers are the freakiest. They like the idea of being up there where you can't get at 'em and getting you excited. "You can see me but you can't touch me!" That turns these dancers on, it's like having a orgasm to them. I would say ninety-nine per cent of 'em have orgasms mentally, and then they go home to their little girl friends. Sure, it shows a hatred for men, but most of these girls have been physically and mentally destroyed by men, so they get back at 'em by teasing from the stage. The only thing they hate is a man masturbating in the audience. They—freak—*out*! They feel, You're getting something for nothing out there! I've had girls cry, or run offstage, shaking, they're so mad! They want to tease, but they don't want you to ejaculate.

Well, I try to help women like this. I try to convince them that they're doing something for themselves before they even get their clothes off, to convince them that when they walk out on that stage they own it. I say, "Just go out there and take out your problems on the fuckin' stage and on those fuckin' customers. Dance away your problems!" It's a strange concept, but it works.

I really feel for these women, mostly the dancers. They make the least money, they have the least going for them. Sixty-five percent of them marry hippies, zeroes, nothings, and then they have to spend the rest of their life supporting their husbands, while their husbands are out on the street playing guitars for nickels. One of 'em I know, she works day and night, dancing for her husband. She says, "My old man's gonna be a great musician someday." In the meantime, she's taking the baby down to the club, downstairs to the fuckin' cold dressing room, every night.

Forty-five percent of the women who come to Sweet Street wind up destroyed by it. No, let's push that up to sixty-three per cent. Why? 'Cause you're mixing three elements together. One, a girl that's mixed up, totally sick, running away from problems. Two, dope, heavy dope, from one end of the street to the other. And three, you got the main item: people who hate, people who have no consideration for others, who think of people as numbers, they run things here. You put those three elements together in *anything*, I don't care if it's football, politics, whatever, and you have trouble. People getting destroyed. People turned into vegetables, literally, man! Turned to *vegetables*!

Out of all the women who ever came to Sweet Street, only five found happiness. Amber was one. She was the finest professional on the street, an asshole, a bitch, a cunt, a nothing, a zero broad, but a fine dancer. She met her multibillionaire, and now she's married and she's happy. That's rare. That happens to one and two-tenths per cent of the women that come here.

Well, I don't let myself feel down. I keep looking for the way out, and I know I'll find it. I'm not boasting, but I know Cappy. Cappy's one hundred per cent Cappy, and whoever digs me, I'm gonna give him one hundred per cent of Cappy. And Cappy has a brain and ability to make things. People have made money off me for years. One guy's making a fortune right now off an idea that I talked over with him. He had the capital and I didn't. Right now I have another idea that nobody's never gonna know till I can find the capital. So I'm saving, and I have a old lady, Olive, that's behind me, trying to help me. And I'm getting a lot of managerial experience, executive experience, on the street, plus money to use for bigger purposes. By the end of this year I should be fairly well set up mentally to start a million-dollar business. I don't even doubt it for a second! No ifs or ands about it! It is *gonna* happen and not in ten years, twenty years, but s-s-s-s-

soon! All I have to do is turn a few more doors to make sure the foundation's right, so I don't make no more mistakes.

I feel confident that I *will* make it in life. I don't know if I'm gonna be a trillionaire, but I'm gonna be close to it. Right now I'm a millionaire, although I don't have a hundred thousand dollars or even *six* thousand dollars. I'm a millionaire emotionally, 'cause I'm not worried about how to pay my rent. I'll *always* make it. Because there's seven million four hundred and eighty three trillion ways out. This is my year, ninety-five per cent of the way.

KIP DONEGAN, 25

"Assistant Manager"

> Who thought of the lilac?
> "I," dew said,
> "I made up the lilac
> out of my head."
> —Humbert Wolfe, *The Lilac*

KIP DONEGAN IS A large, baby-faced man with fleshy lips and sloping, sleepy eyes. He looks like a junior politician shouting mindless slogans or a provisional member of the Kiwanis Club in a small American town ("meets Thursdays, twelve noon, Frosty's Eatery"). He appeared on the street a few years ago, announced that he was bored with the insurance business even though he was earning a king's ransom, and found employment as barker at the Paris Lido, Cappy Van Fleet presiding. Two weeks later he was fired, and caught on as barker and handyman at the Lion's Tail. When a feud between Connie Lea and Pete Stang broke out, the young Kip earned a new title (though no increased emoluments): Connie Lea's production assistant. "Connie just used him to get back at Pete," Olive Calzolari explains, "but don't try telling that to Kip. He's so *pompous*. He tries to give himself power and authority. On Pete's night off, he goes around referring to himself as 'assistant manager.' We tell him to fuck off."

As *son-et-lumière* consultant to Connie Lea, the young Kip Donegan takes his profession with utmost seriousness, as though he were solely responsible for the health and eupepsia of a rare and frangible blossom. "I value this opportunity," he says with an astronaut's proud tunnel-vision. "I value the importance of my work. Too bad management doesn't." By this phrase, Kip refers to the fact that he makes only $440 dollars per month, barely a living wage in the city. In an effort to get a raise, he quits frequently, and now has offered "absolute final notice." One senses he is dubious that the Lion's Tail will survive his departure, and perhaps even entertains a mildly fantastic hope that while his bus is en route to his old hometown and his old job in insurance, the walls of Sweet Street will collapse on those who failed to give him his due. Poor Kip, artist in the midst of tastelessness, off to the boondocks to search for class and culture.

This club is an acoustic nightmare, 'cause it's L-shaped, and there's not many people could keep it alive around here, and the only way to do it is volume. *Volume*! Of course a waitress standing underneath a speaker may get too much, but it'll be perfect for a guy in the rear.

I handle all this sound and light the way somebody else handles a palette and his different paints. There're four different colors on the wheel: green, blue, red, white. I can spin the wheel real fast to create a strobe effect. In all, there's twenty-five lights focusing on the stage, plus another twenty on the wheel, and I've got to manipulate them at exactly the right time. My excitement color is the bright red. When Connie comes onstage and she's dancing to that hot Beatle music before she takes her clothes off, I do the bright red flash. That even turns *me* on! Then a quick snap—*snap snap snap*—and I create an effect, I convey excitement, with bright pinks and reds. I convey another mood with soft pinks and low reds, a sensuous mood. And I make a bouncy mood from bright reds and the strobe, turn the strobe on, come up with a bright pink, turn the music up, give it a little volume, and then just start flashing *everything* on and off. You create a wild fuckin' strip mood!

As you can see, there's a lot to it. Take the opening show. That's the one where Connie goes up on the piano and kind of lays on her side and sets a kind of sexy mood. There I use a very soft pink light, 'cause she's creating a sensuous type mood, she's singing very softly and the music is very mild.

Then all of a sudden—*bang*! she goes into the strip! That's when the lights go on, the music comes up, and I turn on bright flashing light, from soft pink to strobe, and then I turn the soft pink off and she comes off the piano, and I go into the bright flashing pink to create an entirely different mood. This creates a wild mood in the audience.

The way Pete used to do the lights, *nothing* was happening with the audience. They'd hardly even applaud. But when you take them through experiences, the way I do, from sensuous smooth, smooth soft, and into a wild strip, in a matter of seconds, and you can keep 'em with you, why, YOU'VE GOT A SHOW!

Don't get me wrong, Pete's a good guy, but he's a very negative person. He doesn't care what's gonna happen a year from now. He doesn't even have hopes. As far as the show is concerned, he has no empathy. He seems to get along with everybody but Connie. They're like an old married couple.

When I first came here and watched Pete doing the show, it was drab, man! There was no bounce to it. And Connie wasn't satisfied. One light'd stay on and on, and then they'd switch to another one, a strobe here, black light there, and that's all. No bounce, no turning the audience off and on to create a mood. There was no imagination.

None of this happened overnight, believe me. It took me three or four months to get my ear trained till I knew exactly what was right, exactly what Connie wanted to hear. It wasn't a matter of training or education. It's sort of like a talent that I had that I never discovered till I got here. Either you got it or you don't have it.

There are times when you wonder if it matters to anybody else. The street's getting lower and lower and lower, and before you know it there's not gonna be anybody left that knows what they're doing. The public doesn't know and doesn't care. All they come to see is tits. They don't give a damn about the entertainment. And the managers are cheapening things. A dancer won't show up, and the manager'll go out and pull a prostitute off the street and put her on the stage.

This street's got a maximum of three years left, the way it's going. Where would that leave me? I've got this beautiful talent, I'm Connie Lea's light-and-sound-production manager and assistant manager of this night club on Tuesdays, and I don't get paid for it, or any recognition at all.

So I'll be leaving for good this time. I won't be coming back! I love my work, but I can't starve for it. I was accustomed to making fifteen, twenty thousand a year in the insurance business. Now I'm making slave's wages. I have to go. I'll sure miss all this.

BILLY WILSON, 22

Barker

The barkers? Well, if this was a carnival, them poor bums'd be the geeks.

—Buddy De Young

HE IS THE PROTOTYPIC alienated American, one of the millions stamped out with cookie-cutter uniformity during the cultural revolution sputtering continuously since World War II. His family life in small-town Illinois was demoralizing, with step-parents and half-siblings and clergymen and policemen moving in and out of the *dramatis personae* as in a bad Italian play. He used drugs and sold them, fled to college one year and from college the next, dragged his barbiturated body to a commune, dodged the draft, lived in rags and tatters, ate beans and fat and meadow weeds, and pondered and brooded about the dragon called "the system" all the while. "I never knew where my head was at, but I realized that there has to be more to life than what's going on in front of our faces. The system's geared so you retire by the time you're sixty-five, your house is finally paid off, and you're put out to pasture. I wish they'd change it. We're no more 'n slaves."

Physically, Billy is reminiscent of nineteenth-century daguerrotypes that still perch on mantels in rural regions. He has the ingenuous look of the faithful milk-boy, wavy brown hair parted straight down the middle, and the silhouette of a barber pole. His voice is pitched a tone or two higher than most, and his manner is intense and lively. He has a long history of truculence—fist-fighting with his stepfathers, flouting the rules in the freshman dorm, cutting classes in high school—and an equally long history of withdrawing into the woods with a sleeping bag to "get my head together." He gives an impression less of deep intellect than of deep thoughtfulness, looking for answers to unformed questions, chronically puzzled and disturbed. He lives with Lydia Rubini, the waitress, and the liaison is always shaky, though it has endured for three years, an eternity by Sweet Street standards.

Before he starts to speak, Billy breaks the seal on a new bottle of whiskey and sets it on the table next to him. He has kicked the dope habit, but a barker needs an analgesic.

I came out here because I was tired of the screaming and hollering in my family, and the constant moving around from one town to another, and the hassles of my life. I met Lydia at a rock and roll concert. I was broke and in rags, my blue jeans were torn and shattered, I had a grubby shirt on. I was dealing a few psychedelics for a living, and Lydia'd just left the carnival and gone to work on Sweet Street, and we decided to move in together.

One night I found out there was a barking job open at the Heat Wave, and I figured I'd be closer to Lydia, so I went to work. They had to show me everything. It was a shocking moment to stand in front of the club for the first time and know I had all these people behind me, and I'm the man that's gonna get the people inside, and all these people on the street are hustling by, ignoring me. I'd open my mouth to say something, and the guy'd be ten feet past, and I'd feel like an idiot.

I got so frustrated, I just started hollering, jumping up and down. I'd say, "Take a look! TAKE A LOOK!" and I'd physically *pull* people inside the door. I did it out of panic. I knew I had to make the money to hold the job, I had to show 'em good business inside. I've seen other new barkers trying out, and I know that awful feeling they have in the pit of their stomach. They're scared stiff, they stand there with their hands in their pockets, and they're just dying in front of the club. You're out there performing to an audience that doesn't want your act.

Well, I worked so hard I set a daytime record on my

fourth day. It's the all-time record and it still stands: almost seven hundred dollars gross, which is more than the night shifts are doing now. I filled the joint with Coasties—Coast Guardsmen—and all of them minors. The manager didn't care. He said, "Get *anybody* in here today!" The Coasties were all drunk and buying drinks and throwing their hats around, and the girls were dancing and hollering, and people outside could hear all the commotion and they came inside and bought a drink just to see what was happening. What a day that was! I knew I was a natural-born barker.

Believe me, not everybody can do it. I don't say it takes brains, but it takes something. Guts, maybe. You stand out there all alone and you have an area of maybe twenty feet to sell the person on your show, or he's past you and he hits the next place. So you have to size the dude up and down, and jive with him on his level. Like a Texan will come up, and it's pretty hard to talk to a Texan with hair over your ears. So what do you do? You act like a complete dummy and an idiot, and let him joke at you and make fun of you. "Boy, we like this clown!" After you've got his attention, he finds out you also have booze and broads to offer, and you take him by the arm and act dumb and lead him right in.

Or say you get some guy from the financial district. He's got the *Wall Street Journal* under his arm. So you say something like, "Hey, man, this is better 'n the *Wall Street Journal*! Come in and take a look!" Usually you have to present yourself as more or less a fool. It's a degrading type of job.

But if you get a straight-looking person with his wife and they look fairly high class, you come on like you have a little bit of class yourself. You say, "Come on in, folks! Take a look inside. It's only two seventy-five a drink." When they get inside and order, they find out it's a two-drink minimum per person, and the two seventy-five has all of a sudden turned into eleven dollars, but now the guy is on the spot. He's got his wife with him, he's in a strange surrounding, and it's dark and he feels the walls caving in. He's afraid of the new environment, and he feels a little perverted just being there, so he pays with a smile.

I realized very quickly that the first rule is to look 'em in the eye. People try to avoid you, but once you lock eyes with 'em, it's almost like they're afraid to look away. People like hands, too. You stick your hands up in front of 'em and you say, "Hi, there! How you doing today? Why don't you come in and take a look at our show? It's a good one! Come on in!" And all the time you keep 'em following your hands and your whole body movements, always toward the door.

It's no problem getting people into a packed house, but if they walk in an empty place they'll turn right around and walk out. They'll say, "If the show's so great, where's all the people?" and you've lost 'em. Lately we've had a lot of empty houses on Sweet Street, and sometimes on the day shift it's a half-hour, forty-five minutes between prospects. When I do see a guy, I'm ready! I make an instant decision on how to bark at him. You learn to sort them out. Dark-skinned guys, Arabs, Armenians, Turks, they'll always peek, but they'll never go in. Never! Chinamen are a little that way, but if you can get one Chinaman inside and seat him near the door, pretty soon you have the whole club filled with Chinamen.

People are like cattle. I barked last New Year's Eve, and it was a mob scene on the street, like Times Square. All these people stampeding down the sidewalks like Herefords, drunk, throwing confetti into your mouth, and every barker on Sweet Street screaming his tonsils out. But we weren't getting our share. So I started blocking the sidewalk. That's an old technique. You just go out in the middle of the sidewalk and throw out your arms and say, "Hi, folks!" and you back up this big crowd. I had two helpers, and as soon as I had the crowd I said, "Hey, just start grabbing 'em and throwing 'em in the door!" It's easy. You pat somebody on the back, "How you doing there?" very showy, and then you shove 'em right in the door. If you can get four or five guys inside, pretty soon you can turn the whole sidewalk, and that's just what we did. Within a few minutes we had a hundred and fifty people where we had three before.

I personally don't like to go into a vulgar spiel, but sometimes you have to do it to get certain types inside. I know barkers that'll say, "We got open dripping oozing pussy! Hard-core action inside! We've got three bearded clams with the monthly red sauce that'll give you a hard-on up to your collarbone!" Or you can tone it down a little: "You want to see a big furry one right in your eyeball? Then come inside!" Imagine the type of customer that gets turned on by that! Well, there's millions of 'em!

The worst part of the job is the punk kids, seventeen to twenty, the tough guys. They're gonna bully their way inside, even though they're too young, and if I try to stop 'em, I'm called every name in the book. You'll get some punk who'll come up and show you an ID, and you'll see that it's fake, and you say, "I can't do it, I can't let you in. The club is hot right now, the whole street is hot. Please move on."

Now he's gonna get tough. He says, "Well, fuck you, you skinny runt!" And he starts mocking you and making fun of you, and you know you can hit this guy and lay him right out, but what purpose would that serve? When I first started, I got into three fights in six months, but it isn't worth it. If you lose, you lose, and if you win, you still lose. What do you get out of bashing a guy's face in? But I didn't know this at first. I wasn't used to backing down, to swallowing my pride, and one guy threw a punch at me and missed and I hit him a few times and really hurt him. Later on I felt terrible. Now it's gotten to the point where I don't have any ego left. I'll take *anything*! To do the job right, you have to get that way. You have to realize that you're on Sweet Street to collect a paycheck, not to impress people.

This new place where I've been working, the Blue Marble, it prides itself on having the dirtiest show on the street. Most of the beat cops are on the take, but you never can be sure, so whenever we see a cop coming down the street we walk inside and flash the light, and it kills the stage light for a second and the girls know the law is coming. So they get up off the pillow. Sometimes a cop'll sneak up on me and say, "Have you flashed the light yet?" And I'll say hold on, and I'll go flash it. That's a very important part of the barker's job, watching the door, 'cause we have all kinds of things that go on inside. Like this girl Rhoda used to smoke cigars with her box, or pick up dollar bills with it, just as wide open as she could be. And she'd climb all over the guys in the audience. Legally, she's not supposed to be any closer than six feet.

You'd think you'd get used to it, but it's the other way around. To me the whole scene gets uglier and uglier. The first day I worked, I thought it was fun. I'd never been in these places. Here's a naked girl, and she was my friend, and it was fun. But then you begin to realize you're getting twenty-five bucks a day for what? For being exposed to a filthy, disgusting place. I mean, one day a Jesus freak got knifed seven or eight times right down the street from where I was barking. Some psychotic weirdo did it. All the guy was doing was carrying a sign: LOVE JESUS, and they took him away in an ambulance. What a place!

But I stay here, 'cause I don't know what else to do. I'd like an acre or so in the country, and build a small A-frame on it, and get completely away from Sweet Street, never even hear from them again, maybe learn some kind of trade like woodcarving that I can do right in the house. Or maybe candle-making. Or farming. That's the trouble. I never knew what I wanted to be. I still don't know. I guess I'll be a barker for a while.

JONATHAN "BIG JOHN" KEEFE, 24

Unemployed Barker

The minds of different generations are as impenetrable one by the other as are the monads of Leibniz.

—André Maurois, *Ariel*

THE GIANT APPROACHES WITH disproportionately short steps, as though he has learned to gear himself down for ordinary humans. He wears jeans, a dark-blue knitted cap, and a heavy pair of silver earphones with tiny built-in dials: a completely contained portable radio. His clothes are threadbare and holed, and his body radiates a heady effluvium. "Jesus Christ!" a night reveler cries out to his companion. "Is that thing alive?" The giant shuffles along Sweet Street and turns the corner.

I'm seven feet tall, that's the main thing. I don't look on myself as being tall, and when people ask me how tall I am, I say, "I'm average." They cannot accept that. But our souls are the same size, aren't they?

I feel like a normal person when I walk down the street, till I run into somebody who notices me differently from the way I notice him, somebody who notices me as a strange object. Then I feel strange. Sometimes I'll talk to people and they won't relate. They've got to talk about how I feel about being so tall, and why I'm not working someplace as a giant. Let me tell you, I know what it's like to be a black man, I know what it's like to be a woman in a society that's prejudiced against women, I know what it's like to be a minority member, even though I'm a white Anglo-Saxon Protestant.

I'm a person with energy, with a mind, with desire, but I'm not used, except as a slave is used, as an object is used.

People ask me why I'm not playing basketball, as though playing basketball were all you could expect of a big stoop like me. It's a negative question, and it's hard to answer in a positive way. If a black asks me, and he's being a wise-ass, I say, "I'm not playing basketball so *you* can play. If I don't play, that means there's an opening for you, and you can make money and get out of the ghetto."

That's not the answer they want to hear. They want to hear that I'm too stupid to play basketball, or too uncoordinated, something that'll make them feel big. Some people like to come up and say things like, "How's the weather up there, Shorty?" They do this in front of others, to make them laugh, regardless of my feelings. They try to make a freak out of me, but that still doesn't make me a freak.

What most people don't realize about being tall is how much harder it is just getting by. People can't see, for instance, the trouble I have with clothing. I need a new pair of jeans right now, and they cost eight dollars, and they're hard to find in my size at *any* price. I can get straight-leg jeans, the kind that were popular seven or eight years ago, but I can't get bells, the pants of my own peer group. Little things like that can be annoying.

Tallness causes shyness. The giraffe is a very shy animal. A tall creature is more open to offense by others, more visible, and he makes the other creatures feel vulnerable and inferior. They don't like someone standing over them; it makes them a child again, and Daddy's standing there, and they react aggressively. In my senior year of high school I got jumped by a bunch of junkies and they smashed my nose, just because of my size. They thought it'd be fun. I didn't fight back because I didn't know how to fight, I'd never been in a fight before, and I didn't comprehend. They broke my nose so bad the doctors had to do surgery on it. I'm always afraid something like that'll happen again. I still don't know how to fight. It's hard to learn things like that when you're seven feet tall. I find that my body is very difficult for me to grow into. In some ways I still think the way I did when I was fourteen.

My body grew so fast I haven't had a chance to grow into it mentally.

BIG JOHN KEEFE LIVES in a single room two blocks off Sweet Street, in a neighborhood renowned as a supermarketplace of narcotics. The residents of his flophouse hotel are junkies and whores, petty thieves and street peddlers, welfare recipients and winnowers of garbage cans, panhandlers and deviates and submorons. Big John is none of these; he lives in the flophouse because the room is cheap and because the landlady is tolerant of slow payers. At the moment, Big John is eight weeks behind in his rent. "She'll get after me in another week or two," he says matter-of-factly.

His third-floor room is like a pack rat's nest, every inch in use, out of economic necessity. Big John scuffles for his living by selling carvings and leatherwork that he tools in a corner of the room. Shavings are everywhere, even on the single steelposter bed. He slaps his leg, and a puff of wood-dust appears. The air is hung with millions of microscopic particles, suspended in the broad shaft of silver sunlight that slides into the tiny room in the late afternoon, banked off the top of the church across the square. "If people saw this room, they'd say I'm living in a goddamn pigsty," Big John says semiapologetically. "If my stepmother came into this room, she'd go into a swoon. But it really isn't that bad. With these yellow walls, you should see it in the summer. It gets so bright, it's like taking a suntan in the mountains. The whole room glows."

Big John talks softly, in an early Jimmy Stewart voice. When he gets excited and speaks up, his voice cracks, like a prepubescent schoolboy's, and big John does not like the idea of standing seven feet tall and talking like a child. He is constantly in search of the *mot juste*, but seldom finds it. In his gropings and grabbings for images, he sometimes sounds like a stammerer, but his speech is normal, and as he rambles on he becomes more relaxed and fluent.

Big John prefers to sit when he talks, perhaps to diminish any differences in height, but he retains the look of a giant Christ-on-the-cross no matter what his stance. He has long black hair, a dark mustache and beard shot with highlights of copper, and heavy-lidded brown eyes that make him resemble Jesus in the old poster ("Look into His eyes! See them open and close! One dollar"). But Christ was usually better dressed. Big John's jeans are split along the inner seam, and he sits with his legs tightly crossed to spare the visitor a gleam of hairy thigh. He is shod in flapping high sneakers, size sixteen, with holes in the bottoms and rips in the sides. He sees the visitor watching, and he quickly says, "Hey, man, I'm poor and I dress like a hippie. It's all I can afford. If I wanted to wear a suit, it would cost me three hundred dollars, and that would take me months to earn. Right now I'm making twenty dollars a week."

The bare overhead bulb flicks out, and a few minutes later a Slavic-looking woman enters the room. "Someone is using a hot plate in here?" she says menacingly. "The fuse blew."

Big John stands up, his knitted cap brushing the ceiling. "No, not in here," he says. He resumes his seat in the corner, and carefully covers the tear in his jeans.

I'm a craftsman, I'm not a barker at heart. See this pipe I'm working on? It's gonna show a man and a woman doing sixty-nine. The wood is African teak, aphromosia, very hard and dense. I also carve wooden pipes shaped like penises. I call 'em woodpeckers. And I make roach holders and watchbands and belts and things like that. There've been times when I could make fifty or a hundred a week on these things, but right now money is tight, and I hate to try to go anyplace but Sweet Street. I'm shy about meeting people, and at least I know everybody here, and they're used to me.

I don't disturb people's privacy when I take my wares into the clubs and restaurants to sell. I used to go from table to table, but then people started complaining, and Raffaele was the first one to ask me to let the people have their privacy, not push myself on them. He told me to sit with people only when I was asked. So now I just go into the places and kind of hover around, and once in a while somebody'll find me interesting to look at and ask me to join their table, and then it might get down to, "Gee, what's in your box?" and maybe they'll say, "Oh, gosh, I need one of those," and that's the way I make my living. It's a game I gotta play to be allowed in the places at all.

The way I make ends meet on twenty a week is mostly to go hungry a lot. Right now I'm living on peanut butter and honey and organic bread. That's a healthy diet. Two weeks ago I was eating nothing but salads, because they're cheap. I hardly eat any meat. I can't concentrate on my crafts when I have a lot of meat in my system. There's too many chemicals in it. Sometimes I get handouts from the restaurants. I have a friend in the business. I survive. My weight is down right now, but times are tough for everybody. I should weigh a minimum of two sixty, but I'm down to two forty. For me, that's skin and bones.

I came from a broken home. Who didn't? My mother and father were divorced when I was two, and my mother got custody. She was a liberated woman, tall, five-ten, with a big-toothed smile like Joan Baez, long hair. She was very kind to me, but she liked to run around with movie stars and writers, artists, musicians, people like that, so she put me in different homes where I lived with people. When I was seven, I went to live with my redneck conservative father and his wife. They thought that Dr. Spock was a commie plot, and they couldn't figure me out. They sent me to a psychiatrist for masturbating when I was ten, and I was honest with the psychiatrist, and he turned around and told my parents what I said, and they told me, "You shouldn't have said all those things, it's none of his business," and my father beat the crap out of me. So after that I'd lie to the psychiatrist, and he diagnosed me as a withdrawn paranoid schizophrenic.

After a while, my real mother got to be more like a distant aunt. She'd come and see me once in a while, take me to the park, but my father discouraged the visits. I think he thought she was a commie plot, too.

When I was eleven, my mother closed the windows and turned on the gas and went to sleep on her couch. I told a friend about it, and he said, "Yeh, your mother killed herself because she didn't like you." After that I didn't tell anybody. I didn't think about it, either. I was very withdrawn anyway, and I wasn't able to cry. I was watching a TV program with my friend and I burst out laughing, and he said how could I laugh when my mother just died. The effect of her suicide didn't reach me till years later.

She left a note that said, "To Jonathan to be read when he turns twenty-one." My father kept it, and I was curious about it, and when I turned twenty-one I demanded it. He said he didn't feel that I was mature enough to understand, and then he said he lost it. But I finally got to see the note. It was full of apologies and guilt; she said she hoped that some day I'd understand why she killed herself. And I *do* understand. She did it because she didn't have anybody. She didn't even have me. If I'd have been aware of how much my mother needed somebody, I'd have left my home every day after school and I'd have hitchhiked across town to stay with her. I still have the note.

When I was in high school, I came home one day and opened a window and sneaked in to use the bathroom. My father and my stepmother both worked, and they used to lock the house so that I couldn't get in after school, and I'd have to sit on the steps and wait for my stepmother to get home after five. But on this particular day I had to use the bathroom bad, and I just sneaked in.

When my stepmother found out, she said, "You broke in the house *blah blah blah*!"

I said, "Well, I had to take a goddamn shit!"

She was terrified. She'd never heard me use language like that. My father was away on a business trip, and she just locked me out of the house completely. I went to live with some hippie friends, and when my dad came back, I said, "Dad, can I live in the house?"

He said, "She doesn't want you in there."

Later they both told me if I'd gotten on my knees and asked their forgiveness, they'd have let me back in. But I wouldn't. That was six years ago, and I've been gone ever since.

I learned how to do crafts, how to make sandals and belts and bracelets and the things I'm making now, and I hitchhiked here and lived in crash houses with thirty or forty other people. They were shooting up, balling, and whatever came into their heads, and I was right in the middle of it. I'd do nothing but smoke grass and sleep, day after day.

Then I got interested in Scientology, and I moved into a Scientology commune and stayed there for two or three months. I finished the basic Scientology course, and then I discovered that the Scientology people were like robots. They weren't human beings any more. No feeling, no emotions. Their trip was to try to eliminate the emotions of reacting to other people, and they were trying to train you into being able to manipulate people. They'd have sessions where you'd sit there for four or five hours and stare into somebody's eyes.

Three years ago I moved into a hotel on Sweet Street and went on welfare. I sold leather goods and I sold newspapers, but I was getting further and further behind financially, and then one day Bill Gold saw me walking down the street and offered me a job. He bought me a red, white, and blue outfit and a pair of white shoes, and taught me what to say in front of the door of the Lion's Tail. I'd bark, "The world-famous Lion's Tail! Birthplace of topless and bottomless! We got Jimmy Moses the double gold record winner and we got the funky lunky monkey band and we got free admission, no cover, no door charge."

Behind me, there'd always be this boss pressure. "Don't stop barking! Talk talk talk talk talk! *Sell sell sell*! Bring people in! You haven't brought in enough people, you haven't filled your quota! The other clubs are beating us! *Blah blah blah*!" Every five minutes they'd come out and bug me.

Pretty soon I caught onto how to do it, and I developed a good line of my own. I'd lean over to the women and get 'em to brush their hair back from their little ears, and I'd whisper, *"Sex!"* I'd tell the men, "It's supernaked inside! Faster than a speeding nudist, more powerful than a Persian orgy. Bring the girls in, get 'em hot for later on!" Or I'd say, "Gentlemen, this show's so hot it'll burn your pants down." The police didn't like that one. I'd say, "If you come in here, *you'll come in here*!" Or "Our girls got big ones in here, gentlemen, *big ones*! Faster than a speeding phallus, you get it up in a single bound! More powerful than a hundred hot hussies!"

Sometimes I'd get horny working the street. Every night you see women dressed and undressed, sexy women walking up and down, and you're out there barking about sex. Some of the hottest bodies in the world are going by, and they're giving you, "Hello, there, big boy!" It's just too much. But at two o'clock they're gone, you can't find 'em, or they're waiting for their boy friend. There's no bunch of dreamy women waiting for Mr. Superman to come along.

I got very frustrated, and I'd stay up till five o'clock in the morning, just from sexual tension, because I'm repressed with women, very shy, and I could never approach any of these hot Sweet Street chicks. I have Scientology eyes, and when chicks hit on me, it scares them. They think I'm gonna hurt them. And most of them don't even think of me in sexual terms. I'm just Big John, the freak. Plus I didn't speak their language. All the Sweet Street people are into astrology. I've learned something about the stars only to communicate with other people on the street, the way you'd learn French if you were going to France.

When I was barking, I'd do things to get chicks near me so I could hug them or touch them. I *love* to touch women. One night I was luring a bunch of chicks closer and closer and this long tall thing came down the street and she had platinum hair and she's swinging her hips, the whole trip, and I was about to lean over and kiss it when I noticed it had five o'clock shadow. I made it so fast inside the club! He wanted me to come out and kiss him, but I stayed inside till he left.

After a while, I really got into the job. I worked fifty-six nights in nine weeks, and I developed my voice so you could hear me all the way across the street at the Silver Peacock, and I really became a good barker. It's no easy job. The owners don't put prices on the doors, and you can't tell the people the prices, because if they knew the real prices half of 'em'd turn away. They're not supposed to find out the price till they get inside and start sipping their drinks. They're suckers, just plain suckers, but if you don't bring the suckers in, you lose your job. You're only supposed to tell 'em the price if they ask you directly. You'd have some party on the way inside, and some asshole would turn and say, "How much does it cost?"

Well, there's no way to ignore those words. Once they start

thinking about money, you're in trouble. I'd say, "Would you like to see the show?"

And he'd say, "*How much?*"

And I'd have to say, "Two seventy-five a drink, two-drink minimum," and they'd all walk away.

The worst nights were when Connie Lea was off, because all the signs advertise her, and your lines are about her, and if you can't bark Connie Lea it's like being castrated. It's like trying to climb a greased pole, and the manager is always running out to put the pressure on you.

I had a lot of trouble with Bill Gold. He wants to fuck every woman on Sweet Street, but he doesn't want anybody else to score. He'd come out of the club and catch me talking to a chick, and he'd glare, especially if I was kissing or hugging the chick. Or he'd catch me when there was a lull, nobody in sight, and maybe I'd be chatting with somebody, and he'd show up like magic! The second I started to talk! He'd say, "You're not doing your job. You should be barking!"

I'd say, "There's nobody to bark to."

And then just like magic a whole lot of people would turn the corner and he'd say, "Whattaya mean? They're right here!"

So he put me on a guilt trip, and this made it tough to get a raise, and the money he paid just wasn't enough. I was clearing a hundred, a hundred and ten a week, and eating fifty-five dollars worth of food, and paying forty-five for my room, and it just didn't add up. One night I asked for a raise, and Bill Gold said, "Well, if you give us a good night every night, if you make us number one on the street and stop pinching the girls' asses, we'll see about it."

So I *really* started barking. I barked six nights a week and I tore my voice out, standing there sipping orange juice to keep from going hoarse, and the second I stopped yelling Bill Gold'd appear in that door like magic. So how could I get a raise?

I began to get frustrated in every way. And I began to get scared. Every night somebody wanted to beat the shit out of the giant in the red, white, and blue outfit. I had guys pull knives on me, guns on me. I had a guy beat me up on the hottest night of the year. He hit me from behind, blackened my eye. My head looked like an unbalanced watermelon. The guy was nuts; he's in prison now. That's why I wear big leather clodhoppers on Sweet Street, 'cause there are assholes down there that are gonna fight me, and if they try it again I'm gonna ruin 'em.

One night I talked about a raise with Pete Stang, the manager, and he read me the reports of the spies, the guys that go from club to club and act like customers and write reports. They told about times I'd ignored 'em, or I was off on a daydream, or I'd be holding some girl, or I wouldn't tell 'em the facts they wanted, or I wasn't kind and courteous. And I believed these reports! Now I know better, I know it's mostly a phoney, to keep you working hard and to keep you from getting a raise, but I was naïve then.

This made me more tense, and I thought everybody was a spy, and I began barking at *every* person that walked by, barking at shadows, for fear I'd let a spy get by without being barked at, and I did this hour after hour, and I was coughing up my lungs. I worked harder than ever, and when I asked for a raise, Bill Gold said, "We're still not satisfied. Try it for another week." So I saw that this could go on forever, and I worked one night and announced that I wasn't coming back the next, and I left 'em in the lurch. When I came back a month or two later, they didn't want me. Neither did the other clubs, unless I got on my knees, and I'm not getting on my knees for twenty-five dollars a night.

That was a year ago, and my voice is still shot. I really don't know where to turn. I have no money at all, and no one to help. I hear from my father about once every six months, but mostly it's just to ask me not to embarrass the family or embarrass him in his job. He makes me correspond with them through a P.O. box, 'cause they don't want me to know where they're living so I won't visit them in person. I don't have the slightest idea where they're living now.

Well, I still have the red, white, and blue suit. Bill Gold took two dollars a night out of my pay till the suit was paid for, so it's legally mine. Maybe I'll hitchhike to New Orleans and bark some of the clubs on Bourbon Street. It's warm down there, and I've been through five winters of starvation and cold and that's enough for any man. I'm getting more desperate every day. People say this is America, nobody is poor and hungry, but *I'm* poor and hungry. I'm honest, too, but I may not stay that way, 'cause I'm tired of being poor. A person can be hungry enough to steal. Have you ever read *Les Misérables*, where the man goes to prison for stealing a loaf of bread? I understand that book very well.

It enters my mind to steal, but it's only a fantasy. At least I hope it's only a fantasy. I can't imagine a seven-foot thief.

Les Artistes

Christ, they take off their clothes and they're standing still and you say, "What a beautiful body!" And then they start to move and—forget it. Truck drivers look more appealing. I'm still waiting for the one Sweet Street dancer that comes along and surprises me with her talent. I'm still waiting for a Venus with beautiful liquid movements and some artistic ideas. But right now our dancers have one thing in common. From Connie Lea on down, they're all lousy.

—Raffaele Pirini

CONNIE LEA, about 32

Dancer

Some day she's gonna have the biggest kneecaps in the world.
—Josey Costello, Sweet Street dancer

FOR AN HOUR, THE barkers at the two entrances to the Lion's Tail have been yelling little more than "Connie Lea! CONNIE LEA!" At the doors of other clubs, barkers must deal in felicity of phrase, high pressure, and a certain *chutzpah* and flair. But the Lion's Tail barkers make do with their simple litany, "Connie Lea! *Connie Lea*! CONNIE LEA!" The advertising is equally monolithic. "Home of Connie Lea," one sign says, and another presents the simple statement that CONNIE LEA IS NUDE!

By nine o'clock the club is half full, a good crowd for the early show. Tittering couples sit in shadow toward the rear; soldiers and sailors and conventioners position themselves closer to the front, and hard-core "newspapermen" and advanced students of flesh salivate at stageside. No one seems especially interested in the two naked go-go dancers of contrasting pigmentation who grind their pelvises and flap their breasts at opposite ends of the stage, whiling away the heavy time between shows.

The music fades. The two dancers mince off the stage with little geisha steps and disappear up the darkened rear stairway, demurely adjusting their robes. There is a momentary hush, and then a tape-recorded announcer shouts, "Ladies and gentlemen, the moment you've all been waiting for! The beautiful CONNIE LEA!"

A crescendo of machine-gun fire rattles the walls, and a short blond woman bursts on stage, energetically waving a rippling orange scarf back and forth over her head and firing rounds of "extra loud report" blanks from a pistol. "Well," she shouts into a cloud of acrid smoke, "my gun was always good for a few shots! Like most of the men I know!" Her voice is husky, a contralto transposition of Louis Prima's growl and Dean Martin's slur. There may be audience reaction to her sally, but it is impossible to hear above the tape-recorded music and sound. Three rows back, a fuzzy-faced young sailor covers his ears with his hands, while his eyes bug out at the apparition above him.

Connie Lea wears a metallic spangled purple dress, V-slashed to below the navel. Her ponderous breasts, lightly restained, wiggle and jiggle like two large molds of jellied madrilène. As she begins to sing, she dashes back and forth on the small stage, interpolating grunts and groans, as though in a passion at the sight of so many handsome young specimens. Her head is crowned with a squirrel's nest of golden wig, her eyes are accented top and bottom by thick mink lashes, and her slim legs are encased in yellow boots coated with golden scales. Through the rising blue-gray smoke, she gives the impression of an animated succubus constructed by a lecherous boatswain's mate. Insofar as one can tell in the oscillating light, she has a pretty face, with large dark eyes, and her skin is smooth and glowing. She is not especially graceful, but she moves with extraordinary power, strutting and striding back and forth across the stage, all appendages in motion at once, now and then leaning far over the footlights to shake her embonpoint in the face of a leering voyeur. She grabs the microphone and begins bantering in a voice amplified by four giant loudspeakers into a peal of thunder: the voice of Thor from a 110-pound female. "I'M LOOKING AT YOU, TOO! DO YOU NEED ME, HONEY? FOR A LITTLE WHILE? THAT'S WHAT THEY ALL SAY!"

She points to a front-row Babbitt in bow tie. "Hey, how about you and me together?" she says. She turns to another man. "Yeh, and *you* can come along too! And *you* could be the referee. YOU? THERE AIN'T NOTHING FOR YOU TO DO! WE'RE HAVING ORGIES! Oh, no, no, this is a family show. I keep forgetting."

At a lull in the accompanying tape-recorded caterwaul, she spots a familiar face. "Hey, you're the man that came up to our dressing room looking for the men's room! Did you ever find it? YAAAAAAH, YOU THOUGHT I WASN'T GONNA SAY THAT! Don't you stick out your tongue at *me!* Ooo-*ooh,* with a tongue like that you could rule the world! OH, YOU DEVIL, YOU!"

The music explodes again, and she struggles to keep abreast of the doubled beat, sometimes succeeding, sometimes becoming entangled in lyric and ad lib. "Oh, you're still laughing about the bathroom?" she says over the music. "I can't *believe* this audience. Now I know where your head's at. IN MY DRESSING ROOM! OUTA SIGHT! Tell me something, IS EVERYTHING ALL RIGHT?"

A small male voice replies ambiguously, "All the way."

"ALL THE WAY?" Connie answers. "My God, are you from St. Louis, Missouri? See, I guessed it, huh? Is he with you? AH, THE HELL WITH HIM! No, I don't mean that. Where *you* from?"

A chubby man in the front row turns the same color as the star's dress. "I'm from Boston," he says, and squirms in his seat.

"Oh, really? Is this a doctor's convention or something? What are you? A gynecologist? NO WONDER YOUR EYEBALLS ARE ON THE STAGE! What do you *do?*"

The Bostonian retreats to a safe *non sequitur.* "I came to see you," he says.

"All the way from Boston? That's a long way to come, *ha ha ha ha!*" She turns to another man. "Where're *you* from?"

"Tibet."

"Oh? I've never been there. What are *you* looking at? Look at *him!* He's leaning on the stage! ARE YOU TRYING TO TELL ME SOMETHING? LET ME TAKE MY CLOTHES OFF BEFORE THIS MAN TRIES TO ASSAULT ME!"

She returns to her dancing, flinging articles of apparel into the wings until she is defiantly naked except for her boots. The strobes flash purple and pink and red as the master light-and-sound man Kip Donegan displays his virtuosity. The music growls a dirty low-down rhythm, and Connie Lea faces the audience and slumps to the floor. Kneeling, she performs a complete back bend, thrusting her twin peaks up and over her body as her golden head disappears behind her, the finished position placing her shaven genitals almost in the eyeballs of the front-row spectators. All that is lacking for a medical examination are stirrups and speculum. A strobe of hot white light starts its high-speed pulsations, and the supple hands of the dancer begin to slip around her body and stroke her abdomen, while a young man wearing war ribbons shouts, "Go go go!" Then the star hops atop the piano and performs a series of old-fashioned bumps and grinds, ending with another Cook's tour of her pubic region as the piano slowly rises and carries her into the trick ceiling.

There is scattered applause, a refreshing moment of silence, and then a tape-recorded voice that sounds like a middle-aged man trying to imitate a young swinger. "Oh, come on *back*, Connie!" the voice says. "Ugh! Don't go up-tight, let it all hang out! Oh, baby, you know what I want, I WANT YOU! Now let's go down. Come on, little girl, you went up and now, LET'S GO DOWN TOGETHER! UP-TIGHT!"

Miraculously, the piano floats back to the stage, bearing the beautiful Connie Lea, now modestly clutching a diaphanous wrap. She starts to sing a love song, and reaches out to take the hand of an old man in the front row. "*Ooooh*," she says in mock horror, "your hands are *wet*!" Another few lines of song, and then, "What've you been doing to get such wet hands? I CAN'T BELIEVE IT! WHAT A GROUP! This one's up in my dressing room and this one's got wet hands. You guys should get together! *Ha ha ha ha ha!*"

An emboldened stag cups his hands in her direction, apparently in tribute to her mammaries. "Oh, you'd need bigger hands than *that*!" she says, and doubles over with stage laughter. A few more shakes and pulsations and she shouts, "GOOD NIGHT EVERYBODY, THANK YOU FOR COMING," and levitates again into the ceiling.

The MC pays tribute in a weird admixture of words: "HOW ABOUT A NICE ROUND OF APPLAUSE FOR LOVELY, THE LOVELY CONNIE LEA AS SHE DEPARTS THE BANDSTAND? COME ON, LET ME HEAR IT OUT THERE! WHAT IS IT? CONNIE WILL BE BACK WITH YOU VERY SHORTLY WITH A NEW ENTIRE SHOW!"

Up in the eaves, Connie Lea crawls along a grimy passage-way and into the dressing room. There are stains on the walls, trash on the floor, an unshaded light bulb hanging from the ceiling, and an unfinished Scrabble game on a table in the center of the room. A hand-lettered sign admonishes the dancers, "Bring your fucking glasses back to the bar!" and another warns that "Possession of marijuana is a violation of the law. Any employee found using or possessing marijuana or any drug will be terminated," to which someone has added "Cement galoshes!" Costumes hang on a rack in an adjacent alcove, visible through a doorway, and an astrological chart showing free-floating positions of sexual activity occupies a place of prominence on the wall.

Along the baseboard, an electrical socket has been wrenched out, leaving an ugly scar in the plaster. There are wooden chairs and lighted mirrors for making up, and a rusting set of lockers that look as though they were lifted intact from a bombed-out railroad station. Two tinsel-top party hats lie crushed among other debris in the hall; the general housekeeping level is that of a fresh archaelogical dig. A typical Sweet Street admonition is handwritten on a door: LOVE TO FUCK, DON'T FUCK TO LOVE, and local laureates have added a lubricious display of graffito poetry, suitable for a junior high school boys' bathroom.

Connie Lea, a Scrabble enthusiast, takes a seat in front of the board and tries to figure out a way to score. After a short peek at the dictionary, she slips her letters into place. "Okay, Maxine!" she calls down a hallway to a dancer puffing on a small, misshapen cigarette. "It's your turn."

When I was a little kid, I always wanted to be a showgirl. I was brought up in a farm area, and my parents were part Italian, Spanish and German. I picked prunes when I was eight. The press is always writing where I picked prunes for a living, but it was just for something to do in the summers. It was a good way to earn a few bucks and stay outa trouble. They also write that I crushed grapes barefooted when I was a kid, but that's just something I said. See, I never do two interviews the same. Some people in showbusiness have standard answers, but my answers are never standard. Like the other day I told some interviewer about crushing grapes barefooted when I was a kid, and he wrote it all down. But I was just ad-libbing. I never stepped on a grape in my life, except by accident.

When I was a kid, not too far from here, I had to learn to care about myself and whether I became a bum or did something with myself. I came from a broken home, but I don't want to go into that. It's due to people not caring that I had to learn to care for myself. Nobody's gonna do it for you. People help, but you've got to struggle. Everything was a struggle for me. It still is.

When I was under age, I got a job as a cocktail waitress on Sweet Street, and I worked hard, because I had to prove myself. I had to act like an adult woman. I had to act like I knew what I was doing, when I really didn't. I was scared to death and I tried so hard that I became a great cocktail waitress. I guess I'm still scared to death and trying to please everybody. I guess I'm still immature. I have to be the best. That's just the way I am. I have drive and persistence, and I keep after things all the time.

When I'd been a cocktail waitress for a while, they let me dance around the tables, just for fun, and from that I started doing a little dance number up on the stage, between drinks. We had a guy playing the piano, so I'd jump on the piano and dance. Then one of the bosses saw this picture of a baby in a topless bathing suit, a Rudy Gernreich creation, and he bought one and handed it to me. "Here's your new costume."

I says, "Yeh, why not? It's a way to break into showbiz." It was the only way I knew, and here I am.

CONNIE LEA'S TOPLESS VERSION of "The Swim" turned the city inside out. Soon after she made her first seminude appearance, angry delegations called on the mayor to protest. One newspaper called her show "a grim tawdry commercialization of sex," luring "harlots, panderers, narcotics pushers, perverts, and an array of violent misfits." City fathers drew up a resolution declaring that toplessness attracts "punks, muggers, cutthroats, and molesters." The Salvation Army staged an "evangelical witness action and march" on Sweet Street, with fifteen marching bands and a squad of hand-clasping speakers and an all-girl tambourine brigade. A press release pointed out "Marge Johnson, one of the Salvation

Army Tabrettes, also resplendent in uniform. She is a very attractive young lady who will have a tambourine and can give a demonstration of timbrel brigade action." The release quoted a variation on the Apostle Paul: WHERE DO EXCESSES SUCH AS . . . topless exhibitionism for monetary gain . . . LEAD THE HUMAN RACE?

One night soon after the Salvation Army parade a bald man jumped atop Connie Lea's piano toward the end of her act. Connie figured he was just another bumptious stud trying to impress. "You'll have to get off," she instructed. "I'm doing my act."

"You're under arrest," Officer Rarc Brakhage replied, and Connie Lea went along with twenty-seven others charged with obscenity. The city quickly chose sides, headed by the two competing newspapers, one of which pointed with pride to colorful Sweet Street and one of which viewed the street with alarm. A liberal preacher wrote a letter to the editor: "The bare-bosom shows at least . . . glorify the human body which God has given us. The shows may be coarse and they are juvenile, but they are not obscene. The clubs in the city which are obscene and dehumanizing are the ones which discriminate against Jews and Negroes in their membership." The forces for purity, led by the scrappy little Father Johnny Boyle, returned the fire, and made life miserable for the old Italians who owned property on the street and now rode the crest of the nudity wave. The ultimate arbiter, Judge Cays, ruled for Sweet Street. He found that there was nothing obscene about the human bosom, whether Connie Lea's size 34B or anyone else's, and threw the case out.

A decade later, the publicity rolls on, encouraged by the clever Natie "Fatso" Cohen and by Connie Lea's alacrity about almost any publicity stunt, even those that bring her perilously close to another arrest. "She's a beautiful person," Natie Cohen says. "She's our superstar, and she deserves her success. She didn't sit on her ass and wait for others to do things for her. She pulled herself up by her own brassiere straps. Who else woulda gone through that silicone torture?"

Connie Lea paid seven hundred and fifty dollars for a series of shots that swelled her bust measurement to forty inches. She no longer issues press releases on the subject, but her bra size is now 44DD, suggesting that there has been a subsequent implementation of nature's grandeur. Natie Cohen has become imprecise on the subject. "Let's just say she use to have big nibbles and not much else," Fatso says. "Now she's got tits to match."

The entire world of the arts does not stand in unanimous admiration of the plasticization of Connie Lea's bustline. There have been scoffers and detractors, and some have been blunt. "I don't see how she can take it," says Olive Calzolari. "She's been ridiculed to death, over and over and over and over again. On television somebody called her a silicone cow, right to her face. She thought a minute, and she said, 'Well, cows don't have silicone,' and she played the dumdum. But she can't keep taking that guff forever, just to make money. Or can she?"

When they're injecting, the needle hurts. It's like a big horse needle. So *big*! I was one of the first to do it, although the Japanese had been doing it a lot. I can't wear a normal bra any more, I'm too big. I just wear a half-bra, to support me underneath. I don't like anything that binds me on top because it breaks down your tissues. I exercise to build up my pectorals. For a long time, I got the shots every week, and now I'm up to forty-four, a little bigger in summer, when the heat expands the silicone. I make a joke out of it on the stage. I say, "Turn down the heat, they're getting too big!"

Nobody understood at first. This was an old neighborhood, full of Italian women in their black dresses, and they'd walk up and down Sweet Street till they saw me, and then they'd whisper, '*Strega*.' That's Italian for witch. I don't blame them, because they didn't understand what was happening. The big bust and the make-up and stuff, they just weren't used to it. They hurt my feelings, but I got over it. I get over everything. One time Raffaele's wife threw me out. I had a low-cut black dress on, and they were taking a picture of me, and she got uptight. The same thing at Vino's. I was wearing a low-cut dress, and the manager told me to put a coat on. Now I could do a strip in there and they wouldn't care, but this was a few years ago.

What? How old am I? Are you kidding? What the hell is age, anyway?

"SHE'LL NEVER, NEVER, NEVER tell you her age," club manager Pete Stang says. "She's really uptight about that trip. Once there was an interview with her in a magazine, and it said she was thirty-three years old. She blew up! She called Fatso Cohen at three in the morning and then she called Bill Gold on his boat, and he was balling a chick, and she did a long number about suing the magazine and everything else. Oh, fuck, man, what an ego trip! She really gets me pissed off. Right now she's going around saying she's twenty-nine, but I happen to know she's thirty-six."

There are as many estimates of Connie Lea's age as there are suitors for Connie Lea's hand, and they range high and low according to the orientation of the guesser. Robert Benni, the restaurateur who romanced her when he was in his early twenties, says, "She'll be forty on her next birthday, I *know*, and you can take that information to the bank. If you look at her minced pies, you can see all the lines." In Robert Benni's rhyming slang, minced pies are eyes and tin lids are kids. "She's got a couple of tin lids stashed away, maybe three or four," he avows.

Olive Calzolari, seldom overly generous about others, accepts thirty-two as Connie's true age, but is insistent that "she's getting too old for the street now, and she's on her way out. The other night I caught her at a bad angle, and she's getting wrinkles all around her eyes. I flashed that she's very paranoid about getting old. If she would just portray the mature woman that she is, instead of trying to portray a young go-go type, she'd last longer."

Sally Bob Tiner, a dissipated dancer who is herself twenty-four going on forty, calls Connie Lea a "tragic" figure. "She gives you this trip about age isn't important, it's how you feel, and blah-blah-blah," Sally Bob says, "but you get the idea age is all she thinks about. How come you never see her with anybody over twenty? All those young, fruity boys she goes out with! She says she doesn't think about time, and that's why she won't wear a watch. I think there's another reason. I think she's scared of dying."

People say, Well, aren't you afraid of growing old? How long can you do your act? It's as though life *had* to be that way, as though you *have* to grow old. Well, I don't believe it. To me, old age isn't inevitable at all. If you listen to America, you can let yourself grow old, sure. They say, Gee, we *all* grow old. Well, if I thought like that I'd get a wheelchair right now. If a person is forty, he should look like he's twenty. Like in the Himalayan mountains, they live to be a hundred and fifty without batting an eye. The people in the United States just *make* themselves old.

Aging never did make any sense to me. I believe everybody should be like Jack LaLanne, take care of themselves. You wouldn't believe how old he is, and look at the shape he's in. Look at Mae West! She's eighty, and she looks good to me. You can always look good. Why can't you? I don't know the word of old. I don't know the word of deteriation. Not if you watch your mind, your diet, your exercise, everything. I work out three, four times a week, not just to build up my pectorals, but to build up *everything*, to keep my body young. It looks young, don't you agree?

I'm into health food. I don't smoke. I smoked for a month once, and it made me sick to my stomach. It didn't make sense, so I put the cigarette down and I said, "This is the most stupidest thing I ever did." There was no purpose to it, so I quit it cold. I did the same thing with meat. Now I'm a vegetarian, and I feel fine and happy.

"ONE THING ABOUT HER, she's a working fool," says Pete Stang. "She comes in afternoons to rehearse, has her own key, which shocked me because I thought it was just another case of *yatata-yatata*, the great Connie Lea trip, give me a key of my own, 'cause I'm important. For our purposes, she gives a good performance, very smooth, very professional, very well cut. In any one direction, she's not that good. She's not that great a dancer, she's not that great a singer, she's not that great a stripper. But the total package is good. She's like Sammy Davis, Jr. He's not that great of any single thing, but the total package is an entertainer."

On Sweet Street, there is more gossip and innuendo about Connie Lea than any other person. She is the vent of the neuroses, annoyances, frustrations, and deprivations that bedevil the lives of the others, especially since she makes five times as much as any performer and has been the street's top attraction for nearly a decade. "Yeh, she's a star," the former Broadway dancer Cappy Van Fleet says scornfully. "Stars show their clits, d-d-d-d-*don't* they?"

"She's just not a talent," says her old friend, Raffaele Pirini. "Poor Connie!"

"She's always seemed unsexy to the people on the street," Carrie Hess says, "but now she's beginning to look unsexy to the customers. That's the one comment we hear the most. If nothing else would turn you off, that beaver shot would have to."

But for all the mingled fact and fiction on the subject of Connie Lea, there is not a soul who denies her energy and dedication. "She was the hardest-working fuckin' cocktail waitress we ever had on Sweet Street," says Rocco Cardi, "and she's the hardest-working fuckin' dancer. Even now, when she's got it made."

"She couldn't sing," Rocco's buddy Mickey Martin chimes in, "but she wouldn't give up. She went and took singing lessons from the same woman that taught Johnny Mathis, and she just *wouldn't* quit. One night somebody told her, 'Connie, Why don't you save your money, you plain can't sing.' She was hurt, and she went out and tried twice as hard. She *still* can't sing, but she's still trying."

Bill Gold says of his superstar: "She's something. Not the brightest person in the world, but far from the dumbest. She's not exactly what you'd call an adult, but she is a professional. There's *nobody* more professional. She's never late, she wants to work, she rehearses two, three times a week by herself. She's a perfectionist. She's a little bit of a ballbreaker, too, which all stars are. But she loves me, so I get away with a lot with her."

Look, I want that show to be perfect. I want those people to get their money's worth. I'm only on fifteen minutes, so I've got to make the maximum impact, and believe me, I make it! The club has bad sound equipment, and the room is shaped funny, and I need the volume up because I'm not in a bedroom doing a show, I'm in a nightclub, and people want a sense of excitement. Also, I've got to be able to hear myself, so I can project. I don't want the music turned way down to satisfy the waitresses that're making fifty, eighty dollars a night. I've got to hear it so I can do a good show for them, so they can benefit also. I gotta feel the vibrations. Nobody understands that. If they had good sound equipment in the Lion's Tail, we wouldn't have this problem. But they won't spend any money. They're stupid. They don't have any conception about showbusiness. Look at the conditions we work under! Check our dressing room! No air-conditioning, nothing! We're lucky we got a door that opens.

Some of the people at the club, I don't even associate with 'em. I'm friendly to most everybody, except if somebody does me wrong. Like, with one person at the club, I took a year and a month of abuse from him, and finally I just don't even rap to him any more. He *forced* me into that. It's a sick thing, but the man is very sick. A sick person!

The one thing they can never take away from me is my persistence. I have an eye for showbiz, a flair for it, and a flair for publicity. And I *work*, I never quit. That's the whole thing. Other people can't work the way I work. You have to have an unsurmountable amount of energy, and an emotional drive. The other girls say they want to make it big as dancers, but as soon as their act is over they go home, and you don't see them till the next night. Me, I'm back in the club the next afternoon rehearsing a new act. Talk's cheap, action speaks.

The way I work goes back to childhood security. I never thought I had it made. Nobody should ever think they have it made, or they'll just give up. I didn't have it made as a kid, and I don't have it made now.

Sometimes I feel I pay too high a price—working on my body all the time, rehearsing, the silicone shots, trying *so* hard—but there's nothing I can do about. It's just the way I am. I'd feel guilty if I didn't work so hard. I was even that way when I was serving those stupid drinks. Sometimes I'm tired and I don't feel like going on, but I pull myself together and I do fantastic shows! 'Cause I'm overcompensating for being tired, and my shows become fabulous, and then I start enjoying myself so much that I forget I'm tired.

Listen to my singing. I've had six years of study. I *still* take. I never had any training as a kid, and I never identified with music, singing-wise. I didn't know what I was doing up there, and I went to a teacher, and she didn't want to take me at first. Now she loves me. I used to be so envious of singers. I'd say, Jesus Christ, if I only knew how to sing like that! I had a drive to get voice lessons, and I'm getting better and better.

The one thing I have to avoid is wearing myself out. I'm gonna try and get myself into a position where I can relax without feeling guilty about it. It's ridiculous the way I work. I work harder than the men. Sometimes when you're success-ful, you ask yourself: is it all worth it? Fortunately, I have the capacity to get insecure, even today. And that makes me straighten up my act. Insecurity keeps me going. I don't want to be like a Cheshire cat, sitting there with a big grin on my face saying, "Well, I made it, ha ha ha!" 'Cause then I would *really* lose. You gotta keep on your toes to be a success.

Sure, I get depressed, I'm like Lady Macbeth, but I snap out of it in a few minutes. I don't waste time. I'm not a manic-de-pressive; I don't dig that. I may get depressed a lot, but it only lasts a few minutes. I'm an emotional person, that's all. Some-times I just need a day off. That's the one thing that bugs me the most about my whole life, that I can't have two days off a week. One day at a time doesn't get it for me. But I hate to take off that second day and lose all that money. It costs me so much! I'm not money hungry, but I can count.

I used to get more out of the audiences than I'm getting now. I mean, I can read 'em, and lately they're not happy. They should be in the club enjoying themselves, but they got a lot of hangups. I try to make 'em have a good time, and you can't always do it. But I'm glad I got into this business. I don't regret the stripping end of it. It was the only way I knew how to get into showbusiness. I don't have regrets about dancing topless *or* bottomless, there's nothing wrong with it. It's not the *only* thing I want to do in show business, but it's how I got a foot in the door, or a bust in the door, one or the other.

I think I'll get into television. I like it, 'cause you hit a mass media there. Movies I'm not that thrilled about, but TV excites me. I like nightclub entertaining, but I was unhappy the one time I tried Vegas. I'll never go there again unless I have a fantastic production behind me. 'Cause everybody else does! But I was stupid and naïve and innocent in Vegas, and I just went in as one of the strippers. Only I wasn't stripping, I was *already* stripped, and that was dumb. I learned my lesson from that.

No one seems more pleased than the Sweet Street personnel when Connie Lea shows strain. "Hey, Connie's drunk tonight!" Olive Calzolari says gleefully. "One of her little boy friends came in and she was drinking wine with him all night. *Whoo-ee*! But she had it together onstage."

Jessica King, young and newly jobless, talks about Connie with barely concealed joy. "All dancers are sad, and Connie's the saddest. A very lonely, lost woman. She's been hurt a lot, you can tell. Underneath her exterior she's soft, but she's also a strong, dominating lady. That's why she travels with very young men. She's a Don Rickles type. She castrates men."

Mary Hawkins, faithful retainer to Bill Gold and Natie Cohen, says that Connie is riddled with neuroses and fears. "When Sharon Tate and all those people got murdered, she spent the night at my house, 'cause she was afraid to go home. She thought she was gonna be next. And she has this funny attitude about the rest of us on Sweet Street. When she's in a good mood she talks to you. When she's in a bad mood—swish, she passes right by."

Robert Benni, the former suitor, is harshest of all. "She's been all routes, that broad. She's been with boys, with girls, with spooks, young boys. As soon as I came to town, I was a waiter, and she snatched me. But now I'm twenty-eight, and I'm too old for her. She's been married twice, divorced twice. She has no judgment. She makes seven hundred a week and I'll guarantee you she's broke. She spends all her money on singing lessons and psychiatrists. She's a super-untalented chick and a super-unintelligent chick. She thinks she's intelligent, but she's a sad case!"

Only Natie Cohen is resolutely complimentary about the

street's troubled diva. "A beautiful person!" Natie insists. "She goes into a shell sometimes, and everybody takes it his own way. But she's not out to hurt nobody. *Nobody!* She takes the hurt herself. How many people can you say that about?"

Early evening in the Lion's Tail. The place is empty and hollow, and words carom like jai-alai *pelotas* off the walls. Connie Lea arrives, punctual as always. Her eyes are blood-shot, and she has neglected to remove her facial cream, which now appears shiny and slick where tears have run from her eyes. A rust-colored wig is flattened against her head, slightly off center, damp and misshapen. Even at this disadvantage, she is a handsome woman, especially now that her soft brown eyes can be viewed without their exaggerated edging of centipede lashes. She tries to speak, falters, sits down and pats at her face, and tries to speak again. Every word is said with difficulty.

Oh, I'm a nervous wreck. Oh, God . . . I didn't sleep all night. I don't want to go back to my house. There's so many bad memories there. It just surrounds me. I hate it there!

I'm suffering from a hangover today, and from being reject-ed. A whole lot of things, and all *so* unnecessary. This guy I been going with, I used to see him on Sundays. But it's a big mess, he's married and he's *not* married. It's all so stupid. I must be stupid for being in the relationship, to stay in it. But I can't see it through any longer. It's making me unhappy, and I can't stand unhappiness. But it's my own fault, for get-ting mixed up with the guy.

I have to break off this affair, something I've put so much time into. I'm thinking, Jesus, I got to break up now. How can I do this? Nobody can help me. How can you! Even a psychiatrist can't help me.

I'm the one that's been giving everything, and he's the one that's been taking, and when he does give to me it's beautiful, but then I have to suffer for a whole week behind him being nice to me. Does that make sense? I never let things like this interfere with my work, but I can't even think straight.

I can't think! There's your intelleck and your emotions. My emotions are covering my whole intelleck right now. I can't function. I hate to say it. But I'll function onstage tonight. I've done it so many times, so I can do it. It's automatic, but it's dancing with tears in your eyes. It's awful. I hate to be like this, 'cause this is not my style. But I'll work tonight. I *have* to work tonight.

THE SHOW GOES ON, but with noticeable variations. "Good evening," Connie says, followed quickly by a surly, "Fix this mike, will yeh?"

She sings a song and then challenges a customer: "WHAT ARE YOU HOLDING YOUR EARS FOR?" When there is no answer, she shrieks, "WHAT'S THE MATTER WITH YOU? TAKE YOUR FINGERS OUT OF YOUR EARS!" She tells another customer to put out his pipe, "You're *killing* me with that damn smoke," and after the finale says, "Good night, everybody, thank you for coming. I hope you enjoyed yourselves, because I have. You're still smoking your damned pipe, eh? YOU'RE KILLING ME WITH IT!" And she pops into the ceiling.

I don't know *what* I want out of life. Yeh, I want to buy horses, but I can't afford to. That costs real bread. It's a very happy moment in my life when I can go to the race-track. It's opening soon! Thank God!

Oh, yes, I'd like a nice mate someday. A *mate*, I don't say a husband. We'd be like Tarzan and Jane, swinging through the trees. Or just swinging.

Happy? Generally I'm happy, yes, and I'm happier now than I've ever been in my life. I'm not *completely* happy, no. Who is, crazy people? There's that song lyric, "Happiness is just an illusion," but to me it's the real thing. When I'm happy, I can feel it, it's no illusion to me!

There's a great sadness in me, too. It's like the clown, Pagliacci. I've been up on the stage when my heart was breaking, and there's been tears in my eyes, and I smiled that much more and acted happy, but I was crying inside. I just wouldn't let my audience see it. I have self-discipline. I'm Virgo, an earth sign. That means I'm very dedicated, very earthly, very particular, very affectionate. But, see, I'm near Leo, and that gives me fire. I'll be okay, I'll be fine.

Dancer

"THIS BROAD'LL DO ABSOLUTELY anything I tell her to,"
Buddy de Young brags to new friends at Raffaele's. "You
don't believe me? Come on!" He leads the group across the
street to the Paris Lido. "Sally Bob here yet?" he asks the
barker.

"No," the barker says. "Maybe the rain kept her. It's always something."

Buddy De Young takes the two men down a dingy, uneven
set of back stairs and into a dungeonlike dressing room that
smells of mold and stale smoke. An angular woman in disha-
bille spins around and clutches at a towel. "It's all right,
honey," Buddy says. "We all work here. You're new tonight,
aint 'cha?"

"Y-y-y-yes," the woman says.

"Well, we'll sit here and wait for Sally Bob. You just go
ahead and get ready."

After a few minutes, a series of wracking coughs is heard,
and a bulky woman wearing a short raincoat and open-toed
slingback shoes explodes into the dressing room. "Shit!" she
says, and coughs again. "Fifteen fuckin' blocks in the rain!"

"Why didn't you take the bus?" Buddy De Young asks.
"No, don't tell me. You didn't have any money. You should
take a couple nights off for your cold. But don't!"

"Don't worry," the woman says. "How can I take any time
off? I don't have a cent, and you won't give me an advance,
and even if you did I'd have to work to pay you back."

The coughing woman is removing her outerwear and
throwing it in a heap in the corner, and soon she is down to a
black half-slip. "Say, honey," Buddy says, "I'd like you to

meet a couple friends of mine. Fellas, say hello to Sally Bob Bumfuck."

"How do you like your name?" one of the men says.

Sally Bob smiles doggedly through another concerto of coughs. "I like it," she says. "He gave me that name last year. Sounds kinda Polish, doesn't it?"

"Hey, honey," Buddy De Young says, "how about showing us your beaver, your wooly-bugger?"

Sally Bob obliges. "Ain't it pretty?" Buddy De Young says, winking at the two men. "Now one more look, Sally Bob, and we'll let you dress for the show." The dancer lifts her slip while the other performer sits impassively in the corner, and then the men climb up the stairs and take seats in the back of the showroom. "See?" Buddy De Young says. "I told you she'd do anything for me. That's why she's at work tonight, when any other broad'd be in the hospital. She's faithful to me. What the fuck, I wrote that wrestling act just for her, she *oughta* be faithful. She has that big gut and nobody'll use her except me, but she's perfect for the wrestling act. That gut runs in the family. I seen her mother. As soon as they have a baby, the Tiner women get a permanent roll around the middle. So I had to figure out a way to keep her eating and taking care of her various tragedies. I even got her a job as a barker one time. But the wrestling act fits her better. She really hams it up."

The club is nearly dark. Five other men sit wide apart at an arc of bar, just below a small stage. The rest of the place is empty. The stage is in halftones of light and flanked on both sides by chambered sea shells made of plastic. Filmy curtains drape the proscenium, muting a series of colored lights set in a glitter-impregnated ceiling. Miniature flying saucers emit a yellow glow from their portholes, and a quarter moon made of tin hangs in the background like a scarebird on an Italian *podere*.

Loud chords and a peal of bells herald the tape-recorded voice of Buddy De Young, the old master: "Ladies and gentlemen, you are about to witness the battle of the century, between none other than that wild Amazon Nasty Nanette direct from the Folies Bergères in Paris. Watch her carefully! Here she comes!" Sally Bob Tiner staggers onstage and flexes her muscles desultorily. She is wearing a *sumo* coat, unbelted, and her large breasts are revealed in all their ponderous glory. To complete her frank and honest warm-up, she turns around and exposes her bare posterior, then coughs and skips to one side and nearly falls off the stage. ". . . And her challenger direct from the Dunes Hotel in Las Vegas, Muggsy Mary!" Another chubby figure rambles into sight.

Sally Bob steps to center stage and begins mouthing words to the sound track as a melodious female voice speaks in French. "*Ecoute, mon ami . . .*" Buddy De Young's stage whisper interrupts, "Ladies and gentlemen, we will interpret Nasty Nanette's words. 'I am going to turn you inside out. I am going to throw you so far you'll have to hitchhike back. I'll tie your legs in a knot! I'm going to twist your arms until they look like corkscrews. I'm going to jerk your hair out till you look like the mayor. I'm going to kick you so hard you'll look like Lana Turner's sister, Stomach Turner!' "

The other wrestler acts panicked and announces in lip-sync, "I think I've got to go to the bathroom." She disappears momentarily and returns to the recorded sound of a toilet flushing. Sally Bob's lips mouth "*Maintenant, es tu prêt?*"

Muggsy Mary says, "I'm ready! I'm gonna fracture you and tie your French knuckles in a knot, tear you apart!"

"Here they are!" Buddy's voice says, "Nasty Nanette and Muggsy Mary! At the sound of the bell, ladies, adjust your trunks and come out fighting."

The mock contestants throw off their *sumo* jackets and advance to the center of the stage. Sally Bob's face is flushed redder than the stage-lights, but she reaches out and gamely puts a headlock on her competitor. For several minutes the two large women move gracelessly about the stage, barely simulating a wrestling match, while the sound-track emits loud catcalls and enthusiastic grunts and groans. Everything is hopelessly unsynchronized. The sound-track voice says, "Stop pulling my hair out!" as the wrestlers stand yards apart, surveying each other menacingly. While the track is conveying the sounds of torture and pain, Sally Bob walks to the far side of the stage, leans away from the audience, and tries to get her breath through rasping gasps and coughs. "Ladies and gentlemen," the announcer says, "we give you the winner,

Nasty Nanette! From Paree! Take a bow, Nanette, you did it!"

Sally Bob lurches to the center to accept an ovation that the audience does not offer, and the other wrestler lip-syncs, "What the hell do you mean? I smeared that rotten French whore all over the goddamn place. I'll do it again!"

The two wrestlers lock arms, and the waltz of the pachyderms resumes. Finally Sally Bob slumps slowly to the floor, and the announcer says, "Oh, oh, oh, hold it! Ladies and gentlemen, I believe that makes it a tie between Nasty Nanette and Muggsy Mary." There is a trumpet fanfare, a solo bugle sounds Retreat, and the "Battle of the Naked Lady Wrestlers," one of Sweet Street's most famous acts, has come to its inevitable conclusion, as it does six times every night.

We start at seven, and we go till two in the morning. The whole show runs an hour and ten minutes, and I'm on about half the time. There's four of us girls, and first we all come out and do a take-off on National Airline's "Fly Me" campaign, and then an orgy in orbit, which is a take-off on the television show "Star Trek," and then the wrestling, and then a coupla stewardess things that are take-offs on hijacks, and then a female love act, on a pillow. Mostly it's just two girls fooling around each other. We can't touch, that's against the law. If you accidentally touch the body, you're in trouble.

I'm an artist on stage, that's the way I feel. I do what I want to do, I express myself through my motions. We all do. Like in the wrestling act, it can get rough. I've had chicks up there actually hurting me. I swear to God, some of them are sadistic. I was fighting Addie the black chick the other night and I swear to God she was trying to hurt me, and she got pissed off when I mentioned it. She kept hitting me hard, and then she kept saying, "Oh, you're not hurting!"

I said, "How the fuck do you know? You're not feeling it."

I also do a topless and bottomless can-can. That's my own act, nobody else can do it. I work with a stuffed snake, interspersed with jokes on the tape. Every once in a while the music stops and this voice says something like, "What's the difference between a big cat and a little cat? A big cat'll scratch yeh, but a little pussy'll never hurt yeh." Things like that. I stand there and laugh and then I resume my naked can-can. It's a popular act!

I get along okay with Cappy. He's hell on others, but he likes me. He has a tendency to pick on me, but he says that's just because I have more talent than the rest. He knows I'm a good draw, because I have the biggest organic tits on Broadway. Forty inches, no silicone. My breasts are so big that it hurts me to dance naked, and it's not good for them, either. I'm trying to learn bellydancing, that would be easier on me. I bellydanced on a trip to Spain, and the Spanish all liked me, except that one man told me I bellydanced like a go-go dancer, doing kicks all the time. He had his bloody nerve saying that! Well, you don't get a swelled head in this business. Anybody can be a topless dancer. When you get right down to the heart of the matter, I'm inferior. I've never done anything worthy. I'm just a natural-born fuck-up.

Usually I'm here a half-hour early or so, to put on my make-up. I do it all myself, and it takes a long time. I use eyelashes, eye shadow, eyebrow pencil, mascara, eyeliner, foundation, blusher, and lipstick, and I have to buy all that stuff myself. I make thirty dollars a night, five more than the other girls, but don't let on. Buddy fixed me up with the extra money.

Most of the other girls turn tricks to supplement their incomes, or else they live with black dudes to cut down on expenses. The girls from the South and the Midwest farm areas seem to get into living with black dudes more than the rest. Indiana-type chicks! Whenever I see one with a black dude, it reminds me that Indiana was the birthplace of the Ku Klux Klan.

Some of those rural types, they're very uptight on the subject of lesbianism. The other night when we were doing the National Airlines take-off, I ad-libbed, "Don't fly us, we like each other!" Bessaline gave me a very dirty look and she said, "You better not yell things. They won't appreciate it!" She practically accused me of being a lesbian. Another time she called up Cappy and told him I bit her on the tit during the wrestling act. I feel like I'm walking on eggs around here for fear I'll accidentally touch somebody and they'll think I'm a lesbian. I have a habit of patting people on the ass, and that makes some of these girls mad. Bessaline, anyway. But she's an Aries.

EXCEPT FOR HER SUBSTANTIAL waistline, Sally Bob Tiner looks like thousands of young ladies who come lurching and yawing out of finishing schools each year. She has a long, straight nose of the type that is usually called "patrician." Her eyes are gray blue and her medium-length hair is the color of her choice, chestnut brown at the moment, perhaps bright red in the near future, "that's what I'm thinking of dyeing it, anyway." She has a heavy, prognathic jaw, which she juts forward at the slightest provocation, as though daring the house to put up its dukes. But this turns out to be a sham, a horned toad's bluff, since Sally Bob is frightened of ephemera, and gives way the instant she is challenged. She entertains no grand illusions about her looks or her figure. "I got blond hair and blue eyes and big tits," she says. "I'm *saftig*, that's all."

When she dances, she is every pimply adolescent's dream. Her breasts bob heavily up and down like sacked Crenshaw melons, and her nipples are the size of Perigord truffles. Her posterior is by Botticelli; her thighs are marbled like prime beef. Unlike most of the other dancers, Sally Bob dresses like a strip dancer, appearing at high noon in purple miniskirts with white ruffled tops cut deeply, or bare midriff outfits that show her breasts top and bottom and attract attention as she walks. In many ways, she is reminiscent of Christopher Isherwood's character Sally Bowles. There are the same flights of fancy, the same giddy good nature, the same outlandish devices: green nail polish, weekly changes of hair color and style, grotesque costumes, gamy speech.

"I'm Pisces," she explains, as though that covers the matter. "You know how your Pisces people are." On a street where astrology is king, Sally Bob has made herself a high priestess. She rejects whole shiploads of human beings solely on the basis of their zodiacal sign, and makes vast general judgments based on juxtapositions of stars. "Gemini people talk a lot," she says to a Gemini, "and they tell a lot of lies." Those who fall under certain signs, Leo, say, or Cancer, will never enjoy her favor. And pity the hapless fool who mis-guesses Sally Bob's own sign. "Are you a Sagittarius?" an innocent young woman asked her one night in Raffaele's.

"Sagittarius?" Sally Bob screamed, as though harpooned. "My ass! I'm a Pisces sun, Gemini moon, Scorpio ascendant. Don't give me that Sagittarius shit!"

Sally Bob has perfected the veteran analysand's art of rattling on for hours and saying nothing, fending off questions and steering the conversation exactly where she wants it to go, maintaining control and thereby showing how desperately she fears its loss. When an unpleasant subject comes up, a cloud falls over her face and she retreats into sarcasm or hyperbole or truculence. "What was it like, having a baby?" she is asked.

"Oh, I loved it!" she says. "I came ten times!"

"No, I mean what were your feelings?"

"Nothing. I just had the kid."

Or, "Well, why *can't* you go home this summer?"

"I can't. I *can't*, that's all!"

Although she is renowned as one of the most promiscuous women on Sweet Street, Sally Bob acts stricken when the subject of her own sex life comes up. She gulps, changes the subject, and rattles on till the awful subject is forgotten. "Don't interrupt me!" she says. "I'm trying to make a point." The point she is trying to make is that she would rather not discuss sex.

Even to the most untutored examiner, Sally Bob gives an instant impression of imminent breakdown. Sometimes she talks very softly, almost inaudibly, as though striving for equilibrium, but then her excitement builds and her voice becomes rapid and hollow and Julia Child–like, finally breaking into high grace notes and appoggiaturas. In public places, her speech is sometimes so loud that people stare, and her shrill laugh fills the room, only seconds before her eyes flow with tears. She scatter-shoots her attention, studying the exits, looking for menace. "I want to find Scorpio before Scorpio finds me," she explains.

Often Sally Bob will manage to turn the most benign relationship into an adversary situation, as though she were more comfortable in disagreement, in the role of stubborn opponent. She shows her hostilities in small, nettling ways, breaking up a toothpick and distributing it about the rug, or hefting her large booted feet onto the new divan. She seems to flout the cliché of stylized good manners usually associated with Southern women. She is offered a bowl of fruit just coming into full ripeness, golden bananas with chocolate spots, dark green avocados, speckled bosc pears, and a single papaya dappled in watercolors of yellow and green. "No," she says, "I don't want any of that shit." Sally Bob seldom says "no, thanks."

Her companions are presumed to have memorized every detail of her personal history and legend, and are promptly castigated if they forget a single line. "So Lamar and I—*My brother Lamar?* Jesus Christ, don't you even remember my brother's name?"

To fail to get the punch line of a Sally Bob Tiner joke is also to invite a dressing down. "Here we are at Tit-freak Street," she says as the car crosses Chestnut Street.

"Huh?"

"*You don't get it?* Jesus Christ! Chest-nut. Tit-freak! You don't get *that*? You're stupid! You may have brains, but you sure don't use them."

And when at last one's patience is exhausted and one informs Sally Bob that she is becoming unreasonable, how does this difficult young woman respond? She turns away, rubs her eyes, finally reveals a tear-stained face. "You mean I'm rude?" she asks.

"Yes, you're rude."

Sally Bob turns sharply away, and it is several minutes before she speaks.

So what if I'm rude? It's cool to be rude! A lot of people *like* it. Somebody told me just the other night that *everybody* likes me because I'm so rude.

I do have a way of infuriating people, though. Like I do a lot of hitchhiking and the other day I told one guy what I did for a living, and he said, "It must get kind of tiring to see the seamy side of life, all those con artists and hustlers." I didn't like that, and then he asked me where I was going, and I told him to a bellydancing class. He asked me if bellydancers take their clothes off, and I said, "Of course not."

He said, "They do down at the Rubaiyat."

I said, "They most certainly do not!"

He said, "Well, they advertise it outside."

I said, "They do not! And if the owner ever heard you say they have nude entertainment, he'd be outraged." One thing led to another and I finally called him an asshole. He said, "*Nobody* calls me an asshole," and I said, "*I* call you an asshole," and he said, "Okay, get out!" This kind of thing happens fairly often.

Once in Hollywood a guy picked me up and asked what I did for a living, and I told him I was an actress. He said, "How'd you like to make some money? How about a blow job?"

I said, "No."

He said, "How about a hand job?" I didn't answer 'cause I was pissed off.

He said, "Aren't you gonna answer me?"

I said, "What the fuck makes you think I want to do a thing like that?"

He said, "All right, you can get out right now!"

But then most people seem to like me. I was reading this thing about Pisces; it said some Pisces are very shy and some are very magnetic. I've definitely decided that I'm the magnetic Pisces type. I have a very high IQ. My father tested me at 150, and I made 129 and 135 on other IQ tests. But being a Pisces, I'm scatterbrained. It limits me, because it's not a strong sign. Pisces are very emotional people. They have a sense of universality as opposed to egotistical signs like Aries where you have a very strong sense of self. Pisces people are more influenced by their environment, more mutable, more plastic.

My family was bright. My mother majored in music; she had the best record at Sophie Newcomb in nineteen years, graduated *summa cum laude*. My father got into a dispute over his dissertation, so he didn't graduate, but he's very bright. We lived all over the South when I was growing up—rural Louisiana, then New Orleans, Atlanta, Sewanee, back to Atlanta again, then Augusta, and finally to Texas. I lived in Texas from the age ten on.

We were always going from one extreme to another. In our house in Atlanta we had a ten-foot grand piano, a tiger rug, six fireplaces, a great big kitchen where my mother used to make crabapple jam, and a bunch of fig trees and a black walnut tree and a rose garden with seven fishponds. My father was a minister then, and our house was the rectory. We had magnolia trees, and they had a way of growing down on the sides, so that we could climb inside and up to the top, like a ladder, and look outside, and people couldn't see us looking at them.

My father was different from most Episcopal ministers. He used to go on a trip where he told me I was a witch, and that I was always thinking evil thoughts about people, and he would spank me. I wasn't a witch, but I had ESP for sure, and he had it, too, and we used to talk for hours without opening our mouths. He was overly involved with me, and sometimes he'd decide that I was in a bad mood even when I wasn't, and punish me for it. And whenever I'd get nervous, he'd spank me. I talked to my father long distance the other day, and I got him to admit that he spanked me too much, and I thought that was quite an accomplishment, to get him to admit that he'd done *anything* wrong.

My mother doesn't have ESP, so she couldn't get in on the sessions with my father. In Augusta there was an old woman who was paralyzed and had her head shaved, couldn't speak, but she and my father would have long talks by ESP. We went to visit her a lot. She was fond of Browning. She used to sit in her living room and recite Browning by ESP, and say things about me to my father. Then she died.

My father never stopped telling me that I was a little witch. He also told me that I was belligerent, and that I didn't honor my father, and that I was trying to create dissent with my brother and sister. He made me afraid to play with them. I didn't have a lot of friends anyway, and I couldn't play with my brother and sister because of my father, so I was pretty much on my own. I had tremendous imagination. I used to imagine that when I grew up I'd be a flamenco dancer. I had fantasies about it all the time.

We had a swinging parish. The rector was Father Laneville, and he used to drink before he went out and preached and he'd drink so much gin that he couldn't drink the wine left over from the Communion. You know, you're supposed to drink any leftover wine because it's consecrated, it's the blood of Christ, and you can't just throw it away. So my father always had to drink it for Father Laneville, because Father Laneville was always too drunk. Then my father'd get a little tipsy himself, and they had a high old time. I hear that the Methodists use grape juice, but the Episcopalians use port, pretty strong stuff. I don't believe all that church jazz any more, but I do believe in a prevailing spirit that governs the rest of everything. Call it God, call it whatever.

When we moved to Texas my father got involved in a big dispute with the church fathers. We never did find out why they were all against him, but the formal accusation was immorality. What they really meant was he was too liberal for them, the same old issue. So my mother got a job, and my father taught school and drifted into science, and he's become pretty good at his work, but others have taken the credit for what he's done.

All the time I was growing up, my nickname was Toothpick, because I was so narrow and skinny. But when I was fifteen my bust had grown to thirty-five inches, and I kept adding an inch a year till I was twenty. The boys kidded me about it, and my father did too. One day he told me I walked with my chest sticking out. He said, "Everybody notices it." Then he started making fun of my tits. He said one of 'em sticks out one way and the other one the other way, and he said he didn't want me to wear sweaters any more. God, I felt like I wanted to crawl under the table! The next day, I still felt awful. Fathers are funny. Their daughters' sexuality embarrasses them. I discussed this with my analyst, and he said my father was attracted to me. He said this was quite common with fathers.

My father worried about things nobody else worried about. After high school, I began going with a doctor, and one night I stayed out all night with him. It was six o'clock Sunday morning, and my father said, "You just stayed out because you wanted me to worry about you and make me think there

was something wrong with you." So he had my sister pack
my bags. She kept a few things that she wanted.

I went off to college and took zoology, and pretty soon I
found out I was pregnant. By this time I'd started a new love
affair with a psychology grad student, Bennie Williams, and
he told me he'd take me away with him when he interned, but
he didn't want the baby. That was okay with me. But then he
telephoned me one night and said he had a new chick and he
didn't ever want to see me again. He had to do it by telephone! I was crushed. I woulda killed myself if I hadn't been
living with relatives. For a week I didn't eat. I stayed at
home and cried and drank.

The baby was born May 17, 1968. I was nineteen years
old. I gave the baby up for adoption because I was still
hoping to get back with Bennie, and he didn't want the kid.
My son's father was a Virgo, and the kid was a Taurus
Capricorn, and the man that adopted him was a banker,
which I thought was very good. It fit very well, 'cause the
baby was an earth person, and the banker must have been an
earth person, too, because banking is an earth trip, a money
trip. The banker paid for all the doctor bills. The doctors
didn't want me to see the baby at all, but I went down to the
delivery room and looked at him through the glass. He
looked red, like his father, a sweet baby. He didn't cry. The
doctor told me, "You'll never regret giving him up. I had a
son and it cost me thirty thousand dollars to put him through
law school." I thought, Fuck you, man, what's that got to do
with anything?

Before I left the hospital, I told 'em I wouldn't sign the
adoption papers unless I could see the baby once more. So
they brought him in, and he wouldn't open his eyes. I wanted
to see if he had brown eyes like his father, but he never
would open them and I never found out. That's one thing I
regret. My other regret is I always wanted to name a child
Jonathan, but it wasn't up to me. The law says when the
child is twenty-one years old if he wants to find out who his
mother is he can. I'll be forty then.

Well, that same year I tried to kill myself for the first
time. I'd been suicidal since I was six years old, and in 1968 I
decided I'm gonna do it now or else I'm not gonna do it at

all. This is the test. But I chickened out. I cut my wrist, and I watched it bleed for a while, and then I decided to get help. That really cured me on suicide for a while.

When I ran out of money, I quit college, and I went to Denver to visit some friends and look for a job. Did you know there are more FBI agents in Colorado than any other state? Why? Because there are more trips going on there than anyplace else! Denver is an overgrown cow town, boring, and all these con artists are running around conning all the straight people that live there. What a place!

Denver was where I first danced topless. I was living at the YWCA, and I tried to get a straight job, but I don't type or take shorthand. A friend took me to see a strip show, and I got a little drunk and they were having amateurs up to dance, but I wouldn't do it. The next day I went back looking for a pair of lost earrings, and they gave me a couple of drinks and I ended up dancing and working there. At first I was very frightened. I said, I can't really be doing this, it's ridiculous, but I did it. That night when I worked for the first time in front of a big audience, they gave me some tequila sours, but it was still a very heavy trip. The people liked me, and that helped. I made nine dollars a show for three shows, twenty-seven dollars a night, almost as much as I'm making now for six shows.

Some of the girls turned tricks for money, and a lot of them went out with black dudes. This one black dude used to talk to me and express the opinion that dancing topless was really bad. He said he wanted to take me out, and he sounded like a nice guy. He said he was a computer programer. So I went out with him, in his car, and we went down an icy road, and he was teaching me how to drive. I'd had a few drinks, and out in the country he told me to stop the car, and he made all these threats, and he said he was gonna get his friends to beat me up, and finally I just sort of gave in. He drove me home at five A.M.

I woke up the next day, and my roommate said, "What's wrong with your arm?" I looked down, and there was a rash all over my body. It was nerves. Then I looked at my urine, and there was blood in it, and I was bleeding from my vagina. I went to the emergency room, and they fixed me up.

The funny thing is, the black dude called me up later and said he was really a psychology student from the University of Tennessee and he was doing an experiment to see how a victim would react to rape. I said, "Do you know I have neurodermatitis?"

He said, "What's that?"

I said, "If you're a psychology student, you should know." I wrote the dean of the University of Tennessee to find out if he was a student there, and there was no such person.

I never did go to the cops about the rape. It was already done. Besides, the cops won't do anything unless you've got a broken jaw or something. The black dude came back into the club, but I just ignored him. He kept trying to act like everything was perfectly normal. Then I found out I had gonorrhea, by giving it to somebody else. The guy I gave it to acted like I did it on purpose. He said, "It cost me twenty-five bucks to get rid of it."

I said, "Big deal!"

I had a lot of trouble with the chicks that danced with me. One day I happened to mention that one of them was a little strange. I said, "I hope they don't think I'm gonna work with that bull dyke." A little bit later a black dancer said to me, "Are you gonna call me a bull dyke, too?" I realized it was coming down heavy, and I ran next door. A little later, here they came, the bull dyke and the black girl, but the drugstore owner saved me. He put me in his car, and the bull dyke tried to bust the window to get me, and she was hollering that I was the dyke, not her. So later on I got all my stuff and split, and after that one of my girl friends and I got it on with a vibrator a few times, but when I told somebody my girl friend was a dyke, she got after me and I wound up having to run again.

Two days after my twenty-first birthday, I cut my wrists. I'd been going with this Gemini, and Geminis are very flirtatious people, and his wife was a Cancer, and Cancers are homebodies. They like to sit home and watch television and then they get pissed off when their old man goes out and fucks around. One thing led to another, and my boy friend got involved with this Libra chick, and then this Pisces guy got after him, and it was all too much for me and one night

I got drunk and started crying. My boy friend saw me and he said, "Look at you! You look like a German washerwoman. Why don't you do something with your face?" So I ran out into the snow and started walking away, dragging my clothes, and he hollered, "Why don't you go home and shoot yourself?"

When I got home I threw my clothes on the bed and got into the bathtub and turned the water on and cut my wrists with a razor blade, just one slash, deep. It bled for a while, and then I called up Dolly the bartender, and I said, "I've got three hundred dollars and I want to leave it to that waitress that just lost her two children in a fire. The black chick. Will you take care of it?"

Dolly said, "What's the matter with you?"

I said, "I don't know, I gotta go now," and I started crying. I said, "There's blood all over the floor!" So she sent somebody over and they took me to the doctor and sewed me up. I told the doctor I cut my wrist on a bar glass, so he wouldn't send me to the funny farm, but all through the sewing I was crying, so I don't think he believed me. When my wrist healed, I went out to Los Angeles to look for Bennie, my old love in college.

Well, Bennie didn't want me back, and I stayed up all one night watching his house, waiting for him to come home, but he never did come home and I got this funny feeling that something weird was going to happen. I stayed drunk for a few days, and then I started to hallucinate. I started walking up into the Hollywood Hills and taking off my clothes and trying to communicate with Bennie through ESP, but of course he didn't have ESP so it wouldn't work. I became very frightened about Pluto and Saturn. Saturn is the disciplinary planet: Saturn and Satan are the same thing, and Pluto is associated with Scorpio, and that's the main guy of the underworld. When I got all my clothes off, I just kept walking up the hill, and I was frightened to death because there are snakes around there, and I still think I was bitten on the ankle. I felt them biting me, and I started crying, and I peed all over my legs, and the snakes went away. I kept thinking about that thing in the Apocalypse where the virgin steps on the head of a snake.

I got to the top of the hill, and into the sagebrush, and I knew I had made it out of Scorpio into Sagittarius terrain, and this was very symbolic because it was the twenty-first of November and this was the exact cusp between Scorpio and Sagittarius, and sage is associated with Sagittarius because of the first three letters being the same.

When I got to Mulholland Drive, I said to myself, "Keep walking like nothing's going to happen and nobody'll pay attention to you." But then I walked through a guy's backyard, and I was scared to death I'd run into Scorpio, and this man was standing there and I said, "Are you a Virgo?" and he said, "No, I'm a Scorpio," and I freaked out and began screaming and yelling. The policeman that arrested me was a Sagittarius, so I knew that everything was gonna be okay. He said, "You know you can't walk around in the nude, because people don't like it." He said, "I don't mind myself."

I said, "I thought this would be a good place to be doing it."

He said, "No, it isn't." I thought, wow, this guy is cool!

He took me to jail for indecent exposure, and they put me in a little cell, and I could see a Viking king in a chair and a golden goblet on the floor, and I thought I had died and gone to purgatory for doing something wrong. But it just turned out that I was having a nervous breakdown, and I wound up in the hospital till I was cured. Then I came here and got a job dancing. I like it, but I wouldn't want to be here forever.

"WHEN SHE FIRST HIT Sweet Street, she lived across the hall from me," says Carrie Hess, the waitress. "She used to ball the owner so she wouldn't have to pay rent. Then she started borrowing. Every day she'd be over here with two pieces of lettuce in her hands, and she'd say, 'I'm making a salad but I don't have any vinegar,' and she'd wind up borrowing a chef's salad and dessert. Then she wanted to move in. Well, I'm not sure if she's bisexual or what, but she kind of scared me."

Sally Bob quickly built up a reputation for brashness and gall. "She's just a broad that'll say *anything* to *anybody*," says Buddy De Young. "She don't mean to hurt anybody, but her mouth can really hurt you."

"She has no shame," says Bill Gold. "You can tell her to go up and grab somebody by the ass and she'll do it. If I tell her to walk down the street naked right now, she's out there naked in the rain. I've never had any association with her, except that I balled her, but *everybody*'s balled her. She's really quite accommodating."

"She talks just like the men around here," says Mary Hawkins, Gold's secretary. "She comes up to one of the barkers the other day and she says, 'Hey, for my birthday how about giving me a head job?' I was standing right there! But most of the time she doesn't bother anybody."

Ginny Thomas, who threw Sally Bob off the tugboat *Venus*, says, "She's just got to go out and learn responsibility. I admire her boldness. She knows everybody on the whole street. I've been there for years and people know her better. She's never been a stranger, you know? You have to admire that quality."

I don't know if you'd call this living, or what. I call it subsisting. I mean, I eat okay—things like yogurt, eggs, milk, bananas, juices. I eat too much cheese and I drink too much milk, and I drink 'way too much wine, rum and brandy. Usually I live with somebody, or if I'm living alone I have a lot of people over. I have to have people with me. Buddy and I have been friends for years, and I've lived with him on his boat, but Ginny's become too jealous. Three years ago I went to Los Angeles for a couple weeks and when I came back, she was there. Buddy had told her I wasn't coming back. So I had to sleep on the sofa, and she just assumed this position as his old lady. She acts like its her boat. She does carpentry on it, and she goes out and gets the wood for the fireplace and chops it up. She's always burning fires on the boat, she's afraid of mildew. That's her trip, being afraid of mildew and collecting knickknacks and doing the laundry. One morning we had a big fight and I went and packed my stuff, and I've been living with a young guy ever since.

Well, I knew none of this made sense as a way of life, so I went to see a psychiatrist, and he said I was unhappy. I still see him once in a while. He likes me. He's a Gemini. Even if I'm not very happy, I don't really think about killing myself any more, except when something bad happens and for a fleeting period of time I'll think about it.

I don't know what happens next. I don't enjoy dancing topless any more. I have a lot of friends in the film industry, but nothing seems to be materializing. I've even written a scene for a movie. And I enjoy acting. I'd like to act. I'd like to write. Writing's my most long-range goal, a book about myself and my life. I can't go back to college. I just can't. I don't want to be a zoologist any more. I'm just not into the college trip. I'm an artist.

Gee, you know what I didn't do this year? On New Year's Day you're supposed to eat black-eyed peas and spinach, or it's gonna be a bum year. Well, I didn't do it! I forgot! You have to eat three hundred and sixty five black-eyed peas, one for each day. That's what my father used to tell me. Oh, Jesus, I forgot to do it! I wonder what kind of year it's gonna be.

ROCCO CARDI AND MICKEY Martin are analyzing Sally Bob Tiner in Raffaele's. The word is out that she has been spending her spare time at the Rubaiyat, a nightclub that specializes in Middle Eastern dishes and bellydancing, and the two old friends profess to see a deep significance in her new tastes. "She fucked everybody on the street," Rocco says, "and now nobody wants her. Except the Arabs. You know they do it a special way. They like fat young girls, sheep, and horses."

"That crazy broad," says Mickey Martin, twirling a third helping of spaghetti Bolognese under his fork. "She'll reach thirty and that'll be the end. Some night you'll see her walking out toward the bridge, it happens all the time. To a girl like her, life is practically over when she's thirty, youknowwhatImean? Where does she go from here? She lives in a mythical world, like chasing a rainbow and finding out there's not a pot of gold there, and then you have to face the reality that you should have been facing for years and years, and then you're finished."

"Yeh," says Rocco. "She'll have a short run with the Arabs."

Dancer

> I never saw a wild thing
> Sorry for itself.
> —D. H. Lawrence, "Self-Pity"

SHE IS SECOND FROM the left in the four-girl chorus that opens the show at the Seven Seas, Sweet Street's newest and least solvent night club. She is the one who moves a little more fluidly, kicks a few inches higher, bestows her professional smile with warmth and charm. Josey Costello is proud of being a dancer, and she is convinced that the most disreputable member of her audience deserves exactly what he paid for: a good performance. For six shows a night, six nights a week, she whirls and kicks and pirouettes as though she were trying out for the Joffrey Ballet.

But Josey Costello's professional future does not appear to reach beyond Sweet Street. For one thing, she lacks the natural or unnatural voluptuousness of her colleagues. Her bust is small and unimpressive, and she is a bony five feet two and a half inches tall, with a lustrous mane of brown hair that falls below her waist, green eyes, a Pinocchio nose, pinched lips and the oval face of a Rembrandt peasant. She is sweet, cheerful, and forgettable. Dancing alongside the Brunhildes of Sweet Street, she quickly becomes absorbed into the scenery: a prop, a foil, as replaceable as a spark plug.

Happily for her equanimity, Josey entertains no illusions. "I suppose I could solve everything with silicone," she says, "but I find the idea revolting." Her voice is lilting and musical, her sentences grammatical and precise, and she enjoys playing with words and inflections. She in a natural linguist, wrapping her tongue around the swallowed r's and tortured vowels of French as though she were a native of Lyons. Hers is the dubbed voice of "Nasty Nanette" on the Paris Lido's wrestling tape, and she is available to Buddy De Young whenever he needs a resonant female voice in his work. Gratis, of course.

Along Sweet Street, Josey is regarded as the steady work-horse, the honest journeyman, the "harmless drudge." It is not generally known that she is a heroin addict.

I grew up right here in the city, which is unusual for Sweet Street people. My dad works for the post office, always has. His side of the family is Italian, my mother's side is Scotch, Irish, Cherokee Indian, Dutch. I had a placid childhood. No, it was better than placid. We had a happy, close family, and I went to Catholic school for nine years, and I was a devout little Catholic child. There are good things and bad things about a Catholic education. The good things are that they teach you to read and write and spell, do sums and fractions and decimals, speak correct English and punctuate properly, which is well and good because most of the students in public schools *don't* learn those things. I value my Catholic education, and I'm a lifetime member of the National Honor Society because of it.

The bad thing about the Catholic education is the nuns. They may have put me where I am today, dancing in a cheap show on Sweet Street. They began telling us about sex around the ninth grade, and they told us all the things that were sins—necking, petting, French-kissing, and of course quote doing it unquote. Also impure thoughts. I mean you couldn't even *think* about doing it, that was a sin. I'm serious! And I was devout, and I took all this shit seriously. I was so uptight. When I was fifteen, I wouldn't let my steady boy friend put his hands up the *back* of my blouse. Really! I'd say, "Stop that!" Poor guy, he tried everything, and nothing worked.

That was the year we'd always go out on weekends to dance, and one night we all went to Sweet Street to see the animals. They announced that there was gonna be a topless dancer, and this little chickie comes out with a robe on and she steps into this glass booth which is supposed to look like a shower stall. She turns her back to the audience, hangs up her robe, and turns around. Ta-*da*! Everybody was disappointed because she wasn't overly endowed, and it was all kind of funny, and sad.

When I was just about to enter college, I started smoking dope and my head opened up a little bit. I rejected the whole scene and got a little diddly-shit job as a salesgirl and went off to the country to live with some hippie friends. Far out! I saw the seasons really change for the first time. I discovered that grass starts to get green after a rainfall, and the trees begin to blossom in the spring. I was just wigged! I couldn't believe it! All those things had been going on in nature all my life, and I didn't even know. I saved my money and toured France, and then I came back and went to college for two years, till the money ran out, and then one day a girl friend and I were paging through the want ads.

We noticed that these same ads kept appearing day after day, advertising for cocktail waitresses and dancers, and we decided to take a look. The place was so dark inside the waitress had to hand-lead us to a table. She sets us up drinks and comes over with a bill for four dollars. *What?* I told the waitress I was there to apply for a job. She said, "Wonderful! One of our girls is sick, and she wants to go home. How would you like to dance for the next three hours?"

I was astounded! My girl friend kept egging me on, "Go ahead. Do it, do it!" I just said, "Er, uh, well . . ." Finally I figured three hours couldn't hurt anything, and it might even pay for the drinks. I said, "Okay. Do you have any costume I can wear?"

She said, "Oh, just your sweater and your panties'll be fine."

I said, "Where's the dressing room?" and she escorted me into the girls' can. I took off all my superfluous clothing, walked out barefooted in my bikini underpants and my sweater, climbed up the stairs to the stage and started dancing.

I really didn't know what to think. *This is me?* I did a couple of numbers and then the waitress comes over and she goes, "Well, now you got to take your pants off."

I said, "Oh? Okay. Fine." So I took my pants off and I turned around just in time to see my girl friend waving good-bye and leaving me stark raving nude in this club. Luckily I didn't have time to think or feel, I just did it. One minute I was thinking about a job as a waitress and the next minute I'm up on stage dancing naked.

They liked me! They hired me! In the next five days I found out that dancing is exhausting. I'd come home at night covered with salt and dead tired. If I were doing that gig now, it would be nothing. But I wasn't in shape in those days. I didn't really mind being naked. In those days you stood up when you danced, you didn't have to kneel down, you didn't spread your legs, and nobody grabbed at you. It was sufficient to have a nude chick up there dancing. I even discovered that I liked it. It gave me an opportunity to get rid of my exhibitionism and get paid for it.

But there was another part to the job, hustling drinks! I—hated—hustling—drinks! With a passion! And that turned out to be the most important part of the job. The cash register was the only star in that club, and it didn't matter how well you danced or how pretty you were, man. *Nothing* was happening if you couldn't hustle drinks! There was this constant pressure to hustle, hustle, hustle. When you ordered, you were supposed to order champagne, and if the customer wouldn't buy you champagne, you were supposed to order a double anything. Champagne was twenty dollars a split, or some ridiculous price. Till I held that job, I never realized how many transients the city has—conventioners, salesmen, service men, and *all* of them looking for a girl, right? They don't know where to score, so they wind up in places like Sweet Street and they get screwed. I learned very early in my career, a man might get screwed in those joints, but he's never gonna get laid.

I couldn't take it after a week. I quit, and they paid me my hundred and twenty-five dollars, and I was looking for work again. My girl friend had found a job as cashier in a dirty movie, and they had an opening and I snapped it up. I worked there for nine months, selling tickets to men who carried overcoats in warm weather and always bought popcorn. Luckily I didn't have to clean up. It was a pretty boring job, sitting around on my butt all day, getting backaches from this tiny little stool in this tiny little cage in this tiny little room in one of the most horrible parts of town, Skid Row.

We actually had some customers that would walk up and pay their two dollars at ten o'clock in the morning. Others came in because it was the cheapest porny movie in town, and they'd spend the day out of the hot sun. From noon till two, we'd get the most customers. The businessmen would come in for a quickie. It was hilarious. They were so furtive and so embarrassed! They'd be looking over their shoulder all the time. Till I got that job, I'd always thought that only dirty old men go to porny movies, but we had all kinds: businessmen, older people on Social Security, real heartbreakers. I got to know some of them. They'd come in and say hello to me and they were very old, sad men who didn't have anything to do. I guess this place was their whole sex life.

The movies were so terribly boring. I've seen so many, and they're all the same. I still haven't seen *one* good pornographic flick. For the first three or four weeks, I never missed the change of feature on Thursday or Friday, but then I got bored and quit watching. The manager was seldom there, unless we were gonna get busted, and then it was his job to take the bust. Before each election, the city busted right and left, and made it nasty for everybody. Then they'd get into office and relax. The same owners owned a burlesque theater in the city and also a couple of burlesque houses in other towns. They paid two dollars an hour; I cleared sixty-six dollars for a forty-hour week. Two of us ran the whole thing—me and the projectionist. There were no ushers, nobody inside except the customers, breathing.

The manager, John, was a very cool black dude, and one day he told me they were short a girl at the burlesque theater, and would I work?

I said, "God, I haven't danced in so long."

He said, "Well, come on down and do the last two shows and see how it feels."

So I trotted down there and I said, "Well, John, what do I wear?"

He had a box full of shit and I pawed through it and came up with this short white peignoir, very dirty, and fortunately

I was wearing white panties. I asked him a million questions: "Which way do you come out on stage, and what music will I be dancing to, and *blah blah blah.*" He took me downstairs to the dressing room, and then—*ta-da-ta-da-da-da,* here I am out on a stage again, only this time it's a big stage, and there's a spotlight shining in my face. That was two years ago, and times had changed. I was instructed to take off my clothes on the first number and spread my legs on the second. I didn't know anything about how to work on a floor or a mattress, how to show anything gracefully, and I hated it, I just hated it! The mattress was old and filthy, the floor was filthy, and the stage was filthy. My feet were black before I'd gone three steps.

I did the first show, and I decided, No, I can't do this. After the second show, I said, Well, I guess this is tolerable, at least it beats sitting on my ass at the Owl Cinema. *I'll do it!* There were only a few more days of the engagement left.

I took the old peignoir home and washed it, so it would be white instead of gray. I dragged out some shoes that I could dance in to keep the black off my feet, I got some fancy underpants together, and the next day I was ready. They hired me at a hundred and fifty a week for a seven-day week, six shows a day. I played the rest of the engagement, but I really didn't learn much. That place was pretty goddamn scuzzy. Pret-ty, pret-ty scuzzy! And not very professional, either.

By Christmas I was broke again, and I got in touch with John. He'd been transferred to a Seattle burlesque theater by this time, and he was crying for girls. The people in Seattle are a little behind the times, five or six years anyway, and there aren't as many chicks in Seattle that are willing to take off their clothes and dance.

John says, "Come on, Josey, I need broads." So I got my shit together and a friend bought me this beautiful purple satin gown, and that became part of my burlesque costume, 'cause this was going to be a professional show. It wasn't just sit down and spread your legs. You had to have something nice to strip out of. I also needed underwear, but it was too expensive to buy, so my roommate and I made some up. Great! I made a G-string out of an old silver lamé dress, and a little bra with silver lamé straps that looked like butterfly wings, all lined with pink satin and reversible. So I had my drag together, and I headed for Seattle.

I checked into a grungy hotel where the top floor was reserved for the strippers, and the next morning I went to watch the show. I just kind of shrank! Oh, God, no! How *can* I? The first girl that came on, Baby Fran, was so impressive, so young, very pretty, and limber as a dish rag. She did a novelty strip, with lots of acrobatics and gymnastics, and she was just marvelous. I said, Oh, my God, *me*? What am *I* gonna do up on that stage?

Well, I learned a great deal during that week. The attitudes of professionalism. The old cliché about the show going on. At one point a dancer was having a minor freak-out and running around breaking windows and throwing bottles and breaking mirrors while I'm trying to get into my costume to go onstage. But when her turn to dance came, she *danced*! I found out later her trouble wasn't drugs or anything like that. It's just that she'd been in Seattle three weeks.

It was up there that I learned things about the professional attitude that you never learn on Sweet Street. You have an obligation to the audience. You have to be on time. You have to have your shit together—and you can't go onstage still zipping up your dress or brushing your hair. You have to do your best, your *very best*, every time you go on, and if they don't like you, goddamn it, you work fuckin' harder and *make* 'em like you, and if they still don't like you, you smile and take your bows and walk off just as if they loved you. You can't take the attitude that the audience is a bunch of slobs and sex fiends and degenerates. No, *no*! They've paid their money, they've fulfilled their half of the contract, and I'm gonna fill mine.

But it's exhausting! When I got through my first show, I didn't know how I was gonna make it back to the dressing room. I was completely spent. I spent the next two days trying to figure a way out of the job without losing money. It was such a physical drag, because I wasn't in shape. And I was all alone. It was work all day, eat between shows, come home to my hotel room, take a bath, sleep, wake up and get ready for another show. Imagine spending all those days turning on men in the audience and then going home to an empty hotel room and taking a bath and washing my G-string! Terrible! Just dreadful!

Then New Year's Eve came along, and we worked really hard, lettering the Happy New Year signs on fluorescent cardboard, blowing up balloons to release at midnight, getting the whole trip together. We did seven shows that night, had our dinner brought in, and the management bought champagne for the cast. On the New Year's show at twelve-thirty, I was dancing fine. I got out of my dress, and I was twirling it around, and I hit a prop lamp post and it started to teeter. I'm still dancing, and I steadied the lamp post, turned around, and I heard this resounding crash! I gasped, and kept right on dancing. But it was just the right touch for the New Year's show for somebody to knock down a lamp post. *Antic!* That's part of professionalism, too, covering your fuck-ups. I'm sure the whole audience thought it was part of the script.

After the last show, at two A.M., we went to a cast party, and I met this really hot number of a cat, a really attractive man. I asked him to give me a ride home, and he drove me all around the city on the sightseeing tour. Fine! We were snuggling and cuddling in the car, and everything's groovy, just what I'd been missing for four days alone in the strange city. Then he took me back to my hotel room, and he sits on the chair across the room and talks polite nothings. Then he says, "Well, it's getting really late. I guess I should go."

I said, "Well, yeh, I guess so. I mean, you can stay if you want, but if you gotta go, go ahead on, you know?"

So he said, "Yeh, I gotta go," so I opened the door and he gave me a Happy New Year's kiss and walked away. I said to myself, Oh, shit, shit, shit! You blew another one, kiddo!

The next night I got a call, and it was him, and we started the same trip all over again, driving all over town and going back to my hotel room. Finally I said, "Hey, man, what *is* this trip? Why don't you sit down here beside me?" So he stayed the night, and like we spent three or four fantastic days together, and fell properly in love, the whole shebang, and when I went home we wrote love letters back and forth before the romance fell apart. *Wonderful!*

Well, I'll always have good feelings about burlesque. To

me it wasn't dirty or disgusting or tawdry at all. You can laugh, but to me it's a real art form. I mean, the audience knows you're gonna take off your clothes, right? But it's *how* you take them off. The MC says, "And now we present, direct from Portland, will you welcome with a big round of applause—the beautiful Josey!" Usually I'd be standing in the middle of the stage with the curtain open, and the footlights and overhead lights are on, and then all of a sudden the spotlight hits you, and you—are—on. YOU—ARE—*ON*! Everyone is watching *you*. It's *your* show. You are the center of attention and you do whatever you have to do in order to present a sexy, classy, graceful, appealing show. Everyone does it differently. There are strippers who walk, strippers who dance, strippers who clown, who do acrobatics, who juggle, who sing, who do all kinds of things. Baby Fran did a beautiful act, with walkovers and backbends and Japanese splits. She'd bend forward from the waist and touch her forehead on the floor. Amazing! Just amazing!

A good strip act is ass with class. You don't just take off your clothes and show 'em your body, like Sweet Street. You have to have little tricks and movements. I always admired Baby Fran, she had it all, and I copied a few of her movements, little things like arabesques, and I brought them back to Sweet Street, where nobody even notices them. Ah, that Baby Fran! She was *so* sweet. I would have loved to make it with Baby Fran, but I didn't because she's from Seattle and she's really straight and she would have freaked out and I would have lost a friend. I don't consider myself bisexual, but I admire her terrifically.

After our final performance, I was out of work again, and I went to Sweet Street to see what's happening. I still thought Sweet Street was big shit, Sweet Street was "making it." I went into the Heat Wave and the bartender asked to see me naked. Then he said, "Why don't you dance a number and we'll see how you look." After I danced, he said, "You got the job," and I went to work on a regular basis. It was hard work. I was both dancer and cocktail waitress, for fifteen dollars a day plus tips. Well, I got the applause as a dancer, but I seldom made any tips as a cocktail waitress. There was one girl that came from the tough part of town, and she didn't get applause, but she made a lot of money. She'd get pissed when they'd applaud for my dancing, and I'd say, "What're you fussing about? You're the one that's taking home the bread!"

She'd say, "Goddamn it, all they do is clap for you. The least you can do is clap for me, and then maybe the men will, too!"

I said, "Wow! Jesus! What an ego trip!"

The customers really weren't too much trouble. Occasionally I'd have to set somebody straight. "Say, listen, honey, the price of a drink does *not* include a free feel." Twice a day I'd get propositioned, and I'd usually say, "Thank you very much, but I'm not into that," and try to tell them how to find a whore. I'd say, "Look, I'm a dancer, I'm for looking at, but if you want somebody to take to bed, they walk up and down Sweet Street all the time." That usually worked.

I've had my ups and downs in the two years since then. I've even been fired, something I thought would *never* happen to me. There was a nutty manager at the Heat Wave—he was fired himself later on—and he told me I was a pushy, aggressive broad. He thought *everybody* was a pushy, aggressive broad. I mean, on Sweet Street, if you say "good morning" to a man before he says "good morning" to you, you're pushy and aggressive. So he took me to the side of the bar after the show one night and he said, "You're not gonna be working here any more."

I said, "What? *What?*"

He said, "I don't think you fit in around here."

I said, "What'd I do? What *is* this?"

He said, "Well, I don't think you're a good part of our crew."

I said, "Oh, yeh. Okay, Tim, thanks a lot, I'll see you."

The shock didn't hit me right away, but then I freaked. No shit! I had driven to work eight miles, struggled to find a parking space, walked four blocks to the club, all ready to work, and he tells me I'm fired. I spent half an hour running up and down the street looking for Buddy De Young so I could work somewhere, and I couldn't find him, and the shock set in bad. I started to cry. I said, "You've finally been fired. You—just—got—canned!" My friends comforted me.

Since then I've danced in two or three clubs and gotten along fine with everybody. It seems as though I keep doing more and more work for less and less money. We were supposed to get paid for all the rehearsal time at the Seven Seas, but we didn't get it. We were supposed to get a costume allowance, but we didn't get it. Bill Gold's attitude is if you don't do the job, somebody else will, maybe not as well, but what's the difference? His attitude is the public doesn't care who's on stage as long as it has two tits and a pussy. I've seen some dogs lately. Real dogs! And dummies, people who can't even remember what act they're doing.

I *know* I'm being used. Every dancer on this street knows it. I do too much work and I devote too much energy for twenty-five bucks a night. But we're all expendable. Half the time the bosses don't even know our names, and they have no respect for us. They keep tromping in and out of our dressing rooms indiscriminately, and they bring their friends, to take a look at the bodies! Really! And if we complain, we're pushy and aggressive! We're ballbreakers!

This work seems to age you fast. You use your facial muscles quite a bit, and you put on all that garbage every night and wear it for six or seven hours, indoors, smoky rooms. Oh, God! It *can't* be good for your lungs and your system. It *has* to age you. When I worked at that sleazy Heat Wave, I'd take my costume home and wash it out and the water'd just be gray and smell like cigarette smoke. Awful!

Well, Sweet Street is fucked, it's really fucked, and it's getting worse and worse. They're reaching the lowest type of customer, and they're paying their help less and less and charging more and more for the drinks. They're cutting their own throats. We have nights at the Seven Seas when the whole joint doesn't gross two hundred dollars. Why, these same clubs used to pack people in. They charged two drinks per show, and if you didn't order two more drinks, *out*! There was always somebody else waiting for your table. But in almost a year now I haven't seen one full house. There's too much nudity around, for one thing, and the naked body gets boring very fast. Sweet Street offers nothing to the imagination, it just gets grosser and grosser until it can't get any more. What happens next?

I wouldn't be here at all except that I desperately need money, because of certain disasters that have happened lately. I got busted. They really wanted my roommate. She was a social worker, always getting in the cops' hair. The cops' attitude is that these social workers are on the side of the creeps and the freaks and the dopers and the weirdos, the whores and the junkies. All the cops, but especially the narcs, hate social workers. And the thing they hate the most in the world is social workers who deal dope, and that's what my roommate was doing. She's the one that turned me onto speed, and we became good friends and roomies, and may I say I deeply regret the whole experience?

One morning these strange men knocked on my door and introduced themselves as friends of friends. Well, I didn't have anything to hide, so I invited them in for a cup of coffee. They said, "We're gonna do down to McDonald's for something to eat, and we'll be right back." Five minutes later a man knocks on the door and says, "Is Josey here?"

I said, "Yes," and he kicked the door in and cops came running in like those clowns that come out of the circus car, tons and tons of cops, in uniform and out, yelling things like, "Police! *Police!*"

My first impression was it's a bust, my second was it's a joke, and my third was it's *gotta* be a bust. I said, "Let me see your badge and search warrant," and one of the cops waved it in front of my face. They ransacked the place and found exactly two tabs of prescription codeine, two phenobarbital capsules, and an ounce and a half of marijuana, and behind that I got charged with three felonies and a misdemeanor! I copped to felony possession of marijuana, and I got thirty days in the county jail. *Me!* Me, with a clean sheet, never even had a traffic ticket! For my first offense, I get thirty days in jail. I screamed. *Ahhhh!* I'll die! I'm a felon now!

All this happened at the Hall of Justice. It's true, it's true, it's *true!* In the Hall of Justice the only justice is in the hall. The whole thing cost me nine hundred dollars for an attorney and several months of head hassles, but still I got off better than my roommate, and she wasn't even there for the bust. She got one to ten years, which means she'll have to serve at least six months. That's what happens to social workers that deal dope!

I don't understand the law. I consider myself a nice self-respecting doper, causing harm to no one. I do my job, and I make enough money to cop whatever dope I want, and I figure that as long as I'm not stealing or dealing, I'm cool.

I like grass well enough, but it's a little too obvious and too bulky, and now that I'm living back with my parents I can't try to smoke it in the house. I used to be a speed freak, but I quit that three or four years ago. Downers are my favorite: Seconal, Quaalude. That's second best to junk, heroin. Oh, yeh, I do junk. I've never gotten strung out on it, and I keep my junk habit entirely to myself. Nobody on Sweet Street knows about it. If anybody's ever noticed my tracks, they haven't said anything.

I've been on dope for almost four years now. My boy friends used to shoot it, and I always used to knock it, but then I decided I couldn't knock it without at least trying it once. So I stuck out my arm and looked the other way and my boy friend shot some speed in my arm. I flashed! There was a zinging sensation all over my body. It felt good! I was speeded up to the gills, buzzing all over the place. They decided to really do me up right later that night. They said how much do you weigh and they were gonna calculate the convulsive dosage and give me just a pinch less. They said, "We're gonna *really* do you this time!"

I said, "Okay, okay, far out!"

They put the needle in and all of a sudden, *whoosh*! The top of my head started to fly off! There was blue light in front of me, and it was like I had butterfly wings, and I started flashing on and off, and it was like a fifteen-minute total body orgasm. Ooooh, wow! Not fast, but slow and quiet and orgasmic. Not just good, but fuckin' orgasmic!

Each time I shot up after that it was a positive reinforcing experience, and that's how you get hooked. Then I got a roaring case of serum hepatitis and went to the hospital and quit everything except smoking dope. But then toward the end of 1970 some of my friends copped some junk, a whole lot of it, and they invited me over to their pad, and said, "Here, have some."

I said, "Fine, far out." It was really a pleasant trip, a pleasant mellow setting, a nice beautiful place, a nice house, lawn, and very pleasant company. I didn't get nauseated or anything, and I felt fine. I wasn't worried about becoming addicted, 'cause I'm not oriented that way. I can take things or ignore them. Like I had Quaalude up to my ears one time, and they're addictive, and when I ran out I just ran out. So what? Big deal, you know?

I like junk now. If I had enough money and it was legal, I'd get strung out in no time. I love it! It's basically not bad for you. Speed *is* bad for you, it rots your brains, rots your teeth, produces toxic psychosis and paranoia. You can't sleep, you can't eat. But with junk, man, I can do everything. I can function quite well. It's just terribly expensive.

It's good for most things, but it's not a good sex drug. It may be good for foreplay, but it's bad for the actual intercourse, especially for the man. Even in me, too, I can never come when I'm on heroin, no matter how healthy my liver is. Junk is the best analgesic known to man. It deadens everything, including your sexual sensitivities.

I've been doing it on and off now for several years. I go off it when I feel like it, and I never have any withdrawal symptoms. I figure if I eat properly and sleep properly, I can be a junkie for years, especially if I don't burn out all my veins. Look at how good my veins are! I haven't even used one of them up yet. I figure I've got about three more years on Sweet Street, and I can handle it okay for that long.

No, I don't worry about becoming a junkie. Yes, I do, sometimes. Lately I've been needing a little more.

Dancer

PANIC ON SWEET STREET. Two dancers have called in sick at the Paris Lido, and Buddy De Young is scraping the bottom of his reserve supply. At last he fills the final vacancy. Angel Perkins, a shoe clerk who has never danced before, arrives fifteen minutes before show time, a frail and dainty brown-haired girl with a finely wrought face and dominating cocoa-colored eyes. She says she is twenty-six, but she looks like a teenager. "Okay, kid," Buddy De Young says, "just go out there and show a lot of beaver."

I came here three years ago from New Jersey, just to see the country. I spent one year on unemployment and one year as a file clerk. *Yuck!* Now I sell shoes, and I don't make enough money to get by, so I decided to do a little moon-lighting. The Heat Wave hired me, but after I saw a few of their acts I didn't show up. They had one about a virgin bride who did a tremendous amount of giggling. The show was humiliating, degrading, ridiculous, and absurd. There was all this dumb talk about being a virgin, and you wore a little white veil. No way they were gonna get me to go onstage and do that!

I guess that's how they got my name on their list, and when Mr. De Young called me, I said I'd be willing to give it a try at the Paris Lido. The dressing room was something. There was a fat black girl, and Mr. De Young came down and made some comment about her dancing, and she took it to mean she was gonna be fired, and she didn't have a high school education and she'd just had a baby, and she was bawling her eyes out. All the other dancers were completely insensitive to her. One named Sally Bob Somebody told her to shut up and dance. I told the poor thing to just collect welfare and go to school someplace, but she said she's not into going to school. Just totally ignorant, I guess. She told me she couldn't even hold a job as a waitress, 'cause she couldn't talk right. Pathetic! But personally I don't think she had any complaint coming. If you're gonna do something like dancing naked, you should be in shape, and she wasn't. If I'd had her body, I wouldn't even have applied.

I wasn't afraid about going out on stage, in fact it really felt good. I got high doing it! I mean, I wouldn't do it at a party, and I wouldn't think of walking up and down the street naked, but onstage it's sort of safe and impersonalized, and it's a fun way to make a few extra dollars. It's fun to turn the men on, very safe, and then not have to take the responsibility.

On my first number, I came out in little exercise slippers, and the bartender whispered, "Get those shoes off!"

I just leaned over and told him, "Fuck off!" After that, nobody gave me any problems. The swing broke under me when I was doing the lost-in-space act, but that didn't bother me. The whole thing was so ridiculous anyway, that I should be out there naked on a swing. Who's gonna get embarrassed when the swing breaks?

I wonder what it means that I like it when people are watching me naked. I'm still trying to figure it out. I'm about to go back to my therapist for one more session. I suppose it means I'm an exhibitionist, but isn't everybody? Some people are just more hung up than others.

I do know I enjoy stripping. I'm thinking seriously about a career as a dancer. It really felt good! I got high! Maybe I'll get a manager and try to work some private shows, things like that. I've had fantasies about becoming a big-time dancer ever since that night. I see myself in Las Vegas, surrounded by a huge chorus and all these white feathers and pink spotlights. It's become my goal. Do you think I can make it?

The Ladies of Night

I walk by Sweet Street every morning and night, and I've represented a lot of the people there. It used to be a whorehouse area, saloons and bars, real bust-out. A regular Tenderloin red-light district. The streetcar conductor used to say, "All out for the whorehouses!" William Randolph Hearst was the one that harpooned the whorehouses. I guess he thought fucking was too good for the common people. He was gonna reserve it for himself and Marion. He ran the crusade that put the cribs out of business.

Well, I hope we keep 'em working. You need whores in any city. Of course, they're a little too expensive for the high school children who need whores the most. But I say more power to 'em. They're just what the town needs.

—Elliot Brown, lawyer

NANCY DAVIS ("ROYAL"), 25

Prostitute

Fortunately analysis is not the only way to resolve inner conflicts.
Life itself still remains a very effective therapist.

—Karen Horney, M.D.

MIDNIGHT SATURDAY. THE CITY is drawing itself in for the
night, but Sweet Street continues to seethe: a neoned anthill
drenched in mist. Barkers work in caldrons of noise, and in
their competitive Dexedrine frenzies even shout at strollers
across six lanes of honking, fuming traffic. Prostitutes are
cruising the sidewalks in twos and threes, trying to break luck
and appease their pimps, and close behind are undercover policemen, whistling merry tunes and smiling like rubes, as each
side plays the nightly game of trying to penetrate the other's
cover. At Raffaele's every outside table and most of the inside tables are flush with revelers. Raffaele and Rocco and
Mickey Martin and a few cronies sit around chewing old
bones: the dismal future of the local professional football
team and the sexual orientation of a television reporter.

Suddenly customers jump up from the outside tables,
stream to the sidewalk, and peer down the block. Sirens
growl in the distance, and at this official portent Rocco
sprints through the door like an Olympic dash champion. A
minute or two pass, then a pair of middle-aged men come
staggering down the street, hands pressed to faces, blood oozing between their fingers. One drops his hands momentarily,
revealing a crimson slash from hairline to chin, like the loser
in a duel of sabers. The other man, nicked around the cheek,
gives uncertain support, and the two sufferers lurch unaided
around the corner and out of sight.

279

Another four or five minutes pass. Two ."harness bulls," uniformed policemen, engage in spitting exegesis with several overdressed women, their brightly sequined dresses and loud costume jewelry and long wigs attesting to their occupation. Then the women strut off, the policemen ease back into their "black-and-white," and the denizens of Raffaele's, chattering and clucking about the free entertainment, resume their seats in front of steaming cups of *caffé latté* and mountainous plates of lasagna and daintily upturned thimbles of Galliano and green Chartreuse and other adult entertainments.

Rocco returns to report the news. "These two guys with foreign accents are walking up the street in search of some fuckin' pussy," he begins with his customary grace and style. "Down walks Royal the spade whore and another spade whore name of Wanda and a white whore, I don't know her name, and these two foreign guys accost 'em. The one guy's got a heat on, he can hardly stand up, and the other guy's been drinking and he's teedely toddely too. So this spade broad in the middle—Wanda, she's a dangerous motherfucker Wanda—she says, 'You guys got any money?'

"The guy says, 'I gotta mooney, I gotta mooney.'

"She says, 'I don't believe it. If you got no money, you can't even talk to me.'

"He says, 'You gotta big titties?'

"She says, 'Yeh, I got big titties. Now lemme see your money.'

"So the guy takes his wallet out and she makes a grab for it, right there on the street. She's gonna take the money and make a quick getaway.

"But he reaches down and grabs her by the hair and her wig comes off, and she's got that short frizzy hair. He grabs ahold of her by the sweater, and she reaches in her pocket and pulls out a penknife and *zum zum zum*, she makes hamburger on his face. Slit his cheek open and then sliced the other guy.

"The police car come along, and the guys told the cops, 'Forget about it. We don't want to prefer charges,' and they take off, and that's it. That's the whole thing."

"Who told you all that?" Mickey Martin inquires.

"Who told me?" Rocco answers, a puzzled look crossing

his heavy features. "Why, you dumb asshole, nobody told me. But I know it happened that way. It *had* to happen that way. That's the way it *always* happens."

Hey, that's not the way it went down! Hey, that Rocco don't know nothing! Why doesn't that stupid dago keep his mouth shut? Hey, I *know*, I was *there*! One of the old dudes made a nasty remark about Wanda. She shoved at him and she said, "Hey, you don't know me, man!" More words were exchanged and then he shoved her and called her a black bitch. So Wanda hit him with her umbrella and the guys began slugging and swinging with their fists. I mean, they were really dukin' there, all out, like they were fighting with men. Hey, it was a free-for-all, and then Wanda got kicked in her stomach and she let them have it with a knife. Hey, it was ugly, but hey, it happened. What was she suppose to do—let those big ugly gorillas stomp her to death?

THE LADY THAT'S KNOWN as Royal can usually be depended upon to cut through rumor and hyperbole to the heart of Sweet Street history and current events, sparing no sensibilities in the process. Once in a public restaurant she referred to a local civic leader as a "ten-dollar whore," and was immediately asked if that was any way to talk about a director of the civic opera, deaconess of the church, patron of the arts, and leading philanthropist. Royal answered, "Yes, that's the way to talk about a ten-dollar whore."

"Well, I never!" said the socialite's defender, flouncing off.

"Yes, you ever!" Royal called in her rich, mellifluous voice. "Hey, you *ever*! You a fi' dollar whore yourse'f!"

The volatile Royal and her infant son have just been forced by an unspeakable event to move into a one-room apartment in the black part of town, and she is defensive about it. "I'm accustom to living like a movie star," she says, "but not now. Right now I'd be better off on the welfare. I'm down in the dumps, but you gotta take the goods and the bads. A coupla years ago I was paying $450 a month for bedrooms I never even slep' in, only moved my wardrobes. I used to give things away: wigs, hats, leather coats, suede jackets, dresses, after one wear. When I got tired of sumpin, I'd give it away and replace it."

A whole corner of the temporay new apartment is devoted to children's toys: a train, a toy phonograph, records, hobby horses, a plastic tricycle, trucks, play telephones, dolls, hammering kits, games, Teddy bears and pandas and other gewgaws, bulging in one large mound halfway to the ceiling. The rightful owner of this treasure, Benjy AKA Bird, twenty three months and two weeks old, walks in tightening circles around his mother, makes squeaking noises like a baby song sparrow, and keeps a wary coal-black eye on strangers. He is dressed in a sailor suit straight out of Saks Fifth Avenue with matching blue tennis shoes that look about three and a half inches long and are always coming unlaced. A perfect hemisphere of Afro hair-do frames his tiny face in tight black spirals. Now he stops, ominously, and begins to pull his pants down. "Bird," Royal says softly, "why is it you just like to pull your pants off and let your little bootie hang out! Huh? What *is* it with you? I don't want you to grow up to be no kind of freak or nothing."

The child sniffs a few times and walks spraddle-footed to his mother. "Oh, I see," Royal says. "You pee-peed, that's what it is. Poor sweet thing. He went through such a little trauma when his father left, and he began to wet again. I guess that was his only means to express hisse'f. At first I didn't understand and I spanked him, but lately I've been giving him a lot of love and he really don't peepee on hisse'f much now. He just needed a *whole* lot of love."

Nancy Davis looks like the idealization of every native woman in every sultry South Seas movie produced by Hollywood in the thirties and forties, except that she is real, not a white starlet in brownface. Her sable eyes are set far apart and slanted a few degrees. Her nose is slightly flattened and her nostrils flared wide. Her high cheekbones push against a tawny-brown skin completely devoid of blemish. Her gleaming white teeth are even, and her lips are full and moist. Her make-up is carefully understated, as are her clothes, except when she is wearing the necessary advertisements of her profession. Her hair is a mystery; Royal is partial to wigs, owns several dozen, and is never seen in the wig-less state. "Hey, I got a wig for *every* occasion," she says. "I got blond, red-head, black, auburn, chestnut, platinum, whatever. I got a long blond showgirl wig that cost $150 and a bouffant wig and several Afro wigs like the one I'm wearing now. The Afro's one of my favorites, especially when I'm in my own neighborhood. This one cost five fingers. Five fingers, you dig? That means somebody stole it for me."

Sometimes Royal wears stacked hair-pieces that make her look long and statuesque as she preens at Raffaele's bar, but the illusion dies when she gets off the high stool. She is five feet four inches tall, "most of it in my legs," and the other Sweet Street prostitutes tower over her. But Royal makes up in volume and energy what she lacks in physical stature. After a warm-up drink or two, she begins holding court in highly dramatic manner. Her elocution is like the political commentator William F. Buckley's, tending toward abrupt stops and starts and shadings of emphasis. Sometimes she speeds up her words and runs them all together, then slams on the brakes and lowers her voice almost to a whisper, moving into a herky-jerky cadence accented by frequent interpolations of "hey," her favorite word. The whole performance is marred only slightly by a tendency to pronounce a few words like the Cockneys of London and the blacks of the deep South: "birfday," "wiv'out," "mouf'." Her delivery does not translate easily from spoken to written word. "Hey," she says, "the manager at my new place's really sumpin! Like he don't know what-I-do-for-a-living-yet, dig? But—he's—gonna—find—*out*! He's so naïve! Hey. *Hey*! Listen! The other night this white cat takes me home in a—

"Pink . . .

"Cadillac . . .

"Convertible.

"Are you ready for this? Hey, are you *ready*? The dude gives me some money, and the manager says, 'Who was that?'

"I says, 'That's my boss.'

"The next night another cat brings me home in a—

"Black . . .

"Lincoln . . .

"Continental . . .

"Wiv' a moonroof? You dig? and I tell the manager,

'That's my other boss.' He says, 'Gee, you sure got a lot of bosses!' "

These tales are accented by broad sweeps of arm, jumpings up and down, and loud laughs and hand-claps. Like Rocco, Royal is a café minstrel, and her prospective customers are often treated to long hours of effervescent conversation before she will allow the subject of carnal knowledge to intrude. "I'm not interested in no quick turnover," she says. "I want a man to wine me right out in the open, and *then* we'll do business, maybe yes and maybe no. You can't wallow in the alley with me and not want to come out in the light, because I could never count on you after that. Hey, I don't want customers that just roll in the hay. Hey, if that's what you want, then the best thing I can do for you is get you one of these little jive hookers down on the back streets!"

Sometimes Royal's lengthy reminiscences sound like Grade B scenarios, sometimes like the golden dreams and cotton-candy fantasies of a deprived child, sometimes like the everyday horrors of the poor and oppressed. Are her stories gilded? Only Royal knows. Perhaps there are resemblances to Utrillo's mother, Suzanne Valadon: "She believed it herself just as she came half to believe anything about the past, not knowing (and not caring) where the facts and the fantasies had become confused. Truth or reality lay in the pictures she had produced . . . Where else it lay was unimportant."*

Or as the matter was put in Sweet Street style by Raffaele, one of Royal's patron saints and defenders, "Royal is the epitome of the whores. Their stories are all the same: they started at twelve or thirteen because somebody raped them, an uncle or somebody they trusted. Some of it is bullshit, some of it is true. What's the difference, as long as they believe it themselves?"

Hey, my family life was so confusing, I wouldn't even try to sort it out myself. My real mother I hardly knew. She was an addict, and she was always into her own thing. When I was seven or eight, she just dropped out the picture. Then my father married a Mexican woman, and we went to live in

* John Storm, *The Valadon Drama* (New York: Dutton, 1959).

East Los Angeles, and I had a new stepsister, Haydee. I was a little black kid, and Haydee was a Mexican, ten years older than me, and she treated me so nice, she loved me right from the start. Hey, she'd had her troubles! She'd been in a school for girls, and she was a butch, dressed in men's clothes, and she was very prohibited about everything. She really showed me affection, and I just loved her right off. I guess I was looking for love, 'cause I didn't get all that much.

After a while, Haydee started stepping in between me and my stepmother, which was her real mother. My stepmother would have other men, and sometimes she'd take me in the car when she went to meet them. Then we'd get back home and my stepmother would put me in the bathtub and whup me with this big belt. "If you open your mouth and tell your daddy where we been, I'll beat your little ass." What could I say? I was seven or eight. I said, "Okay."

One day she was whupping me for nothing, she was drunk, and Haydee came home from school and made her stop. She'd say, "No, Mommy, no! Mommy, you can't hit Nancy, you're drunk," and my stepmother called her a pervert and they had a big fight, and all I could do was cry, 'cause it seemed like it was my fault. And then Haydee would cuddle me and hug me, and I'd play with my two canary birds and my stray dog. Something to love, you know? Dogs! I had dogs forever.

It wasn't even six months before my sister and I got *that* close, both of us needing something to love, hey, and this was it. She'd take me on her dates with lesbians, and they'd buy me Hershey's kisses and her and her girl friend would be kissing and hugging in the front seat and me eating my chocolates in the back. A lot of times the girl friend would want to get it on, but Haydee would always say, "No, no, not over my little sister."

But hey, she had a hard life, you know? Prohibited from this, prohibited from that, and being a lesbian you're just always against the grain. She used to get these terrible depressions. One morning she was in the restroom and I pushed the door open and she was cutting her wrists. I started screaming when I saw the blood. I was patting her wrists to make the blood stop. Somebody called the police, and Haydee told them, "I was getting ready to kill myself, but my baby sister means so much to me. My mother would beat hell outa her if it wasn't for me, and I'm not gonna leave my baby sister 'cause I want her to grow up wiv' a good life. She's all I have to live for."

I really went through a thing behind that, because now I knew how you made blood come outa yourself, and one day I tried to do it, too, but Haydee stopped me. Hey, I tried to do everything Haydee did, *everything*, because I loved her so much. If she said, "I'm going bye-bye," I'd say, "I'm going, too," and like hey, I wanted to be with her every second. She was just my knight on shining armor in a pant, you know? If you wanted to do anything bad to me, you had to whup Haydee's ass first, 'cause she was good with a knife, and she wasn't afraid to fight men and women both.

One night it was very drab, and there'd been a big family fight. It was raining, and Haydee sat there and looked at me for a long time. I was playing on the floor, and pretty soon she said, "Hey, it's time to go to bed." I whined and whimpered, and after a while she tucked me in and she said, "After I go bye-bye tonight, give this to Daddy," and she hands me a note all folded up. She says, "Now remember, don't give it to nobody but Daddy." She started out the door and when I tried to follow, she said, "No, no, Chiquita! Not this time." She pushed me back, really hard, and I couldn't understand this, this was sumpin new, she'd never denied me her attentions before this. I looked at her, and I knew within my heart that if I let Haydee go I'm never gonna see her again.

She went out to the car and I ran after her, and I'm hanging on the latch, and she's saying, "No, Chiquita, *no!*" and crying real loud.

I says, "No, don't leave, I'm not gonna see you no more."

She pushes me away, crying, really crying, and I'm crying 'cause she's crying, and she just hauled off and slapped me, and she said, "I said go. *Go!* I don't love you no more."

I said, "No, no, Haydee, you love me. You love me, and I love you."

She slaps me again and knocks me down, and she says, "I hate you! I hate you, you little black girl!" and she jumped inside the car and drove off, and I stood out on the street and I screamed and cried. After a while my father drove up from work, and he took me back off the curb, and I handed him the note.

He says, "Oh, my God!" and the phone rang and he ran to answer it. Then he told me to stay in the house, he had to go someplace. I said, "No," and so he takes me with him, and we drive to a place three or four miles away and there's Haydee's car with all the police around it, and my father tries to lock me in our car and he runs over to the police. So I get out and go around the other side of Haydee's car to see what's happening.

My sister's head was lying alongside. I picked it up and cradled it in my lap. Her body was still on the front seat, and I'm sitting in the gutter rubbing her head. I'm telling her, "Wake up, Haydee! Wake up! Where are you, Haydee? *Wake up!*" It wasn't for a long time that I understood what she'd done. She stuck her head out the window and cranked up the handle and stepped on the gas. That way she knocked her head completely off her neck. I guess she wanted to make sure she didn't just get a gash in the head. I never did know what the note said.

Right after the accident they put me in a mental hospital for six or eight months. At first I had to be fed intravenously. I did a lot of fantasizing and dreaming. A guy'd be chasing me, and I'd run out the window of this hundred-story building and fall down and down, and when I got to the bottom this guy'd still be chasing me. And I was forever thinking about death and fire. Still do. Nothing's been the same since. I dreamt of Haydee for a whole year. If I met somebody that looked the least little bit like Haydee, I'd burst into tears.

When I got out the hospital, my father sent me to live with my grandmother in Detroit. They were down-to-earth people from Georgia and they couldn't understand a kid that lied and fantasied a lot. I kept saying, "My daddy coming to get me in a Cadillac." I didn't understand how they ate things like powdered eggs, and cornbread and okra. Hey, the first time I saw okra I almost threw up. And brains, and chitlins. I thought, *Gaw!* They gimme some cornbread and I choked on it. And beans, greens, pig ears, pig feet, neckbones, we never had no food like that back in East L.A.

Altogether in that little house there was me, four other children, a aunt, a uncle, my grandmother, and an occasional friend that would stop in and stay a few months. The rest were dogs, lots of dogs. It was a filthy place, and I was always being made to get down on my hands and knees and scrub it. That's the trip my grandmother put me on. I guess she was trying to make something outa me. Maybe she thought I was such a 'bitual liar or whatever, 'cause when I got a whupping I got *four* whuppings, and then they'd make me clean the house all day. My grandmother would never allow me to play, and my cousin used to chase me with the gardener snake, and they was always glorifying my cousin Annette. I was getting A's and B's on my report card, and they was glorifying Annette. I worked hard to get the A's and B's for approval, but then I never got the approval. So I'd try to get approval from my teachers, but by the time I got into the ninth grade, I was in a bad class of teachers, you know? They didn't like children that were too inquisitive, they just wanted a bunch of dummies to sit there and shut up till the bell rang. Like I'd ask a question, and they'd say, "All right, Nancy, that's enough," and I'd say, "Well, I'm *trying* to understand, and I want you to hallucidate a little further for me," and they'd say, "You're disrupting the class," and I'd say, "Hey, I'm just trying to find sumpin out! I come here to *learn*." And I'd end up in the office with Miss Collins, and she'd call me a arrogant little black bitch and hit me with the terribilest paddle in the world, a long heavy paddle with air holes in it, and they'd suck into you and hurt all the more, and hey, I felt it was unjustifiable, and one time she hit me and I let her have it right in the face, and there was all kinds of trouble.

Two weeks before my thirteenth birfday, I ran from that life. On a street corner I met this black dude named Larry and I told him I ran away from home and I didn't want to go back, and he was very gentle with me and took me to his room. His brother came on real strong, but Larry protected me, and that knocked me out, and I said, "Okay, I'll stay with you for a while." Larry was a little dense, he'd been in the penitentiary and he was very illiterate, very immature, for a grown man. Like I asked him a question about some law, some rules, and he said, "I don't want to hear about that shit." He was just ignorant, but I figured he hadn't had a chance to go to school, it wasn't his fault, and so I would condone him. He can't help hisse'f.

Pretty soon he asked me if I ever had a man before, and I said no. He put me in his bed and he began screwing me very very hard, through my rectum. I'd never heard about that before. I'd had sex education, but they weren't giving up that much information. He just put me in a crouching position and held both his arms under me to pin me in position, and then he just rammed and rammed and rammed, like he was doing it to a grown woman, really pounding me, and while he's pounding he's calling all these little derogatories—"You're gonna be my little bitch! I'm gonna turn you out to be a dog, little bitch! You gonna be my star whore."

I was screaming, I only weighed eighty-nine pounds wet, but nobody came to help me. People in Detroit are like that—they'll hear a person screaming for his life, and they'll just close their ears.

After he did that to me, I told him, "I want to go home. I don't want to be with you 'cause you hurt me."

He said, "You're not going anywhere." He takes me down to the street and he's dragging me along, and I'm screaming and hollering, and I guess he figured that was unsafe, so he takes me back inside and threatens me. He scared me so bad that he could leave me upstairs in his room and I would be scared to pick up the phone. He promised to kill me ten times a day, and he'd beat me up and hurt me and then start screwing me in my rectum again, for hours and hours till I was really sick, feverish, just weak and sore all over.

Then one night he drug me down to the corner of Canfield and John R., that's where all the whores hang out in Detroit, and he set me down on a packing crate waiting for my first customer. He brought the johns around to look at me, and then they'd take me in their cars out to the country. At first it felt so good to sit in a car, on a soft seat, 'cause my rear end hurt, and then we'd get out in the country and they'd

park the car and say, "Hey, what's wrong wit' chew?" and I
would say, "I'm sick."

A white guy drove me out on Eight Mile Road, and when
we parked he pulled out a hammer, but he didn't hit me
'cause I guess I just looked so pitiful to him, El Weirdo and
all. First he said, "I'm gonna beat your ass," but then he kept
looking at me and he says, "You're not gonna try to run
away or anything?"

I said, "Mister, I'm sick, I'm sick. Would you please help
me?"

He turned on the light and he took a good look at me and
he said, "I couldn't see you before, but you're just a baby.
How old are you?"

I didn't have enough sense to lie. I told him, "I just had a
birfday. I'm thirteen. I'm sick. Would you help me? Would
you give me a aspirin?"

He said, "I'm gonna take you back," and I kept on telling
him all the way back, "Please don't leave me, don't leave
me!"

Larry musta thought he had a gold mine now. All day long
he kept me locked up in his room, and at night he'd turn me
out at Canfield and John R., and in between he'd screw me in
the rectum. I kept getting sicker and sicker, and one day I
just crawled to the phone and called my cousin and told him
I was being kept in a room.

He said, "Where are you? Get up and look out the window
and tell me what you see."

I said, "I can't."

He said, "Why can't you?"

I said, "I'm sick, I hurt, I can't walk."

He begins screaming at me. "Where are you? *Where are
you?*" And finally he tells me to just lie there and leave the
phone off the hook so he could put a police tracer on it.
Pretty soon Larry comes back in with a sandwich for me,
and then we hear a voice down the hall, "Open up! Police!"

Larry grabs me by the mouf' and he says, "You better not
say nothing. Shut up! Shut up!" I squirmed loose and
screamed, "Help me, help me, I want my cousin!" The police
rushed in just as Larry's lifting me up, and this big cop turns
him around and hit him to where his body almost went

through the wall. The big cop looked at me and he said, "Oh, my God!" He turned to Larry and he said, "You bastard, if you do this to her, I can just imagine what you'd do to my child. That's a *baby* lying there!" And he starts pounding Larry's head to the point where the other officer's trying to hold him back.

Then all of a sudden the big cop gets gentle, and he picks me up, and I'm screaming, "Oh, my God, save me, save me!" He picks me up, and he says, "It's gonna be all right, baby, don't worry. I'm gonna take care of you. You can trust me. I'm your friend." Pretty soon he begins asking me, "Did that guy have you? Did he have you down there?" Like he's talking to an infant.

I said, "He had me sexually. We had sexual intercourse."

He said, "Oh, you're smart, too! Bless your heart!"

By the time they got me to the car I was screaming from the pain of being moved, and the big policeman was in tears. I hate to think about the shape I was in, it's so repulsive. I had stuff secreting from me, I got a odor that won't wait, and like, hey, my stomach was all bloated. And I'm so hot and feverish that I had a reddish tint on my skin, and I'm prespiring and eyes all bloodshot, and I'm bruised badly around the face.

Well, it was a long case, and good old Officer Eddie stuck with me right through the hospital phase and every other phase. Larry was sentenced to natural life. In the trial Larry's lawyer tried to say that I was an incorrigible child, but Officer Eddie he told the court, "She's just a mixed up, confused child and needs a break." He says, "Hey, and you don't need to lock her up." So I'm paroled in his custody and the first thing he does is take me for a tour of the jail. He says, "Look here, this is the life you were getting ready to go to." He showed me junkies puking up, and when I tried to turn away he snatched my head and made me look. Then he took me to the hole. He said, "You wanna know where the restroom at in here? On the floor!"

I said, "Where's the bed at?"

He said, "Same place." He said, "You wanna go in there?" and he shoves me inside and slams the door and he says, "How you like it in there?"

I says, "I thought you was my friend!"

So after a while he let me out, and he said, "If this is what you want I'll take you right back to the corner of Canfield and John R. and one of the patrol cars'll pick you up and I'll see you here tomorrow."

I said, "I wanna go back to school. I wanna go back to my grandmother's." So he took me home, and after that he came to see me, and I spent a lot of time with him and his family. Officer Eddie. I'll never forget him.

Things went all right for a while, but then there was a big family fight, and one of the relatives shot me in the knee, tore the flesh all off, laid the bone wide open. Look here. See all that scar tissue? After that I got hysterical and crazy, and they sent me to the hospital for ninety days, in the mental ward, and when I came back home everybody called me crazy all the time, and they put a rod in my knee and it hurt.

My daddy came and brought me back to LA, only it was worse this time. It was another messed-up house, he'd remarried, and he kept two of his wives home, and some of the kids belonged to one mother and some to the other, and it was just a lot of hassle all the time. One day one of my half-sisters said, "You need to go back to juvenile court, you little black——" Then she interrupted herself.

I said, "You were gonna call me a black bitch, weren't you?" and I just launched right into her. That was the first time I ever fought anybody. She was twenty-seven years old and I whipped her ass, I beat her ass good. And my stepmother came in and started hollering at me, and I said, "The hell wit chew, too, fat lady! You big fat out of proportion nothing you! You're a zero!" She ran to the phone to call the police, and I ran away and got caught, and the rest of my childhood I just watched TV and went to school.

Right after I graduated high school I got a job dancing in a club, and then I became a topless dancer, and I won an exotic dance contest and danced in costume after that, and I was billed at places like the Whiskey A Go Go. Once I asked this other dancer, "Hey, why do you be so groovy all the time, always groovy?"

She said, " 'Cause I pop pills."

So I took one that night, and it was a sleeping pill, a Tuinal, and I really came on strong on the dance floor, I just forgot about everything, I was in this haze. Pretty soon this cat walks in and he begins playing for me, and I said, "Like you wait for me after." The other dancers were shocked! I was always the one that would have nothing to do with men. It blew their mind.

I went to a motel with this cat, and we were dancing to the radio, and then I came down from the pill and started crying. I said, "I don't know what I'm doing here with you. I don't even know what a orgasm is."

He's saying, "What?"

I said I didn't know how to go about sex, other than to be used and abused.

So he says, "Well, you can do it if you want to." He's talking to me and talking to me, and finally I tried it, and it wasn't bad. I said, "Ummmmm, how about that!" And the guy left me a hundred dollars. I said to myself, "That's pretty nice." So I seen him a couple times after that for the money. But other than that I wasn't having any sex life, and I certainly wasn't turning any tricks.

Then I met Aaron, and he was sumpin else. He had almost killed a boy in a fight, and he'd served big time in the penitentiary, but now he was straight. He was selling ladies' clothes for a living. He'd claim they were hot, but they really weren't, 'cause people will pay more for things they think are illegal. He'd go out and buy a whole lot of clothes wholesale, and then he'd say, "These boots are hot. I'm gonna let you have 'em cheap. Thirty dollars." He'd use fake price tags and all, and he was making a lot of money.

Well, you would not believe how intelligent Aaron was. We intercoursed verbally for a month! So refreshing. And hey, we would discuss the administration of Cambodia, and oh, hey! *hey!* it would be beautiful, and I was absorbing everything he said. To me he looked just about perfect, just what I was looking for. He didn't smoke or drink, he never spoke about prostitution, and I left it out of my talk, too. I told him everything else about myself, about my chronic heart trouble, my asthma, and I guess I got his sympathy. And he was such a good-looking cat. When he walked down the street they all stared at him, white, black, purple, green, yellow, all of the women turn 'round and drool! He was very masculinely build, only slightly bowlegged.

One day we went to the motel, and tried out sex together, and I didn't reach a climax. I said to myself, "Well, maybe I was just looking for it too hard." I told him I had a big orgasm, I put on a act, and I was such a faker. I said, "Yes, I'll marry you, Aaron."

The day we went to get married he was looking at me so loving, so sweet. I just thought this guy's got to be too much. After the ceremony, we come outside on the courthouse steps, and I'm looking up at him, and I just know I'm gonna get a little kissypoo, and he slaps me in the face! Then he whirls me around and bends over behind me and kisses me on the cheek and kicks me in my ass, and he says, "You're mine now. And I got to have my money each and every night, fresh money." He says, "That's how it is, or else go back inside."

I went home and I stayed a week, but I was hung up on him, and I went back and said, "What do I do to get the money?"

He said, "Don't ask me what you do. Just go out and get it!"

I said, "Hell, I'm making three hundred a week dancing. What's wrong wit' that?"

Well, that wasn't enough for him. He wanted to live the fast life, and I made him the money to do it.

This went on for a few years, and he had other women, too. There was women laying all over the place, and then I found out he had a habit, and he was kicking our asses right and left to make money, and one night I counted up how many women it took to keep him in his habit, and it was fourteen—thirteen others and me, and half of us wondering where he was gonna sleep that night, and him going around full of junk.

One night he almost killed one of the girls, and he broke his arm and had to go around in a cast, and I came home and looked at this pitiful thing and I said, "Listen, you punk fag motherfucker, I'm full of red devils, and what you gonna do about it? You're a fuckin' junkie, and you ain't no man. You been professing to be a man all this fuckin time, but you're not shit. You just live off women. You're lower than a gigolo. I'm ready to kick your ass." I weighed 102, and he weighed 198, but I was full of reds.

He says, "Little bitch!" and when he said that I hit him with all my weight. It came up from my toes and surged all the way through my arm, and I knocked him completely across the bed.

He was shocked, "What wrong wit chew?"

I said, "I'm gonna kill you, you bastard. You been kicking my ass for the last three years. You been pimping my drawers off, boy, and I been going for it, and you been taking my money and belittling me and degrading me, you know? You've had me selling my bod to every Tom, Dick and Harry. I've come home bloody and all you asked me was how much money you got. Now I'm about to have your ass!"

I got me a sawed-off shotgun he had and I just chased him and beat him and beat him and beat him and beat him and beat him. I kicked the door completely off the hinges going after him, and I picked up a bureau and threw it at him. Then while he was trying to figure out where I'm getting the strength at, this little weasel he'd been kicking around, I put on some clothes and I told him, "See yeh," and walked out.

Well, I left with nothing, but I guess God take care of all fools and babies. It wasn't long before I had me another man, and I was just twenty-two years old, and my new man was a con man, a bunco artist, and it really pays off. Oh, yes, it do! He could go out and spend thirty minutes and come back with ten thousand, fifteen thousand dollars, and he had me and other girls working for him, too, but he didn't need us, and it used to give me a hangup 'cause I was competing against him to see who could make the most money and he'd just go out and tell one lie and make more than I made in a year.

I loved him. He turned me on sexually. In three years I'd orgasmed with my husband once, but now I was orgasming with George just about every night, and enjoying every second. And I spoiled him rotten. I catered to him, spoon-fed him. I'd wake him up and wash his face and brush his teeth right in bed, and like hey, I'd serve him steak and eggs. Then I'd dress him. He'd be all washed and fed and dressed before his feet hit the floor. Then I'd go out and warm the car up, so he wouldn't have to wait. I guess I needed somebody bad. I wanted to make up for all the love I'd missed.

We traveled, him doing the bunco games and me working the streets. We went to Seattle, Portland, San Francisco, Denver, and I showed him a few things, too. Like in Seattle he came home with this white chick, and we're looking at each other funny, her and me, and she's sashaying around showing off her beautiful bod, no clothes on, you know. The next morning it was raining, and I told him I was going for a walk, and I guess he thought I was leaving, 'cause he knows I'm a good leaver. He says, "Yeh, you're leaving, but the trouble is you don't know how to come back when you leave." Because destination means nothing to me. We'd been through that. Like once up in Saskatchewan I went out for cigarettes, and the next time he found me I was in Los Angeles. I hitched-hike all the way.

He got all uptight about me taking this walk, and two blocks away I turn around and he's following me. In the rain! Mad! Ready to hit me!

I told him I wasn't going back to the place, I didn't want to go on no sex trip with him and the white girl.

He drug me home and he took me into the bathroom and he had this wire clothes hanger, and he told me to bind over. I said no. He said, "Bind over!" I said no. He said, "Do you hear me? I'm gonna knock you out in a minute."

I said, "Knock me out then. And when I wake up I'm gonna fight you back. I'm not taking any beating!"

So he goes out and beats up the white chick instead, and he tells her, "Look, I got a woman I want, and I'm not gonna lose her behind no bullshit with you," and he throws her out the place.

After that I got real sentimental with him, and I told him my life's dream. I told him I wanted to bear his child. And that just turnt him on! He said, "No one's ever said that to me before."

I said, "Well, I want to do it, call it selfishness or whatever. I made my pick out the litter, George, and you're it."

So right then he got turned on and we started making love

in the bed. He said. "Relax! Stop trying so hard to conceive!" And sure enough, I conceived soon after that.

Well, there he is over there in the corner, the main dream of my life come true. Good old Bird! He was everything I dreamed he'd be. I don't know, I've never been materialistic. I just wanted a child, that's all. The day the doctor told me I was pregnant, I wanted to scream, "Thank you, God!" but I was scared if I screamed I'd wake up and it'd be a dream. So I helt it all in, and I walked around holding my breath.

When I told George, I blurted it out so fast he couldn't even understand me. He said, "What?"

I said, "I'm pregnant. I—*am*—*pregnant*! That's what I am! Me! Nancy Davis! Me! *I am pregnant with your baby*! I'm gonna have *your* baby!" And he just lit up and we screwed for a week straight, and then we called up everybody and told 'em, over and over again.

After a while the gynecologist wanted to take the unborn child because there was complications. I said, "You gonna have to kill me first."

He said, "You're gonna die if you try to have this baby."

I said, "Then I'll die." But the delivery turned out smooth and easy. The doctor said it was because I had such a will to have a child.

I spoiled the bird from the word go. He slep' on my chest. George was a perfect father, too. There was no end to his love for his son. But he had one bad strain in him, too. He was selfish, and it made him do something ugly one day. I hate to even talk about it.

He had a chick over my son! Oh, I don't want to discuss it. Ugly, *so* ugly! I told him I wouldn't tolerate that, and I packed up Bird and me and we left him. That's all it took: one moment of lust. My baby's two years old and he's very perceptive. He knew what went on over him! So I just walked outa my own house and we haven't been back. George has been leaving messages all over, but he hasn't found us. We'll tough it out, me and Bird. That's why you see us in this little apartment, but we won't be here long.

I'm going out and I'm working harder than ever. Yeh, working. Let's don't call it tricking. That sounds like—Yuck! Let's call it making the scene, or dating. It's a complex thing, dating. Not everybody can do it. You got to have qualifications, good street sense. You have to know how to sell it, and you have to have great confidence in yourself to do it. You have to stand in front of the mirror and build up your confidence, and even then there'll be some nights you can't even give it away.

I always try to perform, but I'm not a good phony. I can act like I'm enjoying it if I really put my mind to it, but sometimes I really hate it, too, and I'll have to say to myself, "Well, you're making a hundred-dollar bill," and I'll think about the hobby horse Benjy wants, and that thrills me. But if the trick wants to talk all night, I can get very very uptight if I'm in my bitchy ways. Sometimes I'll talk and talk and talk, but other times I'll tell 'em, "Hurry up! You're taking too much time. I'm not your wife or your woman. I don't want to be up here all night. And don't be sitting there telling me a bunch of lies that you love me, 'cause I don't love you. You know why I'm here, and it's inside your wallet."

Sometimes they'll say, "You don't even act like the same girl I met a little earlier."

And I'll say, "Well, I'm *not* the same girl. I got a split personality. You get away from me! Don't touch me on my breast! Leave me alone around the rear end too! See if you can do it without touching me!" That's very rare, but I get my bitchy ways sometimes, I'm only human.

I run on certain rules. One is I always let the man do the soliciting, so when I come to court and say I didn't solicit him, I'm telling the truth. Another old rule is "ho money's not show money." "Ho" means "whore," and the rule means never give credit. Never let a guy say, "Hey, tomorrow I'll give you a hundred dollars." It's cash and carry in this business.

Usually we get along with hotel people, restaurant people, but sometimes some little clerk'll try to make it harder for you. Like I walked into a hotel and this clerk comes up and says, "Hey, what are you doing?"

I says, "Whattaya mean what am I doing? I'm sitting down to have a drink."

So a white guy came over and spoke to me, "Why don't you come up to my room?"

I said, "Well, I may and I may not. It depends."

He whispered in my ear a little offer, and I said, "Oh, that makes me feel like I *want* to come up! I'll be up later on, now that you've sweetened the pot."

So he walks away, and immediately the clerk comes over and says, "You're gonna have to leave!"

I says, "Now wait a minute! You're defaming my character. I don't know you from Adam. I could be a female impersonator for all you know. You don't know what the hell I am or *who* the hell I am, and yet you're drawing a conclusion. You could be sued for things like that, so don't make that remark again."

Just then one of the big Motown music guys comes on over and he says to the clerk, "Look, if this lady can't stay here, we'll just check out of the hotel. I have two hundred guests here and we'll all leave wit' her!" And his people get up and start for the door. The clerk said, "Well, I'm sorry, I didn't know," and I sat down and they all come back.

Something like that can shut me down for the whole night, ya know? It used to be I took it all in stride. Nothing bothered me. I used to be much more active. I'd think nothing of walking away with six or seven cats and put 'em all in a cab and go by myself with 'em. Fifty, forty dollars apiece. And it wouldn't take me no time to do it. Like I might leave by ten o'clock and be back by eleven-thirty.

One night I ran into a whole platoon of Marines, a even dozen men. I said, "How much you guys planning on spending?"

They said, "Depends on the chicks."

I said, "Well, you're not gonna find no whole bunch of chicks. Now I was getting ready to go home myself, 'cause it's late."

They said, "Well, would you go with all of us?"

I said, "Yeh." It was three cabs full, and myself in another cab. Hey! And I give 'em all the address in case the police stop 'em.

So we all got together in this transit hotel—the desk lady says she'll never forget it—and I walked in there first, and as the Marines come in the door I got their money. I said, "No refunds, no nothing!"

The desk lady said, "All the rooms are filled. You'll hav to wait. How many are there?"

I said, "Altogether there's thirteen."

"Royal, you're putting me on!"

"Uh uh, I'm not."

"Well, what am I gonna do with the other girls?"

"Ain't no other girls. Just twelve men and me."

By that time the other hookers were coming out of their rooms and saying, "Oh, look what Royal got! Royal got a platoon!" They'd grab a Marine and say, "Come here, come here, baby!"

I says, "Hey, I got 'em all! They're *mine*! I'm not sharing no money! I'm dating 'em all!" I says, "If anybody tries to date one of my Marines, I'll make such a ruckus all of us'll go to jail."

Then I began taking 'em into the bedroom, eight in the room and four waiting outside in the lobby, and I just went down the line, like a little rabbit, jumping from hole to hole. By the time I had did the eighth one I was so tired, but lucky they was quick, 'cause they'd just came from Vietnam, and they was healthy, so they couldn't last very long.

After the first trip at forty dollars a man, they said they wanted to do it again, but I told 'em I was too tired, I was going home, I wasn't going through that again. So they raised the stakes to fifty dollars, and we went through the whole thing again. Then one guy says, "That was so good I'm willing to pay double for one more."

I said, "I'll go wit chew!" and I went through most of them again for double. That brought it up to around two thousand dollars for the night, and they took me home in a cab, and I was so swollen! They waited outside in the cab till I got in my apartment and my light came on, and then they hollered, "You all right?"

I said, "Yeh, go home!"

They said, "Can we see you tomorrow night?"

I said, "No, *just go home*! It was nice seeing you all." I took the money and threw it on the bed and took a shower with my clothes on, I was so tired, and hurting. And like I didn't work for a week or so. But hey! it was worf' it.

That was back when I was working the downtown hotels

and all over the city. Now I mostly work Sweet Street exclusively, because you eliminate so many bad things that can happen in other areas. In the course of the last three months can you imagine the number of young girls under the age of seventeen has been killed down in the black area from various tricks? No, it's *not* just one maniac. It's a whole bunch of crazy people. They operate in the dark. They very seldom come up here in the bright light. So when you work Sweet Street, you eliminate those crazies right off.

But not *all* crazies. I'm in a dangerous business, and there's minny and minny a night I worry that I'm not gonna get back home to the Bird, I'm gonna leave that poor little sweet thing stranded to hisse'f for the rest of his life. Just last night I had a guy maybe six five, maybe seven feet tall, weighed around 250, 270, and like he was a perfect gentleman when I met him at Raffaele's, and after we got into the cab he said, "I hope you know I'm a karate expert."

I said, "Why do you say that? Do you say that 'cause we've left the bright lights and you're beginning to feel insecure?"

We drove up to a hotel, and the guy begins taking off his watch. He jumps out the cab and he says, "All right, now, get out!" So the cabdriver steps on the gas, with me inside and the door still open, and he says, "Hey, baby, it's not worf' it. That guy some kind of nut."

Well, you never know till it's too late. When I'm talking to a john I look him deep in the eyes, 'cause I got a few seconds to figure out, Is it safe to go with him or not? It's a hell of a thing when you shut that bedroom door behind you and he was the sweetest person in the world when you met him, and now you turn around and he's a shell-shocked veteran from Viet Nam, and start calling you Charley, and grab you around the throat and start choking you. Yeh, it happened to me, it happened to me. More than once.

When you close that door behind you, you're in a different world altogether. You might have a *anything* in there with you! There's a lot of the girls getting killed every day. *Every* day! Coming up dead in a motel or a alley. 'Course, it takes a lot of heat off the children, this killing. The maniacs work out on the prostitutes instead. As far as I'm concerned, I'd rather have a prostitute killed than a child killed, even if the prostitute was me. It's just a occupational hazard.

Four, five years ago I was working a cattleman's convention, and I went back to my apartment with a great big Canadian, very well off, with a huge diamond ring on his finger. When we got into the room he said, "Are you gonna give me what I want?"

I said, "Yeh, I'm gonna give you everything you want that's reasonable, but I have my rules and regulations, too. And I have limitations, too. I'm not a degenerate. If it gets too far beyond my reach, I'll try to accommodate you with somebody else that can help you."

So we get into bed, and he says he wants to do it the Greek way. I told him no, I'm not doing that. He hauled off and hit me in my mouf' and I felt like all my teeth had fell out my head. My tongue was cut, my mouth was one big mass of blood. I screamed, and some of my friends came running and sank a knife into him. He ran away bleeding, and I went into the hospital to have a broken jaw set.

The next day when I came out of it and went back home, I opened up the briefcase he left behind. Inside he had forty-two thousand dollars worth of unsigned travelers' checks, and a diamond ring, five and a half carats, and ten thousand dollars in cash. I had the ring broken up and made into a ring for me and sold the other pieces for cash. I held onto the TC's till I found out what to do wit' 'em, and then I unloaded for ten percent of the face value. That's the going rate for unsigned TC's. My jaw hurt so much, I figured I deserved every penny. I had to leave town for a while. My mouf' is still a little off.

But that's not the worst thing that ever happened. The worst thing that happened was a nut, a real genuine crazy. I'd been dating him off and on for five years, out in the suburbs, a guy that used to have five or six thousand dollars, sometimes fifteen or twenty thousand dollars, laying around his place in cash, and I never touched any of it. One day I went down to his house to meet him on a call, and he told me to go in the bedroom and get ready, and I opened the door and blood was spattered all over the room. He comes in behind me and he says, "My wife had a good face, and you have a good face, and I have to save the whole world from women like you. If I didn't love you, I wouldn't do you like I did her, 'cause I loved her a whole lot."

Now I can see he's got a hatchet in one hand and a gun in the other, and I start to scream, and God knows how but we scrambled and I wound up with the gun back in the living room. He threw the hatchet at me and missed, and I shot at him, and then I heard a noise and it was the police breaking in.

I'm standing there wide-eyed, buggy-eyed. My wig was snatched off and I'm yelling at the top of my lungs, "Help me! Help me! God, help me!" And I told the cops, "This man has killed his wife!"

One cop says I'm under arrest for prostitution, and the other cop tells me, "Shut up, tramp! Shut up, you black bitch! What were you doing out here in the suburbs?"

I'm begging, "Please, sir, *please*, go into the bedroom. If you don't believe me, go into the bedroom! Yes, I'm a prostitute, take me to jail! I'd rather go to jail than die! This man has cut up his wife, and she's in the bedroom."

Well, you could smell something bad, so the one cop says, "There *is* a peculiar odor," and the other cop says, "Don't listen to what that trifling tramp has to say."

So I just break and run into the bedroom, and I'm standing in the middle and the cop runs after me with his gun out. He comes in, and he says, "Oh, my God, you was telling the truth!" And he's looking around at blood splattered all over the ceiling, and puddles of blood here and there, and little pieces of meat and flesh. *Ughhhh!*

The trick's still in the state mental hospital. One nice thing: he told the cops to be sure to give me my two hundred dollars out his wallet, and they gave it to me, too.

Another weird guy was driving me around in his car one night, on the way to a hotel room, and he says, "Just to show you that I mean well, here's $150. Count it!" We're driving on the freeway about seventy miles an hour and I'm counting the money out loud, and the second I hit "150" he just sort of leaned against me and opened the door and shoved me out. I rolled for three or four blocks, and people stopped and helped me. I was dazed, but I walked off. I'm still scarred a little on my hands.

Dealing with people like that is why I always carry a pistol. If a guy starts getting ugly with me, I say, "Hey, I got sumpin with me. I don't intend to use it against nobody for nothing. I understand that you're a man and I'm a woman, and if it makes you nervous that I'm carrying this pistol, then your ideas couldn't have been too honorable in the first place, so the best thing I can do is say bye-bye." Nope, I don't carry my weapon concealed. I pull it right out and I say, "Look, this is what I got!" And sometimes I'll say, "I got a two-year-old boy that I love very dearly. I will kill you, your mother, and everybody else in this world if you try to prevent me from getting back to my boy." And I mean every word. You can call it a cop-out or not, but little Bird is the reason I'm working, and you'll find that's true of a lot of the girls on the street. Their money goes to buy toys, or to put the kid in a better environment than they had. That's just a simple fact.

The main thing we girls have to fight is the system. Everything that falls down in the city falls on the prostitute. The mayor says, "Hey, I got to make a showing that I'm enforcing the law, so, hey, the prostitutes are the easiest to catch." He says, "Now let's have a six-week drive, and I want you to bust everything walking, right?" Then for six weeks the cops don't do anything but arrest working girls. Everything else can go on. I've seen a black cat robbing a white cat on a street corner and the cops drive right by and make a U-turn and roll right by to chase three prostitutes up the street. This white guy's hollering, "Hey, he's robbing me!" right in prime time, early in the shank of the night, and everybody's standing around hollering, "Help him! Help him!" and the cops roll right by.

And persistent. Man, they're persistent! Two of the undercover cops that patrol Sweet Street have been hitting on me for two years now. They just won't give up even though I know them like my own brothers. Any night now I expect to see one of 'em come up to me with a Hallowe'en falseface and try to hit on me. They must think I'm dumb! One day I passed some tests to see about getting into dental training and I'm feeling so good 'cause I passed, I was eligible to go, and I said to myself, "Well, shit, I'm gonna go out tonight and get smashed. I'm just gonna show my behind and do my thing," and out I went.

So around midnight I truck on out of Amadeo's bar half drunk and giggly, and the little blond cop walks up and says, "Hi! How are you? What chew doing all by yourself on the sidewalk?"

I said, "Hey, you want to come inside and dance?"

He says, "Sure, yeh, c'mon. What else is cookin' around here?"

And I says, "I don't know what's cooking around here, but I know what's cooking on the dance floor." And just then a couple of chicks start to come out the door and they see him and they run back in, so I know right away he's the fuzz, and his come-on was too strong anyway; I was already suspicious. So he talks and talks to me, and I told him all about passing my tests, and pretty soon he lost interest and quit.

Not long after that the same blond one and his partner that looks like a hayseed from the country hit on me sitting at Raffaele's bar, and we got to talking, and the hayseed one, Steve Diggs, he said, "You're really good!"

I said, "What do you mean?"

He said, "Well, you're doing all this talking, but I know, *I know*."

I said, "When God made man he gave him the right to his own opinion. So I guess you've got the right to express your own. Not that it matters much what your opinion is." His partner grabbed him and says, "No, no, that's not where it's at," 'cause he'd already struck out with me before.

Well, all I can say is they must like their jobs, they must like policing, gutter work, arresting people that has little children to bring up. Maybe they should try policing themselves. There's one big cop on Sweet Street that gets drunk every night; he goes from bar to bar drinking free and making arrests in between. If he can't think of anything else to arrest you for, he'll bust you for obstructing the sidewalk. One night he reached down in my bra for my money, just reached down and felt around for it. If he ever snatched any money from me, I'd kill him! Either I'd have his ass or he'd have mine. He's not gonna take *my* money. *NO. Uh uh.* Not just 'cause he's John Law, half drunk. No, it don't go like that.

The other night one of the girls said she was gonna do a favor for a narcotics cop, and I told her, "Look, if you do that one favor, hey, they're not gonna have no respect for you. That one favor's gonna lead to another favor, and another. And you're never gonna be able to get out of it. Somebody's gonna end up putting out a contract on you." I says, "Hey, I don't want to be around you no more!" Then Raffaele asked me if the girl was okay, and I said, "Very uncool. *Very.*" So I don't think he lets her come around any more.

It's not really the cops, it's the system. You can't blame the cops. They get a fifteen-dollar bonus for every arrest, and a twenty-five-dollar bonus for every conviction. The money comes from all the guys up the line that are living off the proceeds of prostitution—the bondsmen, the lawyers, the prosecutors, the police officials, the judges, all of them. I had a police officer tell me hisse'f, came right outa his own mouf', which I'll never name, he told me, "Hey, shoot, I got brand new carpets on my floor, a brand new hi-fi, a beautiful large color TV—all from arresting you chicks!" And yet this same policeman, on his patrol, like, hey, he'll protect us from bad tricks. If a trick jump on us, that cop gives him a good ass-kicking. You don't jump on prostitutes in *this* city. The police don't let you. They say, "Look, we may take 'em to jail once in a while, but we don't let anybody hit 'em." Most of the girls know each police by name, and the police know us. Sometimes they'll even come around and say, "All right, you girls can work tonight."

But when they're arresting, it gets tough. First off, it's $62.50 for the bondsman, right? Then you've got $150 or $200 for your attorney. This is all behind one fifty-dollar date, and the date's gone and *you're* still having problems. So you tell your attorney, "Look, I can't stand another conviction. Take it into chambers." And you begin all the pulling and negotiating to get the case squashed out, you manipulate the whole thing through the court system so you don't have to serve a day. But it costs money. Depending on the case, the judge might want two thousand, three thousand dollars. The hard-nosed D.A., he says you got too many priors, you got to show him some time, but what he really wants is a new refrigerator or a down payment on a new car. He says, "Okay, let your client donate three hundred dollars to the policemen's children's aid society, and we'll cut her time in half." Your lawyer says, "She don't want to do *any* time," and the D.A. says, "Well, you tell her if she donate four hundred dollars then she can walk wit' ninety days, but if she don't want to do that, then tell her she can do that year flat. *No* time off, no work time, no nothing."

So the lawyer brings the bad news back, and you say, "Hey, did you holler and scream and pull out your hair and all that, and threaten to make an appeal, BECAUSE I'M NOT READY TO DO NO NINETY DAYS?" And you keep on bargaining and bargaining till you get what you want and they get what they want. That's the way it works. The going rate on getting a prostitution rap squashed out is $500, if you don't have too many priors. On grand theft, you can buy it for like $500. A murder cost you a little more. In my business, you got to figure $10,000, $12,000 a year just for courtroom procedures. And you still have the big fear left: that you'll get a real judge, I mean a real *judge*, or maybe even a real D.A. who's gonna act on the real law, and when they do, that's it. You're up shit creek. I don't let that happen to me. Leastways, not too often. How'm I gonna take care of the sweet thing Bird from behind a jail door? So I buy my way out, and I stay free, like the rest of the good mamas in the world. For $10,-000 a year.

A PECULIAR SEQUENCE OF events transpires in Raffaele's. A pair of uniformed policemen from the headquarters station arrives and one of them asks Rocco, "You know a broad named Royal?"

"Yeh, I know that whore," Rocco says.

"She been in?"

"Not tonight. Maybe later. What's the beef?"

"We just want to ask her a few questions. What's she look like?"

"Black. That's all I remember. If she comes in, I'll let you know."

Ten minutes later the uniformed policemen are enjoying

espressos in a corner table. Two representatives of the vice squad, looking like a pair of rock musicians on the prowl, are sipping Scotch at the bar. Four "harness bulls" from the Sweet Street substation are eating dinner at a large table near the old-fashioned capuccino machine under the oversize beach umbrella. A policewoman, out of uniform, stands outside. Royal makes a grand entrance in a deep-cut white velours slack suit, and calls out grandly, "Hey, what's happening?" With a little jump-step, she parks her dainty behind at the bar.

Rocco makes a beeline from the other side of the room. "Well, well," he says, panting from his exertions, "How you doing, *Nancy*?"

Royal looks nervously around the room. "Oh, just fine, thanks," she says.

"That's good, *Nancy*," Rocco says. "Say, could I talk to you a minute?"

The two repair to a corner. Then Royal leaves her drink and slips into the street.

The other night there was heat on, and Rocco says to me when I walk into Raffaele's, "Hello there, Nancy." As a rule he'd go, "Hi! What's happening, Royal?" Now he's saying in this stern voice, "Hello there, Nancy. I wanna talk to you for a minute."

Right away I know three things: there's cops around, they're looking for me under the name "Royal," and I better get my behind outa there.

Rocco takes me over in the corner and he says, "Hey, they're all over the place."

I says, "How many of 'em are on my case?"

"Just one that I know of," he ·says. "You better change your street name for a while. Don't let anybody call you Royal."

I didn't know whether they had a warrant out for me or what, or whether I'd be picked up later that night, so I handed Rocco my gun and he gave it to Raffaele and Raffaele put it in the safe, and I split.

I knew what the trouble was. A couple of nights before I went out of Enrico's on a date with a big dope dealer and another working girl. Rocco sees us about to leave, and he says to me, "Don't go wit' them."

I hate to be told what to do, so I said, "Hey, these are my friends."

He says, "Don't go!" So I went.

While the guy and I were having a good time all night long in the bedroom, hey, the white chick was stealing his coin collection, and that brought the heat down on both of us. She did the stealing, but she's white. Now who do you think's gonna take the heat? So I had to stay away from Raffaele's for a while, till somebody made a deal. The deal was the narcotics agents would squash this case out in exchange for a little information from the white girl. I guess she's gonna lead them back to the big dealer.

That's the way things work around Raffaele's. They take care of their own. I don't know what I'd do without the place. I like the people there. All that's required of me is to be a lady. And if you're right the whole place will stand up behind you, and if you're wrong you go out on your ear.

The very first time I went in Raffaele's I had some known hookers with me, and Rocco said, "No, I don't allow that in here."

But I started coming back by myself, using the restroom, and one day Raffaele stopped me and bought me a drink, only I didn't know he was Raffaele, I thought he was somebody that worked for Raffaele. He says, "Remember, I'm not a john now."

I says, "I don't care who the hell you are." I says, "Do you know this cat Raffaele that owns this place?"

He says, "Yeh."

I says, "He must be really a stuff shirt. He don't want people to come in his place. It take all kind of people to make a world. To make a good place, it take a little bit of everything to make it click. If I was Raffaele, I'd let a couple of really classy chicks work this place, and that would be a little color to add to the joint."

So he says, "Well, I've seen you around. You can come in. But be discreet."

A coupla times later, he walks up to me and says, "Out!"

I says, "What chew mean, *out?*"

He says, "Get out! It's hot. The police are here."

I said, "I thought you were cool, but you ain't nothing!" and I split.

Rocco came running down the street after me and he said, "Hey, do you know who you was just talking to?"

I said, "Some jive manager or bouncer."

He said, "That was Raffaele."

After that Raffaele and I made our peace, and we began rapping and getting to know each other, and he turned me on to a lot of things. I promised him, "If you let me come in there, all I can do for you is let the john buy some drinks and possibly a meal, and I'm never gonna disrespect your place, and I'm never gonna come up here and catch a john and take 'em right outa here like some highway floozy. I'm gonna be a lady, be discreet, never be loud."

Ever since then I been coming in just about every night. I know I'm okay around Raffaele's. But I don't let my okayness go to my head. I stay cool. A lot of the other chicks say how can you sit in Raffaele's when can't nobody else do it? Are you screwing the cat? I say no, I couldn't tell you what he look like under his shirt to save my life.

The nice thing about Raffaele's, when I'm in there I feel safe. They back me up. I've slapped a couple guys completely off their bar stools there, and it was all right. We used to have a punch-out in there every night. Night after night there was something happening that endeared Raffaele and me to each other as friends. Like one night this guy had me hemmed up in the corner and I just took as much as I could take and he's like pulling and jerking on me 'cause he bought me a coupla drinks. I guess he felt like he owned me, and I just let him have everything I have in my left arm, and I hit him in the mouf' and his chair went over. Raffaele came by and he said, "I guess he deserved that, huh?"

I said, "He sure did."

Raffaele said, "That's good enough for me."

One night Raffaele and a big party of people are sitting at the big table with the beach umbrella, and I'd had a couple of sloe gins and I was feeling good, and somebody told me the guy sitting next to Raffaele was a big movie producer, so

I sauntered over and I grabbed the guy and I said, "Hey, man, where you staying? Let's go down there and get it on!"

The man said, "Hey, do you act like this all the time?"

I said, "People act a little funny when they get a little money. Gimme some money and I'll act real funny, Jack," and I'm hugging and tugging on him, 'cause he was so cute.

Raffaele grabs me and he pulls me off and he says, "Oh, isn't she the biggest put-on?" and all the time he's pinching me. He says, "Did you think she was serious?"

I says, "Raffaele, I was about to make some money!"

Raffaele says under his breath, "Do you want to go to jail?" He took me by the coat and bodily picked me up and set me down outside and said, "Why don't you shut up! Do you know who you was talking to? *Do you know who you just hit on for a trick?* You dumb broad! That was the chief of police!"

I started hollering and screaming, *ahhhh, oooooh*, screaming hysterically, and jerking around, and my wig was twisted halfway off my head. Raffaele said, "Go in the bathroom and straighten yourself out!" So I went in, still crying and sniffling. I thought sure they were gonna call a whole station of cops to come get me.

Well, that's the kind of thing that happen. Since then they've always given me plenty of warning about cops in the joint. Rocco and I don't get along too well, but he warns me every time. The other night he was standing out front when I got there, and he waves behind his back to tell me to split. Or I'll walk inside, and Raffaele'll say real quick, "You know who's here? And that lady over there's one, too." I'll just say, "Oh?" and take a cab. They give me that much protection.

I know I can always depend on Raffaele, but I'm not positive about Rocco. I honestly believe he's jealous of my friendship with Raffaele, and he's showing it more and more every time. Wouldn't surprise me one bit if he gave me up to the cops some night, if there was sumpin in it for him. A long time ago we had a big fight, and he called me a black bitch, and I called him a fuckin' dago wop, and I didn't come back in the place for two months. Then one night Raffaele saw me walking by and he dragged me inside and he said real loud to the bartender, so Rocco would be sure to hear, he said, "Look, anytime Royal comes in here, I don't care what she wants or who she's with, you serve her! This chick, like, can come in anytime she wants."

But I still have to put up with a certain amount of disrespect from Rocco. Like pulling out his penis and rubbing it against me! In front of all those people! That's really bad! But I'm trying to be tolerant because I can also hurt myself in the same token if I blow my top. I can clean up my respectability around Rocco, sure, I can tell him to put it back in his pants and treat me like a lady, but I also got to tell myself one thing: Rocco is Raffaele's right hand man, and Raffaele not gonna get rid of *him* behind *me*. So I have to give a little bit. I don't want to damage myself in my profession, and I don't want to get run out of the joint either.

Raffaele knows what he's doing for me. He's doing more than I could possibly repay. He's helping me, 'cause he knows I'm helping myself. We have long talks, and I'll say, "Raffaele, I'm tired. Like I've done everything there is to do, and hey, like it's a *nice* life," only I'm being sarcastic, 'cause a nice life is what it isn't. I said, "Raffaele, I been going to school. I'm tired of the life."

He said, "Are you serious? About school?"

I said, "Hey, I really am. *I really am.*"

That's what a lot of the cats around Sweet Street didn't know. For seven months I was going to dental technician school, but then they threw me out because I'd been arrested. They let me almost finish the course, and then they threw me out, and now I'll never be able to be a dental technician. I was really struggling to get out the life, and I'm maybe halfway out of it now, because I went right back into another state program under another name and now I'm studying to be a X-ray technician. I hope they let me finish this time. The trouble is, I don't have much money to cover the training period. I spent all my money trying to buy something that money can't buy: love. I'm so afraid of being alone.

Well, I'll get out as soon as I can. The fast life is no way to live. I have a child, and I want to be a part of the community again, and I want to be *somebody*. I don't want to be just tolerated. Maybe I can get into the movies; I keep hoping. Maybe in ten years I'll be a big famous somebody like Diana Ross. Then I can write my own ticket. But mostly I just want to be a good person and take care of my little Bird. Listen at him now. Ain't he sumpin?

BENJAMIN ALEXANDER "BIRD" DAVIS, a few hours removed from his second birthday, stands in a corner smashing a toy piano and screaming like a baby catamount. "Come here, sweet thing," his mother says softly. "Don't cry. Come here and let Mommie hold you close." The child toddles over, digging at his eyes with infinitesimally small brown knuckles, and deposits himself in his mother's lap. "Now who should be patient," Royal says, "if *I* shouldn't be patient? Huh?"

Retired Prostitute

Art in the blood is liable to take the strangest forms.
                    —Arthur Conan Doyle, *The Greek Interpreter*

"So THIS FUCKIN' NUN walks into the place, full habit and all, beads down to her knees," Rocco Cardi says with high good humor, "and I walk over and grab her by the tits and give her a little feel, and she reaches up and gives me this nice big slobbery French kiss. That was one of her best stunts. Had the place in an uproar!"

Merle of the super-English last name, self-bestowed when she arrived in the city from the dairy farm of her childhood, lives to shock. When she is not strolling around in her nun's habit, she is performing fellatio on disc jockeys over the air, or making outrageous proposals to the devout as they stroll from evening church services. Why? "For kicks," Merle Farquhar says. "I've been laughing all the way."

At thirty-five, she is handsome in a wild, sunburned, pixie way. Her eyes are big and blinky, her figure as slim as a thirteen-year-old's, her hands and fingers graceful and articulate. She is unflappable herself, and indeed gives the bland impression that she finds life somewhat tedious, until she throws the cherry bomb under the hearse. She speaks slowly and precisely, as though reciting, raising her voice only slightly when she mentions her pet hates: authoritarians, fakers and phoneys, and "those dirty fuckin' motherfuckin pig fuzz cops." Her antipathy to the police department goes back to her earliest days wandering about the city, when she claims she saw frequent cases of entrapment and other corrupt practices against her fellow *femmes de nuit*. Merle has nursed her animus ever since, rushing back and forth to help beleaguered prostitutes, enlisting the assistance of others, harassing the vice squad, making people angry and sad, and always trying to see the silly side. She has the vocabulary of a stevedore and the giggle of a schoolgirl, and she has friends who would take on an army of ocelots on her behalf.

Lately I've become a health freak, a mountaineering type. I don't smoke, and I don't allow the people in my life to smoke. I don't drink, except for a little wine once in a while. I live on a half-acre in the woods, I run two or three miles every morning. I enter cross-country races, I grow most of my own food in the summer, and I do potting and painting and all that artsy-crafty crap when I have time. Oh, yes, I smoke pot, but I'm thinking of quitting. So I make it on about a hundred and thirty dollars a month, seventy-five in rent and the rest for food and gas, and my whole income comes from teaching a private dance class and running a maid service and a gardening service. Look at my clothes. Simple, huh? I don't blow money on clothes. I haven't bought any clothes for five years. I wear castoffs, or I dig around in free boxes, and I make things, because I am not going to be a slave to fashion or materialism! When I was in the business I had a twelve-room house full of furniture and all that shit. And what is it? It's just a big chain around your neck.

Yes, I was a farmer's daughter, up in Washington State. I came to the city on a train with ten dollars and a trunk, and the cabdriver hauled me to the Sweet Street Hotel, and I lived there for thirty-five a month starting in 1959. Back in those days, this was an old Italian neighborhood. These strip joints were neighborhood bars, and all the men played *bocce* ball. There was very little crime. It's changed a little, hasn't it?

The only place that retains any of the old style is Raffaele's. I really enjoy Raffaele's and Rocco and all those funky cats that hang around there. Rocco turns some of the women off, but that's just because they don't know how to handle him, how to flow with him and turn his energy into a trip for your own benefit. Like when he grabs my tit, I grab his balls. He's not gonna hurt me or I'll slug him or kick him, and he knows it. He'll do things like feeling you up just to humiliate you or intimidate you, and it does *not* work with me, because I do the same thing right back to him. But it *is* pretty sexist and racist around here. I just laugh at their male chauvinist jokes and then do and say what I want to do and say anyway. It's not hard, because you're dealing with people that aren't very smart.

Raffaele's has been the scene of some of my biggest theatrical triumphs, my nun scenes, my scenes as a mail carrier, or a nurse, or a Salvation Army lady. I used to use a borrowed Salvation Army outfit to enter topless dancing contests, till the head of the Salvation Army put a stop to it after I won three straight contests. I couldn't lose! Oh, I love theater!

Once this movie reviewer and I went to a preview of a dirty movie, and there were a whole bunch of other reviewers sitting in the row in front of us, and at the appropriate moment we rapped the seats and they turned around and I was holding his cock. I got my nun's habit just for kicks. It's the other end of the spectrum from being a whore, and I have that black kind of sense of humor. I turned tricks in that habit, and I made dirty movies in it, too. But I couldn't make much money tricking in it. Catholics couldn't get it up with that kind of imagery around. Men have a hard enough time getting it up as it is.

There were a lot of incidents in that habit. Once I took the deejay Slim Hollway to the airport in my habit and we French-kissed and he pinched my ass as he turned to get on the plane. I said, "Say hello to Father Berrigan!" There was a bunch of nuns dressed just like me, and I had to rush away before they saw me. Later on Slim told me no one would sit near him on the plane.

Another time a real nun walked up to a friend of mine to ask directions, and he thought it was me, and he said, "How the fuck should I know?" She just vanished! My little fun and games!

Being a hooker was grand and glorious for me, a masquerade in itself, because I came from a poor background, and as a hooker I got to go to all the rich places, all the fine restaurants, meet some beautiful and brilliant and exciting men from all over the world.

But I refused to give up my own sexuality to trick. One of the traditional trips for a whore is not to come with a trick. I refused to fuck myself up like that, because I found that when I did, then I had trouble getting off when I wanted to. So I just tried to get off every chance I could, at least once a day and sometimes three or five times a day. I'd have fun with the two or three tricks I thought were okay and spend more time with them, and just give the others their money's worth.

One of the biggest challenges to a man is he wants to get the whore off, you know? It's like fucking a lesbian, it becomes a challenge. So I became very expert at faking. I can fake better than most anyone I know. I've got all the sounds down, the muscle contractions, that's all you have to know. Body language. It gives the guy a big ego trip, and he gives me one in exchange. He tells me I'm the best, I'm beautiful, so it's a mutual admiration trip.

I can't stand these creeps who go around talking about "loose women." My definition of a loose woman or a hooker is "one who is more accepting and compassionate of other people, someone who can understand and feel empathy for just about anyone else." Most hookers have a tough act, to protect themselves from being hit on by everybody, and most of them are in a degree masochistic. They don't hang onto their money, they give away their money and their housing and their food and everything else. I know that's what I always did; I saw myself as a matron of the artists. But the cliché of the whore with a heart of gold is a cliché *because* it's correct. Most of them *do* have a heart of gold.

The tricks, well, they just want to be told things that their wives don't tell 'em any more, that they're really super. When you find a guy who's been going to whores for any length of time, generally he turns into a pretty good lay. A lot of them get into eating pussy and oral sex and getting sucked off and so forth. A lot of men over forty don't go for oral sex with their mates, because they feel it's disrespectful, and they've got all this puritanical conditioning behind them. So they go to whores to have the service performed, and whores generally get pretty good at sucking cocks, as good as some faggots.

One of my tricks asked me how come I don't hate men? And the answer is because I make fuckin' sure I get off myself. Why don't men hate me? Because I laugh!

The cops, man, they're another story. I balled a couple when I was a whore, and I still sleep with one once in a while. That's the way you pay them off, that's the level they're on. Cops like knowing whores because whores are the most attractive women and a lot of cops wind up marrying whores. But this is one that'll never marry a cop, you can write than down! They're so completely totally fucked up on the subject of sex. Like don't ever report a rapist, because the cops'll treat him like a hero and treat you like a whore. If a guy rapes you, report him for indecent exposure, and he'll be brutalized by the police and picked on by his fellow prisoners. Because it's a sexist society, and any cop that knows of a man that whipped it out and didn't fuck anyone with it—well, that guy has to be supersick and done away with because he's bad for the masculine image, the *macho* trip that they're all on.

Don't get me wrong, I think that most of the men who go into law enforcement have integrity. But then things happen. They always put rookies on the vice squad, because they need young pretty faces to trap the girls. It either makes the rookies sick to their stomachs or they love it and stay on vice for life, and then they become sneaking little immoral motherfuckers. They suspect *any* single woman of being a whore, and they'll entrap you and perjure themselves in court to send you to jail. I know. Entrapment happened to me, ten years ago when I wasn't even hooking. But I was from the country, and I'm an open person, and I didn't understand what was going on. Slimy little bastards! The word fuzz comes from their own fuzzy idea of their own sexuality. If they were sure of what they were, they wouldn't be so afraid of queers. I've never seen two or more vice cops get together without cracking sexiest jokes about homosexuality. *Never!* And within the first five minutes.

The guy that was head of the morals squad in one of our biggest northwest cities was kicked out a few years ago because somebody opened a folio that he had hidden in his car, and in it were eight by ten photographs of himself sodomizing his daughter, fifteen years old. I think that says it all about the vice squad and the morals squad and the whole bit.

Well we're working on the fuzz here in this town. I've just started an organization called *Wolverine* which provides bail, medical and legal assistance for hookers that are busted. We're trying to get the policies of enforcement completely changed, so that instead of arresting women only, the cops either arrest the men, too, or ticket *both* of them for a small fine. Because the way it is now the cops and the vice squad have a really soft fuckin' job. Those yellow motherfuckers feel pretty stinking brave when they bust women and queers. I'd like to see them go out and bust some *real* crooks. Like this young student that I know, she was hooking out of a hotel bar, and she wasn't paying the cops off. They picked her up and put her in a room for three hours without letting her know that they were cops. They got her to call another whore, and the two women did each other while the cops watched and took pictures. Then they booked them for oral copulation, a felony, and seven prostitution charges. Isn't that sweet and fair?

So *Wolverine* is trying to get the cops to change their ways, and we're fighting fire with fire. We print up fliers with the cops' descriptions and mug shots and circulate them to massage parlors and the bars where the street women hang out. We provide an emergency number where a whore can get assistance at any time in dealing with the pigs. And some of our women who are *not* prostitutes are hanging out with sultry looks and tape recorders, posing as whores, just like the cops pose as tricks, and as soon as the cops solicit them for an act of prostitution, we're gonna make citizens' arrests, and we're gonna charge them with entrapment. We'll also publish transcripts of the tape-recorded conversations.

Even before *Wolverine*, I was fighting cops. I got tired of being busted and ripped off at the same time. I got a couple of fancy cops demoted to flatfeet. It took two years of gossiping about them to effect the change, but I did it. I'm not a radical, I'm not trying to lay any trip on the cops that they haven't laid on a bunch of other people. I just got sick and tired.

I'm the worm that turned.

The Law and Beyond

Policeman

The cops used to take a whore's money or a piece of ass and let her go. But they got a bunch of gung ho young suckers now. A whore's better off with crooked cops. These new young guys are terrible. They're dedicated, and that's worse than dishonest.
—Diego Darby, former pander

WHEN HE WALKS INTO Raffaele's, there is a change in the air, as though someone had just lit up a Gauloise, or announced the death of the parish priest. In his sporting plainclothes from Robert Hall, he looks like thousands of other small-towners visiting Sweet Street to take part in the permanent rites of spring. But there are differences: a sly furtiveness to his manner, a false joviality toward the regulars, a subtle swagger in his walk. At his appearance, the ladies of night turn sharply from males and huddle closer to each other. Rocco Cardi dashes about delivering whispers, and several women disappear. Raffaele himself rolls his eyes at the ceiling, like a man oppressed. His establishment is different now. A coyote has appeared on the lambing grounds.

"Yeh, I like cops in general, get along with 'em," Rocco says sotto voce. "But not that Diggs motherfucker. I don't like his racket—busting whores. What harm'd a whore ever do? The rest of the cops, they're different. They know I pack a gun without a permit, and they never bust me. There's one cop I smoke pot with, play golf with, run around with. He's married, and he come in here one night and he said, 'I got two broads right up on the corner here,' and he's in uniform! He says, 'I need somebody to keep the other one company. Let's go!' We had a fine time that night. But when this bum Diggs walks in, the party's over."

"It isn't that he makes arrests," Raffaele explains. "It's the *way* he makes arrests, with so much enthusiasm, so much delight. He *loves* it! He's a sicko. Talk about sickos!"

Steve Diggs, plainclothes patrolman attached to the anti-prostitution detail, takes a seat in a leather-covered corner booth and orders several appetizers and an entree and a double Chartreuse. Back in the shadows, he could be a visiting wheat broker from Burkburnett, Texas. His black hair is parted to one side and lightly tonicked, his sideburns extend precisely to the bottom of his earlobes, and the rest of his face is shaven and pink. Being medium is his specialty. He is of medium height and medium build, his eyes are medium blue, even his nose is indescribably medium. He wears a medium .38 police special under his sport jacket, and a medium smile upon his medium face. When he talks, it is in the common accent known as general American, western rancher subdialect, in a softly pleasing voice that becomes animated and excited only when he discusses his work. He cracks "Hi, whore!" to a painted lady on her way to the restroom, but otherwise takes no notice of Raffaele's clientele. Another plainclothes operative walks over to pay his respects, and a short conversation ensues:

"What you eating?"

"Beats the shit outa me."

"Looks like eye-talian throw-up."

"You cocksucker!"

"Busted any fruits lately?"

"I'm working on one."

For a medium man, Steve Diggs is able to down Olympian quantities of green Chartreuse, an herb-based distillate for connoisseurs of esoterica and possessors of Carboloy stomach linings. Periodically he announces, "One more round and I gotta go to work. Gimme a little more of that green stuff! Then, by God, I'm ready!"

After six or eight drinks of the green, plus orders of lasagna and steak and spumoni, the medium man wobbles over to the bar to begin his evening's assignment.

Those fruits, they advertise in the underground papers. I remember one ad: "Peter Long, a rocking cock busting forth from a hole in his Levi pocket with the strength of an East Texas oil well," and something about a coral snake python coming loose, the most gross ad I ever saw in my life. It said, "He'll fuck yeh, suck yeh," excetera. And we've never been able to bust that guy. He's booked up solid, he makes appointments a month in advance, strictly by mail. Don't worry, we'll get him eventually.

I like to work on the male prostitution cases 'cause male prostitution is a wide open field for subversion, 'cause they can get something on a guy and blackmail him. You turn up some very prominent people working male prostitution. Like a few weeks ago we were working on one of the biggest male modeling agencies in town, a huge male prostitution operation. We had search and arrest warrants and after a seven-month investigation we kicked in the front door and we went upstairs, and the bedroom door was closed. I kicked that son of a bitch open, and here's a very affluent attorney sucking the dick of some male model. When he comes off the prick, it sounds like a cow pulling her foot out of the mud. I turn to my pardner and I say, "Hey, what is this shit but an on-view 288-A?"

The lawyer's frantic. "What can I do? What can I do?"

I said, "Buster, next to disappear, I don't know."

"Well, I know some people."

"Do you know the governor?"

"No."

"Well, it looks like you're shit outa luck."

"Well, I know a judge."

I said, "Well, I suggest that you use one of your phone calls to call him." I said, "Mister, you are in a lot of shit, because you are under arrest, and I don't give a shit *who* you know."

He told us he paid that kid thirty-five dollars and it was his third visit to the house, and he just loved to chew on the banana. A real closet queen! Now you take somebody like that and put him into high office, and somebody who knows he's fruit can put the screws to him. That's why it's important to work on fruit prostitution.

I was telling my pardner the other night, the whole world's becoming fruit. I don't care what they do, but don't do it in front of me. We were driving to headquarters and two guys were standing in front of a night club swapping spit and grabbing each other's swats. We throwed the red light on 'em and you oughta seen 'em run. That showed they was closet queens, or they wouldn'ta run, they'd just turned around and said fuck you otherwise.

Say, order me another green, will you? That's one thing we have to be careful about, drinking, 'cause we have to do so much of it on the job, just to keep our cover. One rule is that we never drink at home. That gives us a cooling off period. You have to watch yourself about booze. If you ever begin to need it, you better knock her off and quit entirely. Or if you have to have one when you get up in the morning. And you should never get tight. If I get a little tight, my pardner notices, and he stays sober, and if I see him getting a heat on, I cool it a little. You never get on your pardner's back about drinking, that's just not done, but you just watch him a little closer when he drinks and you back him up a little better.

Lookit these people in here! What's the matter with Raffaele, anyway? I remember when this was a class joint. Now it's turned back to prostitutes and pimps. I seen more pimps in this joint in the last two weeks than in the year previous. Well, it just gives me more work to do. The broads in here think they can get away with anything.

My pardner met a girl in here the other night, and she was five eleven, taller than him, and she had these terrific long legs. She says, "I'm a working girl. I want you to know that right off the bat."

He says, "Great! What's the yardage?"

"Fifty bucks."

"What do I get for my money?"

"Well, I'm into oral. I'm into anything but screwing in the ass. That's gonna cost you at least a thousand dollars, because I don't really dig it."

"Well, I'm not into that either."

So they sit there talking and drinking their drinks for a while, and she says, "You know, this is really nice in here. I can work in the city and not get arrested, 'cause I have amnesty."

He says, "What's amnesty?"

She says, "Well, I help the guys in the narcotics squad, so I can't be arrested." She lays it out how she helped on all these dope buys, and she keeps saying how she can't be arrested. So Vern, he's heard enough by now, so he says, "You're under arrest!"

She says, "You can't arrest me!"

He says, "Get in the car, you're under arrest." The next day, she cops a plea. Amnesty, my ass! All it turned out was she helped the narcotics on one little dope deal, and there was never a word said about amnesty. But that's the way these broads talk around here. They think they got a license. I arrest 'em all. If they tell me they got amnesty, or they got hot information on the big bad things that're going on, I just tell 'em, "Beautiful! If you got all this fuckin' information and it's good stuff, then it'll still be good tomorrow after you talk to the D.A. He'll make you a deal you can't turn down! But as far as right now, asshole, it's nighty-night and into jail for you!"

Most of 'em go easy, some of 'em are crazy. You can't tell. We're arresting a lot of prostitutes that are different from the usual run, girls that have turned out on a lark. The problem nowadays isn't the sad little girl from the ghettos, the ones that never had any opportunity. Now we're getting the affluent—"My daddy is a business executive, but I don't dig the establishment." It's a psychological thing where the girl's gonna show Daddy how much she hates him by placing herself in a degraded position.

Those are the ones that can give you trouble, because getting busted and thrown behind bars is something that never enters their minds till it happens, and then they go crazy. One night my pardner and I walk into this bar and here's two chicks setting at the bar, and I know one of 'em personally and she knows me, because I've arrested her before. But this high-class broad setting alongside of her doesn't know me *or* my pardner, and the minute we walk in she grabs him by the arm and says, "Hey, are you a cop?"

He just shook his head no, and she says, "How much money you wanta spend?"

So I crawl up alongside the other broad, the one I know, and she looks me over and she says, "Oh, shit!"

I whisper, "Now, listen, goddamn it, just set here and behave yourself. I'll buy you a drink and everything's cool. But if you tell her that my pardner's a policeman you're gonna go to jail. Just let 'em both do their thing."

She says, "Goddamn it, she's my sister-in-law!"

I says, "That's your problem, not mine."

In the meanwhile, this other broad's yelling her solicitation to my pardner, very blunt and uncouth, almost like I'll fuck you and suck you and run you a foot race. So I look down at my pardner and he buys a drink and there's some change lying on the bar and the broad says, "I wanna play some music," and she sweeps up the change like a crooper in a casino, a couple bucks worth of change, and she's gonna do enough music to play the last waltz. When she walks to the juke box, I get off the stool and follow her and nudge her in the ribs. "Hey, dear, I got something rather unhappy to let you know about."

She looks at me and she says, "You're a fuckin' cop!" And she starts screaming "*I didn't do anything!* I didn't say anything! All we was talking about was race cars!"

I said, "Fuck that shit! Now just behave yourself before I add another charge. You're busted!"

She runs behind the bar. I says to the bartender, "Listen, Eddie, get that bitch out from behind there before I have to go and get her out, because if I do it, it's not gonna be so gentle." The broad came out screaming bloody murder. She's crazy. I told the psychologist, "The girl is a classic schizophrenic."

This affronted the psychologist, *me* telling *her* something she didn't agree with, and she said, "Where'd you get your degree in psychology?"

I said, "Right out there on the street, sweetheart!"

We've arrested that same broad a couple of times. She's completely crazy, a skitz. She'll kill somebody some day. That's the weird kind of whore we're getting these days.

It might be better if they were organized, but you can't organize 'em. The reason is most of their pimps are niggers, and you can't organize niggers, or anybody connected with niggers. They've got the whores locked up. They go right down to the bus station and pick up fourteen- and fifteen-year-old runaways, and turn 'em out on Sweet Street. They set 'em up in a six-dollar room and make a terrific profit.

Some of these pimps are very quiet and businesslike, and others will come in here styling, wearing a thousand dollars' worth of shit, or they'll throw big, expensive cocaine parties, spend maybe ten grand on a single party. They like to get their whores up on tables and show their dominance over them in front of their pimp friends. They'll make two of their whores go down on each other, scarf up each other's swanso. That's their big ego trip. Then they'll give each other a snort of coke from their pearl coke spoon, and say, "Hey, baby, cool," and the women'll go down again. They're crazy, those pimps! There's one working around here now, he's twenty years old, started pimping when he was sixteen, driving his mama's Cadillac, sitting on two big sofa pillows to see over the steering wheel. He's a crazy little son of a bitch, very into cocaine.

The big-time pimps, they like to work their whores on Sweet Street. There's people that'll tell you Sweet Street's just a little risqué, that it's not really so bad underneath. Well, I'll tell you it's worse underneath than you ever imagined. There's not a club on this street that won't go bust-out if it gets a chance. And if you've got the bucks they'll rip you off. You show me one son of a bitch along this street that he won't rip you off. . . . You lay out a twenty for drinks, and you'll never see the change. I'm not talking about Raffaele's, no. But it's true in the strip joints, down to the last one. The whole street's bust-out. And the broads that you pick up here—man, I wouldn't fuck 'em with your dick! Dangerous, man! Dangerous!

We got a call from a guy said he was a vice cop from the East. He'd lost two grand, him and a friend. He took this broad in his hotel room and she found his money and ripped him off. He's asking me, "Find the broad. I'm gonna break her fuckin' arms!"

I said, "Listen, Jack, if you want to make a complaint I'll go bust her. I know who she is."

He said, "No, just find the broad. I'm gonna take her down an alley and break her fuckin' arms."

I saw the broad a few nights later, and I said, "Listen, you kissed off all your fuckin' opportunity. If I ever see you on this street again, you're going! So you might just as well go back to your hometown and stay there, 'cause any time I see you in the city you're gonna get busted, because if you're ripping off cops, you're ripping off everybody."

That cop—he was the all-time biggest fuckin' loser. What an asshole! He didn't want to make a complaint, he just wanted the girl. He offered me a yard, a hundred dollars, to find her. I said, "Hey, this isn't New York, asshole! We get paid well enough. Make the complaint and we'll find the girl. The mayor pays our wages, you don't!"

I don't know what a cop was doing with all that cash in the first place. I know on the money I make I can't be walking around with two grand in my pocket. And he wasn't sweating the bread, either. He just wanted revenge. Why, if some broad ripped me off for that kind of money, I'm gonna have a cataleptic fit!

But a mark is gonna be a mark, and there's no way you can stop him. A mark is gonna give some broad his money even if he has to fight her to get her to take it, 'cause he's made up his mind he's a loser, and he's gonna prove it. Last night I'm walking down Sweet Street and I spotted these two black guys hustling an old man. It was the old paddy-hustle—they pretend they've got a broad for him, they collect the money in advance, and then they leave him standing there with a stiff swat. Either that, or they were gonna roll him. So I walk up and I identify myself, and the old man said, "Yeh, they told me they had some broads, and I paid 'em twenty dollars for a little flatback."

I arrested the two guys, took 'em to Central for booking, and then I come back to Sweet Street, and here the old man's talking to three whores! I hear him say, "Don't say anything! Here he comes again!" I said to myself, Why, you trick son of a bitch, I hope one of 'em roll you! What an asshole!

I run into so many guys like that. Born marks! I tell 'em, How old are you, mister? They say forty-five or fifty. I tell 'em, Look, I'm thirty-five, and I'm from one of the smallest towns that there is, and I never been as fuckin' naïve or stupid as you are. I've never met anybody that's as goddamn goofy as you are. But it's like the old saying, a stiff dick has no conscience, and no judgment either. They go plumb off their rocker.

The paddy-hustlers used to take 'em up to the housing projects, where there's a thousand different hallways and exits, and they'd say, "Look, I got this broad waiting for you, but I don't trust her with money. Gimme the money in advance." Or they'd say, "Look, I don't trust that broad, better give me your wallet before you go in there. Don't worry, I'll give you a receipt for it, and when you're through with the broad, just give the guy at the front desk your receipt and you'll get your wallet back." And they fall for it! These assholes from the country, they're begging to be rolled!

Once in a while we'll run into one of the bleeding-heart social scientists, and he'll be prowling Sweet Street looking for some ass, and he'll say to us, Why aren't you out catching killers? Aren't you ashamed of your job, chasing whores? I always tell 'em, Listen, Buster, you just keep right on doing what you're doing, just keep right on looking for ass, and when you find the wrong broad that sticks a fuckin' knife in you clear up to the hilt, *then* I'll be investigating a murder, and it'll be yours. That usually shuts 'em down.

Just last year a man was knifed five times in the chest and twice in the back by one of these whores. He died. Happened right in one of these Sweet Street hotels. The girls that did it were just harmless prostitutes, right? They didn't even have a record, never booked for anything, till they were booked for murder. The pimp was the only one that made out on the deal. He got the man's watch and rings.

Those fuckin' nigger pimps, they're taking over the whole city. They'll hit on anybody, the niggers. My pardner and I were talking to these far-out-looking chicks on the street, and these four black dudes come up, wearing the big long leather welder's gloves, the whole nine yards, and they were tough little street punks, junior-grade pimps, and they said, "Hey, man, gimme some money! Gimme a dollar!" There were four of them and two of us, and one of them says, "Give us a dollar each!"

I says, "Flake off!"

He says, "Hey, man, gimme some fuckin' money!"

I says, "Listen, asshole, get the hell outa here or I'm gonna give you what you need."

He says, "Man, you gonna fuck wiv' all of us?"

So I took my badge out and jammed it in his face and I said, *"That's right, you little punk son of a bitch, you're under arrest for begging!"*

His buddy started to crowd between us. He says, "Hey, leggo! He didn't do nothing."

I said, "All right! You too, cocksucker!"

One of 'em ran, and I took off after him, and my pardner took off after the other one and put his head into a brick wall, the old waffle iron trick, and I caught my man and kicked him in the gut, and he kept saying, "Man, you're just fuckin' with me 'cause I'm black!"

I said, "You're out here fucking with *me* because you're black. You think you can walk up to anybody on the street and just because you're black you can intimidate 'em into giving you money. You son of a bitch, you got another think coming, you asshole!"

I don't go outa my way to arrest Negroes, but you just can't help yourself. They're into *everything*. Last night I'm walking along Sweet Street minding my own business and I see this big crowd of guys, and a black guy's saying, "Get your money down, man! Pick the card and win twenty bucks!"

They're all black, but I can see it's good old three-card monte, and I walk over and I say, "Goddamn, man, that's my game! What it cost to get in this game?"

The guy says, "Anything from one to twenty, man. We'll cover it all."

I says, "Is this what I think it is? Is this a little monte?"

He says, "Yeh, man, you pick the card, you win the money."

I says, "Okay, how's this for a bet?" and I pitched the fuckin' police badge on the ground, and I said, "Punks, we's gwine to de *poe*-leece station!"

It was just like you flushed a covey of quail. They went north, south, east, and west, and left me with the two guys running the game. One said, "Shee-it, man, we just got busted in LA."

I said, "Well, now you're busted here."

He said, "How's two hundred? Here, take it all!"

I said, "Listen, punk, I'm gonna book you for bribery, too." They were brothers, turned out they'd been running this movable monte game for years. They both copped a plea.

There's one thing I will *not* tolerate, and that's broads messing around with the niggers. I can't swallow that and I never will. I been fooling around with a broad, and the other night she confesses that she was seeing a dinge, and I said, "Jesus Christ, you coulda told me you went with a fruit and never done you and me *that* much damage! Now flake off!" She called me up and said, "I ditched my black old man."

I said, "Well, that's cool, but forget it." A beautiful broad, too, one of the most beautiful broads you ever saw. But going with a black, that rules 'em out of the human race. I don't know a white cop in the city that doesn't feel the same way.

I love to go up against those black motherfuckers. They're so *tough*! One time I'm standing outside a whore's door, and I can hear this black pimp inside with the chicks, and he's got a revolver and he's spinning the cylinder and he's saying, "Man, I'm gonna get that sorry mothafuckah, that lousy Diggs!" And I can hear the cylinder going, "*Brrrrrr, Brrrrrr, Brrrrrr,*" and I just stood outside and started to laugh. I felt like kicking the door in and shooting the son of a bitch, but instead I just laughed.

You don't ever worry about a guy that makes noises about killing you. If a guy's really gonna come get you, you're gonna be dead anyway, right? So why pay any attention to it? It's like when a guy pulls a gun on you. If you're not dead the second the gun comes out, he doesn't really want to kill you, and you've got an opportunity to get around him. The professional killer, the man who's really gonna kill you, with him it's—*bang!*

To stay in my business you can never take anything personal that happens. You got to stay cool. It's like I was telling a younger cop that gets pissed off if somebody calls him a motherfucker or belts him in the jaw. I just told him, "He's not hitting *you*, he's not calling *you* a motherfucker. He's calling a cop a motherfucker and he's hitting your badge in the jaw. And if you take it personal and get uptight over it, you're gonna quit or go bananas or blow somebody's fuckin' head off and wind up in jail yourself."

It's like an instructor of mine told me. He taught psychology, and he had about four doctorates, and he told me if you want to work in institutions that deal with people, it's just like you're a garbage collector. You work in the garbage pit of the human mind. And he said, "If you take that garbage home with you, then you're in real bad trouble. But if you can go to the shower and wash the shit off and then go home and forget it, you'll last. But if you go out to get a loaf of bread and you get pissed off because some guy's walking down the street the wrong way, you're in the wrong business."

No, I don't want a transfer, I don't want to go investigating murders. I'm happy right here. I figure I'm investigating murders before they happen.

JIM FLAHERTY, 35

Police Detective

AFTER TWELVE YEARS ON the force, half in the anonymity of plainclothes, Jim Flaherty retains his zeal. The easy-going policies of the city's police officials suit him. He is assigned to the rape detail, and he does much of his investigative work hip to hip with criminals: paid informants and logorrheic brigands. He handles a heavy case load, and his file shows numerous "complimentaries"—special citations from senior officers for courage under fire, unusual resourcefulness in line of duty, or just plain luck.

Jim has the traditional Irish "gift of the gab," preserved in the genes through four generations of Flahertys in the new world. He is a prolix story teller, shaking with laughter at his own anecdotes and nearly bringing himself to tears with nostalgic *feuilletons*. He retains another generation's courtliness toward women. "Say, if the missus will excuse my French," he says, "that's a damn good salad!"

In the classic interrogation technique, Jim portrays "the good cop," while his beefy, taciturn partner, Sanford McQuiston, stands in the background clenching his fists and muttering. The team's forte is making contact with underworld figures and wheedling more out of them than they intended. "What the hell," Jim Flaherty says in his oversized, strident voice, "it's all police work, isn't it? If I have to take a drink with some filthy scumbag con artist to solve a dirty vicious rape, well, who am I to be proud? If I could solve a case, why, I'd even drink with the mayor!" The room swells with his loud laughter. Even in total privacy Detective Jim Flaherty never lacks an appreciative audience.

Police work is different here. I'm not sure I'd enjoy it

anyplace else. We have one rule: *get the job done.* And you can do it your own way, thank the good Lord. You stick to your side of the street, and let the other cops stick to theirs. Take bookmaking. Neither San nor I have ever gotten involved in a bookmaking case; we've never contributed one thing to that subject. Me, I don't see anything wrong with it. I'm not gonna go to a guy and say, It's all right to make book, Charlie, and I'm not gonna go out and tip a bookie off to a pinch, either. I'm just not gonna worry about bookmakers. I know a ton of 'em in this town. They're very helpful people, at times. Once the FBI came to us and said, "You know, Jim, you and San seem to know a lot of bookies."

Right away I said, *"Wait a minute!* I know a lot of bookies, yeh, but I don't know *anything* about bookmaking." He bought my act, and he didn't try to pump us. That's what I mean—it's different here.

Right now San and I are on rape, and we get a lot of our cases off Sweet Street. A lot of our *worst* cases. If a rapist wants to find a victim at two o'clock in the afternoon, he goes to the university area. If he wants to find one at two in the morning, he goes to Sweet Street.

To a rape victim any rape is bad, but to a rape detective, some are worse than others. I mean, every girl that comes into our office and lays her story on us, we cannot possibly allow these stories to penetrate us, or we'd be in an institution. The Sweet Street cases are the worst. When these chickies are sitting in our office telling us what happened, they look like they should be in the hit-run detail. Somebody's really done a job on 'em.

A lot of 'em are raped by pimps, because your typical Sweet Street pimp is mean. The day of the old-style wining-and-dining pimp is fastly disappearing. You don't get the lover pimp any more; you get the sadist. He'll get a chick by hook or crook and break her down as bad as he can by drugs, by force, by whatever it takes. Maybe he'll just beat the shit out of her. Maybe he'll turn her on and then break her down morally. After two or three days she's all the way down. She's wiped out. She's a zombie. You see 'em walking the street. You can tell around the eyes. There's nothing there, no light, no fire, just a stare straight ahead, and they don't blink, or else they blink all the time, constantly, like the light's too bright.

These pimps nowadays are too impatient. They don't want to wait to wine and dine her for a couple of weeks and pork her for a couple more weeks and really make her happy and do a job on her and love her. They gotta have cocaine and heroin right away, and they gotta have that money coming in twice a night, meet 'em on the street corner and hand it over, or get the shit beat outa you in front of everybody.

Me, I hate to see a girl even set foot on Sweet Street. I'm like old Sal Giobbe that owns a couple of the strip joints. Old Sal, he's the closest thing to the Godfather we've got on Sweet Street, and he's a dear friend of San and I. We love the guy. A tremendous person, and a perfect gentleman. And Sal Giobbe wouldn't let one of his daughters *near* Sweet Street. He'd disown 'em if he ever saw 'em pass through in a cab!

'Course, the girls on Sweet Street are *all* there temporarily, right? In their own minds, I mean. Then they find that they hang on and on, they never seem to accumulate any money, or they get interested in one of the pimps, or in drugs, or they get to liking showing off their flesh to the animals. Some of the girls become survivors after a while, like they're there for a means, for a purpose. They need *paga*, they got a kid or an old man or both, and they gotta survive, and some of them even become practical, basic people. Look at Josey Costello, Connie Lea, Lydia Rubini, some of the others. They're survivors.

The funny thing is the church sends nuns sometimes to try to show the girls the truth and the light. It's like trying to stop the Bonneville Dam with a Band-aid. Sister Mary Holypitcher goes up there and everybody smiles at her. "Oh, sister, how nice to see you here!" and then Sister Mary Holypitcher gets her pockets picked and her rosary beads snatched at the same time. Look, Sweet Street is laden with opportunists of all types, be they just streetwalkers, or be they have a sign advertising their business. Watch out!

I remember when it used to be kind of exciting to go up there and look at a coupla bare boobs. That went on for a few years and then it became boring. The clubs went bottomless, and we started looking again, but now that's getting boring, too. So the guys on the street; they're wondering: what do we do next? Do we get a donkey? I mean, that street is fastly becoming Tijuana. Everything gets old, and they keep having to raise the ante. But how long will Joe Blow from Idaho keep paying his money to go inside?

They've got strange financial arrangements on that street; nobody'll ever get to the bottom of them. Everybody has a piece of each other. You get a nickel of my joint, I got a dime of your joint, you got a dime of his joint, he's got a nickel of my joint. We're all holding hands, and we can get anything we want in a few minutes: a drummer, a bartender, a boobyshaker, a barker, anything. And we're not gonna cut each other's throats economically, so all the drinks cost the same. If you're looking for a bargain on Sweet Street, don't bother.

It's like a three-ring circus, society and scum combined. Don't you find that society and scum like to run together? It's a status symbol for both. We're all hypocrites in our own way.

Really good people on Sweet Street? I'd have to stop and think. Raffaele Pirini is really good people. He's a survivor. He's always giving his money away, and he's always in financial trouble. He gives too much away. The other guy that comes to mind is Stanley Hamilton Briggs. Believe me, there are *no* other Stanley Hamilton Briggses anywhere. They broke the mold! He keeps crossing my trail. For ten years, he's been a second career for me. But I genuinely like him. I genuinely buy his act. Stanley gets out of jail two times a year, and when he's clean there's not a better guy to talk to. I sent him to the state penitentiary twice, and he's one of the dearest guys I ever met in my life. He's a thief, a likable thief. He would have been the good guy on the cross. He paints like an angel, he sold one painting for twelve hundred dollars, but he'd rather steal. He has a thirty-five-page rap sheet, and he is without a doubt—signed, sealed, and delivered, and fully confirmed by every cop in the city—he is without a doubt the best fuckin' auto booster in the world. The guys in the auto-boosting detail go fruit when they hear San and I talk about Stanley Hamilton Briggs, and I don't blame 'em! If I was in auto boosting, the first thing I'd do is put a gun against Stanley's head and drive him out of town, and that would cut my case-load by about ten percent. Because he has a big dope habit, and he has to have that *paga*. He's a very institutionalized guy. He's been in the joint for so many years, off and on, and he lays right into the program, feels safe there, considers it home. But when he gets out, he heads straight for Sweet Street and the connection, and he's on the shit from then till he goes back into the joint. He's always running, always surviving. He says he got on the shit in the Korean war. I tolerate that story. It might even be the truth.

Six or eight years ago Stanley was wanted, as usual, and I'm cruising in an unmarked car at Fifth and Sweet, and he strolls by. It's a hot summer night, Friday, steaming, and there's thousands of people on the street. I shout, "Stanley Briggs!"

Zzzzppp! He runs down Fifth. We abandon the car just like cops and robbers, right in the middle of the intersection, and we run after him. Stanley's going like hell—*chmmmmmmmm.* And I'm hollering, "Stanley! *Stanley!* Stanley, for Chrissakes, it's *Jim!*" And he puts on the brakes. Meanwhile there's thousands of Joe Blows from Iowa watching all this.

Stanley says, "Jim? *Jim?* Why didn't you tell me it was you?"

I come running up and grabbed him. I was shaking, I was so damn mad. I said, "Goddamn you, Stanley!"

He says, "Well, you shoulda told me it was you."

I said, "Well, you stupid shit, who the hell did you think I was?"

"I just thought you were a cop."

"Well, I *am* a cop!"

Finally he says, "I have a problem."

I says, "What's in that bag?"

He says, "That's the problem."

So I open it up. Sure enough, in a glass jar in oil is a thirty-two caliber revolver dismantled. He was already a two- or three-time loser, and I said, "Stanley, you know what this means."

He said, "Jim, you know me. I don't fuck with guns."

"What are you doing with this one?"

"I'm moving it from one place to another. That's why it isn't assembled."

I said, "Well, Stanley, you know this is a nickel for you. Five years minimum."

He said, "I know."

So we stand there looking at each other for a while, and I says to my partner, "Well, whattaya think?" You know how we handled the case? I'll *tell* you how we handled the case. The gun's still in my garage. In oil.

Well, you know, Stanley's not useless. I'm not saying he's an informer, because he's not. But he's helpful. He may not steer us into somebody, but he saves us a lot of time by steering us *away* from certain areas, if you get me. I don't think he'd ever put the finger on anybody, he's too con-wise for that, but he believes in that old Latin expression, what is it? *Quid pro quo.* He's fair.

Every time he gets out of city jail, he comes straight to the sex-crimes detail to see me and San. He'll sit down and start BSing, and his mind will be clearer than mine ever was, 'cause he's been off drugs while he's in jail, and he starts this big con game of his. You never know when he's serious and when he's jacking you off. Like the last time, I gave him the James Reginald Flaherty lecture about staying away from Sweet Street and changing his ways. I said, "Stanley, for Christ sakes, you're a talented person. You could write, paint, but every time you go back to Sweet Street you end up on shit."

"No," he says, "I'm through with shit."

"Baloney! As long as you stay on Sweet Street you're gonna be on one drug or another. Why don't you go into some kind of business?"

He puts on this real sincere look, see, and he says, "Jim, I got an idea for something else, but I need some money. Not a lot, but some."

"How much?"

"Just enough to get it started."

"Well, Stan, maybe I can find somebody to help you. What kind of business you got in mind?"

"A whorehouse on Sweet Street for off-duty policemen!"

Son of a gun, he'd been jacking me off the whole time! Then he pulls his regular routine, the same one he does every single time he gets outa jail. He wants four dollars. So San and I contribute two bucks apiece and get rid of him. He doesn't know that we know what he wants the four bucks for. He's gonna take a cab back to Raffaele's! He doesn't want to show up after ninety days or a hundred and twenty days on a bus. He may have a dollar in his pocket, but he arrives by cab. He wants to look like a winner, but he's a born loser. If he goes to the beach, it rains, and he gets shaken down by some beat cop, and he winds up in city jail. *A born loser!*

One morning he's down in Chinatown looking for dope, and he knocks on the door of Lemon Lee, and Stanley doesn't know it but Lemon has just been murdered and his body is leaning against the inside of the door. Stanley leaves his name and telephone number on a note on the outside!

The homicide bureau looked for him for four days. Finally they came to me and they said, "You know Stanley Hamilton Briggs, don't you? We want him for murder."

I said, "Oh, no!" I went up to Sweet Street and I left messages: "Call Jim."

Twenty minutes after I get back to the office I get a call. "Jim, this is Stanley."

I says, "You're wanted."

"I'm wanted? What for?"

"Murder."

"Lemon Lee?"

"Yeh."

"Should I come down, or do you want to come up and get me?"

"Got any money?"

"No."

"Stay right there. I'll come and get you." I took him down and they talked to him for four or five hours. It took homicide two years to crack that case, and they cracked it on a single little remark Stanley Briggs made to them. One little inconsequential remark! And he's not even a fink! But nobody ever said he was stupid.

The main thing that drives him crazy is being rousted, and he's rousted every week. There's some cops that'll stop him wherever and whenever they see him, and I don't blame them. I told him the last time he was in my office, "Stanley, any cop worth his salt is gonna search you every chance he gets. If I was a harness bull, *I'd* search you. For Christ sakes, why don't you move away from Sweet Street? Every policeman in the area has at least one complimentary in his file because of you, and some guys got dozens. Why, we got guys that made *captain* on you!"

He says, "Jim, they don't have a right to search me. That cop last week, he had *no right* to stop me like that!"

I says, "What did he get when he searched you?"

"A couple cameras."

"So what'd he do about it?"

"He arrested me, but they kicked it out of court. It was unconstitutional."

"Well, that cop is doing a service to the public. He's taking cameras back to their rightful owners, and he's not putting you in jail where you belong, Stanley. Look, you're driving the beat cops crazy. For Christ sakes, change your act! Try Worthington Park!"

About six days later I get a message: "Call Stanley Hamilton Briggs in City Jail." So I go to see him in person. "What're you doing here?"

He says, "I got busted."

I says, "Yeh, I can see that, I'm not stupid. Where'd you get busted?"

He says, "*In Worthington Park,* you son of a bitch!"

One night I'm sitting up on Sweet Street in my car, talking to this broad, and Stanley comes along and we get to rapping. The broad happens to mention that she's going bowling the next night, and Stanley says, "Yeh? You want a nice bowling ball?"

She gets all excited. "Yeh! Yeh!" she says.

"Wait a minute," I says. "Hold the phone there, Stanley. Where *is* this bowling ball?"

He says, "It's right around the corner on Second Street. It's in a Pontiac." Oh, that Stanley Hamilton Briggs! The fuckin' Sphinx'll change before Stanley ever does. But I love him. He's a wonderful human being. I buy his act completely.

STANLEY HAMILTON BRIGGS, 40

Burglar

He reaches forth beyond prohibitions, beyond natural instinct, beyond morality. He is the man who has grasped the idea of freeing himself, and on the other side, beyond the veil, beyond *principium individuationis*, of turning back again. This ideal man of the Karamazovs loves nothing and everything, does nothing and everything. He is primeval matter, monstrous soul-stuff.
> —Hermann Hesse, *Glimpse into Chaos*

Well, then, to take something away from someone else—to profit by another's loss—is more unnatural than death, or destitution, or pain, or any other physical or external blow. . . . The tightest of the bonds uniting society is the belief that robbery from another man for the sake of one's personal gain is more unnatural than the endurance of any loss whatsoever to one's person or property—or even to one's very soul.
> —Cicero, *The Unnaturalness of Doing Wrong*

HE SITS ALONE AT Raffaele's, wolfing down a rich Italian dinner, ending with an assortment of *pasticcini casalinghi* from the pastry cart. He is one of Raffaele's charities; the two men are distant cousins, but the family relationship is beside the point. "I just love the guy," Raffaele says. "He's a great human being." Sometimes Raffaele revises his opinion sharply, but in his wildest fits of anger he never denies Stanley Hamilton Briggs the solace of a full stomach, gratis. "The guy needs to be able to depend on somebody," Raffaele explains. "Besides, I can never stay mad at him long."

Stanley's blue-white skin stretches tight across his face and forehead, giving the impression of an animated death's head rigged up by medical students. The outline of his facial bones is starkly visible, his cheeks are concavities, his small upturned nose looks like a hurried emendation by a mortician. The region around his lips puffs slightly outward, giving him a mild prehominid look. His features are twisted a few degrees off center, reminiscent of the paralysis of Bell's palsy, or certain Picasso paintings in which the face is redistributed about the canvas, a cheek here, a nose there. As though to heighten the effect, Stanley's face is remarkably mutable, his mouth opening widely while he tilts his eyes at the ceiling and tries to disgorge a stubborn idea, his lower jaw grinding from side to side as he describes an old hatred, his face breaking into the smile of a freshly burped baby as he recites a favorite lyric.

"You only acquire that frantic pasty look in the joint," Joseph Wambaugh writes of a character in *The Blue Knight*. Stanley has the ex-convict's pallor, and emphasizes it with dark glasses that seldom leave his face. Underneath the gray-green lenses, his eyes are so light blue as to be almost unpigmented, but few have ever seen them. His thin, straight brown hair, flecked with reddish highlights like Buddy De Young's, sits wiglike and slightly askelter, falling in lifeless wisps about his ears and forehead. For no evident reason, he is touchy on the subject of aging, although he professes contempt for death. He wears no sideburns whatever, thus eliminating a pair of tell-tale gray patches, and he guillotined his beard when it showed traitorous flecks of white. His eyebrows are full and severe, black hyphens atop his face.

He stands barely six feet tall, with the figure of a cross-country runner, so narrow that he hardly casts a shadow. He has the burglar's talent for unobtrusive movement. Sometimes he stands in a group for several minutes before being noticed, and disappears as silently and peremptorily, disdaining the formality of a good-bye. His head is always tilted toward the door, looking for an unfriendly policeman or a familiar drug connection; his public life alternates between fears that he will encounter the one or miss the other. He almost always wears a light mackintosh, sandals for relaxation or tennis shoes for work, and simple shirts open at the collar and accented by silken scarves. His hands are graceful and his fingers tapered, and he uses them to make his points. He smokes cigarettes to the nub, and coughs lightly, but has no plans to withdraw. He talks in a low, deep voice, with thick s's like Humphrey Bogart's, and interrupts himself often with a chorus or two, usually hopelessly disharmonic, from a moony love song of the fifties. The music libraries of most prisons are decades behind the times.

That Jim Flaherty, he's a good influence on me, for a cop. He never arrested me unless he absholutely had to, and then he'd write a good report, say that I was no trouble to the city, and recommend my release. One time there were charges that I was paying him off, but it wasn't that. Jim's just a good person. He cut me loose plenty of times when he should have taken me in.

Altogether I've been arrested about a hundred times, and maybe eighty of 'em illegal and unwarranted. But according to the ethics of this culture, I wouldn't have a complaint in the world if they used illegal tactics and sent me to the joint for life, 'cause I'm a bad guy, right? And any way you can get me, it's all well and good for society. A few of the cops think like that.

I've become almost fatalistic about it. I get a sense of God's presence, His prevailing over everything, whenever I think about certain cops. Like there's a couple in Chinatown that're gonna pinch me whenever they see me, even if I just left church having served as altar boy. But I'm not staying away from Chinatown! In fact, I go there at two in the morning and I rip off every fuckin' thing I can get, two or three times a night, because they're gonna pinch me anyway, so I might as well get all I can. I could be walking around wearing a bikini and those guys'd arrest me for stolen property. I went over to the station once and I told 'em, "Hey, these phoney arrests are an embarrassment to me! How do I explain to my friends? If you don't know how to catch me, I'll *show* you!" They were offended.

We've got a few cops around town that want cameras, they want money, they want all the stolen goods they can carry. But they've got all the grass and cocaine they can handle. The police department keeps a little from each bust. Years ago, they used to buy grass from me, but in the last four years I haven't had a single cop hit on me for grass, and I've alwaysh been able to hit on them and get it.

The other night at Raffaele's one of the bad cops came to the outdoor half of the restaurant and motioned at me. So I said to myself this is the same guy that's pinched me four times in Chinatown, for no reason at all, just stopped me and shook me down for burglar tools, and I just said to myself, Aw, this motherfucker's trying to roust me again. I said, "Go fuck yourself!" and I walked back to the inside of Raffaele's and sat down. He comes in, and I hand him a menu.

He whispers, "Hey, come on out and get in the car!"

I thought, Oh, shit! But I got in the car, and he begins driving around, and he was really hot and outraged, as if I was a buddy that had embarrassed him by not coming when he called. A social error! He was screaming and hollering at me. So I said, "Look, if Rocco tells you to go fuck yourself, you laugh. I lose my references sometimes, you know? You don't come to Sweet Street often, and I was so happy and surprised to see you, and I got something on my mind anyway, my broad's visiting me, and I don't know where you're at or what you want. I'm clean. Do you want to take me down? You got a joint? I could use a joint."

He says, "Look, don't you *ever* do that again! Don't do that! I just wanted to say hi to you."

I said, "Well, look, how did I know that? The last four times you said hi, I've said hello in return and then you shook me down without a warrant. There's no reason to shake me down all the time, but you do it and all you're looking for is a nail file or something, anything you can call a burglar tool, and then you bust me, right? So you're bad news to me. Why should I be happy to see you unless I know where your head's at? So that's why I told you to go fuck yourself."

He says, "Well, it's embarrasshing in front of all those people."

I says, "Well, it's embarrasshing to me, too, and a pain in the ash, and an inconvenience." So we had a nice talk, and we drove around and smoked a couple of joints, and he let me off back at Raffaele's, and I haven't seen him since then. Maybe he's gonna stop searching me every five minutes now.

"I KNEW STANLEY BRIGGS when he had it made," says Diego Darby, a pimp and armed robber and heroin addict. "He used to sit out in front of the beer joint with a whole briefcase full of narcotics. He really had it together. He was a debonair dude, a lot of class. Then later I lived across the hall from him at a flophouse, and he had just gotten out of the joint. I thought he was totally insane at the time. He had a young boy living with him, and a bunch of pornography. That was five, six years ago. When he's got his shit together, the right jewelry, the right clothes, the right broads, he's something. But he hasn't had it together for years. He's scuffling now."

Stanley lives on the fourth floor of the Sweet Street Hotel, a residence popular with addicts and dealers. He retreats to his room only when he is coming down from methedrine and cocaine, the rod and staff of his life. The rest of the time he is out stealing, or loitering in Raffaele's, or wandering around looking for a connection. He sometimes stays awake for five or six days and nights, manic on stimulants, walking the streets and admiring the sunrises and the people. When he has stayed up too long, he begins to lose track of time. "Hey, wait right here," he says. "I'll be back in fifteen minutes." He wanders off, and returns the next day. "Oh," he says, "I'm glad you waited."

"He hasn't got long," says Diego Darby, "and he knows it. Things aren't going right for him any more. That broad he met in the penitentiary, the one he brought back here with him? She's down on Skid Row living with a nigger named Riker. Stanley doesn't mention that. Poor guy, I don't know what he'll do now. He's never had a straight job in his whole life; he wouldn't know how to work. I just hope he keeps himself together. I've seen him crazy, insane. I've seen him pull a knife a yard long on a sucker, and if I hadn't jumped between 'em there'd have been blood. He can be a very mean dude."

I've stuck a needle in one part of my body or another every day for at least twenty years. Look at my hands. There's not a vein left. But I've been off heroin for years. I'm the only person I know who kicked it cold turkey on the streets, without going through some program like methadone. I have absolutely no deshire for heroin any more, haven't had for eleven, twelve years. Oh, I've done it four times within the last year, with four different whores that wanted me to share their bag and their bed.

I'm one of the loneliest motherfuckers in the world, and they were such groovy broads that I thought, What the hell, I dig them, I'll try it, and each time the heroin brought me down so fast that it cost me a thousand dollars' worth of methedrine to get back up again.

I do methedrine, cocaine, grass, almost any upper, but you have to be careful. You can get killed very easily. The simplest thing in the world is to take a neon light and scrape the freon from the inside, and you get a white powder that looks just like heroin, and give it to somebody to shoot, and that's it. A hotshot. I've fortified myself against results like that. You go into my room and you'll see a shelf with eight vials of chemicals, to test the stuff I buy. To be an addict you have to be a chemist. In fact I've got an old lady down in Southern California that *is* a chemist. She runs a secret laboratory where they make methedrine, things like that. She makes four thousand dollars a day when she feels like it.

She was just here, and she tried to lay a grand on me, but I didn't take it. That would have been plotting on the grand, and my concern is with *her*, in the way we relate, not in her money. She was in a hurry to get back, and she kept looking at this clock on her arm, so I just said, "Well, fuck it! Get on the plane and go back, I'll see you later." We'd done about fifty bucks worth of cocaine apiece, and a spoon of speed, and I was still yawning. She started giving me some horseshit about not loving her, and I just got out of the car and walked away. She said, "Here, take this money!" But I just kept on walking. I discipline myshelf about money. I can't be bothered thinking about it. Sure, I have to live, but I have to *live*, too, and you can't really live if you're always worrying about cash. I have to be able to get it sometimes, but I'm pretty ungovernable, I'm a psychopathic motherfucker, and I have to be able to get hot and get out of the car and slam the door, too. That's just as important as money to me.

People say, Why bother with drugs, why not kick speed the

way you kicked heroin? And I say, well, it's not impossible. People turn me on more than drugs. Certain women turn me on more than cocaine or methedrine. I'd be glad to kick drugs for any of these women, but they don't want to make the deal. But I also see rich straight people like Sedler Anthony that comes into Raffaele's and he's on the cocaine pretty regularly, and he doesn't have the slightest thought of giving it up. So why should I?

I get energy and a depth of ideation from a few people, but not many. So I use methedrine for the same effect, 'cause there's *plenty* of that around. The big problem with uppers is mediating your life so that you take care of yourself. That's why you see me in Raffaele's, putting away a big meal once in a while. And drinking lots of milk, eating healthy foods, so I don't freak out or collapse. The other danger is jail, but I bought a prescription for my methedrine. It's really methamphetamine hydrochloride, sold as Disoxyn, and as long as I have that prescription to show the cops, I can take as much as I can get my hands on. The courts don't ask where I got it.

Drugs have always made me a whole lot better than I am, that's one reashon I use 'em. When I'm not on drugs, I'm not interesting to myself or others, I'm not spiritual. Drugs are an enrichment to me. At one point, I was about as insensitive a person as you can imagine. If it hadn't been for chemicals I'd still be insensitive. There's a Van Gogh painting that tears me up inside and makes me cry. I think its called "The Bridge at Arles." It hypnotizes me. I love the man for it. I was gonna steal it and bring it to Raffaele's, but I didn't because I'd have cracked the impasto, and I didn't want to harm anything so beautiful.

If it hadn't been for dope, I'd never've known about that painting, or cared. I never would have been thinking about things like that, and I never would have cried about it. If it hadn't been for dope, I'd be walking around with a gun in my hand, scaring people. But dope sensitizes me. *Me*! I don't know about other people. Seeing a painting like that, it's my communion with posterity. I feel like I know Van Gogh, as if he'd spent a lot of time with me, right around the corner.

The only thing you have to be careful about is keeping

yourself under control, keeping your needs in hand, not letting the habit run away with you. Strange things happen when you let go, when you lose control. One night this cat and I were completely stoned and we had a broad in a hotel, and he was a stunt man in the movies and also a drug distributor on the side. So after a while we left the hotel and we were driving along and he said, "I wonder if I left her shoes under the couch?"

I said, "What?"

"That broad."

"*What* broad?"

"The one I threw out the window."

STANLEY HAMILTON BRIGGS WALKS through a children's park on a bright watercolor day, picking his way past the carousel, stepping nimbly around the smelly artifacts of Saturday night, not yet carted off by the city's faithful "sanitation engineers." He passes a short Filipino man, and says out of the corner of his mouth, "You sheen Cherry Bomb Charlie?"

"Yeh," the little man replies. "Chollie was around this morning."

"Was he holding?"

"I dunno."

A hurdy gurdy strikes up, and inspires Stanley to hum a few quavery bars of "Chances Are." He breaks off, his eyes rolling skyward behind his dark glasses, his fingertips twirling in little *s*'s and circles, his footfall light and gentle, like a moth's. "I've had a beautiful week," he says. "*Beau-tee-ful*! There's nothing like getting up in the morning, looking for the connection, finding him, and fixing it. That's one of life's genuine concerto achievements. The others are ephemeral, just constructions of culture, outside of an orgashm and a full stomach."

The words stick slightly in his throat, and sometimes he stops to make a new attack on a balky phrase. "I'm cloudy," he says. "My head's cloudy, like I'm cloudy, I'm woolly. But happy! That's the way I am just before a fix."

The route of search for Cherry Bomb Charlie, Oriental pill impresario, leads out of the children's park and into Chinatown, and Stanley encounters the lifeless hulk of an elderly man, stretched out alongside the entranceway to a noodle factory, his face drained of color, twin streams of terminal urine coming from his pant legs. With a dainty skip, Stanley clears the obstacle, and presses on, searching faces. He is wearing a shorty raincoat, faded blue slacks, a yellow silk scarf knotted about his neck, and red, white, and blue tennis shoes. "Ah hah!" he says. "This'll be a very fine day all over America," and he bursts into song:

> When I see your face,
> Every star is bright,
> Da-da-dum da-da-dum, da-da-dum, da-da-dum
> *Da-dum!*

He does a small hornpipe, and his hands rotate faster than ever, as bemused tourists stop to watch. Then he moves along the trash-strewn thoroughfare with redoubled pace. Cherry Bomb Charlie is in sight.

I've been in the joint fourteen of the last twenty years, but it would have been much less if I hadn't been sent back as a parole violator. They'd parole me, and I wouldn't report to my parole officer, and back I'd go to prison. I'm not the type of cat who ever looks rehabilitated, because I spend most of my time on Sweet Street with the broads, and I had no appreciation whatever of big brother, the authorities, the people who had my welfare in mind and were trying to get me to live a life that would satisfy them. I had no gratitude whatsoever, so I didn't bother to report and kiss their ash. Mainly I didn't report 'cause I didn't have anything to report. I just like to stay away from the authorities as much as I can. Like I never even picked up my gate money, sixty bucks you get when you're paroled. I didn't get a penny of that money yet! And I've been paroled three times. That's a hundred and eighty the state owes me, but I don't want anything from them. I'm not even franchised; they can keep their vote. I don't want a fuckin' thing from the authorities, just the air that I breathe and the space that I'm walking on. And a few skeleton keys.

I like to think I made a good accommodation to the joint, but it wasn't as good as some people think. Like Jim Flaherty, he thinks I'm institutionalized, meaning I'm maladjusted unless I'm behind bars. Well, there wasn't a single minute in the joint when I wasn't either thinking of the outside or jacking off. I was in *plenty* of trouble; I was no model prisoner by a long shot.

One morning I woke up and found the motherfuckers had welded my cell-door shut. A captain did it. He had his own ideas of how to handle convicts. Well, I'd been causing trouble, minor scale. The doctor left the combination of the hospital safe in his coat pocket when he changed clothes to go into the operating room, and I'd lifted it, and we'd taken all the narcotics out of the safe. That same week we'd gotten into the canteen in the yard and stolen maybe two hundred cartons of cigarettes.

So the captain welded the doors shut on about twelve cells, all of us from the city. A lunatic! Nine months later, they unwelded us, but pretty soon I was put into a strip cell for bookmaking and disrespect. For twenty-nine days you're in the hole. No bed, no toilet, you're stark naked, you've got to stand up, and even then they shake you down twice a day for cigarettes, and you're watched all the time by the Death Row guards. Through the plumbing shaft, just a foot or so away, there's the head of a guy on Death Row, and pretty soon you develop some kind of affinity to him.

I adjusted to it. It was my life, and I *had* to adjust to it. I've got the loser's reality, the loser's discipline. When I feel bad nowadays, I tell myself, You don't *really* feel bad, and I just project myshelf back in time to when I was in a welded cell or in the strip cell naked. Most of the time I was a nice guy in prison, *a nice guy!* I was a confused fuckin' cat trying to figure out why his parents didn't get along and why he didn't relate to his brothers and what was wrong with the neighborhood, and why people weren't happy, and I had a lot of time to think about it. So you tell me: what the fuck's gonna bother me now?

I always thought the captain was a lunatic, but later on I saw him in a different light. A guy flipped his lid one day, and he runs into this blind alley going off the prison yard, and he's standing there threatening to kill everybody by inches, and he's got a shank about a yard long swishing around.

Maybe twelve or fourteen guards are standing there watching him, and he tied them up for two hours, because they couldn't get close enough to disarm him and they didn't know what to do.

The captain's waiting for it to be resolved, and he finally loses his patience. He walks right up to the guy, sails his hat into the guy's face and takes the knife off him just like that. I realized: he's a man! The captain is a man! That's when I stopped thinking about "we" and "them." After that, I tried to learn all I could from him. He's been a big success since then. He's a warden of his own prison now, in another state.

I settled in pretty good after that little bit of trouble with the strip cell. I had some consenting relations with other males, and they were better than some of my heterosexual relations on the outside. I found myself in love with a kid who's now an Episcopal preacher in the city. He's a beautiful person. One thing I found, you can't tell black from white in bed, and if you're passionate enough, you can't tell man from woman. It's a matter of taste, like fried ice cream. I tried to reach out and make contact with everybody I could in prison. I spent two years with a Roman Catholic priest who'd had an adulterous affair with a woman and murdered her son. I celled for a year with a big-town mayor, embezzled ninety grand from his city, a typical Irish politician. I got to know policemen, physicists, a seventy-five-year-old symphony conductor in for child molesting and bad checks, a cultured cat, really lovable.

I made it my business to find a way of using all those lost years to my own advantage. Fortunately I was usually able to manipulate the situation, to move myself around as much as I wanted, even better than I do on Sweet Street in some respects. I was able to get in contact with people who were significant in their fields, and I was able to have my own impact on prison circles. I held jobs with psychiatrists, sociologists, and anthropologists for almost the whole fourteen years. At one point I was the warden's secretary. I was fortunate in prison to be deeply involved in psychological treatment with a very competent Freudian analyst of excellent repute. He worked on me, and together we helped other prisoners.

Very early in prison I decided I wanted to incorporate into my life some of the things that others considered important. I thought, Let's see, people speak a lot about the ancient classics. What the fuck are the classics? What makes them classy? So I would read a paragraph here, a page there, trying to find something that I liked. Pretty soon I started to relate to the Greeks and the Romans, and the ones that appealed to me I brought into a fantasy community for myself, and I dealt with them in a fantasy way, inasmuch as I had no prison neighbors at that moment that I related to. I began to find it as easy to deal with 100 A.D. or B.C. as it was to deal with 1950 A.D. or 1952 A.D. In some respects, they had *more* meaning to me.

It didn't take long to find out why they were classics. The first one I hit on was that cat that did all the agrarian writing: Herodotus. See? I mispronounce it. I mispronounce a whole lot of classical names, because I've never heard them spoken, I've only read them. I never talked to anybody in prison about the Greeks and Romans, so I didn't hear the names. Today I could probably lecture on the subject, but I'd fuck up all the names and people'd think I was an idiot. I still don't know if it's Eurydice or Eurydi-chee. I ended up teaching two classes a week in general semantics, with twenty-five to fifty prisoners in my class. They were zealous fuckin' students, believe me! They wanted it all, books, shupplementary material, everything they could get their hands on about general semantics.

The cat I dug the most was Cicero, the original jailhouse lawyer. I would read the Apostles and I couldn't make any sense out of what they were saying, but Cicero was crystalline and exciting. The greatest thing in Cicero is his advice to his son. I read that discourse about twice a week. On Sweet Street, I get really lonely about Cicero. The people here don't respond to him, they don't read him, and they won't even take time out to look at his work if I beg them. So I don't mention the subject any more.

Well, I've had to learn that loneliness is a part of my life, I have to live with it. I spent fourteen years in a corner of the world with no references from home except negative ones. That didn't give me much to go on emotionally. I figure it'll take me four or five more years to get better at people. In the joint, you lose something irreplaceable. I'd never want to go back. Prison doesn't hold any terrors for me, but it doesn't hold any attractions either. I wouldn't even go back to lecture. They asked me, and I told 'em no. There's only one way I'll ever go back to prison, and that's to get caught. And I've never been convicted of burglary in all this time, so I figure I'm sure.

It's twenty-one years since I spent any real time with my family, back in Philadelphia. My mother and father are dead now, and I don't see my two brothers at all. One of 'em came here a few years ago and he was drunk the whole time.

We were brought up just outside of Philadelphia, on the Main Line, but I really don't like to discuss it. My childhood is meaningless to anybody but me, and explanations are of no value. I accept the responsibility for what I am, I don't blame it on my parents. *I* did it, not them. I had lots of time to figure these things out.

For many years, my father was a repugnant subject to me, and I cast him out of my mind. His values were chimerical, and he believed in them, which was all the more absurd. He was an engineer, self-taught, from a South Philadelphia laboring family, Jewish. I haven't used his name since I left home; Stanley Hamilton Briggs is my own idea. My father had respect for everything: the commandments, the laws, parking meters, whatever. I never saw him look at another woman. I always thought he was stupid, but then one day in prison I realized that I'd met a lot of men and my father wasn't a bad cat, in fact he had some admirable qualities. It hit me just like that, and when it did, I felt the tension of years relieved, my shoulders and vertebrae were looser than they'd ever been, and I accepted him. Of course that doesn't mean I accept him as my real father. *I'm* my real father, I don't give a fuck about my biological paternity. I carved myshelf out of Cicero and Sophocles and Herodotus and Plato and Thucydides and all those other cats. That's my true paternity.

My mother was always complex, kind of beautiful, full-blooded Italian. I was never close to her. When I'd been away from home for twelve years, I passed through Philadelphia, and I went to see my mother, and there she was, fifty years old, and absolutely extraordinarily beautiful, and I thought to myself, What a beautiful chick this broad is! At that point a lot of the chaos and confusion inside me just disappeared, and I gave her this warm hello, and all the unspoken realities were exchanged, and it was a powerful experience. That was the first and only time in my life that I ever related to my mother. Before that I'd always turned her off. She's gone now.

I was raised a Catholic—the Ten Commandments, the Pope, and all of it. I went to private Catholic schools and St. Joe's Prep. When I was sheven or eight I was an altar boy, and I was strongly attracted by religion. At the same time I found it vacuous. I kept listening and being attracted, but I couldn't make any sense out of it.

Then my favorite aunt got me the Little Blue Books, maybe fifteen of them, and by the time I was ten I could understand them pretty well, and I wondered why they talked about this man Shakespeare, so I started reading *Hamlet*. I read it again and again and again, and certain phrases just jumped out at me. There were lines that seemed to be saying something directly to me, or seemed to be *me* saying something to others.

> . . . Take thy fingers from my throat;
> For though I am not splenetive and rash
> Yet have I in me something dangerous,
> Which let thy wisdom fear. . . .

Shakespeare was more exciting than Tom Mix, he was more modern than Flash Gordon. I used to squirm around under the covers in a fit of agitation when I'd come to the exciting parts. Hamlet saying:

> How now! a rat? Dead, for a ducat, dead!

when he cuts old Polonius, and Lear saying:

> A plague upon you, murderers, traitors all!
> I might have saved her; now, she's gone for ever!
> Cordelia, Cordelia! stay a little . . .
> I killed the slave that was a-hanging thee.

I'd go to sleep sweating in my pajamas, and I'd dream about those lines, the way they roll off the tongue, the images they conjure in my head, and I'd try to draw my parents out on the subject, but they just didn't know. They just didn't know. I don't hold them in contempt. How were they to know when nobody'd ever told them? They had to keep their dignity. They couldn't admit that I was bringing them something rich and new, something they had no feeling for. So they just had to turn me away. "I'm busy now." "Ask me later." "Remind me tomorrow." And tomorrow they'd say the same things. They were poor, empty, arid souls. Their lives were dull and hollow.

Somebody gave me a book of selected phrases, and a few of them were the same phrases that were dazzling me in Shakespeare, and I cried! This was the first time I felt related to the fuckin' world in any way. *Somebody else liked the same phrases I liked!* It was my only proof that I was a living human being, that inside I was the same as somebody else. After that, I'd lie in bed and repeat the speeches over and over, and I'd play the roles myself. When it was rainy and windy outside, I'd light a candle and pull the covers over my head and do Macbeth, so I'd get a hollow echoing sound under the covers. I'd build a little tent in the bed, and I'd make myself morose and cry a lot. I cried from six to thirteen, trying to figure out my life. I found early that sadness was the only real feeling I had. I could appreciate tragedy, I could *feel* tragedy, nothing else, because the things I wanted had nothing to do with the lives that were being led around me.

After a while my mother and father realized I was a misfit. My mother had a lot of academic-type people come over to look at me. They seemed to think I was reclusive, so my mother bought me a lot of things that I could use alone: chemistry sets, microscopes, telescopes, things she'd buy at the expense of my brothers' toys, and when I was ten she had a lot of money tied up in my things. My brothers must have resented it; I don't blame them. I never had a conversation with either of them, ever. Not one. I had my room and they had theirs. There was no hatred; we just didn't communicate. I don't think any member of my family ever looked me in the eye. They were unhappy and miserable and dissatisfied, and I wasn't gonna live like that even if I had to be shot at sixteen for robbing the goddamn mint. I dreamed my own world, and I created it, and I appointed it with Van Gogh paintings and Graham dances and Mahler's music and Shakespeare's plays, and years later I sensitized myself to it with dope. I was so fucked up emotionally, I never played a game with the other kids. *Never.* All I did was read. Read and jack off.

When I was fifteen, I used to walk all over Philadelphia, looking at the lights, peering at people sitting in living rooms, walking down to the two burlesque theaters, the Troc and the Bijou, and looking in and wondering, Is thish all there is to Philadelphia? Well, then, let me out of here! I don't want any part of it! I joined the Navy. Philadelphia boys have been doing that for years; I wasn't so different.

When the Korean War broke out, I said to myself, This is how I'll reach maturity, I'll be part of the things that Hemingway and all those guys had done in Spain. I figured this has got to be the last war, a nice safe war, and I volunteered. I had twenty-six fuckin' Marines and a tank to land at Inchon, and we were going in on the tide all nice and peaceful when a mortar shell went off and I got blown into the well deck, with both my shoulders torn out of their sockets, and I'm lying there half out of it, and a star shell comes floating down on top of us and almost sears my eyes out. I was nearly blinded; that's why I wear dark glasses.

I was bewildered, in pain and shock, and this corpsman came over and hit me with a needle full of morphine, and just like that, there was a miracle. I was warm, calm, lucid. I wasn't even thinking; there was no need for thought. The anxieties and the tensions that I'd carried, they were gone for the first time. It was an experience of calm, of peace, of being an animal with a proper, functioning nervous system instead of the wreck I'd always been. Instinctively I was aware of one thing: that needle was better than anything else, it was better than all I had known. Psychically, I was hooked from that moment on. I asked the corpsman, "Give me some more!"

For the next couple of months in the hospital, I got

enough morphine to last me into the twenty-first century, and then in Tokyo I began to get into heroin. The Japanese made a fine, pure heroin available to servicemen, maybe to demoralize us, I don't know. Somebody told me it came from the Japanese Communists, but I didn't care. It was a brilliant concept. I'd have sold my soul to the devil and given him his money back just to have more of that Japanese heroin.

You don't realize the fine quality till you get back to the States and try to get fixed. When I got home, I had twenty-eight hundred dollars in back pay, and I spent four days and all my money trying to get fixed on American heroin, and all I got out of it was a lifelong hatred of the Mexicans in San Diego, because I thought they were burning me with rotten stuff. It took me a while to realize that it took much more American heroin to get off; it was about twenty per cent as potent as the Japanese shit. And I was out of money.

I had a Hopkins Allen .38 and a shoulder harness from the war, and it was very clear to me, like a flash of genius, what to do with it. The purpose of the gun was to frighten. The most essential thing was not to fire the gun, then you would never have a serious problem. You go into the drugstore with your finger off the trigger, and it's a matter of demeanor, of poise and presentation, and you bring it off calmly, articulately, and emphatically.

Ben Steiner was my partner, a short, sharp, stocky New York Jew. I haven't seen him in twenty years. He went to Fort Worth to take a cure, and then he disappeared. We agreed that I'd do the robbing and Ben would stand by the door, and he would drive. I didn't drive in those days, and I still don't.

That first night, we went to a drugstore in Chula Vista, and I opened my coat and said, "This is a robbery. I'd like to have the poison box. You won't be hurt. We'll only be a coupla minutes." There were people waiting around, but they didn't bother us. I realized that if the pharmacist reached for a gun, I'd have to shoot him. It would be my ass if I didn't, because I had a partner I was responsible for. I'd have suffered psychologically, but I'd have done it, even though I'd sworn I wouldn't pull the trigger. But luckily it went smoothly. He handed over the poison box and we split.

Ben and I did thirty straight robberies like that, never taking any money, just the poison box: morphine, Demerol, codeine, dilaudid, all the stuff that comes under the Harrison Federal Narcotics Act. It took us a long time to even *think* about stealing any money. Then we rattled off another sixty or so robberies before we were finally caught. It was just as well. I was beginning to enjoy the arrogance, the power, and that's not me. I served eighteen months with the youth authority for robbery, first offense.

When I came out, I went back on heroin. The folklore was that you were addicted for life, and I accepted it. I didn't like being an outcast, being out of step with society, but I was told I would always be a heroin addict. But after a while I realized that it was just plain wrong for my metabolism. Somebody gave me some uppers, and they changed me from a naturally lethargic creature into a new person. The uppers sensitized me to *everything* around me. So I kicked heroin and shwitched to speed, and I've been on it ever since, even in prison. There's no shortage of drugs in prison, don't let them tell you otherwise. There's no shortage of *anything* in prison, provided you can come up with a little cash.

Cicero tells you not to steal, but then he says if you *have* to steal, there's a way to do it and a way not to do it. One way I have of doing it is never to think about the victim. I constantly suppress any thoughts about the people I'm stealing from. I have a long involved psychological routine I go through. Sometimes when I'm boosting a car, I can see that the people aren't in good financial shape; maybe there's a lot of children's food and diapers, and I back off, but that's the only time I ever think about victims. The victims don't exist. I work in a vacuum.

You can learn more about the world through burglary than anything I know. You can learn more about other people by going through their possessions, especially if you have time to do it carefully: looking for the diamonds, looking for the good watch, the bracelets. People are more at home in their own houses than anyplace. You can learn about them from their bedrooms, their drawers, their desks, the way they stack their closets, their dirty linen. Laundry can tell you more than conversation. Almost everybody's conversation is built around the idea of impressing, but your laundry talks straight.

Once I entered a place and there was a broad in a beautiful peignoir, and I got acquainted with her. She'd just come up from New Orleans that day. She wasn't afraid, she'd taken some uppers. I stayed there three days. But ordinarily I don't get any sexual feelings out of burglary, just exhilaration.

I always try to work with information. The payoffs are better. I know when the people are out of town, and I know where the wall safe is, and approximately what's gonna be in it. After I get what I'm after, I play. I just wander in and out of the rooms, look things over, for my artistic and architectural pleasure. That's the best part of a burglary, if the place is inviting. A lot of times, it isn't. I wander through, making their acquaintance, appreciating the place, learning something from the family and their interior decoration and their books and their lifestyle.

I'm not a safe-burglar per se, but I know how to handle those small cannonball safes that you find embedded in concrete. You either cut 'em right out of the wall and take the whole thing, or you can freeze and shatter them with one blow, using liquid nitrogen. It freezes the molecules and makes them brittle, like ice. There's not one policeman in the city that knows what liquid nitrogen is, and it's not against the law to possess it. But it's hard stuff to handle.

The last few years, I've been specializing in car boosting. Sweet Street is the center of the greatest boosting area on earth, bcause it's going every day of the year. Within a five-block area I can turn thirty thousand, forty thousand a season, without making much effort, and never get arrested for it, 'cause it's so easy. I found twenty-six grand worth of jewelry on Brannon Avenue in an open station wagon. It was in a make-up bag. A mink coat was wrapped in a white ski jacket, and a shoulder bag had a hundred Disoxyn tablets and fifty Nembutals and fifty codeines. I couldn't believe it! Another time I found a pound of grass and three hundred in cash and six hundred in traveler's checks. I got into a Javelin one night on Lembeck Street and I picked up a coat and there's three cameras underneath it. I go through the side pockets and there's Japanese passports and eleven hundred in traveler's checks and a thousand dollars in yen, big notes like bedsheets. I took everything there was, without the slightest tremor. These were either successful Japanese businessmen or Japanese car boosters who did far better than I do. I mailed back their passports and their papers. I get ten Honeywell Pentax cameras a season. I saw one in a station wagon tonight, but I left it, 'cause I think the guy uses it in his business, and I try to steal only from tourists. I always boost out-of-town cars, that way they'll never be here to testify against me if I'm caught.

You wouldn't believe how many of the cars are open, and you'd be absolutely appalled if you knew the number of cars that not only have the door unlocked but the window down and the car full of valuables. If you just stole from open cars alone, you'd be good for two or three hauls a day.

Most of the locked cars can be opened with tools, as easily as you'd do it with a key. A screwdriver and a coathanger are all you need. The screwdriver gives you the leverage between the window and the rubber combing, and if you can't get through there you take the screwdriver and force the door away from the frame, and then you run the hanger in and lift the knob. There's a new type of knob that's made of softer rubber and it gives if any pressure's applied to it, but you can defeat that with a lipnoose. I do it all the time. I can open some cars without a key quicker than I could *with* a key. It's just a knack.

I have tools stashed in every block around here, in dives, in chicks' pads, all over. At one time I had eleven tool cases, each one in a shoulder bag with small binoculars and all the custom tools that I could use. I don't carry a gun, and I don't have much respect for those who do, because a gun gives you a false sense of confidence. It gives you an edge that you don't need, and it gives you a hell of an arrogance.

I seldom take anything to a fence. Mostly I sell to friends, contacts. A fence will give you half the wholesale value, or two thirds at the most. I've thrown things away because fences offered me too little. I get a hundred dollars for a Pentax camera with strobe, eighty-five for a Mamiya Secor. Some of those club owners and managers on Shweet Street are like fuckin' sisters, the way they argue over my stuff.

They're jealous of me and who gets the most of my loot, and oh Christ! Rocco goes up the wall if I sell to anybody else. Most of the people I sell to tell me they give it to their son as a gift. Good! Then they want more, and I go out and get it for them. I try to give more and more things to more and more people, so I can make 'em happy all over the street.

STANLEY HAMILTON BRIGGS VANISHES. For seventy days and nights, no one on Sweet Street sees him, and then he materializes in a taxi and slithers into Raffaele's.

I had a gun on me, and I got busted. It's on account of a guy named Rickie Beyler, a hype, a heroin addict, a guy I befriended several years ago, and unfortunately I let him into too much of my business. A long time ago he got pinched and gave me up, and the police found a warehouse full of my stolen merchandise and threw eight hot felonies against me, but fortunately I was able to get them thrown out of court. I had incontrovertible proof that Beyler the Rat informed on me, and then he did the same thing a few months ago. The arresting officers told me.

So I got a gun to take care of him, because he obstructs my vision and he makes me sick. Something has to be done about him. He not only rats on me, he rats on everybody. He puts people in jeopardy; he's out of control. He doesn't want to pay the dues for what he does. He wants to use heroin, but he doesn't make enough money, so when he gets pinched he fabricates, he puts things on other people so he can keep on walking the streets. By any standards, that's unethical behavior.

So I had my gun, and I was in Chinatown looking for him, and two cops stopped me, and I had to serve seventy days for loitering. That was reasonable, don't you think? It could have been five years—ex-con with a gun. But we bargained it down to a misdemeanor.

What do I do now? My first inclination is that nothing's changed, something has to be done about Beyler the Rat. A cop I know very well, we were rapping about it, and he said he might take care of it. Either *he* will or *I* will.

I go back to Cicero to try to figure out what to do about

people like Beyler. Cicero tells you first to determine what is right, and then what is fitting. It's right to kill Beyler, but what way is fitting? Cicero takes things like revenge and vengeance, and he makes them reasonable. They're part of nature, they're impulses that we act on, they're necessary for preservation. Nothing that is necessary for preservation can be considered wrong in the aspect of eternity. By studying Cicero, I learn how to make an art form out of my revenge—to do what is fitting and to do it with style. I think you should bring a little happiness to people, a little class and culture, even if you're gonna kill 'em. So I'm gonna get another gun.

This would be hard for straight people to understand, I imagine. In the straight life, you're molded, you're channeled, you're induced, seduced, and traduced into channeled ways of living. You're not functioning out of your balls, you're functioning out of society's needs, *somebody else's* needs. But some of us are *self*-controlled, we do what *we* want, and that feeling is generally based in the genitals. The games that we play and our basic constructs are based on genital needs rather than social or financial pressures, and in the long run this is better than accumulating money.

Money's never been my thing, anyway. I already have the things that money buys. In fact, some of the richest people in town spend a hell of a lot of time in close proximity to me, in places like Raffaele's, blowing their money. I get it free.

For me, the most important thing is interrelationships with people. Liking people so much gives me a problem. I have a rule for myself: *never* steal from your friends. But who isn't my friend? As soon as I meet somebody, I like 'em, and it's cutting down on my stealing a little too much. I don't know what to do; there has to be an honest solution somewhere. That's one thing I demand of myself: honesty. I have to look at myself in honest terms.

A few years ago I was feeling depressed and unrelated to anything, and I still hadn't finished doing my fourteen years for the state. I was out on parole, and naturally I was wanted as a parole violator, and I was kind of musing on the situation, wondering what was gonna become of me. I went out and spent a hundred bucks trying to get high that day, and nothing seemed to work, and I lay back and closed my eyes, and I don't know how much time passed, but something came over me, like an ocean wave at the beach, and all of a sudden I started smiling inside of me. *Smiling inside*! The smile went from my neck and my shoulder blades right into my face. I kind of sat up, and my mind held the reality that the world was mine. All of it, any of it! I could just reach out and take whatever I wanted. The only problem was learning what was the best, and then to use it for a while, *whatever* I needed to get by, for my allotted lifetime. The feeling was that I was part of the world and the world was part of me, we were inextricably intertwined, and the things that were the world's were mine, because we were the same thing. The city was my plaything, something to amuse myself with. After that, I stopped being depressed.

It's also good for my mental health to be on Shweet Street, around these beautiful people. I've studied them very closely, the small businessmen and working stiffs. One thing you have to admire—they're doing their thing, and they're feeding themselves *by* themselves. And they're all brothers—you can feel the atmosphere of brotherhood from one end of the street to the other.

When I was twenty-nine years old, just out of the joint, I still had clear memories of my own family life, and the people I'd known in Philadelphia, and I remembered how I'd perceived life as a child, and the apathy, the lack of interest, the lack of vitality, the *ennui* that permeated everything in my early years, and then I ran into Rocco Cardi again, after being out of touch for a few years. He's fifteen, eighteen years older than I am, and his mustache was beginning to get a little gray, and he was getting stoop-shouldered, and it was four in the morning and we were rapping. All of a sudden he hears a fire engine, and he jumps up and says, "Let's go!"

We spent the rest of the morning watching a fire on the other side of town, and then driving around looking for another excitement to get involved in, and I realized, here was a guy enjoying life and doing the things he liked to do, things *everybody* wanted to do but wouldn't do, and he was still a pretty reliable, pretty capable human being.

That little incident told me where I belonged, where to go

to school, around people like Rocco. On Shweet Street. Getting my balls enlarged.

I said to myself, I've been around, I've been all over the world, I've been in and out of prisons, but this is the first time I ever met a man. A *man*! Rocco Cardi. I still feel that way. If he'd put on a dress, I'd marry him, except that mentally he's under age. He's a little kid at heart. He does the things that every little kid dreams about. Last night, at four in the morning, there's not another soul in the joint, just me and Rocco and Raffaele, and Rocco's playing around with Raffaele's automatic, and the next thing I know there's a shot. I figure Raffaele's dead, but he's walking around, so I figure *I'm* dead. Somebody's *gotta* be dead when you fire a Beretta in an enclosed place like that. The bullet stuck in the wall. It turned out that somebody'd been bragging about firing a pistol inside a house, and Rocco wanted to see how it felt. Raffaele just reached across and took the smoking gun and said, "Rocco, that's *no* way to handle a gun. You're so clumsy!" He sounded like he was talking to a little kid.

You have to love people like that. Rocco, he's my fuckin' brother. He's one of the great people. It bothers me sometimes that I don't deserve friends like him, people like Raffaele, the other people on the street. It frightens me, the fear of losing them. I'd be satisfied for the rest of my life just to go around cleaning up after Raffaele. I've met a lot of people, but he is the most stimulating person I know, he stimulates me the way drugs do. When he's depressed, I'm depressed, too. I'm more addicted to him than anything else in the goddamn world. For one thing, he is absolutely the only person on the street with a code of honor that he sticks to. Certain things are important to him, and he'll *never* abandon those things. Trees, flowers, plants, friends. The most beautiful time at Raffaele's is after three in the morning, when we do the plants. There's nobody there but Raffaele and Rocco and I, and you can't believe how mellow it is. We water the plants inside and out, all the trees, eight of 'em, and there's no traffic, and Raffaele and I stand there and listen to the trees. He says, "Don't ever forget them. Keep them in your life! Keep the soil in your life, and you can't get too complicated." He manages to verbalize some of the things the Roman and Greek authors were talking about, in almost the same words, without realizing that he's doing it. It's in his heritage, it comes right out of his cells and his DNA, ten thousand years of Mediterranean knowledge.

The Raffaeles of this world, they keep me moving, they keep forcing me to do my best. He won't let me pay for anything in here, but then it's that way all over the street. I pay for cigarettes in the tobacco shop, but other than that I haven't spent a dime on the street in twenty years. I don't drive, but there's always somebody to take me around. Whatever you want, Shweet Street'll provide it for you. And it's a small enough neighborhood so I can handle it, I can encompass it emotionally. It's the finest, friendliest neighborhood in the world. When I'm here, I find myself. The street keeps me from being too kinky. Without it I'd be lost.

ROCCO IS FUMING. A raging fire gleams in his eyes, and his booming voice rattles the fancy liqueur bottles on the wall. He is so angry that he cannot stand still. He paces from one end of the bar to the other, stalks to the men's room and back, opens the outside door and inhales a few angry gulps of air, and returns to his harangue. "I'm *positive* about that motherfucker," he says. "*Positive*! Oh, I'm so hot! My Panasonic portable, a good one, too. I just took it out of my truck and put it in the office with a set of earphones, and it's gone. *Nobody* walks in that office but him and Raffaele and Mrs. Pirini and me, and it wasn't any of them. I called him on it this morning and he said he didn't know anything about it. Son of a bitch! *Cocksucker*! I said, 'Well, stay out of that office! You got no fuckin' business being in there. Stay out of the motherfuckin' office! If I catch you in there once more, I'm gonna whack you right in the fuckin' mouth!'

"What a guy! He says he digs me, he loves me. Well, he digs shit! Imagine! A sixteen-, eighteen-dollar radio, and it's still good, the motherfucker. I use it in my truck, it keeps me company on the road. *Gone*! Oh, that fuckin' prick! He's gonna get killed one of these days. He steps on toes, and as much as he says he cares for me and Raffaele, he'll steal from us. *Oh, yeh*! It's in his character, he'll steal from *anybody*. Don't let him into your place! I guarantee you, he'll set you up, he'll open a bathroom window or something, and when you're out, he'll come back and rob you. That is definitely for sure! He's got no scruples, which he left his scruples in the joint."

"Stanley's very bright," Raffaele says, "and yet he lacks so many things. He's so substandard that it's uncanny. He doesn't really know who his friends are. I don't believe he could work honestly for anybody. He just *has* to be devious, that's part of his nature. Even with me. I don't kid myself about him. Little things are missing all the time. The poor guy, he doesn't measure who to steal from and who not to. I don't think he knows *how* to measure things like that."

Rocco returns from a few seconds' cooling-down period in the damp outdoors, but he is still ablaze. "Listen!" he says to three or four regulars at the corner table, "A long time ago I had a small Sony TV, an eight-inch, that I bought for my mother when she was in the hospital. *Jesus H. Christ, Donald! Why'd you put so much fuckin' whipped cream on that sundae? You know what that fuckin' stuff costs us?* Stanley stole it right out the office. I got my little revolver and I put it in his mouth and I says, 'Stanley, you are a motherfucker!'

"He says, 'Aw, I had to pay some fuckin' bills. I had to get some fuckin' shit, man. I'll see if I can get it back.' We *never* got it back!"

"This is his whole life, taking things from others," Raffaele says. "His attitude isn't, 'Well, *I* shouldn't have taken it,' his attitude is, '*You* shouldn't have left it around.' He has no measurement of values, of friendship, *anything*. Does he know the difference between right and wrong? I don't think so. But he's intelligent and he's loyal, and it really doesn't bother me if he lifts something once in a while. It's worth his friendship. I allow him to go into the kitchen and take whatever he wants to eat. I let him do little things like watering the plants, so he'll feel entitled to his food. That's always easier than giving something outright. I hate to be thanked. And I want him to eat, I'm happy to see him well fed, 'cause he can't work for a living. He never pulled an eight-hour shift in his life. When he worked here for a day, it was like being in jail for him, cleaning tables, picking up plates, waiters yelling at him. He couldn't take that. He went nuts.

He's always on the verge anyway. But I love the guy. I won't do anything against him. Never!"

Rocco has been listening, turning an imaginary key on his temple, and otherwise indicating doubts of Raffaele's sanity. When Raffaele steps away, Rocco says, "He's losing it. I'm telling you, they're gonna come for him with the net! He *loves* being ripped off, he acts like you're doing him a favor when you steal. Well, I don't give a fuck what he says. Things are gonna be different around here. I've taken care of Stanley before, I've bailed him outa jail twice, and he's in hock to me for three, four-hundred dollars, and I've boughten some hot stuff from him, which I give a price. I done everything a man can do. I put him to work here as a busboy, and I brought him home, I made him bathe, I put one of my ties on him, and he looked good. Then *ba-doom!* We don't see him for four, five days, and the next thing we know he's in jail.

"So this is it! He can't be trusted, not in the least. I'm gonna fix it so he can't *eat* here and he can't *shit* here and he can't do *anything* here. Nothing! *No fuckin' way!* I don't give a fuck what Raffaele says. Fuck Raffaele! I won't forgive this time. Forgive? *Forgive shit!*"

The oration goes on for the better part of an hour. At midnight the door opens and the party of the first part slouches in, head wobbling on chest, hand waving a weak hello to his constituents. He is plainly under a baleful chemical influence. He slumps into a chair just as Rocco walks out of the office. "Oh, hello, Stanley," Rocco says. "How they hanging?"

Stanley waves lazily.

Rocco sits down, and Stanley makes one of his instantaneous migrations to the steamtable. "Stan," Rocco calls. "*Stan!* STAN! Get out from behind there! Let a waiter wait on you! C'mon, now, no more taking whatever you want! *Get over here and siddown!*"

Stanley walks slowly to the table and sits. Everyone in the place is staring. His normally ashen face is red, and he whispers from behind a menu, "Jesus Christ, Rocco, why'd you have to holler? Why didn't you just look in my direction? You embarrashed me, Rocco!"

"Yeh, all right," Rocco says. He is shamefaced, like the dog that only meant to shake the kitten.

An hour later, Stanley is finishing a Lucullan feast, while Rocco and Raffaele and several cronies sit at the same table and gossip. Rocco takes out cigarettes and offers them around. He bypasses Stanley momentarily, then squiggles a cigarette from the tip of the package and says, "Here! Want one, asshole? That's it, go ahead, take my last one! *Bring my radio back*!"

Stanley says nothing. Postprandial collapse is setting in, and his head begins to droop again toward his chest. He sings something that vaguely resembles Billy Strayhorn's "Lush Life," the part that goes:

> And there I'll sit
> Where I'll rot with the rest
> Of those whose lives
> Are lonely tunes

Rocco can't find his radio. Anytime he misses something, he thinks I've got it. He thinks I'm the only motherfucker in the world that steals from him, and I'm the only one that doesn't.

How can I take his complaints seriously? It'd mean I was finished in Raffaele's, and I'm not. In the last twenty-four hours I stashed about eighty dollars' worth of hardware fittings and another forty dollars worth of tools in here. I'm bringing stuff in, not taking stuff out.

Rocco's probably ripping Raffaele off for something and laying down some smoke. While he's complaining about me stealing his radio, he's probably going through Raffaele's briefcase. He always projects to me what he's doing himself. A lot of guys do that.

Well, what the fuck. Sometimes it's enough to make a man look for honest work. But how can I go to work when the alternative is just to lay in my room and fuck two or three different broads a week or a day, and get high. I'm lazy. I've been lazy all my life. I don't worry about getting a straight job. I can't even think about it.

This afternoon I was with a chick, she's a little chubby,

about thirty-six, and she hasn't taken care of herself the last fifteen years. But I like her, and I owe her some debts of kindness. She was thoughtful enough to go to court for me once and give me an alibi.

She came down to see me because she had some Disoxyn and she wanted to get rid of it by giving it to me. I could see that she was frushtrated, so I got her to rub my back and she told me she and her old man weren't making it any more. By that time I was pretty well acquainted with her needs, so we went for a walk and I felt I reached the point where I could physically love her, so I took her back to the room and started making love. Well, I'm never in a hurry, and she's a pretty complicated woman, and I wanted her to love *herself* and appreciate *herself*, and she'd never encountered this kind of attitude before. In her whole thirty-six years she'd always been used as a sexual object. I was pretty happy with myself about it. Love was the essence of the situation. I wanted to interject something more than a tangential contact. I wanted to love her for a time, and make her love me, and I think I was successful. She really was smiling when I put her on the bus tonight. Neither one of us had an orgasm, so I told her, "You can always come back tomorrow, Ellen."

To me, love is some kind of electro-colloidal process, actual energy and vibrations. You can *feel* it, a positive charge, and a lot of refinements and niceties can be added on. It's inescapable, love. At least *I* wouldn't want to escape it. I'd like to choke on love. What else is there? I'm scared of it, sure. But it's the only thing worth while. And it's the hardest thing to maintain in your life.

I've had long periods of hunger, but longer periods of loneliness. I have a constant yearning for somebody to fulfill myself with, physically and psychically, both the masculine and feminine parts of my nature. But I end up alone, because I don't find the kind of broads I need on Shweet Street. Most of them are automatic losers in front, and I can see it right away, so why should I fall in love with grief?

I go from day to day. I try to get the best out of the day that's at hand, like the Mormons. Maybe exchange this shirt for one better, some big accomplishment like that. Or get a good old lady and put her to work. I'd like to catch a chick, and I'd prefer one with money, and then I wouldn't have to take so many risks.

I've been going back into Cicero lately, on old age. Very beautiful stuff. He lucidly explains the advantages that come with the years, the strengths that you acquire, and how they compensate for the weaknesses that you pick up. He says, "If, during his long life, a man has failed to grasp that death is of no account he is unfortunate indeed." He calls that section: "Death Has No Sting." The only sting is the possibility of a little pain, but he's even soothing about that.

Me, I don't worry about death. I figure I'm bound to die of natural causes, if I've lived this long. I'm fortunate to be alive. I never expected to reach thirty, let alone forty. I thought I'd be shot by the police or dead from an O.D. So I don't worry about the future. Every day is a bonus that I never thought I'd have.

Epilogue

Daybreak.

The first rays of the sun fleck the tips of the tallest buildings, dappling them with hints of chrome. A soft glow begins to suffuse the harbor, rinsing away the deep grayblack of night and staining the water mauve. Only Sweet Street goes pallid in the new light, its palaces exposed as papier-maché and tinfoil. Neon marquees blink and die, and a furtive quality slips over the scene that a few hours before was throbbing and glittering with mirth and cash; dawn was never the street's finest hour. Even Raffaele's, with its *belle-epoque* air, its hanging plants and marbled tables, looks darkly uninviting. Faint violin music seeps through the locked doors. The *proprietario* himself, having fulfilled his nightly musical obligation to the trees, practices a Mozart cadenza for tomorrow's performance.

Down the street, Robert Benni finishes his accounts, fires twenty rounds from his Smith & Wesson, then turns off the lights and pronounces himself ready for all challengers on his particular field of wheat.

Rocco Cardi lies back on his bed, lights a joint, and fantasizes the imminent arrival of a nubile blonde, seeking lodgings for the night.

Nancy Davis, also known as Royal, gives value for money to the last trick of a long, strenuous evening.

Patrolman Steven Diggs slumps in his bed and creates in his mind a memorable scene: the arrest of the governor for an on-view 288-A.

Merle Farquhar grinds her teeth in a low growl of satisfaction and imagines Steven Diggs caught *flagrante delicto* on the stage of the opera house during a performance of *Tosca.*

Bill Gold, a female veterinarian freshly added to his life-list of conquests, hopes the lady will quietly disembark from his yacht before breakfast.

In another part of the harbor, Captain Buddy De Young of the good tug *Venus* counts naked teenyboppers jumping a fence.

Next to him, Ginny Thomas listens to the hum of the bilge pump and wonders what new bargains may be offered at the thriftshop.

Cappy Van Fleet, his morning's meditations completed, sips lapsang souchong in bed and thinks about the busty new waitress he hired.

Alongside him, Olive Calzolari drifts off, her mind filled with plans for the same busty waitress.

Connie Lea, the one, the only, completes the tedious task of removing wig and eyelashes and layers of make-up, like Madame Pompadour after the Bal Masque.

Jessica King paces her grimy apartment in an agitated state compounded of three double vodkas and pretty pink pills.

Sally Bob Tiner wakes fuzzily from a dream and sits up in bed, searching for her name in lights on the wall of a room where she is biding her time with a Sagittarius.

Big John Keefe dozes in a haze of fine wood-dust, one seventh of his frame extended into space, his stomach gurgling a call for help.

Toby Gomez suffers the agitated sleep of the sodden, his body writhing in nightmare, flushed and drenched in the three-dollar-and-fifty-cent bed provided by the Dominican fathers.

Stanley Hamilton Briggs, his early morning labors rewarded by a new Pentax camera with strobe, looks in vain for a usable vein, and turns instead to Pliny the Elder, another of his addictions.

Along the street, a door closes softly, the last light flickers off, and the silver sun climbs above Raffaele's and drains the color from the block, like a child's paintbox left out in the rain.

Sweet Street sleeps.